Sachi's MONSTROUS Appetite

3

Chomoran

Characters

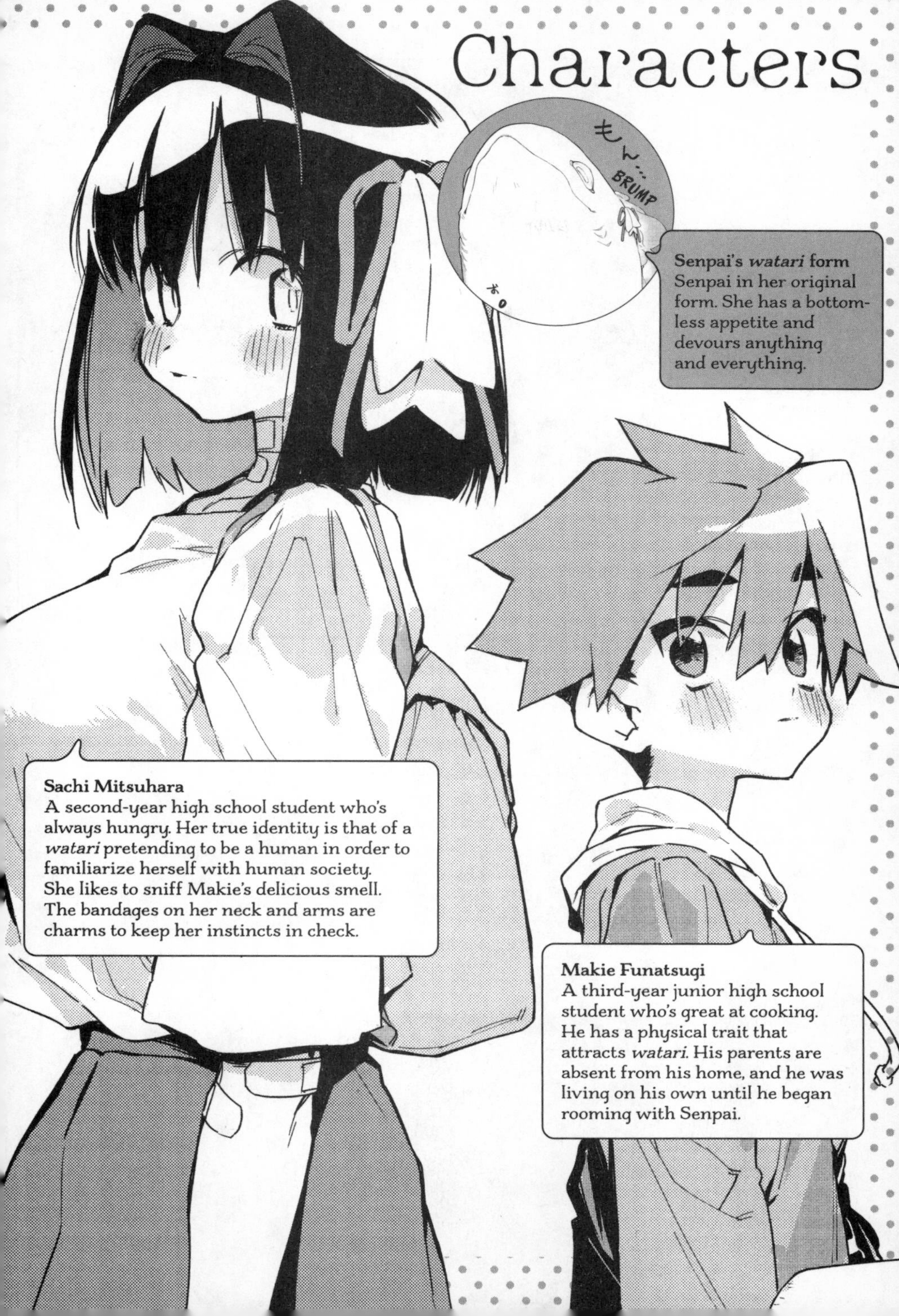
もん…
BRUMP

Senpai's *watari* form
Senpai in her original form. She has a bottomless appetite and devours anything and everything.

Sachi Mitsuhara
A second-year high school student who's always hungry. Her true identity is that of a *watari* pretending to be a human in order to familiarize herself with human society. She likes to sniff Makie's delicious smell. The bandages on her neck and arms are charms to keep her instincts in check.

Makie Funatsugi
A third-year junior high school student who's great at cooking. He has a physical trait that attracts *watari*. His parents are absent from his home, and he was living on his own until he began rooming with Senpai.

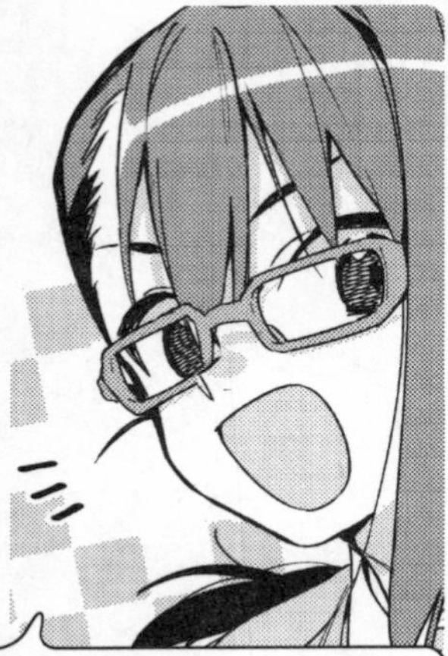

Miss Maid
The Manager's maid. Keep an eye on her headband.

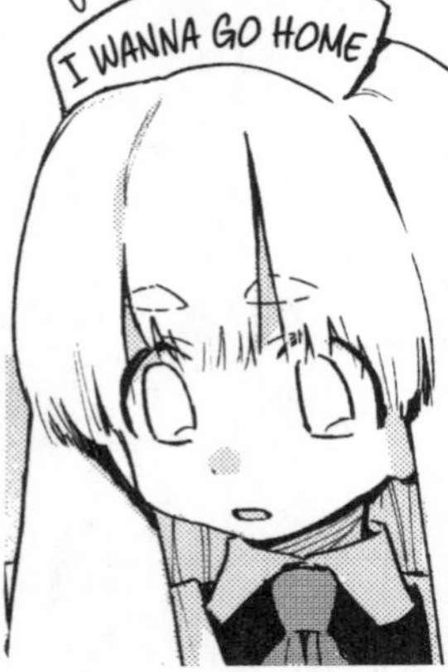
I WANNA GO HOME

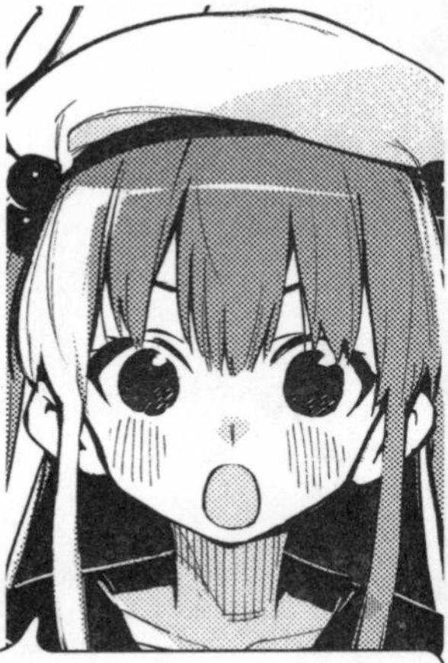

Miss Manager
She manages the *watari* for the town that Makie lives in. She has tasked Senpai with the job of protecting the town from dangerous *watari*.

Izumi Izumi
A *watari* that mimics humans and other creatures, it blends in by planting false memories in those around it. It previously took the form of a girl, as Makie's neighbor, and has decided to continue living this way.

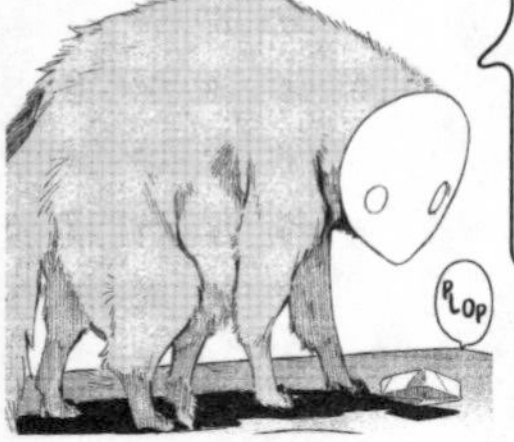
PLOP

Kintsuba
A *watari* that Makie first saw when he was a child. Since then, it's been living in the Funatsugi household, hidden from sight until recently.

The *Watari*
Strange beings that are typically invisible to humans. They act in accordance with their own unique desires and inhabit spaces called nests.

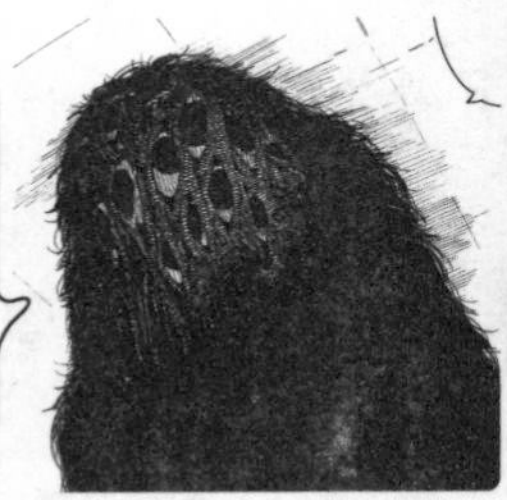

Story

Love strikes Makie, who has fallen for Mitsuhara-senpai, and because she always seems to be hungry, Makie approaches his senpai with a sample of his excellent cooking. But before their love can blossom, a rather large obstacle stands in their way. It turns out that Makie's senpai is a strange creature called a *watari*, and this whole time, she thought that Makie seemed...tasty! Mitsuhara-senpai is doing everything in her power to control her instincts, though Makie resolves to accept her as she is. After Makie confesses his feelings and the two share their first kiss at the beach, their courtship officially begins!

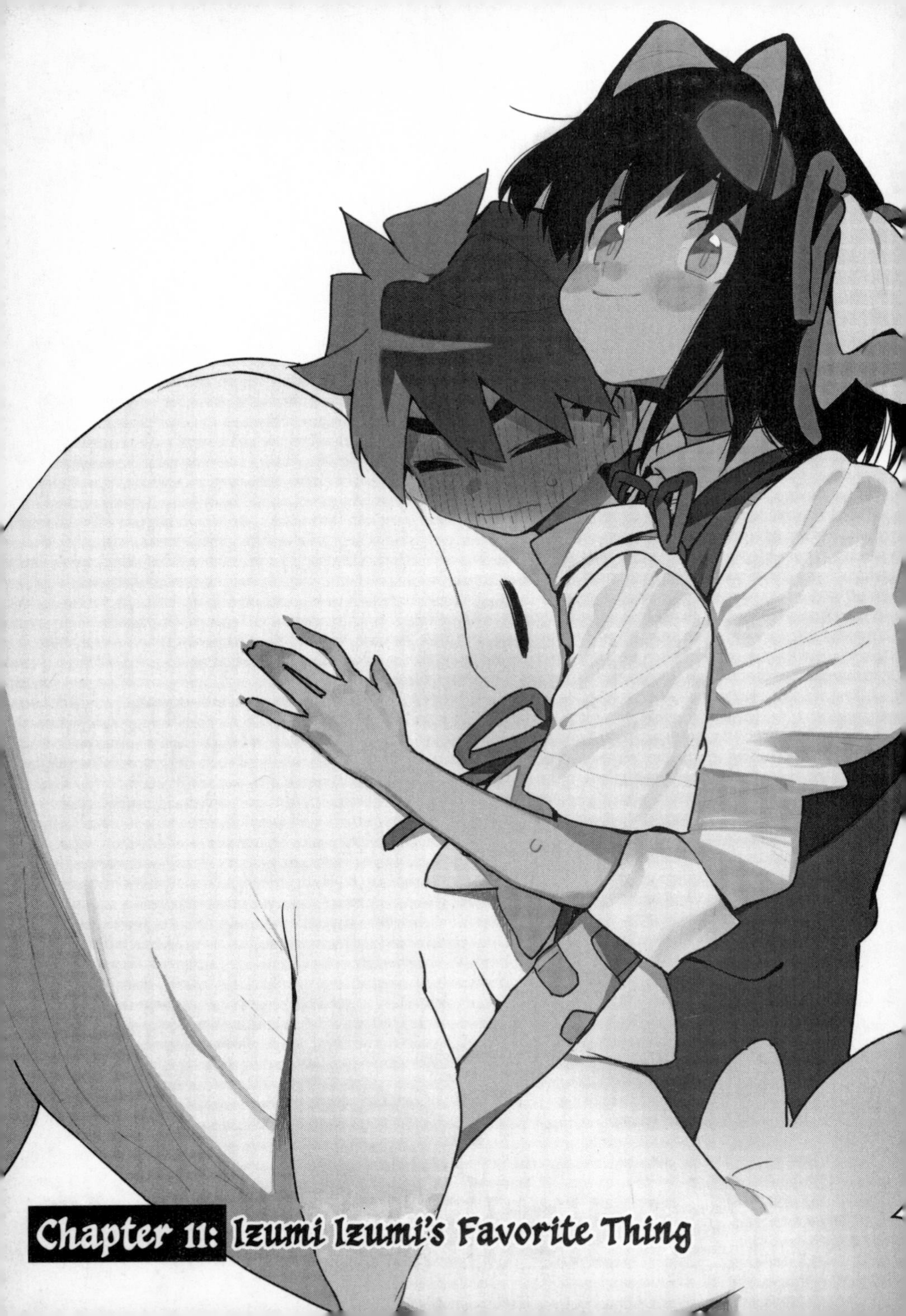

Chapter 11: Izumi Izumi's Favorite Thing

Sachi's
MONSTROUS
Appetite

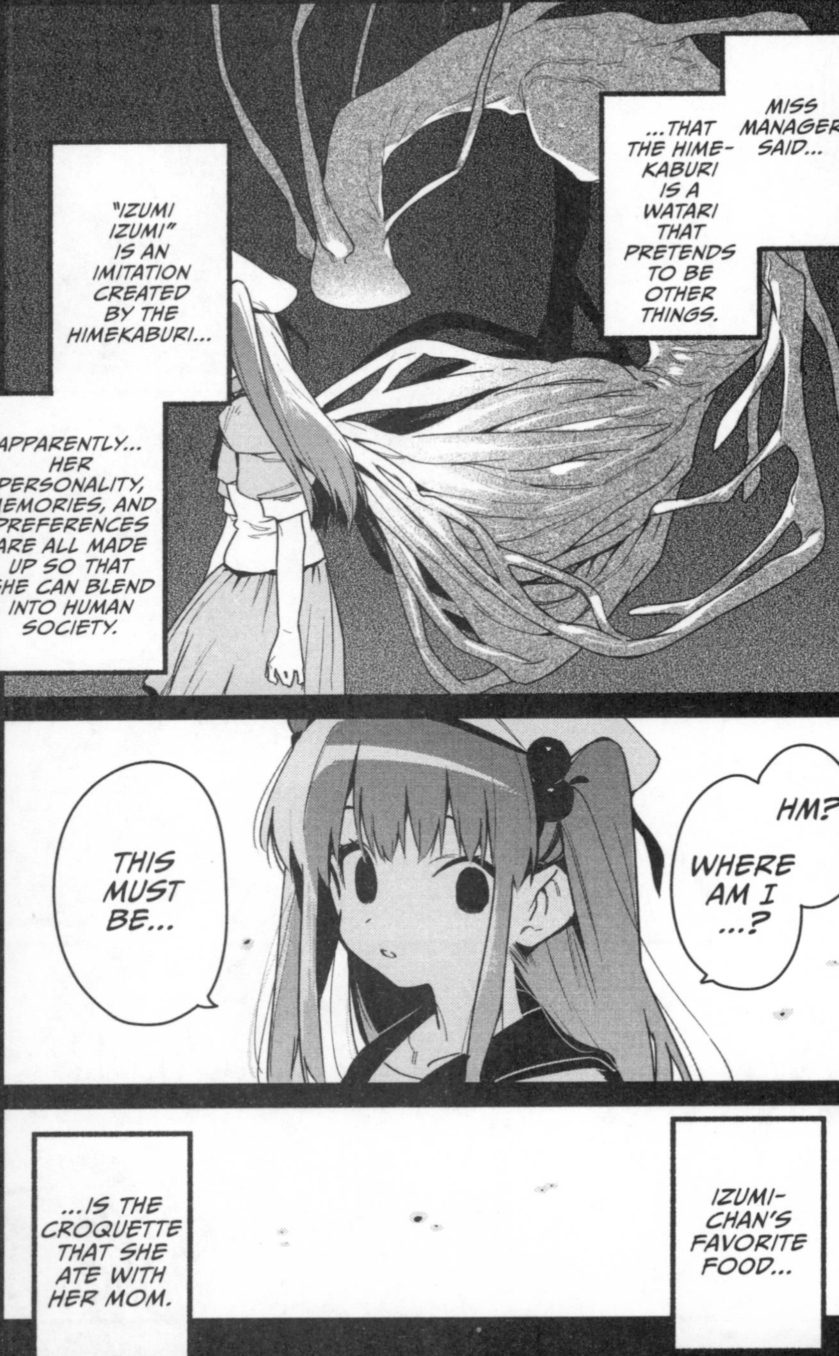
MISS MANAGER SAID...
...THAT THE HIME-KABURI IS A WATARI THAT PRETENDS TO BE OTHER THINGS.
"IZUMI IZUMI" IS AN IMITATION CREATED BY THE HIMEKABURI...
APPARENTLY... HER PERSONALITY, MEMORIES, AND PREFERENCES ARE ALL MADE UP SO THAT SHE CAN BLEND INTO HUMAN SOCIETY.
HM? WHERE AM I ...?
THIS MUST BE...
IZUMI-CHAN'S FAVORITE FOOD...
...IS THE CROQUETTE THAT SHE ATE WITH HER MOM.

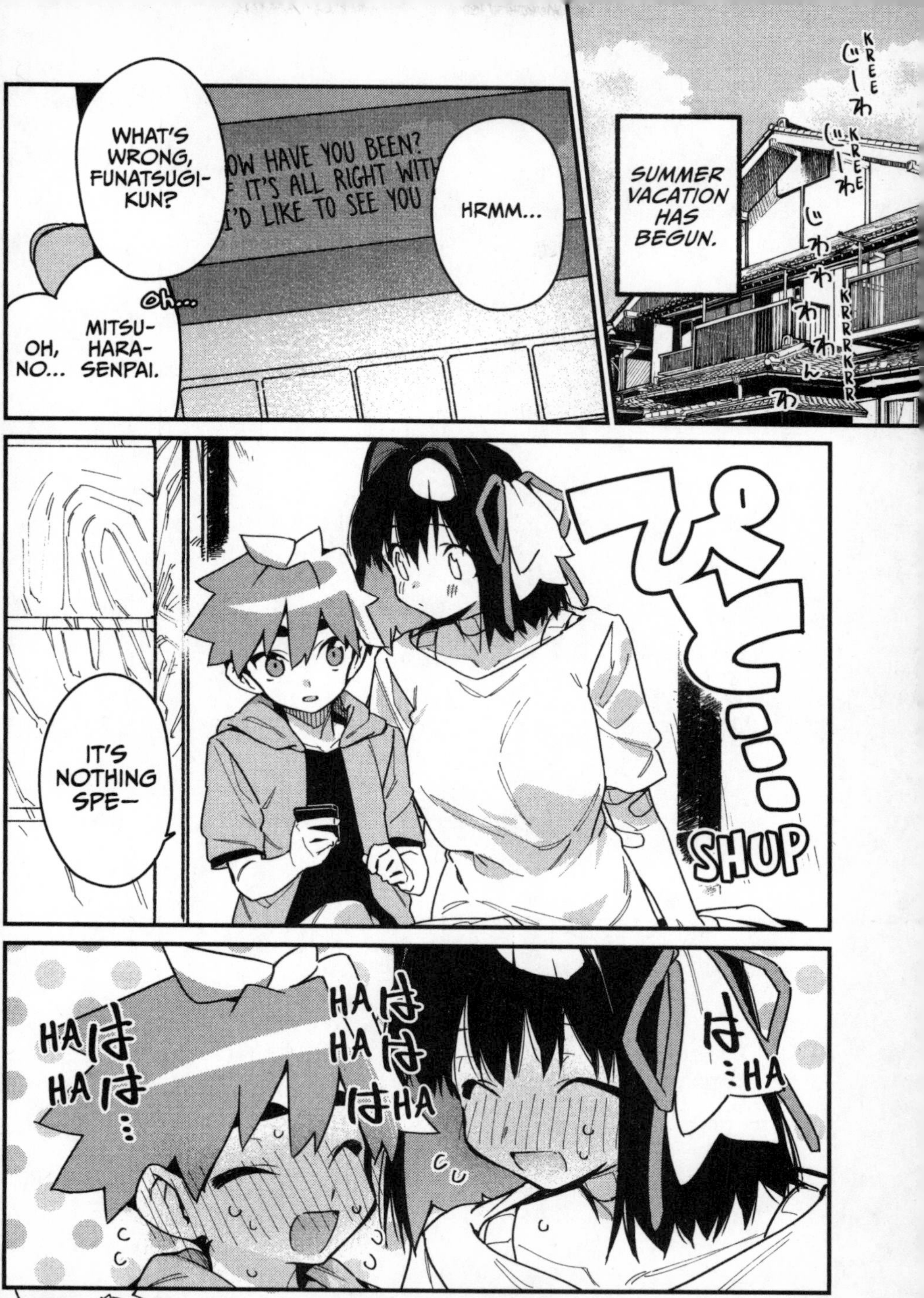

KREE じーわ
KREE じーわ
じわわわわん わ
KRRRKRRR
SUMMER VACATION HAS BEGUN.
OW HAVE YOU BEEN?
F IT'S ALL RIGHT WITH
I'D LIKE TO SEE YOU
HRMM...
WHAT'S WRONG, FUNATSUGI-KUN?
Oh...
OH, NO... MITSU-HARA-SENPAI.
ぴと...
SHUP
IT'S NOTHING SPE—
は HA
HA は HA は は HA
HA は HA は...
I got a smartphone, by the way!
They helped.

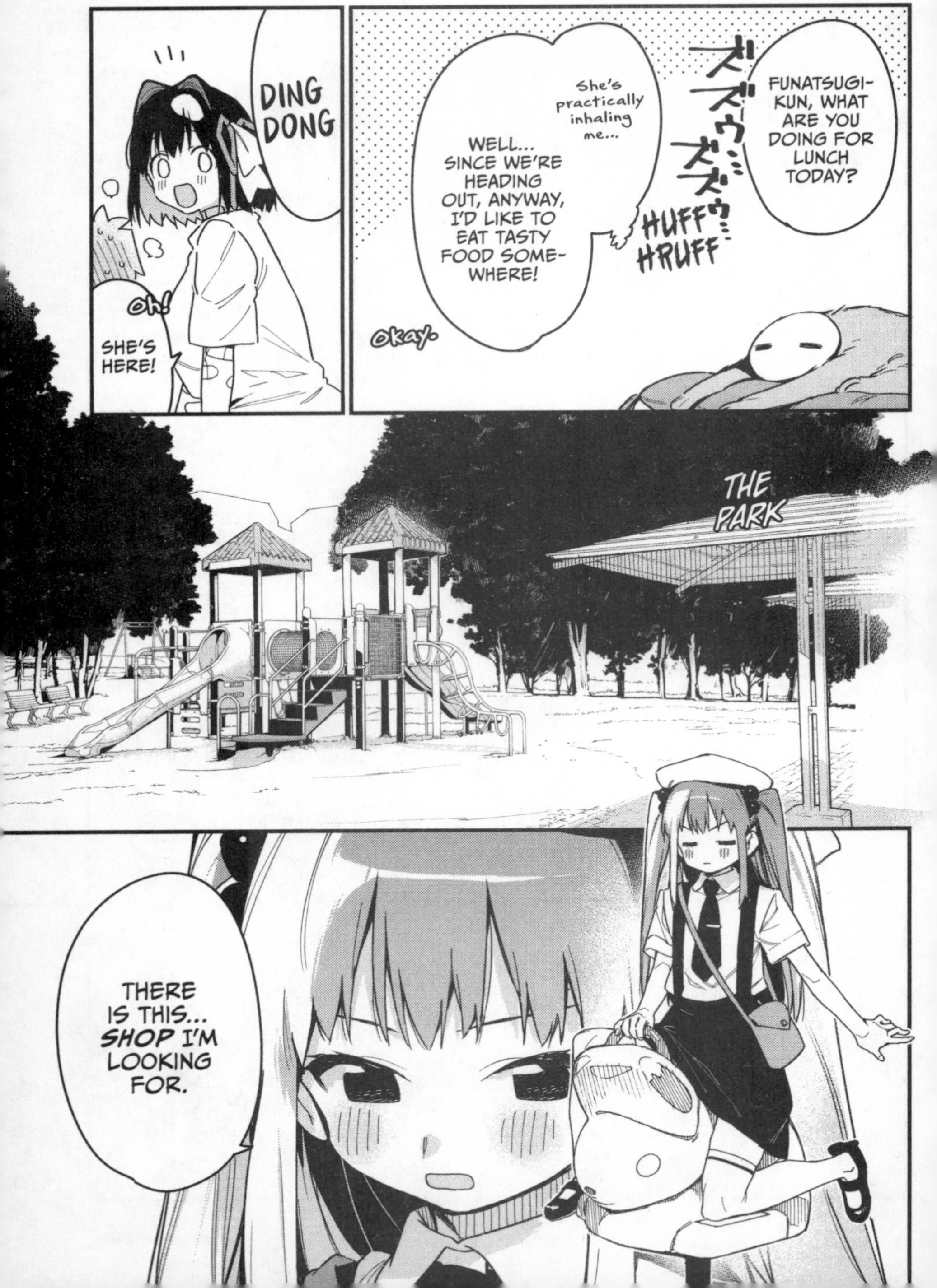
FUNATSUGI-KUN, WHAT ARE YOU DOING FOR LUNCH TODAY?
ズズゥ…ズズゥ…
HUFF HRUFF
She's practically inhaling me...
WELL... SINCE WE'RE HEADING OUT, ANYWAY, I'D LIKE TO EAT TASTY FOOD SOME-WHERE!
Okay.
DING DONG
Oh!
SHE'S HERE!
THE PARK
THERE IS THIS... SHOP I'M LOOKING FOR.

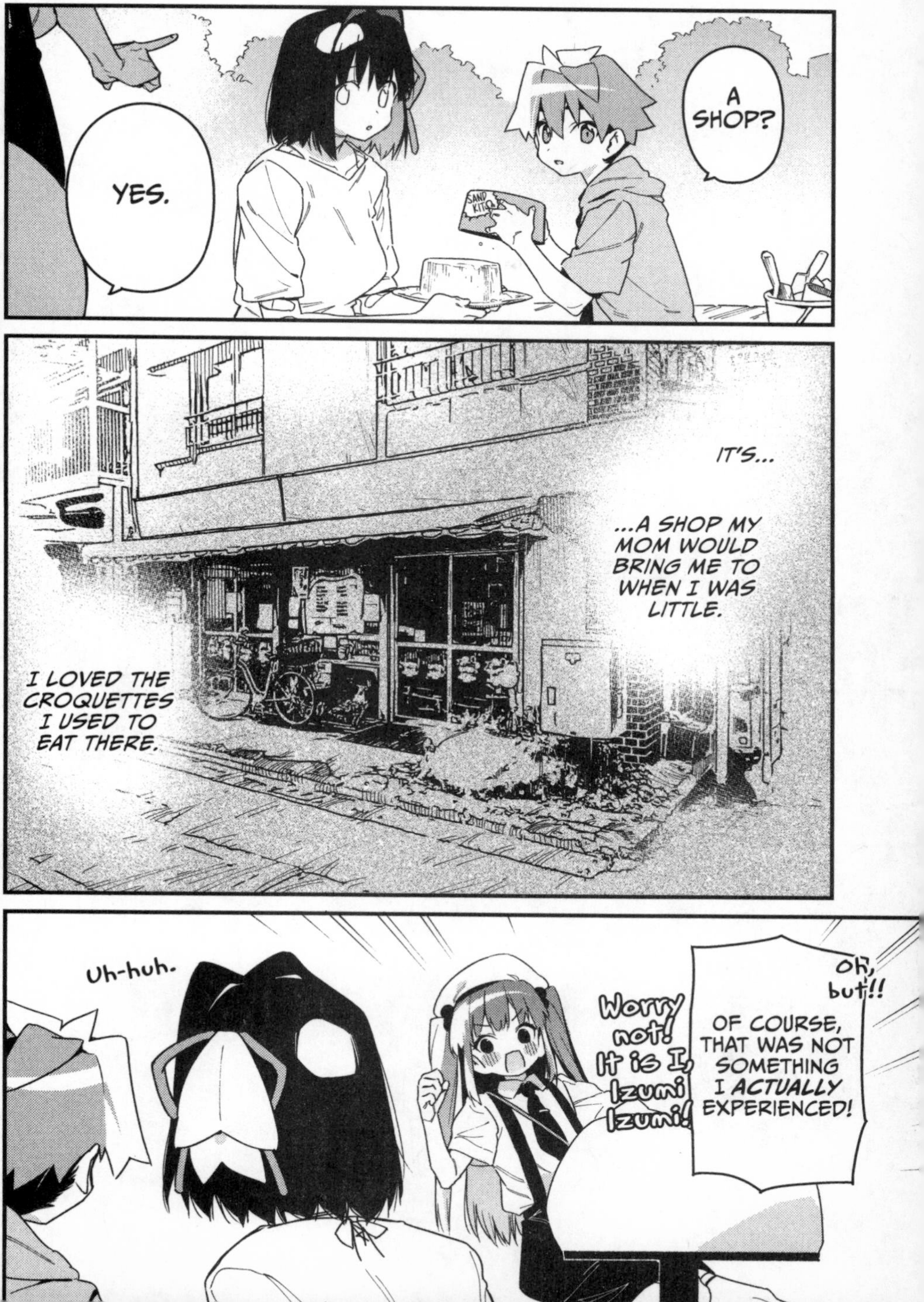
A SHOP?
YES.
IT'S...
...A SHOP MY MOM WOULD BRING ME TO WHEN I WAS LITTLE.
I LOVED THE CROQUETTES I USED TO EAT THERE.
Oh, but!!
OF COURSE, THAT WAS NOT SOMETHING I ACTUALLY EXPERIENCED!
Worry not! It is I, Izumi Izumi!
Uh-huh.

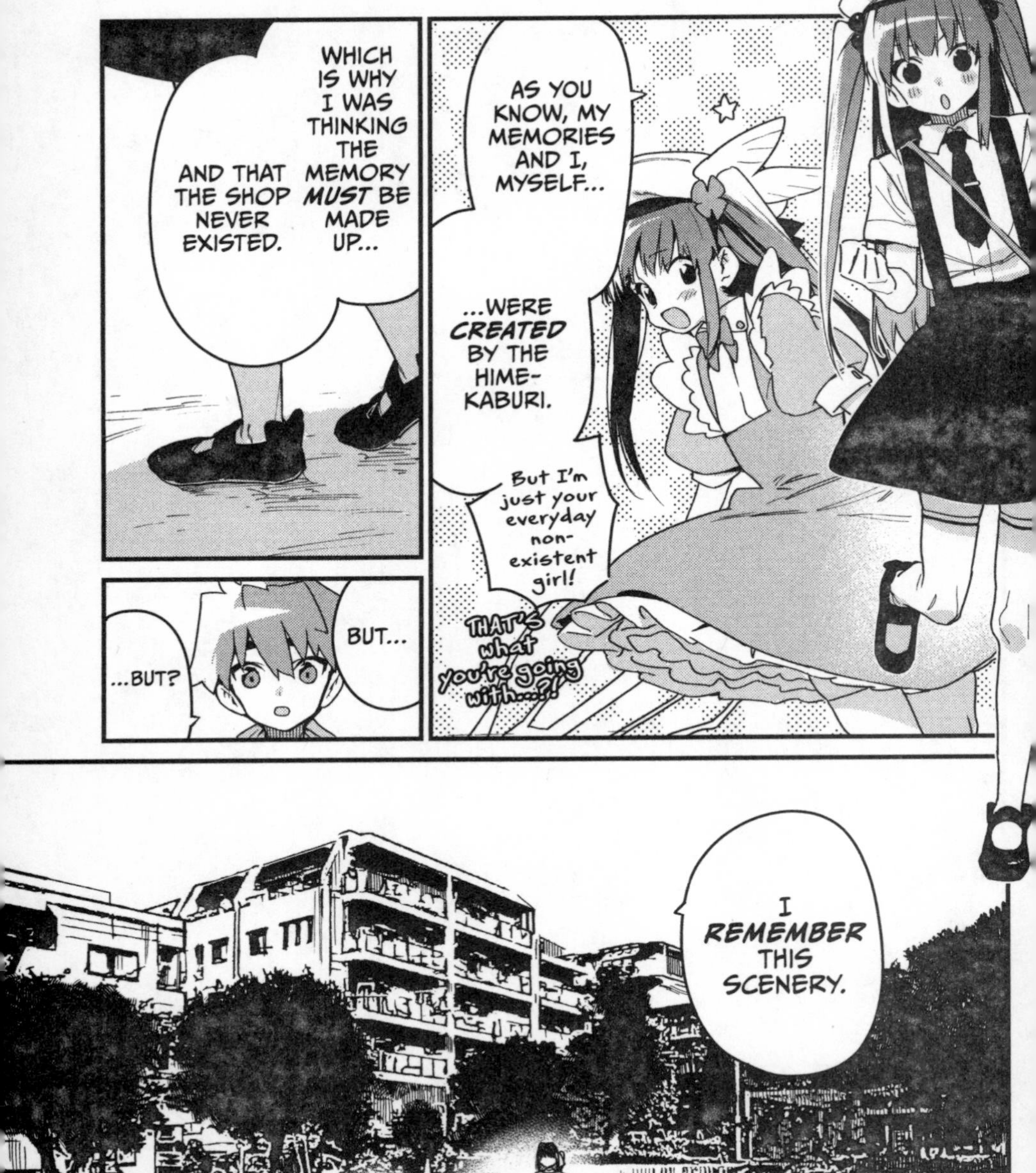
AS YOU KNOW, MY MEMORIES AND I, MYSELF...
...WERE *CREATED* BY THE HIME-KABURI.
But I'm just your everyday non-existent girl!
THAT'S what you're going with...?!
WHICH IS WHY I WAS THINKING THE MEMORY *MUST* BE MADE UP...
AND THAT THE SHOP NEVER EXISTED.
BUT...
...BUT?
I *REMEMBER* THIS SCENERY.

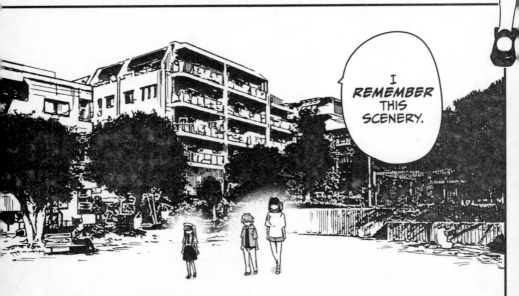

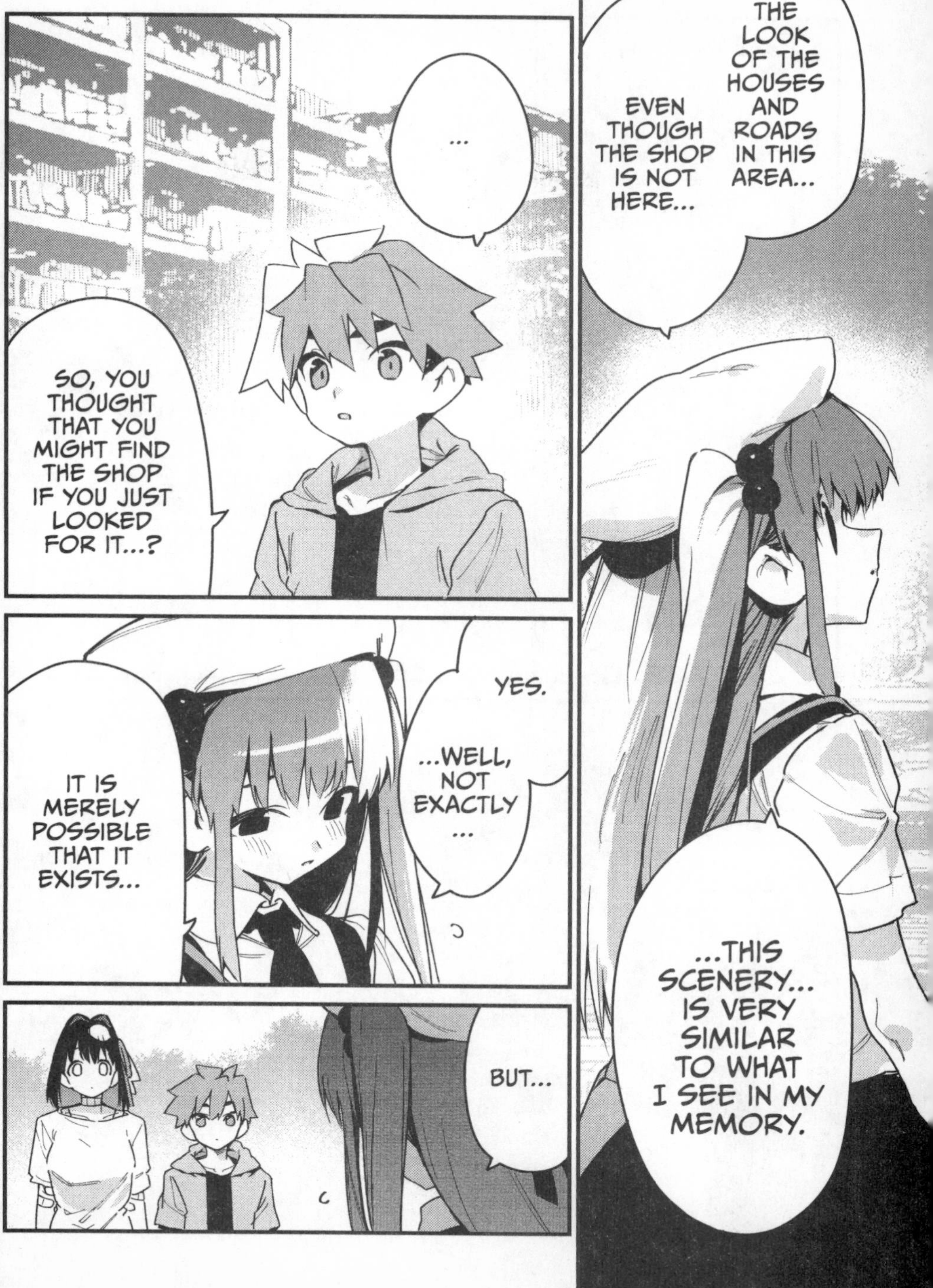
THE LOOK OF THE HOUSES AND ROADS IN THIS AREA...
EVEN THOUGH THE SHOP IS NOT HERE...
...THIS SCENERY... IS VERY SIMILAR TO WHAT I SEE IN MY MEMORY.
...
SO, YOU THOUGHT THAT YOU MIGHT FIND THE SHOP IF YOU JUST LOOKED FOR IT...?
YES.
...WELL, NOT EXACTLY ...
IT IS MERELY POSSIBLE THAT IT EXISTS...
BUT...

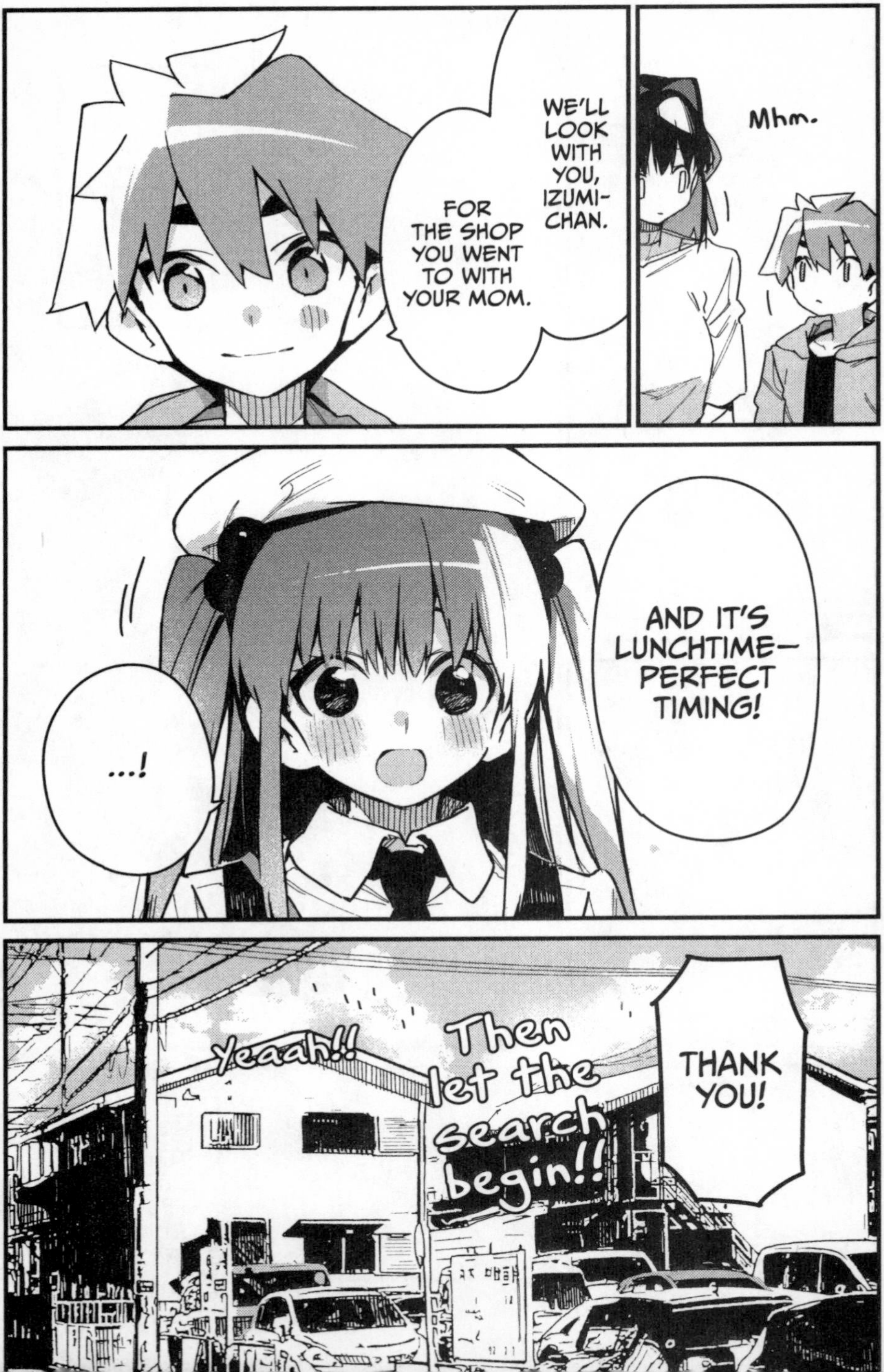
Mhm.
WE'LL LOOK WITH YOU, IZUMI-CHAN.
FOR THE SHOP YOU WENT TO WITH YOUR MOM.
AND IT'S LUNCHTIME—PERFECT TIMING!
...!
THANK YOU!
Then let the search begin!!
Yeaaah!!

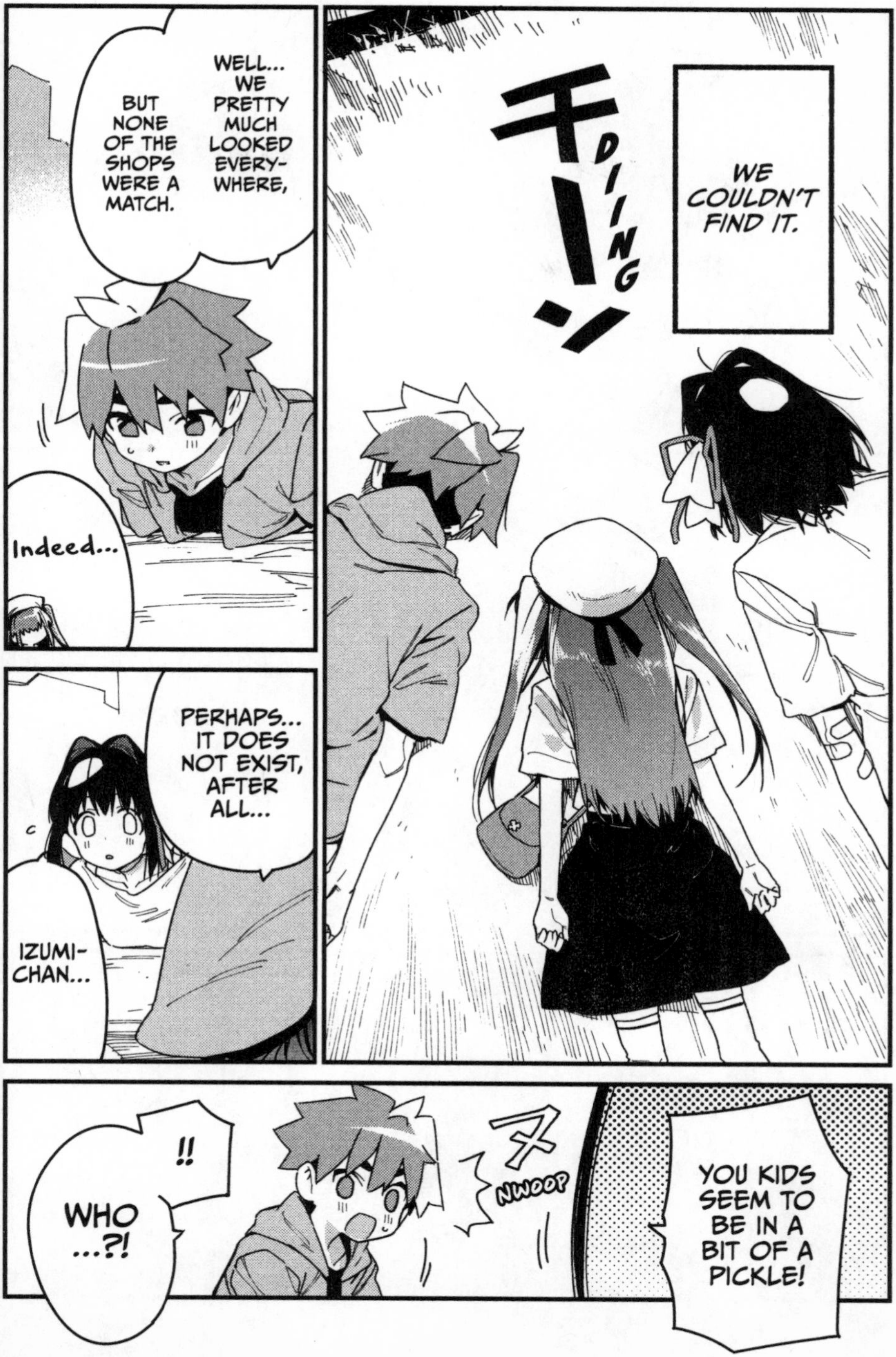
WE COULDN'T FIND IT.
DIING
WELL... WE PRETTY MUCH LOOKED EVERY-WHERE,
BUT NONE OF THE SHOPS WERE A MATCH.
Indeed...
PERHAPS... IT DOES NOT EXIST, AFTER ALL...
IZUMI-CHAN...
YOU KIDS SEEM TO BE IN A BIT OF A PICKLE!
NWOOP
!!
WHO ...?!

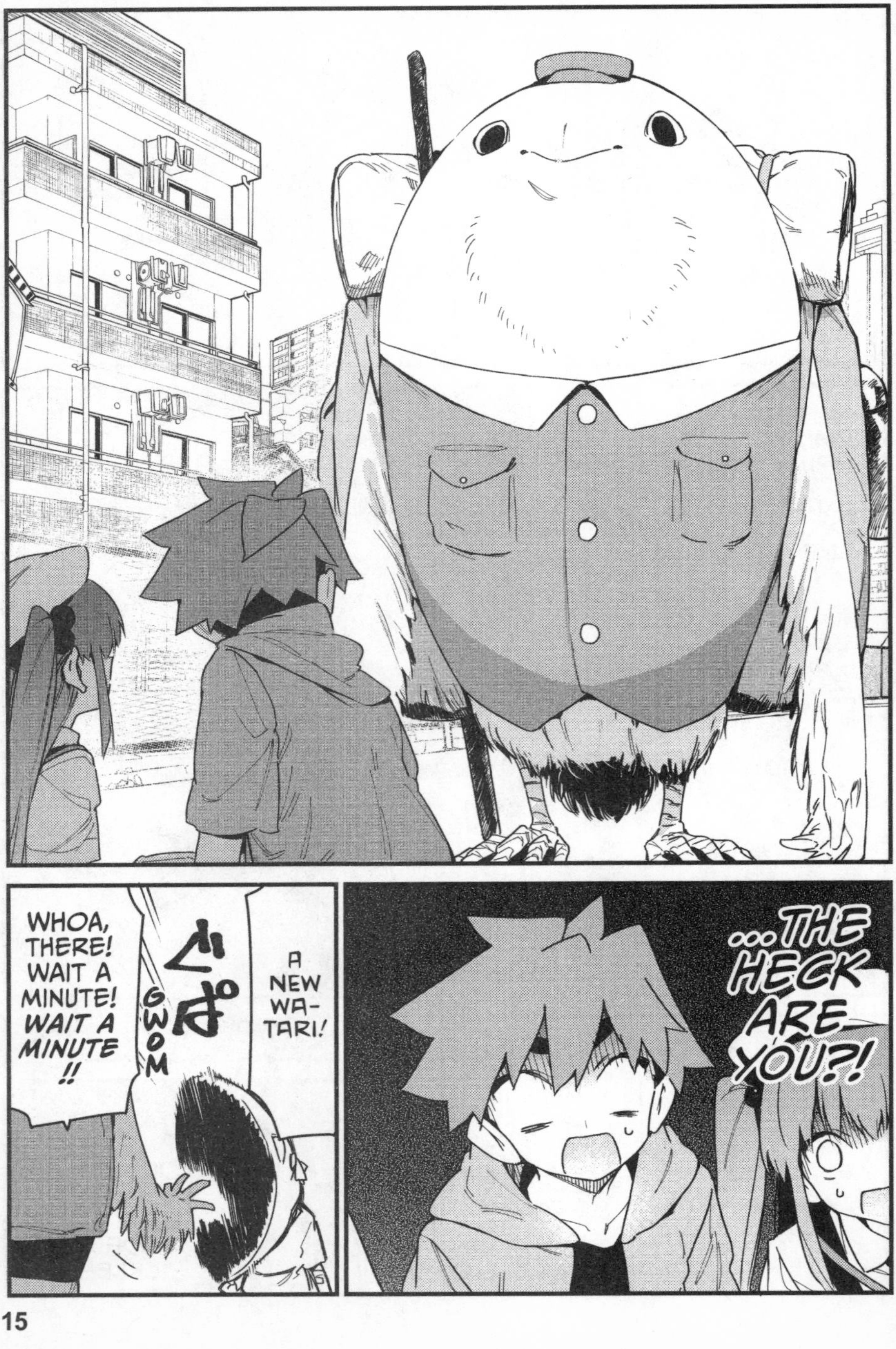
...THE HECK ARE YOU?!
A NEW WA-TARI!
GWOM
WHOA, THERE! WAIT A MINUTE! WAIT A MINUTE!!

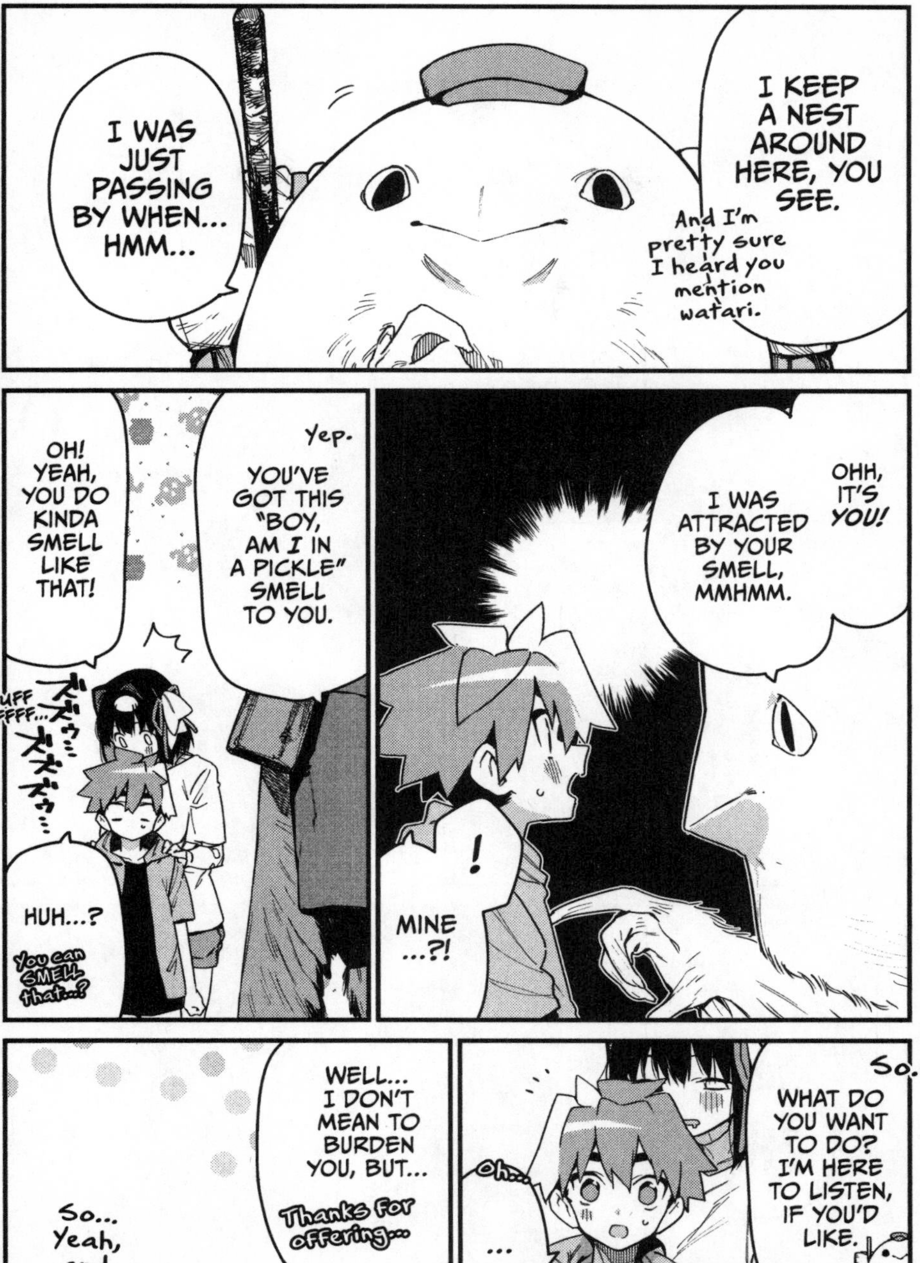
I KEEP A NEST AROUND HERE, YOU SEE.
And I'm pretty sure I heard you mention watari.
I WAS JUST PASSING BY WHEN... HMM...
OHH, IT'S YOU!
I WAS ATTRACTED BY YOUR SMELL, MMHMM.
!
MINE ...?!
Yep.
YOU'VE GOT THIS "BOY, AM I IN A PICKLE" SMELL TO YOU.
OH! YEAH, YOU DO KINDA SMELL LIKE THAT!
HUFF UFFFF...
HUH...?
You can SMELL that...?
So...
WHAT DO YOU WANT TO DO? I'M HERE TO LISTEN, IF YOU'D LIKE.
Oh...
...
WELL... I DON'T MEAN TO BURDEN YOU, BUT...
Thanks for offering...
So... Yeah, and then...

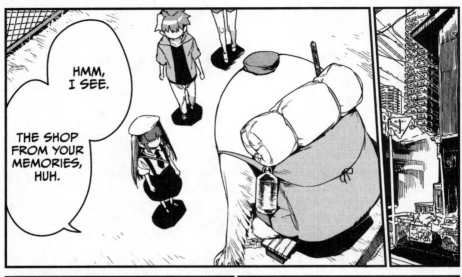

HMM, I SEE.
THE SHOP FROM YOUR MEMORIES, HUH.
IN THAT CASE... YEAH...
I THINK IT'S BEST TO TAKE A LOOK AT THE GIRL'S HIMEKABURI.
TAKE A LOOK ...?
...HUH?
What do you mean...?
Pardon me.
ZH-

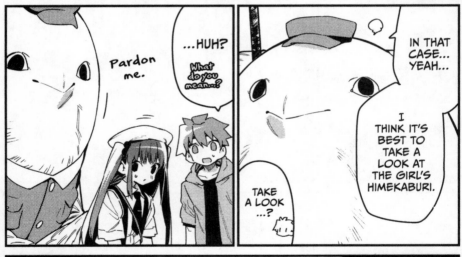

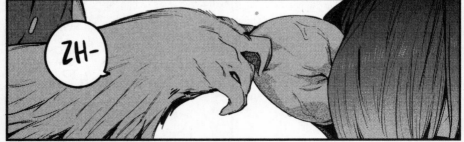

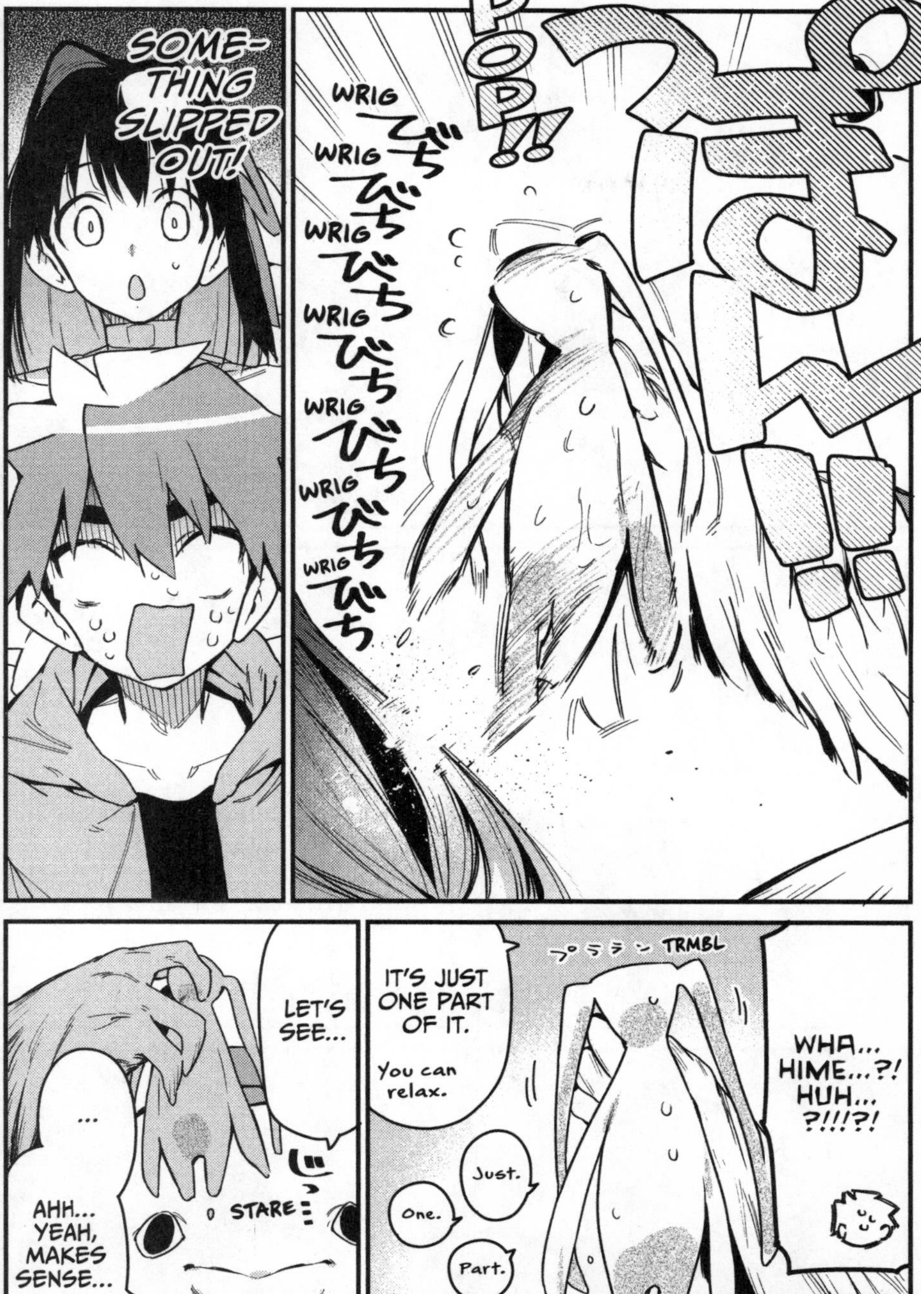

ぽん!!
POP!!
WRIG びち
WRIG びち
WRIG びち
WRIG びち
WRIG びち
WRIG びち
WRIG びち
WRIG びち
SOME-THING SLIPPED OUT!
プララン TRMBL
WHA... HIME...?! HUH...?!!!?!
IT'S JUST ONE PART OF IT.
You can relax.
Just.
One.
Part.
LET'S SEE...
...
じっ
STARE
AHH... YEAH, MAKES SENSE...

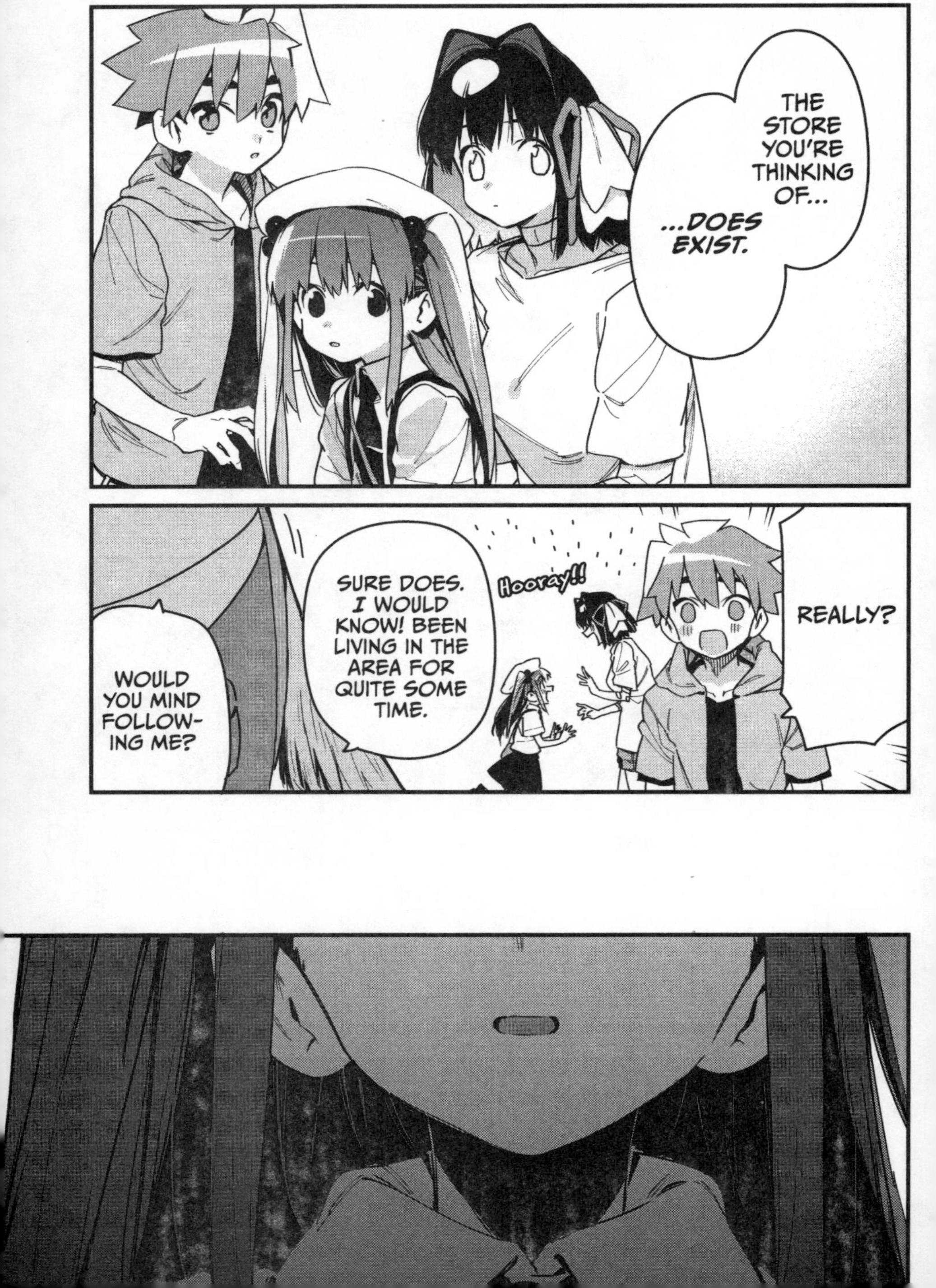
THE STORE YOU'RE THINKING OF...
...DOES EXIST.
REALLY?
Hooray!!
SURE DOES. I WOULD KNOW! BEEN LIVING IN THE AREA FOR QUITE SOME TIME.
WOULD YOU MIND FOLLOW-ING ME?

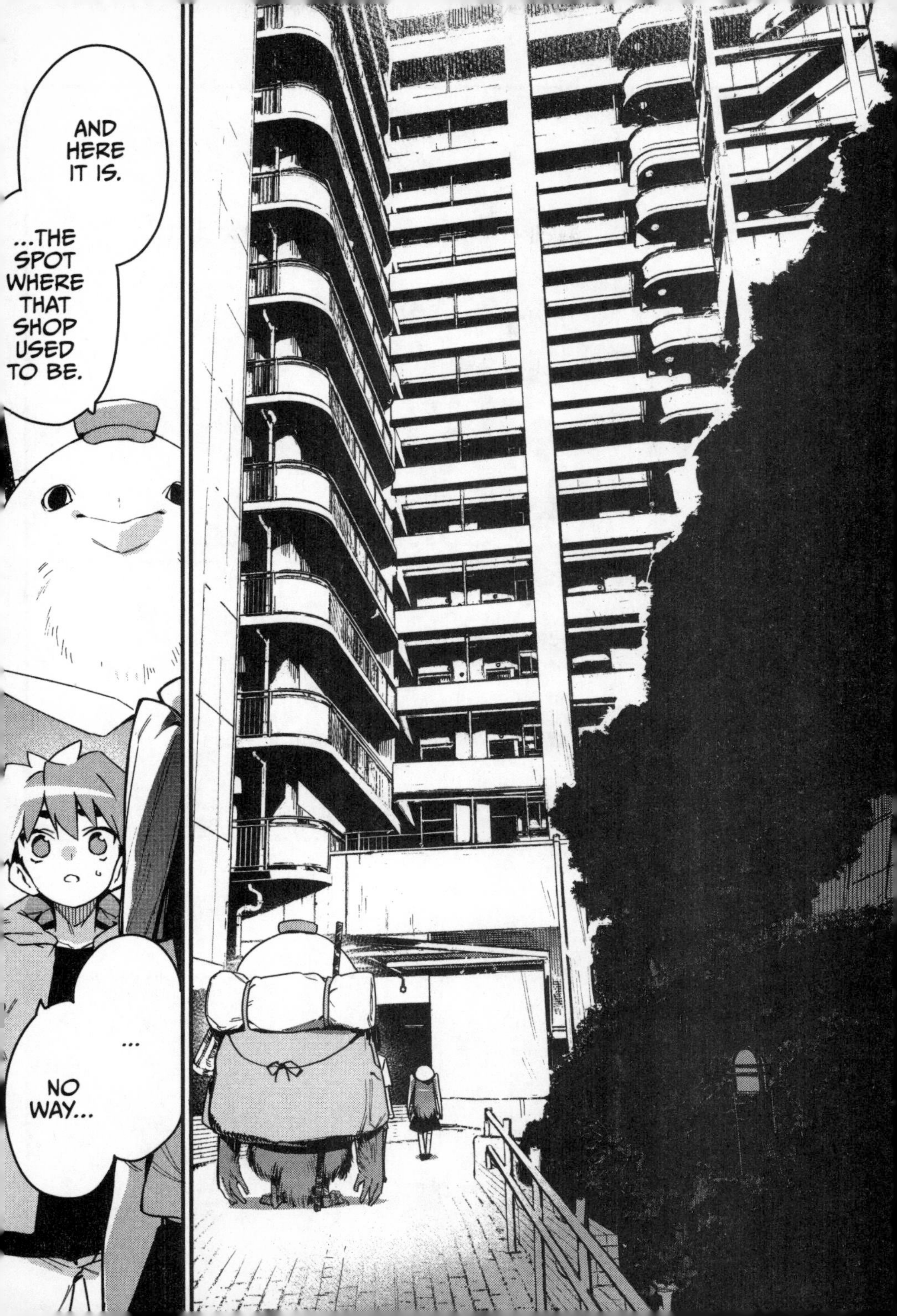
AND HERE IT IS.
...THE SPOT WHERE THAT SHOP USED TO BE.
...
NO WAY...

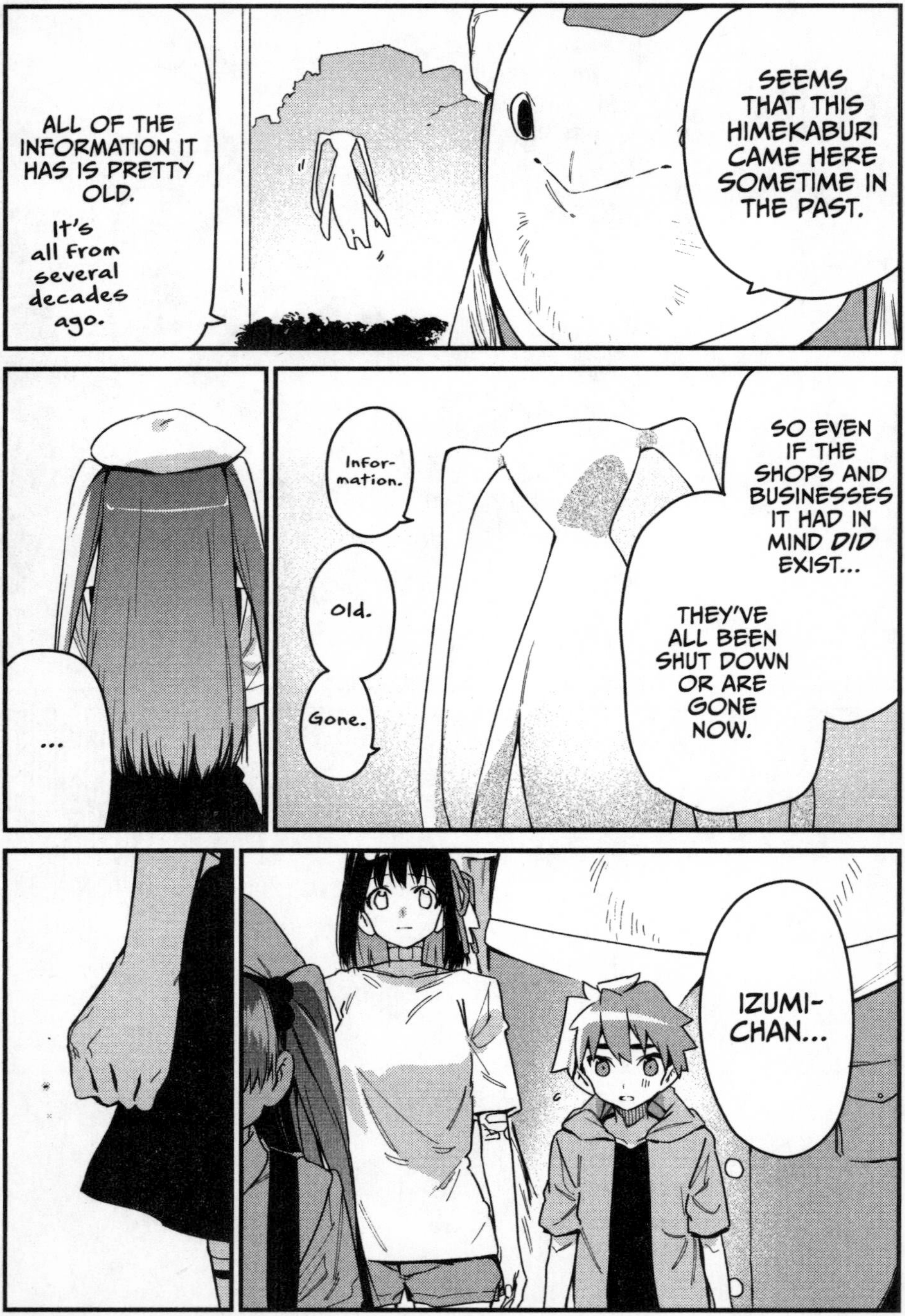
SEEMS THAT THIS HIMEKABURI CAME HERE SOMETIME IN THE PAST.
ALL OF THE INFORMATION IT HAS IS PRETTY OLD.
It's all from several decades ago.
SO EVEN IF THE SHOPS AND BUSINESSES IT HAD IN MIND *DID* EXIST...
THEY'VE ALL BEEN SHUT DOWN OR ARE GONE NOW.
Information.
Old.
Gone.
...
IZUMI-CHAN...

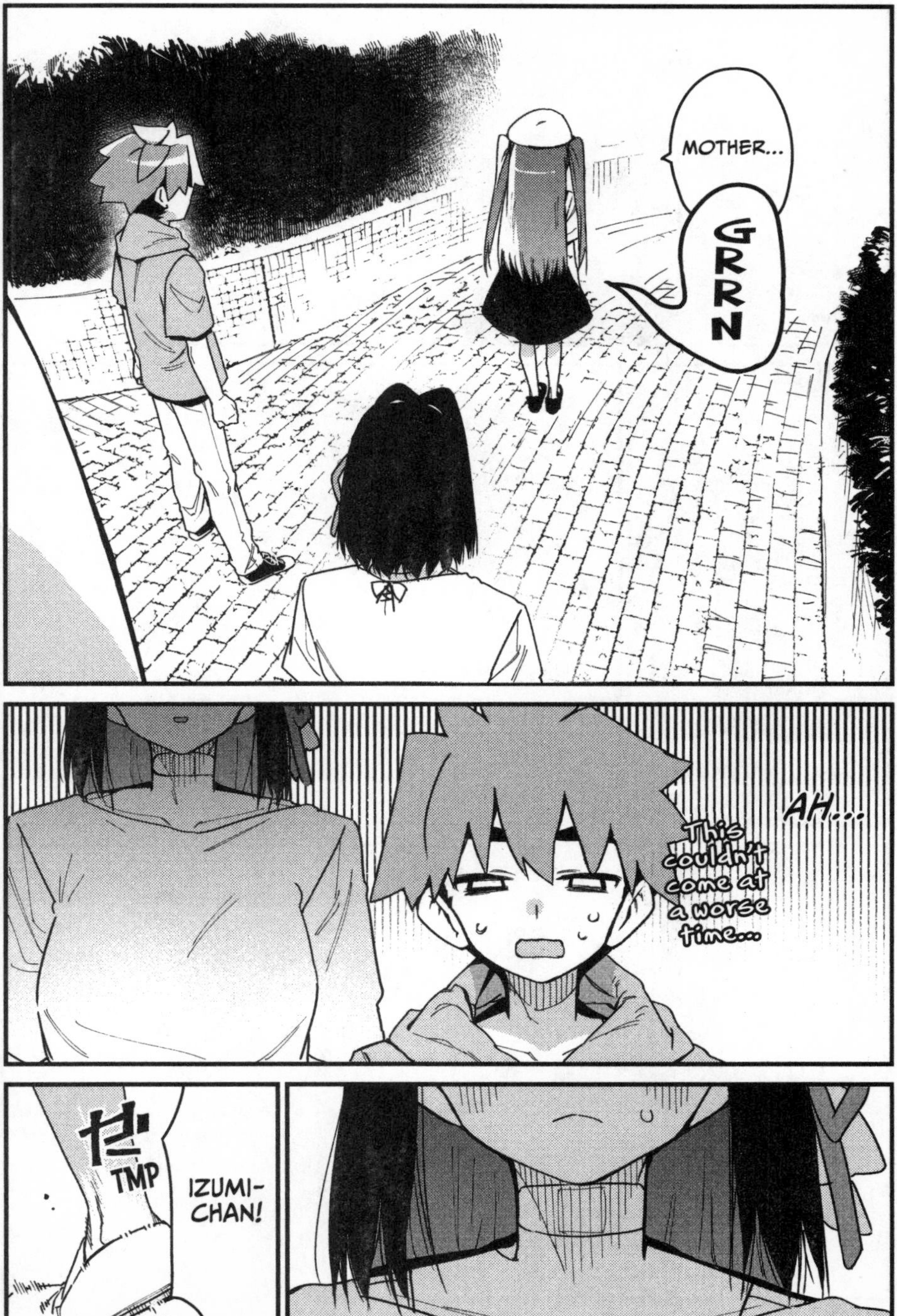
MOTHER...
GRRN
AH...
This couldn't come at a worse time...
IZUMI-CHAN!
TMP

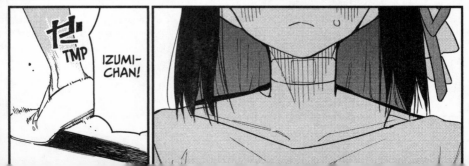

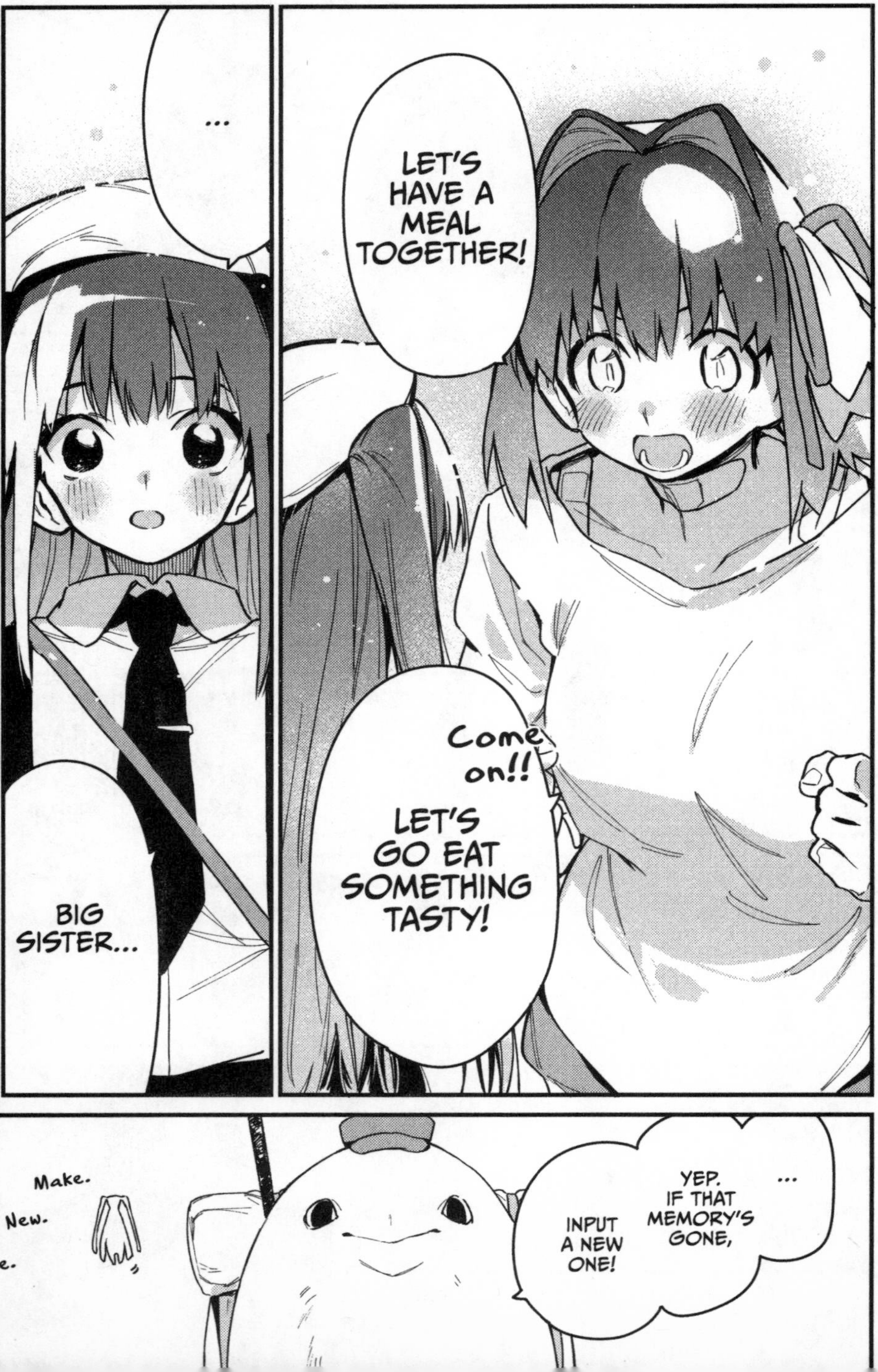
LET'S HAVE A MEAL TOGETHER!
Come on!!
LET'S GO EAT SOMETHING TASTY!
...
BIG SISTER...
...
YEP. IF THAT MEMORY'S GONE,
INPUT A NEW ONE!
Make.
New.
One.

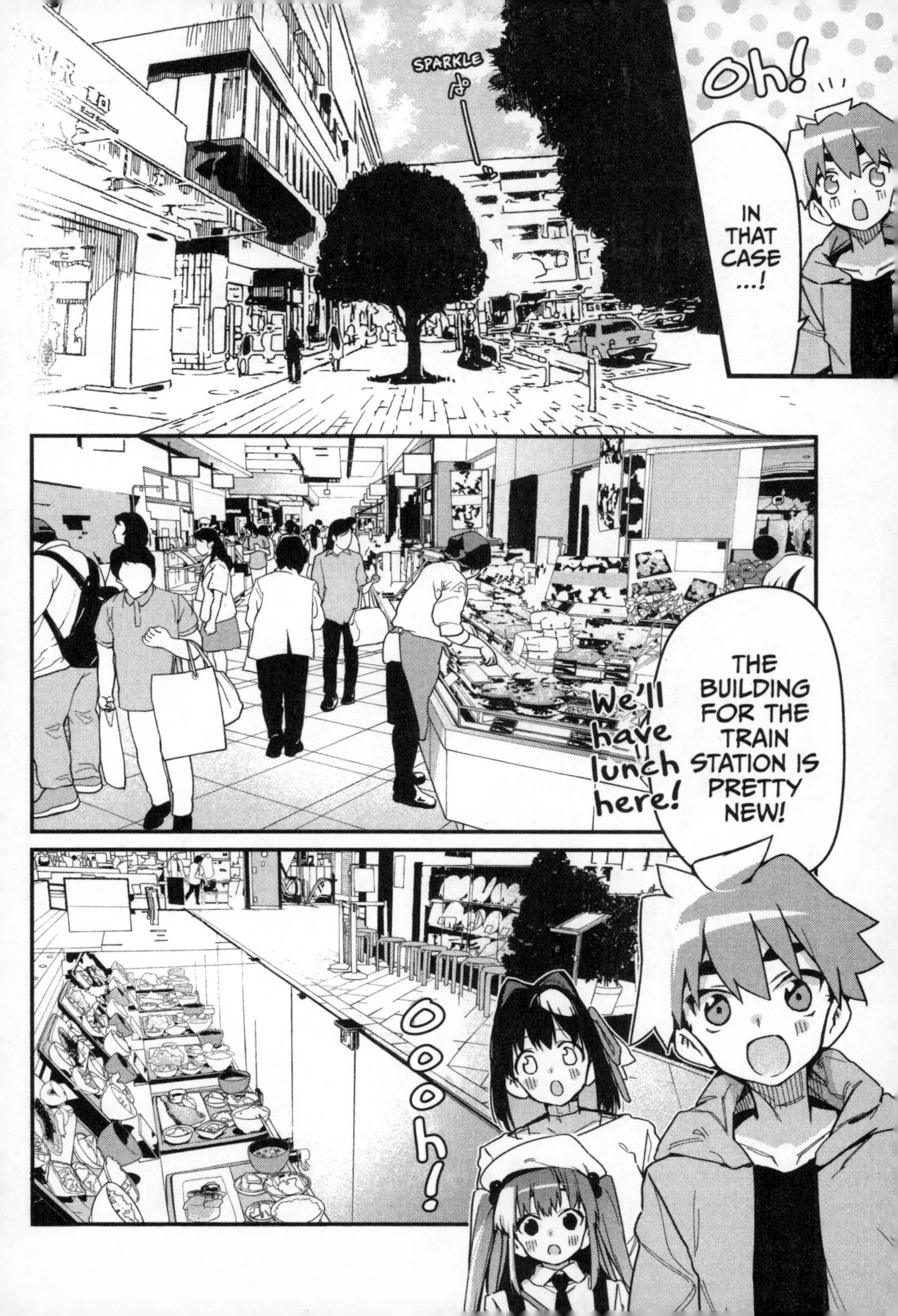
Oh!
IN THAT CASE ...!
SPARKLE
THE BUILDING FOR THE TRAIN STATION IS PRETTY NEW!
We'll have lunch here!
Oooh!

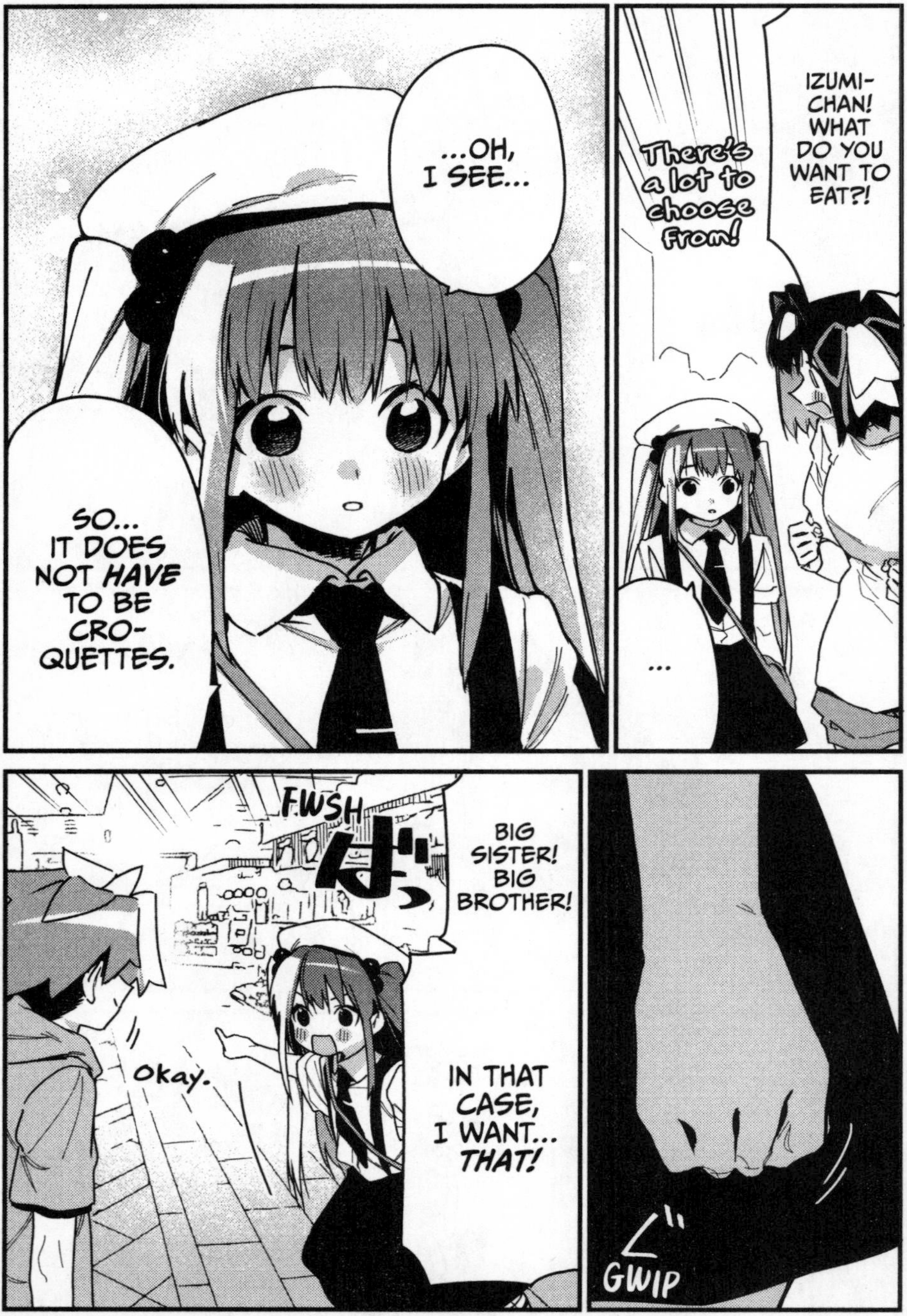
IZUMI-CHAN! WHAT DO YOU WANT TO EAT?!
There's a lot to choose from!
...
...OH, I SEE...
SO... IT DOES NOT *HAVE* TO BE CRO-QUETTES.
GWIP
FWSH
ばっ
BIG SISTER! BIG BROTHER!
IN THAT CASE, I WANT... *THAT!*
Okay.

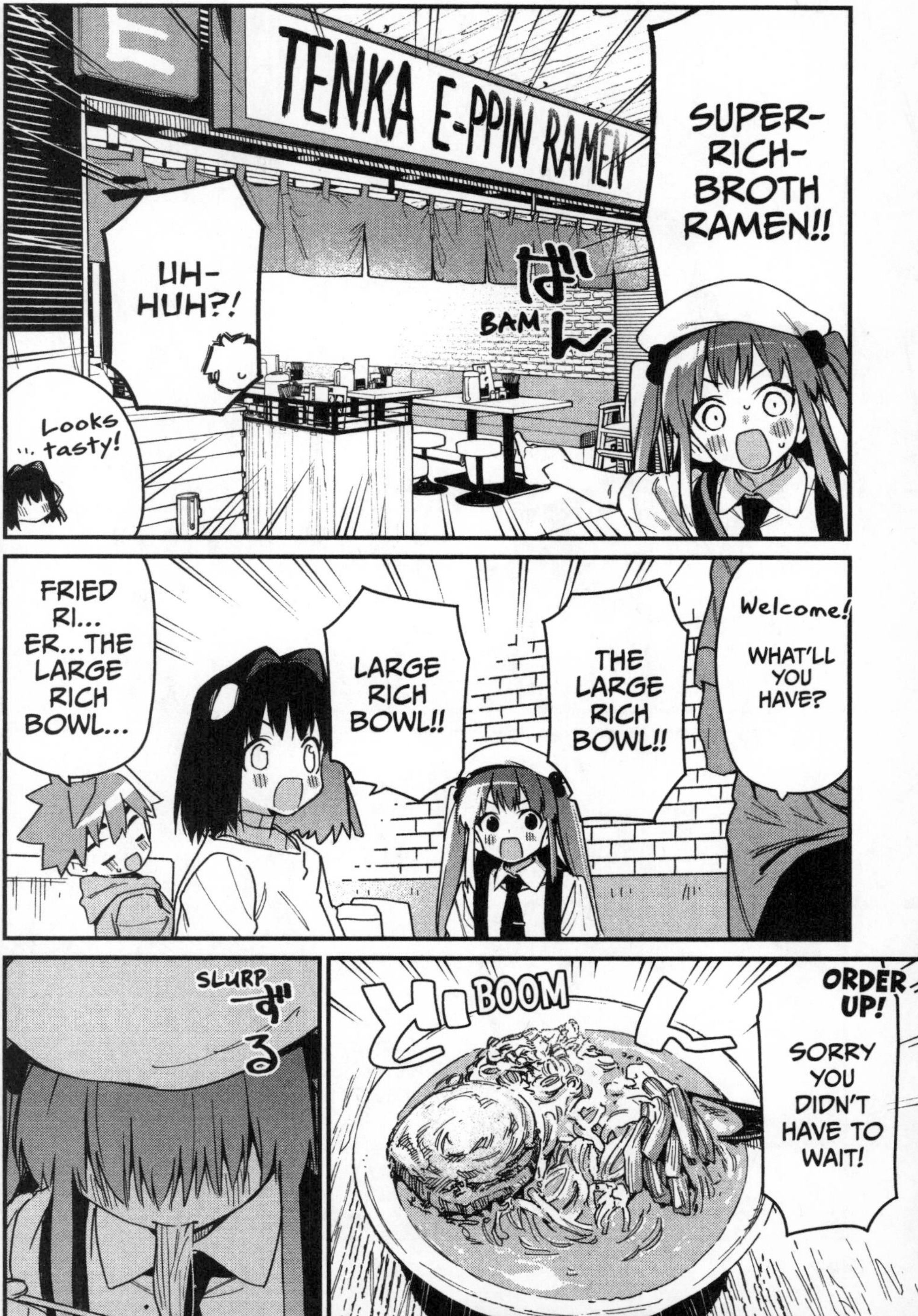
SUPER-RICH-BROTH RAMEN!!
TENKA E-PPIN RAMEN
ばん
BAM
UH-HUH?!
Looks tasty!
Welcome!
WHAT'LL YOU HAVE?
THE LARGE RICH BOWL!!
LARGE RICH BOWL!!
FRIED RI... ER...THE LARGE RICH BOWL...
ORDER UP!
SORRY YOU DIDN'T HAVE TO WAIT!
どん
BOOM
SLURP
ずる

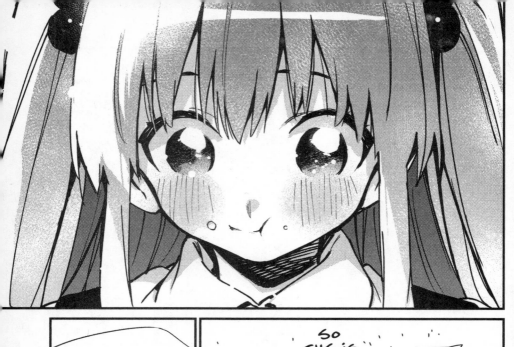

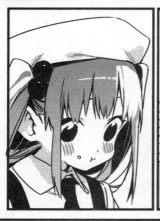

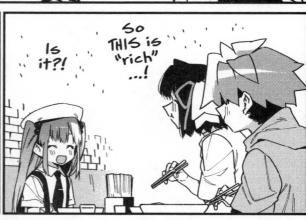

Is it?!

SO THIS is "rich" ...!

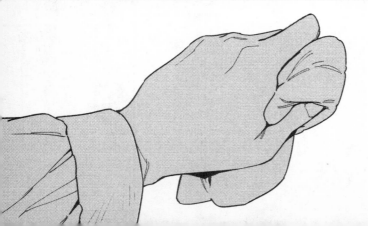

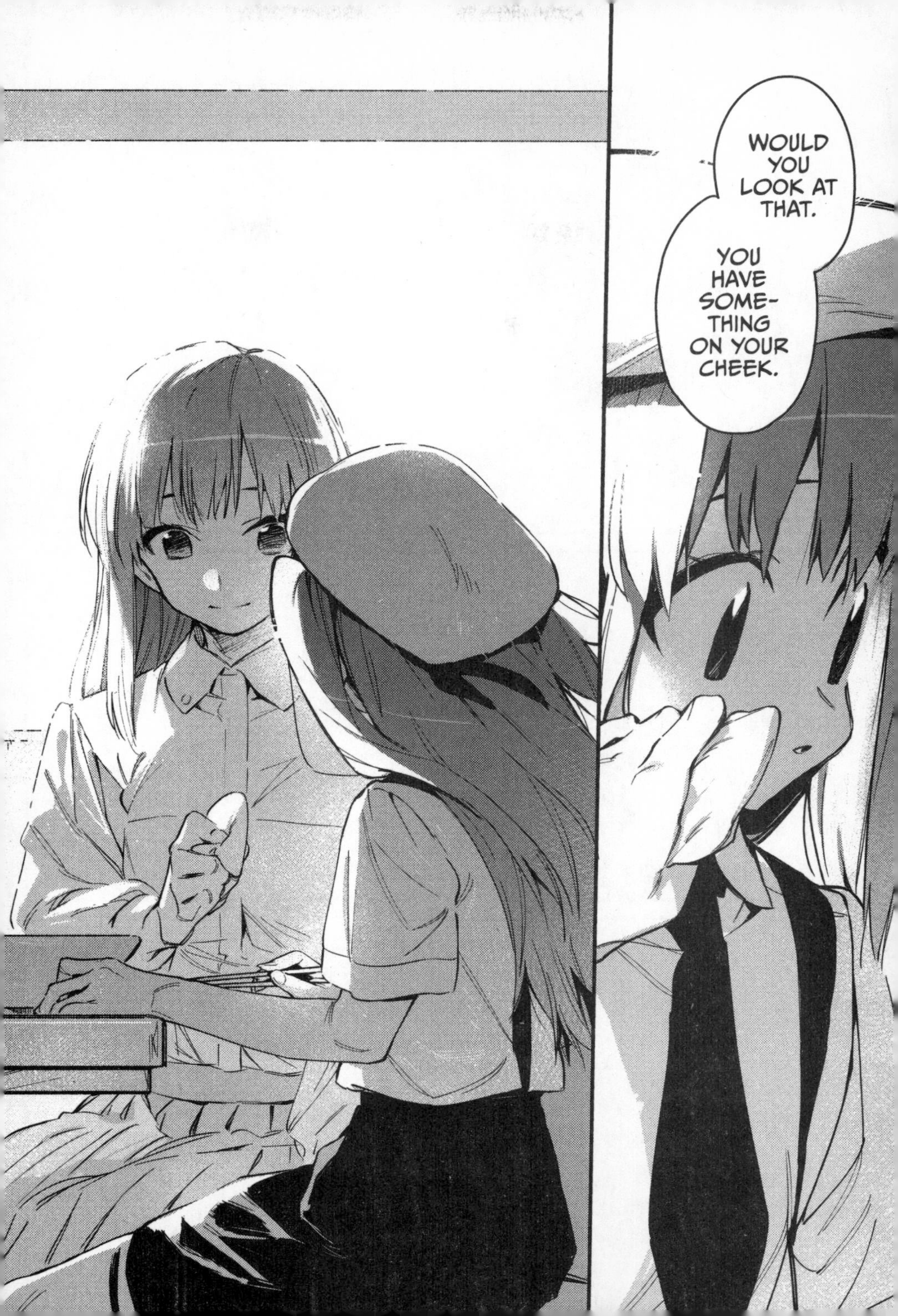
WOULD YOU LOOK AT THAT.
YOU HAVE SOME-THING ON YOUR CHEEK.

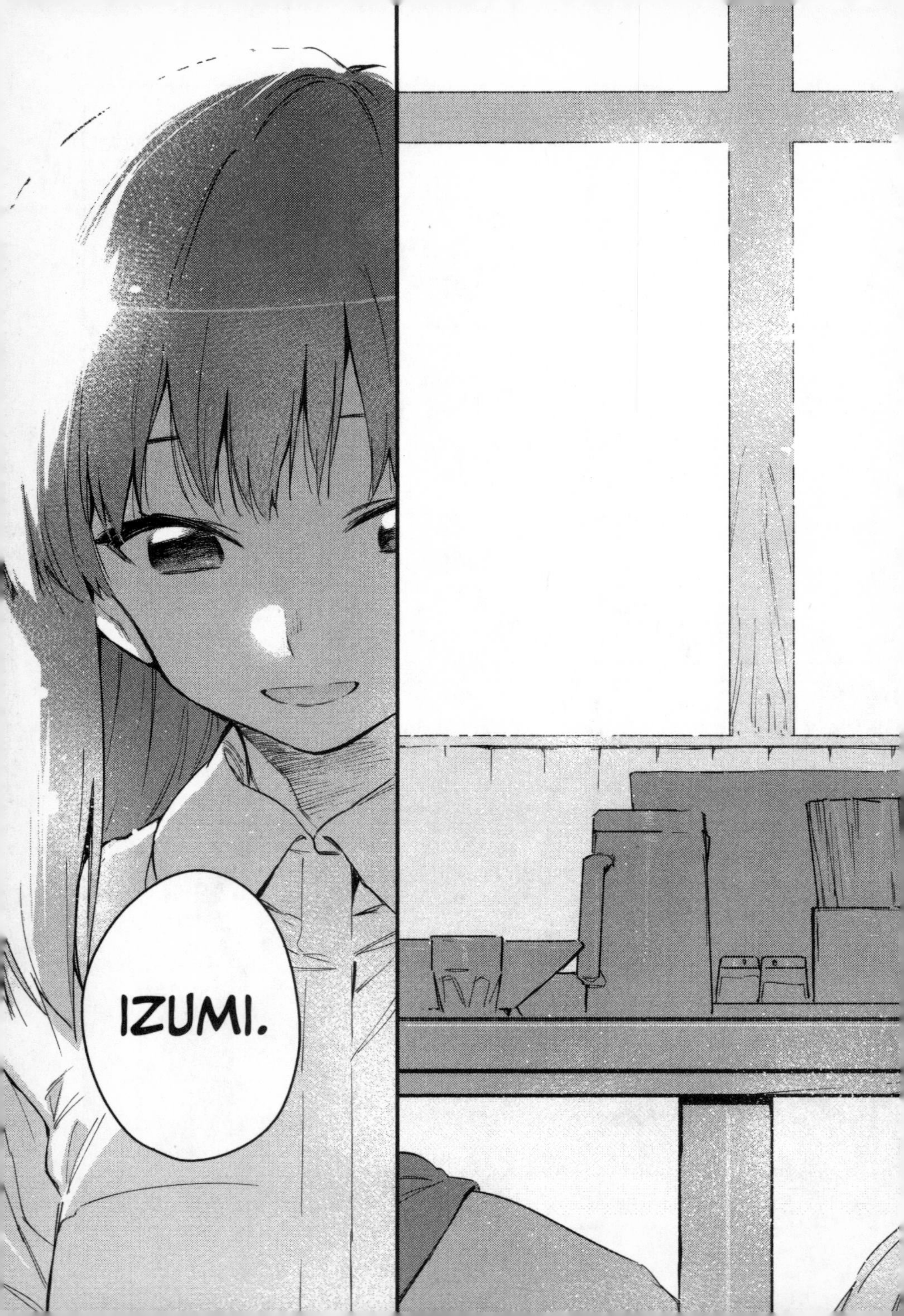
IZUMI.

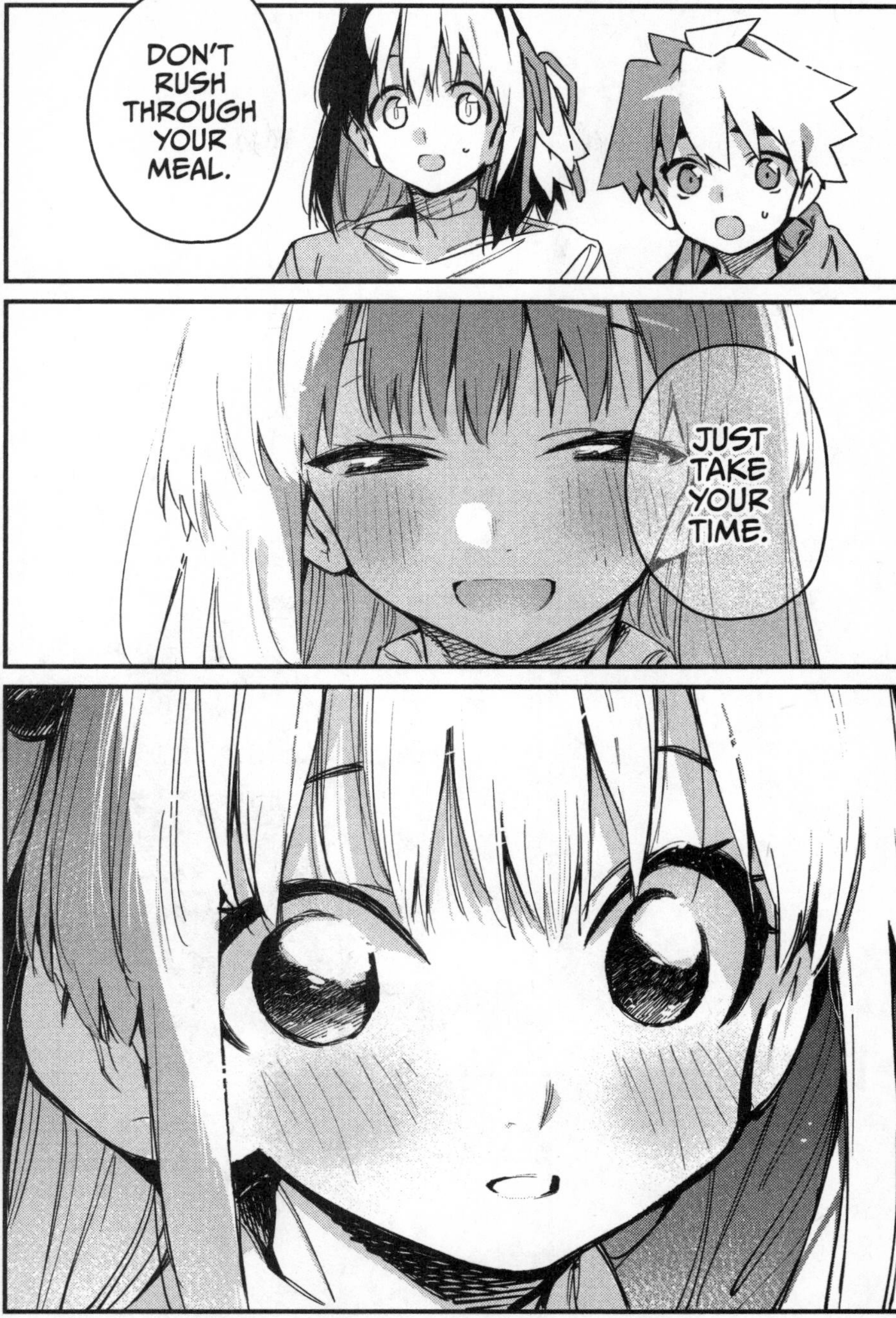
DON'T RUSH THROUGH YOUR MEAL.
JUST TAKE YOUR TIME.

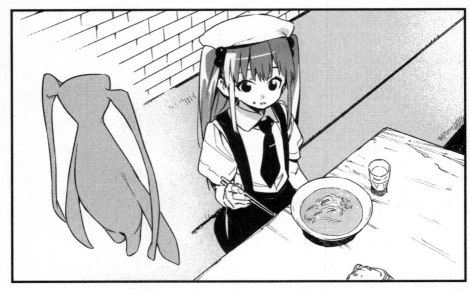

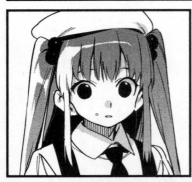

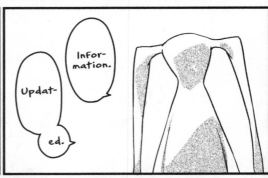

Updat-
ed.

Infor-
mation.

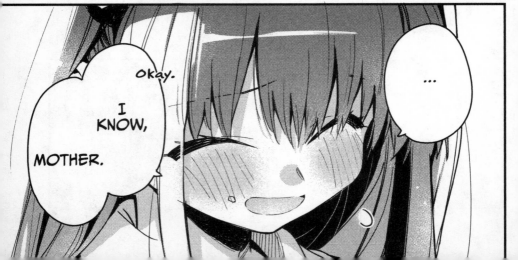

Okay.

I
KNOW,

MOTHER.

...

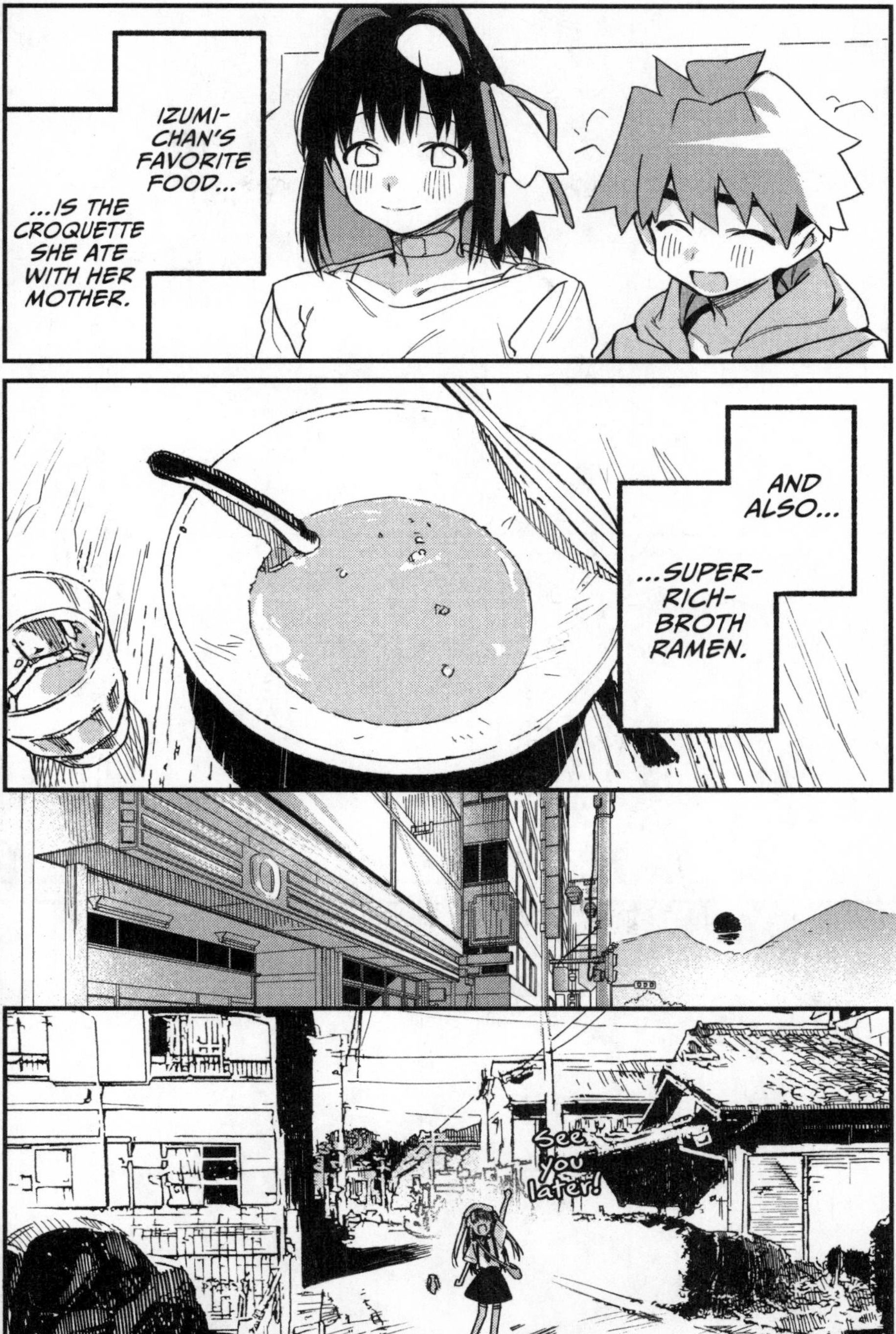
IZUMI-CHAN'S FAVORITE FOOD...
...IS THE CROQUETTE SHE ATE WITH HER MOTHER.
AND ALSO...
...SUPER-RICH-BROTH RAMEN.
See you later!

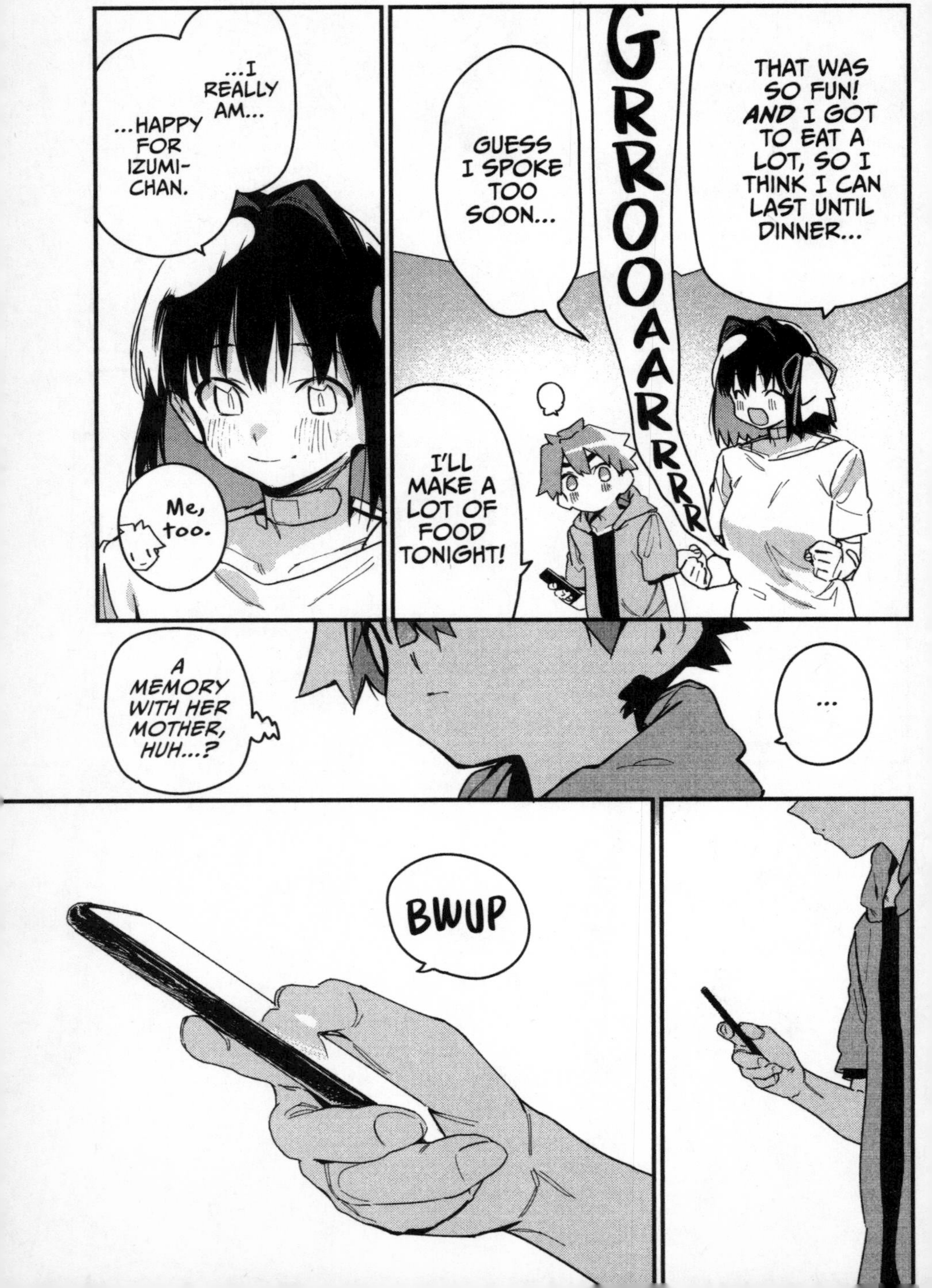
THAT WAS SO FUN! AND I GOT TO EAT A LOT, SO I THINK I CAN LAST UNTIL DINNER...
GRROOAARRRR
GUESS I SPOKE TOO SOON...
I'LL MAKE A LOT OF FOOD TONIGHT!
...I REALLY AM... ...HAPPY FOR IZUMI-CHAN.
Me, too.
...
A MEMORY WITH HER MOTHER, HUH...?
BWUP

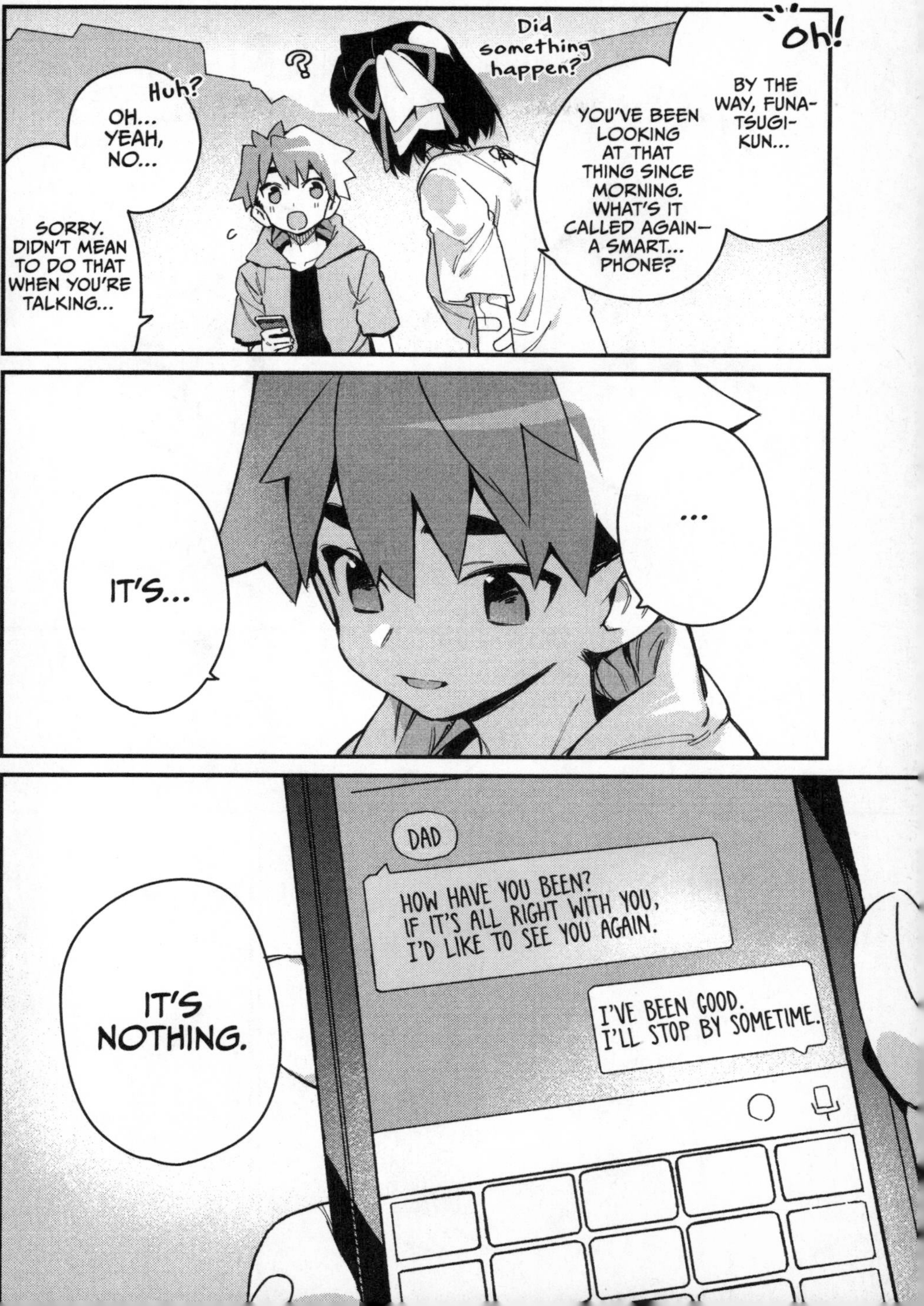
Oh!
BY THE WAY, FUNA-TSUGI-KUN...
YOU'VE BEEN LOOKING AT THAT THING SINCE MORNING. WHAT'S IT CALLED AGAIN— A SMART... PHONE?
Did something happen?
?
Huh?
OH... YEAH, NO...
SORRY. DIDN'T MEAN TO DO THAT WHEN YOU'RE TALKING...
...
IT'S...
DAD
HOW HAVE YOU BEEN? IF IT'S ALL RIGHT WITH YOU, I'D LIKE TO SEE YOU AGAIN.
I'VE BEEN GOOD. I'LL STOP BY SOMETIME.
IT'S NOTHING.

Sachi's
MONSTROUS
Appetite

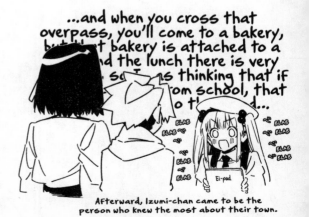

...and when you cross that overpass, you'll come to a bakery, but that bakery is attached to a ...d the lunch there is very ...s thinking that if ...om school, that ...

BLAB BLAB ~~
BLAB ~~

BLAB BLAB ~~
BLAB BLAB ~~

~~
BLAB
~~ BLAB

Ei-pad

Afterward, Izumi-chan came to be the person who knew the most about their town.

Chapter 11.5: Sachi's Monstrous Appetizer

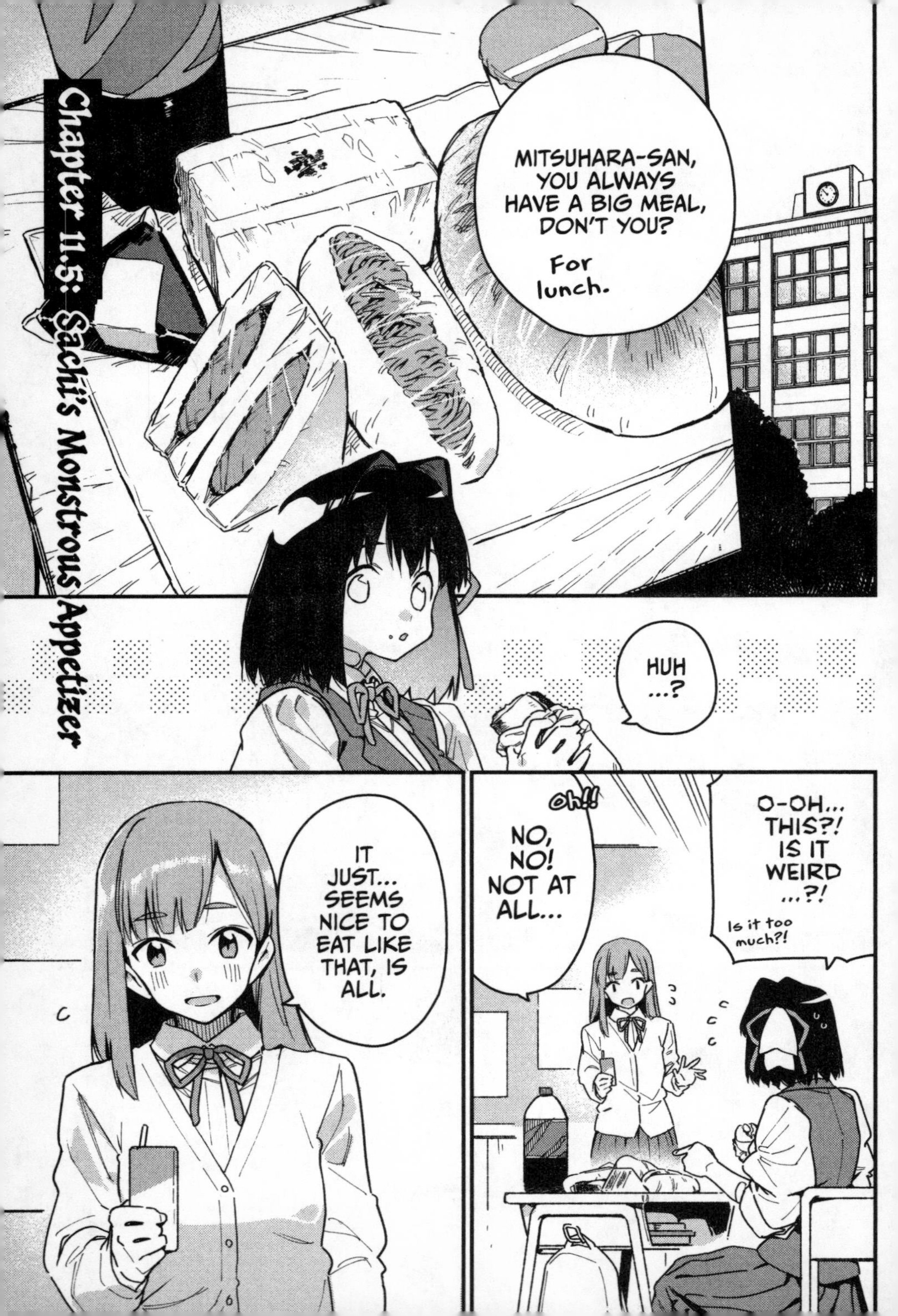
MITSUHARA-SAN, YOU ALWAYS HAVE A BIG MEAL, DON'T YOU?
For lunch.
HUH ...?
O-OH... THIS?! IS IT WEIRD ...?!
Is it too much?!
Oh!!
NO, NO! NOT AT ALL...
IT JUST... SEEMS NICE TO EAT LIKE THAT, IS ALL.

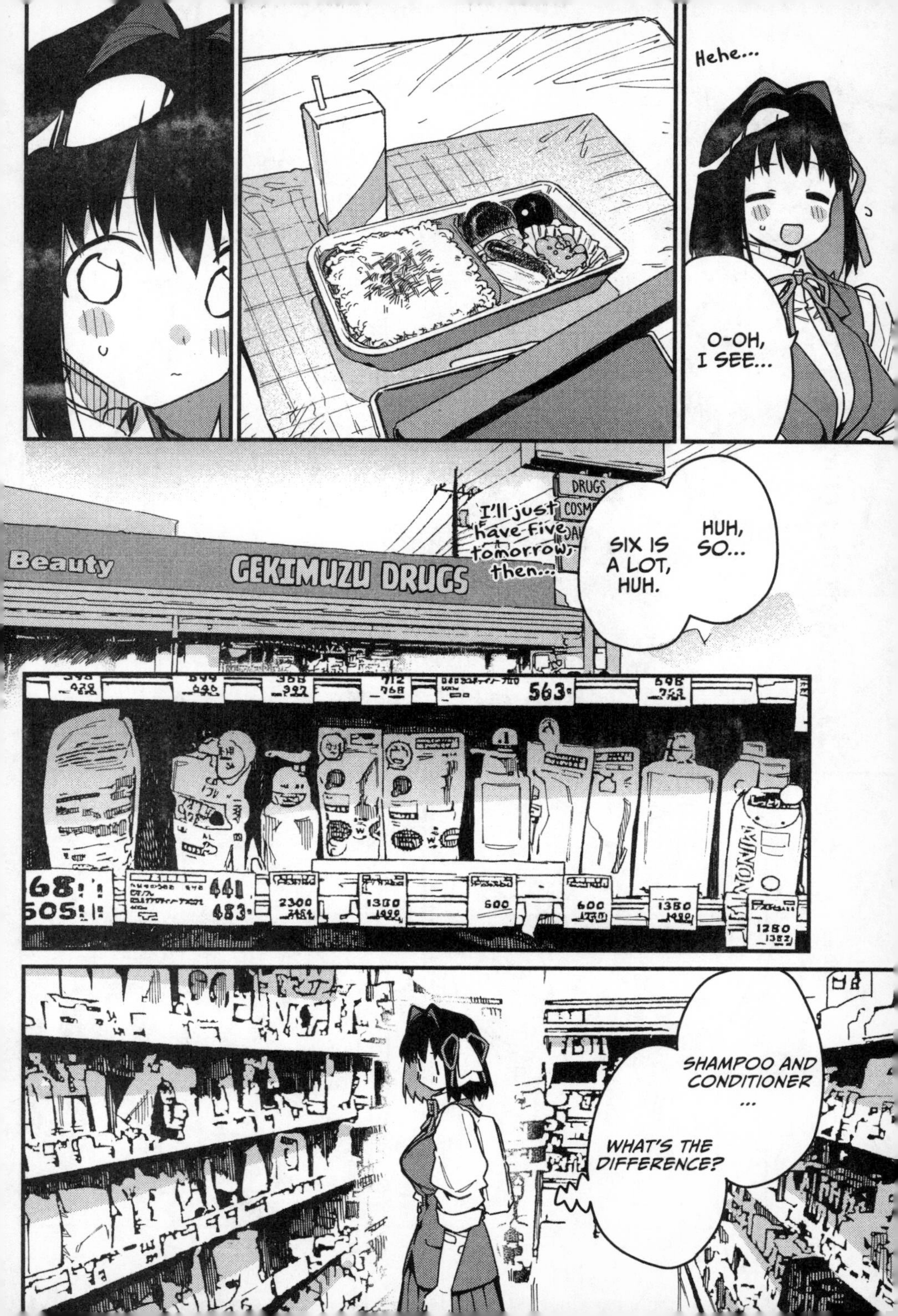
Hehe...
O-OH, I SEE...
HUH, SO... SIX IS A LOT, HUH.
I'll just have five tomorrow, then...
DRUGS
GEKIMUZU DRUGS
Beauty
SHAMPOO AND CONDITIONER ...
WHAT'S THE DIFFERENCE?

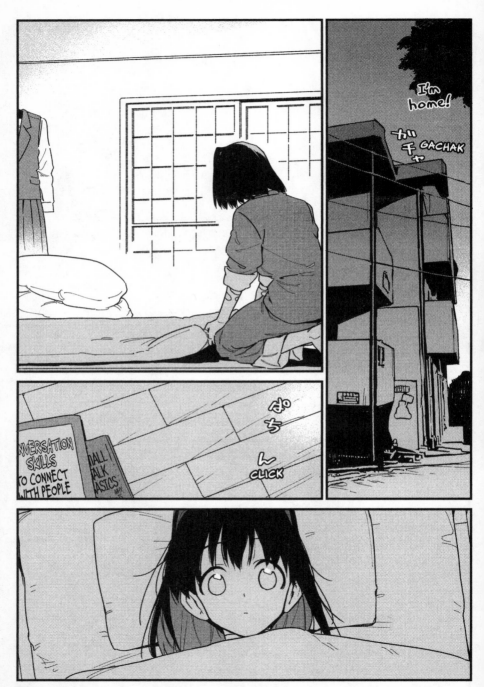

I'm home!

GACHAK

CLICK

CONVERSATION SKILLS TO CONNECT WITH PEOPLE

SMALL TALK BASICS

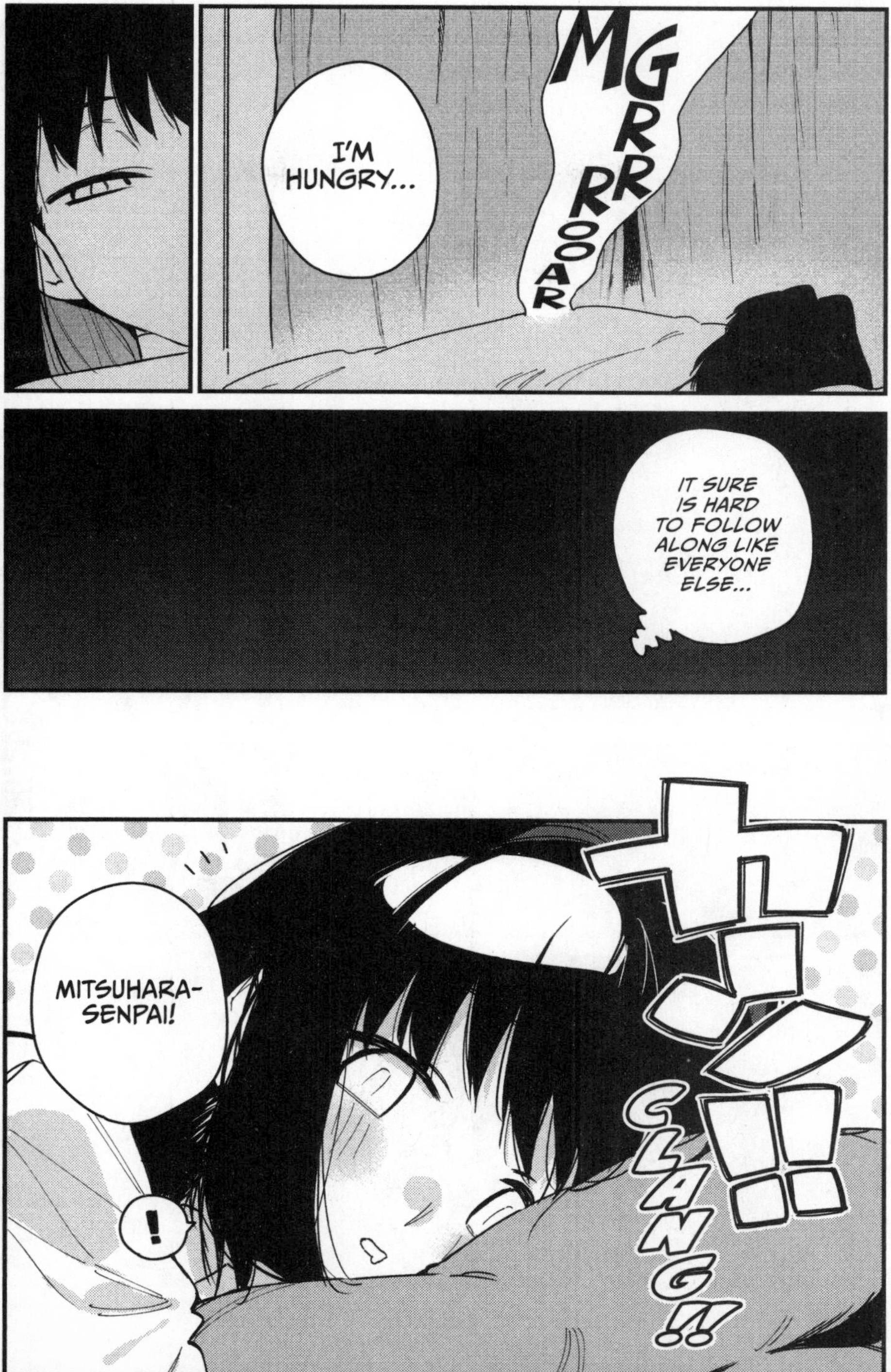
MGRRROOAR
I'M HUNGRY...
IT SURE IS HARD TO FOLLOW ALONG LIKE EVERYONE ELSE...
CLANG!!
MITSUHARA-SENPAI!
!

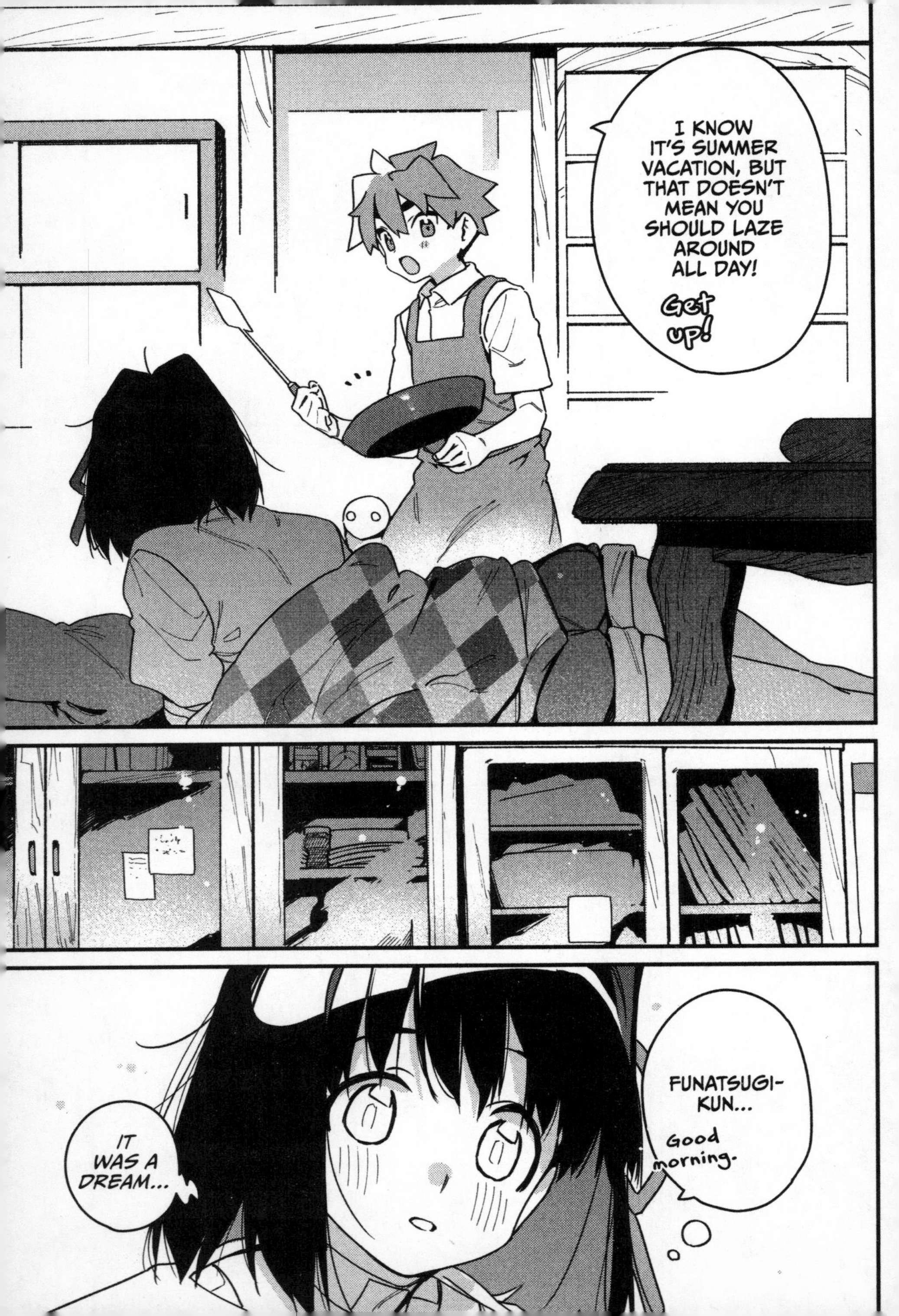
I KNOW IT'S SUMMER VACATION, BUT THAT DOESN'T MEAN YOU SHOULD LAZE AROUND ALL DAY!
Get up!
FUNATSUGI-KUN...
Good morning.
IT WAS A DREAM...

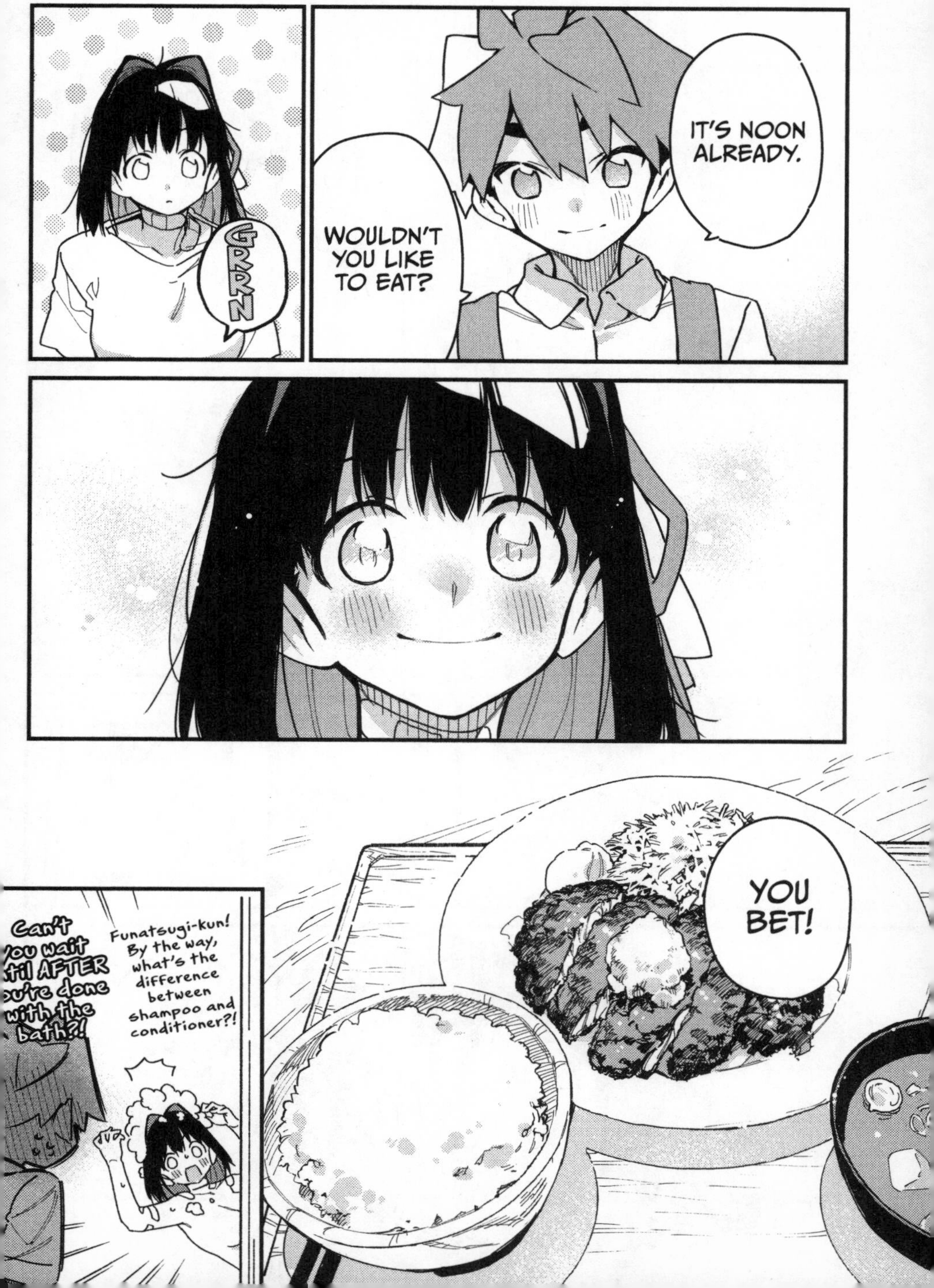
IT'S NOON ALREADY.
WOULDN'T YOU LIKE TO EAT?
GRRN
YOU BET!
Funatsugi-kun! By the way, what's the difference between shampoo and conditioner?!
Can't you wait til AFTER u're done with the bath?!

Chapter 12: Even When It Looks Like You Made a Mistak

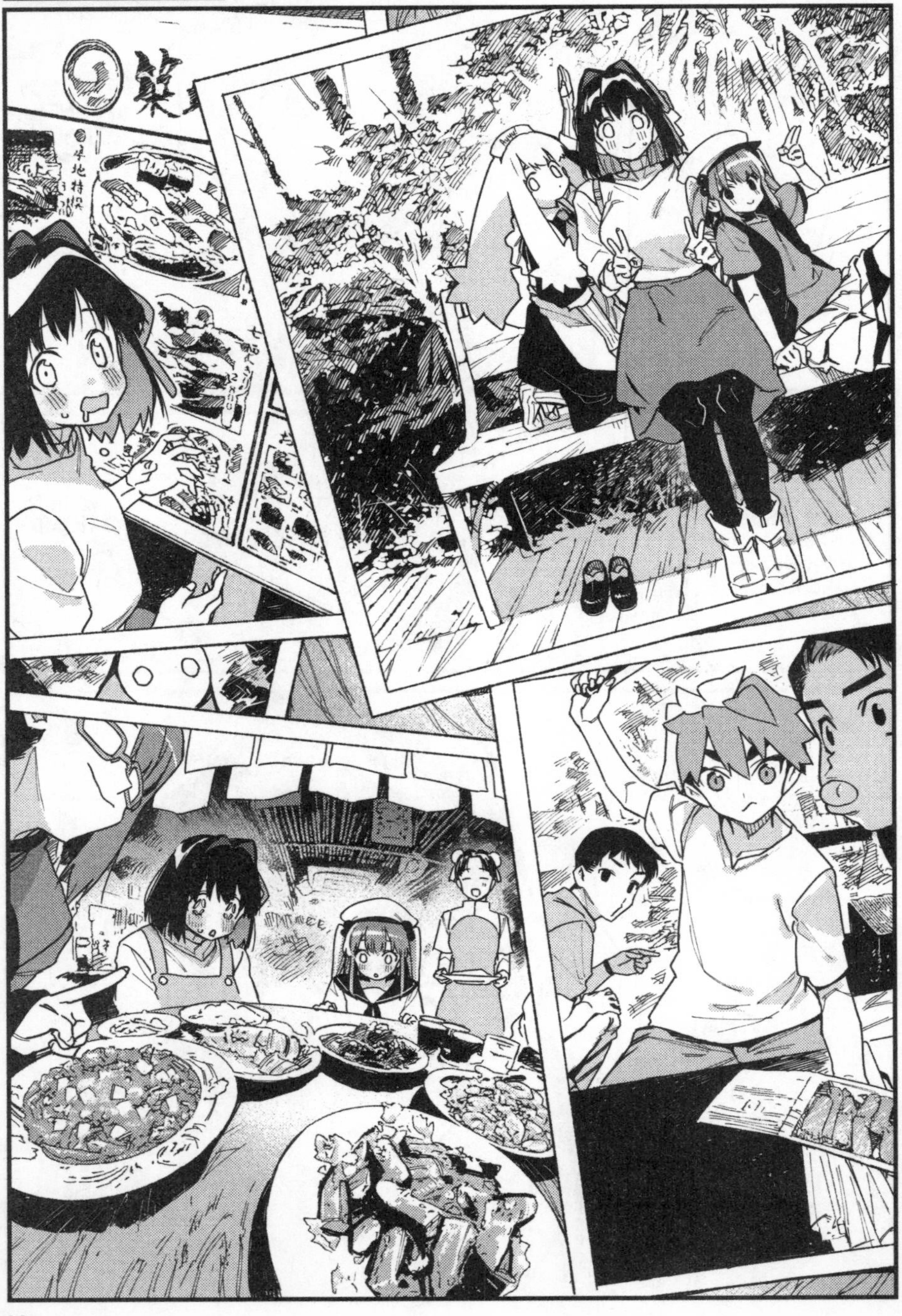

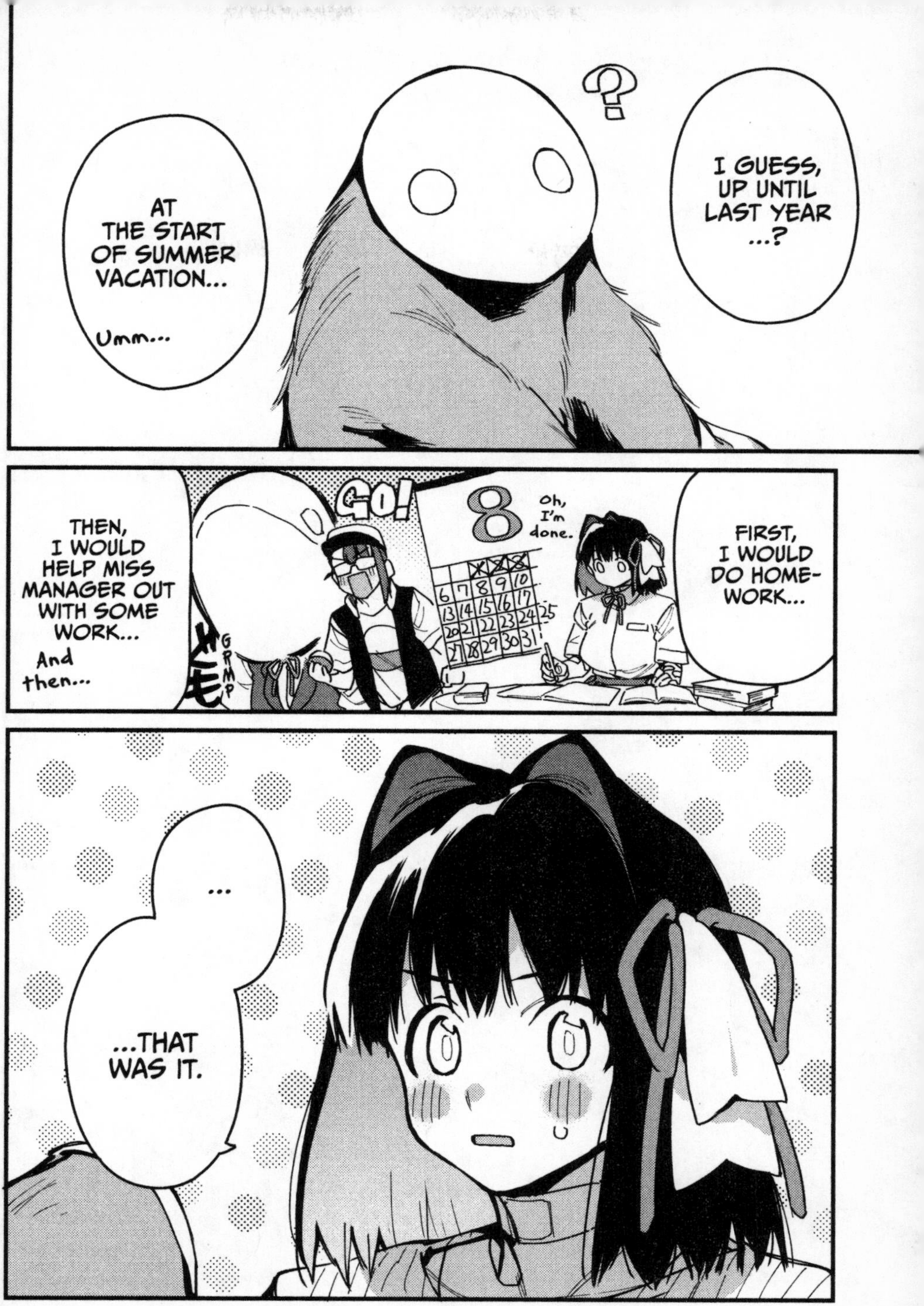
I GUESS, UP UNTIL LAST YEAR ...?
?
AT THE START OF SUMMER VACATION...
Umm...
FIRST, I WOULD DO HOME-WORK...
Oh, I'm done.
GO!
THEN, I WOULD HELP MISS MANAGER OUT WITH SOME WORK...
And then...
GRMP
...
...THAT WAS IT.

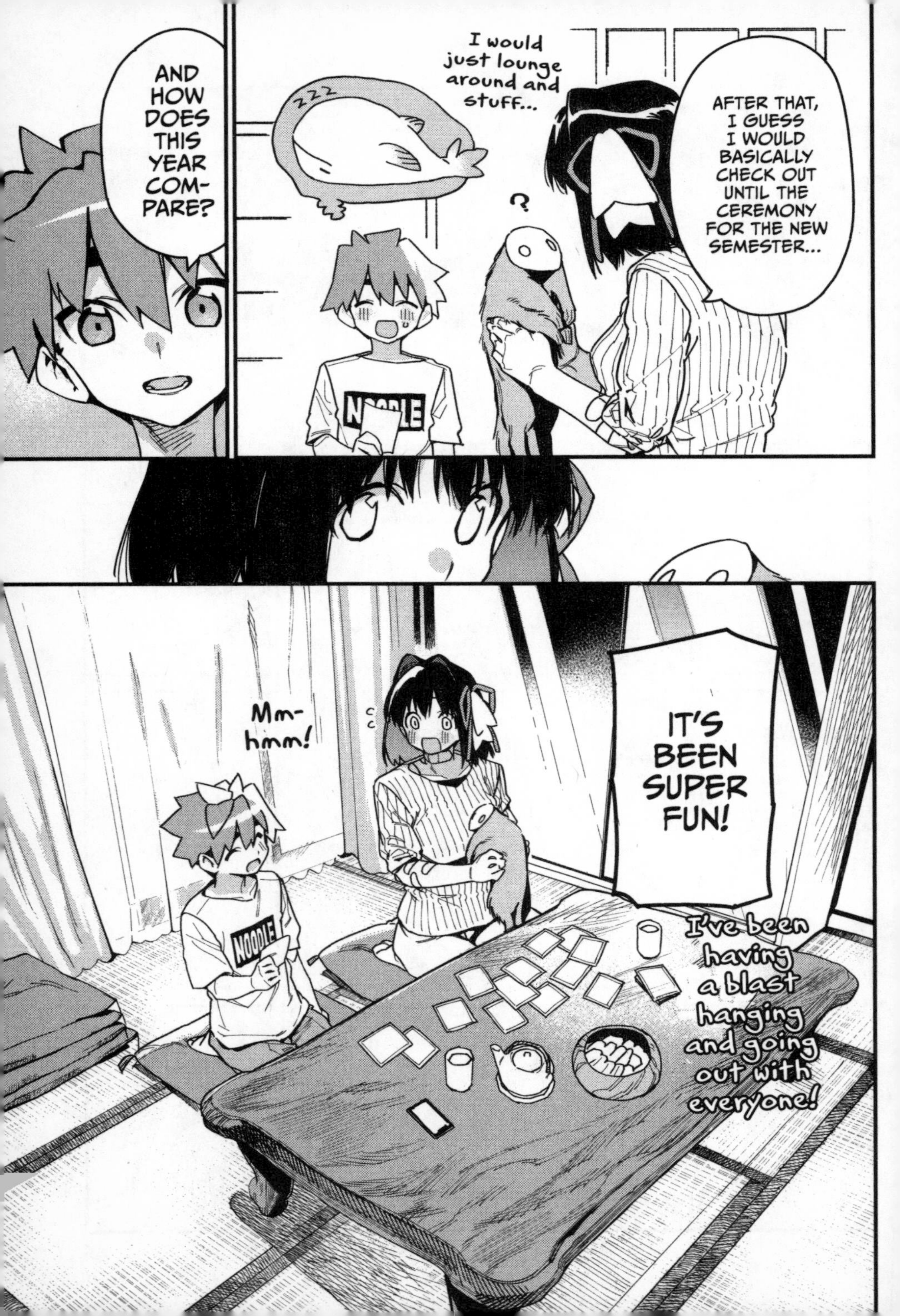

AFTER THAT, I GUESS I WOULD BASICALLY CHECK OUT UNTIL THE CEREMONY FOR THE NEW SEMESTER...
I would just lounge around and stuff...
AND HOW DOES THIS YEAR COMPARE?
IT'S BEEN SUPER FUN!
I've been having a blast hanging and going out with everyone!
Mm-hmm!

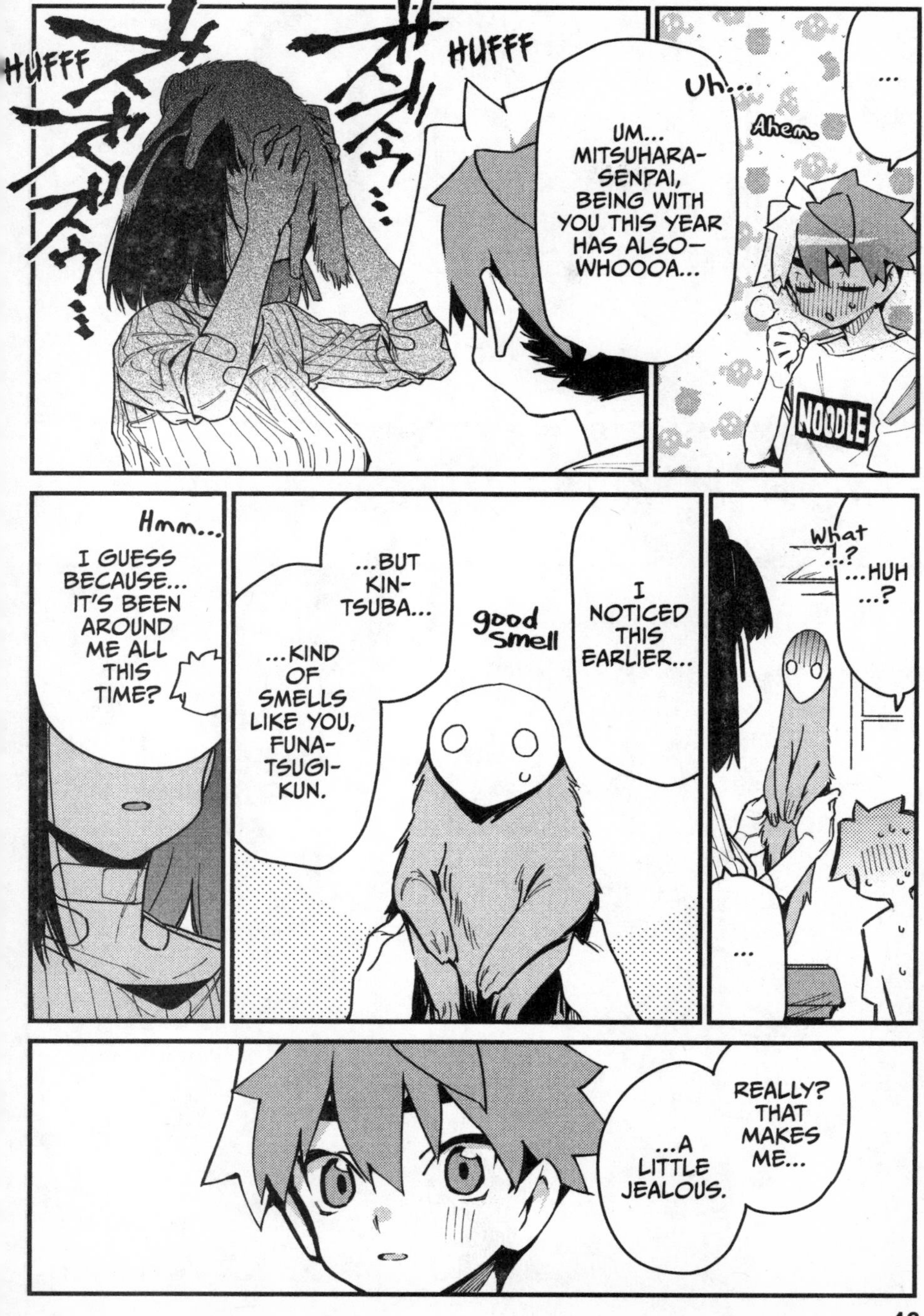
...
Ahem.
Uh...
HUFFF
HUFFF
UM... MITSUHARA-SENPAI, BEING WITH YOU THIS YEAR HAS ALSO— WHOOOA...
What ...?
...HUH ...?
...
I NOTICED THIS EARLIER...
good smell
...BUT KIN-TSUBA...
...KIND OF SMELLS LIKE YOU, FUNA-TSUGI-KUN.
Hmm...
I GUESS BECAUSE... IT'S BEEN AROUND ME ALL THIS TIME?
REALLY? THAT MAKES ME...
...A LITTLE JEALOUS.

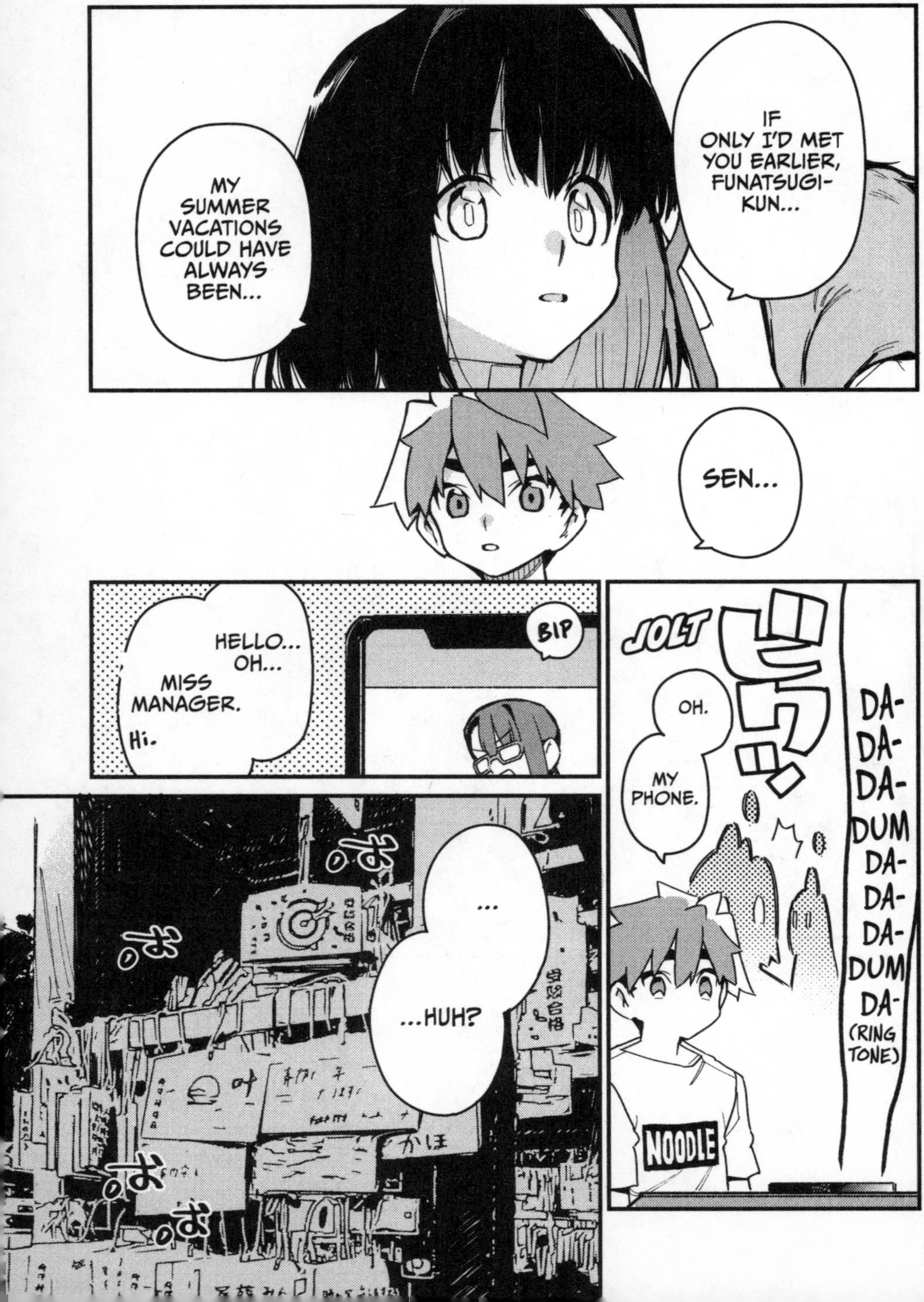
IF ONLY I'D MET YOU EARLIER, FUNATSUGI-KUN...
MY SUMMER VACATIONS COULD HAVE ALWAYS BEEN...
SEN...
DA-DA-DA-DUM DA-DA-DA-DUM DA- (RINGTONE)
JOLT
OH. MY PHONE.
BIP
HELLO... OH... MISS MANAGER.
Hi.
...
...HUH?
NOODLE

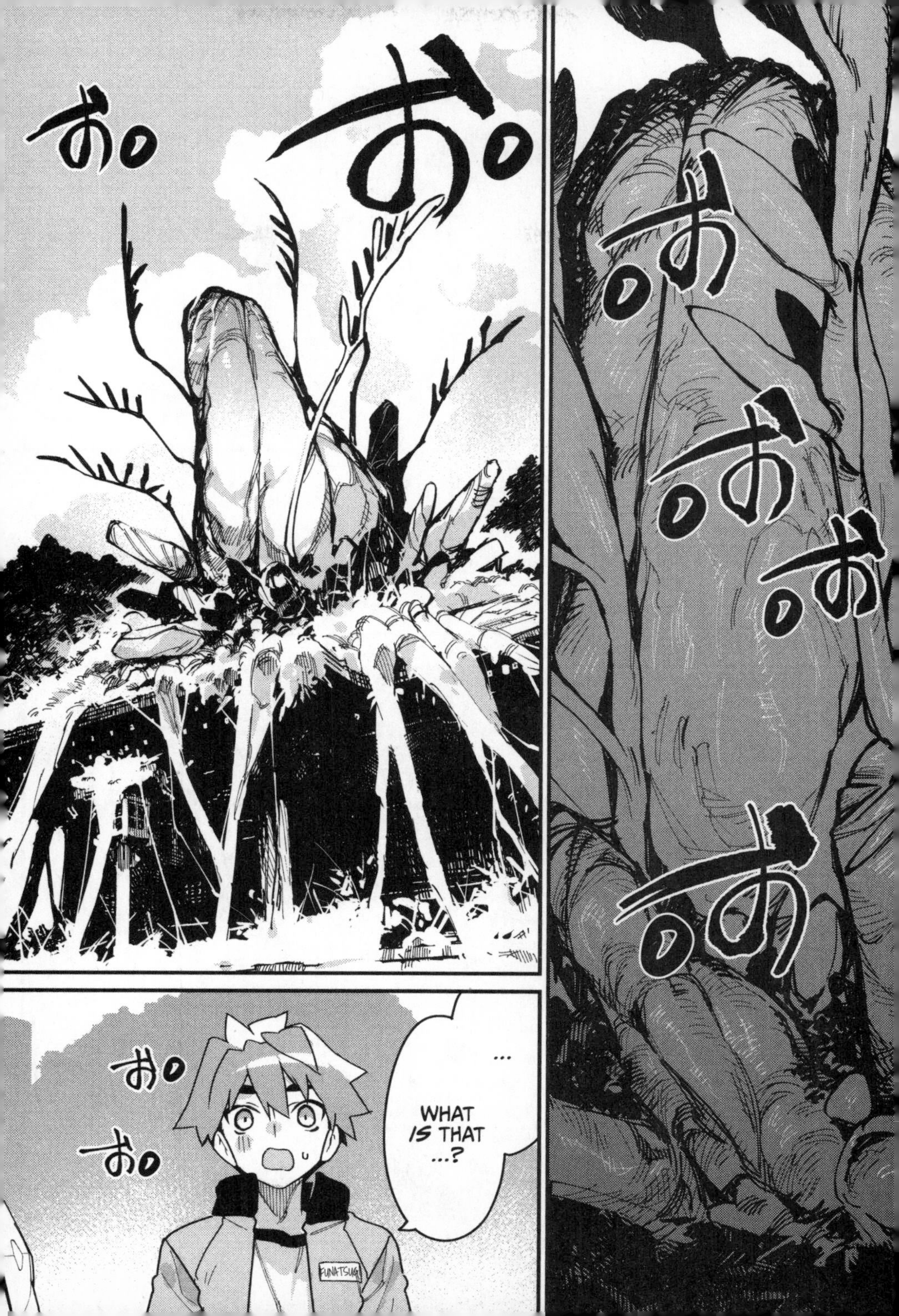
おおおお
おぉ
おぉ
おぉ
おぉ
...
WHAT *IS* THAT ...?

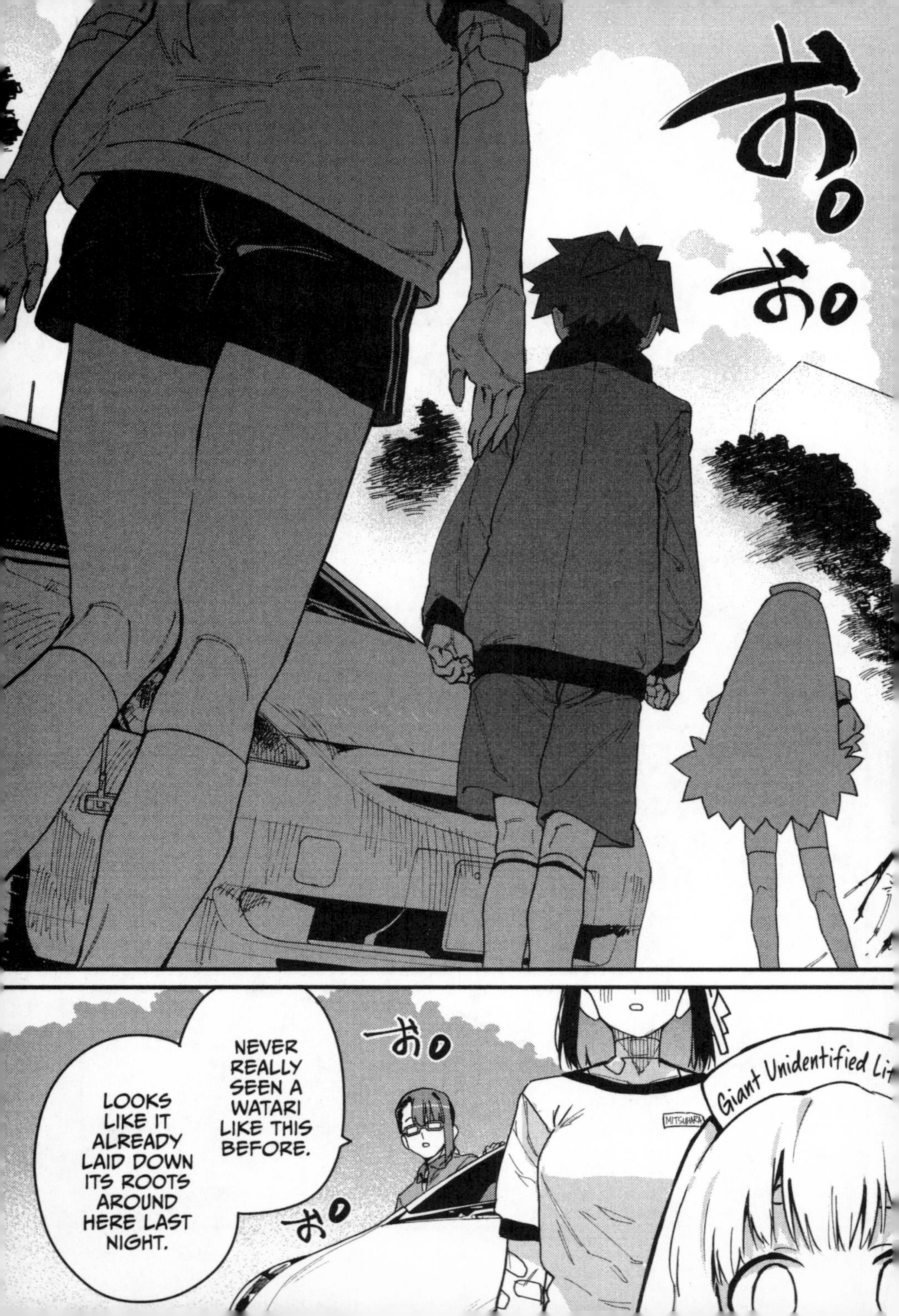
おぉ
おぉ
Giant Unidentified Li
MITSUHARA
おぉ
NEVER REALLY SEEN A WATARI LIKE THIS BEFORE.
おぉ
LOOKS LIKE IT ALREADY LAID DOWN ITS ROOTS AROUND HERE LAST NIGHT.

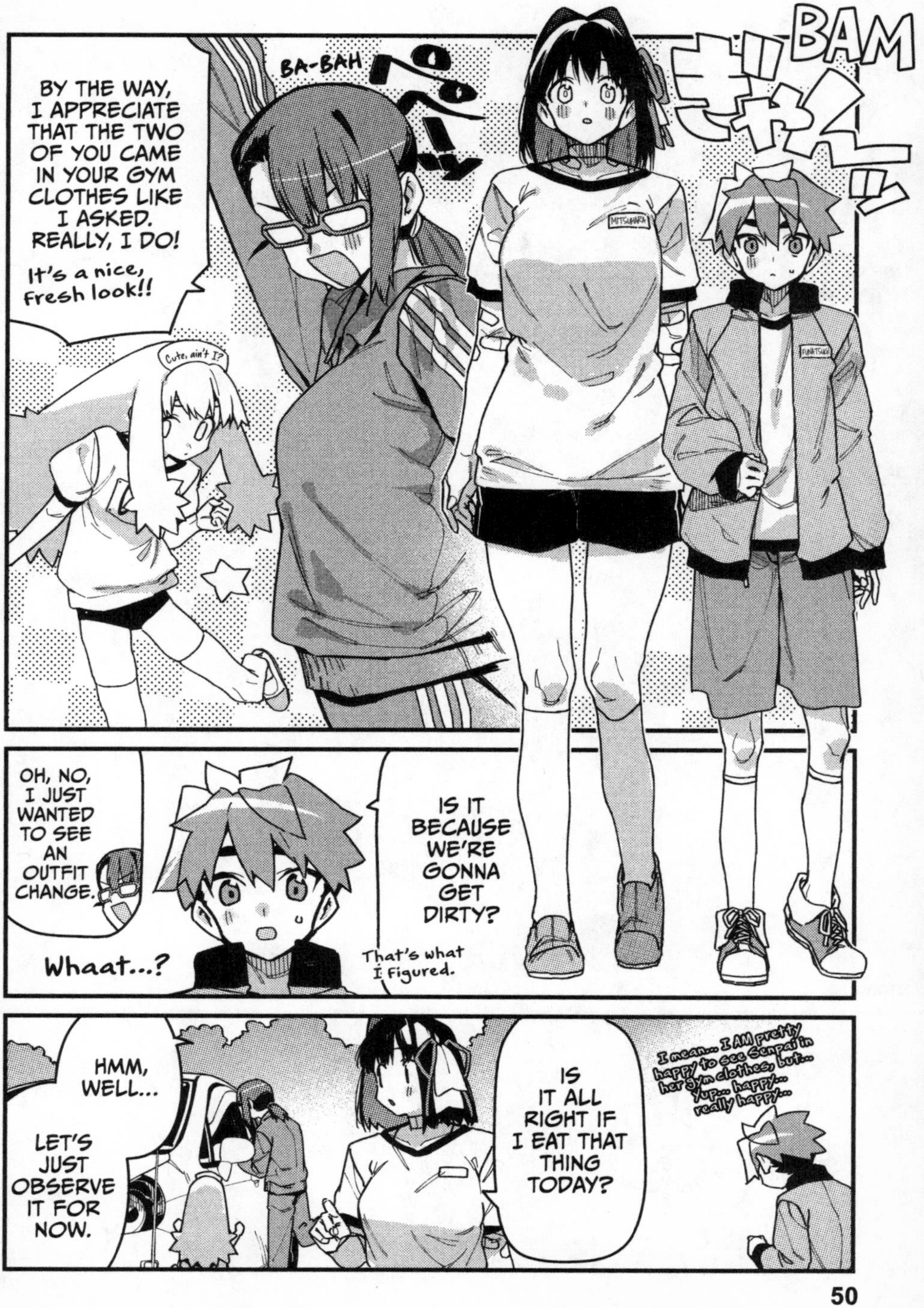
BAM
BA-BAH
BY THE WAY, I APPRECIATE THAT THE TWO OF YOU CAME IN YOUR GYM CLOTHES LIKE I ASKED. REALLY, I DO!
It's a nice, fresh look!!
Cute, ain't I?
IS IT BECAUSE WE'RE GONNA GET DIRTY?
That's what I figured.
OH, NO, I JUST WANTED TO SEE AN OUTFIT CHANGE.
Whaat...?
I mean... I AM pretty happy to see Senpai in her gym clothes, but... Yup... happy... really happy...
IS IT ALL RIGHT IF I EAT THAT THING TODAY?
HMM, WELL...
LET'S JUST OBSERVE IT FOR NOW.

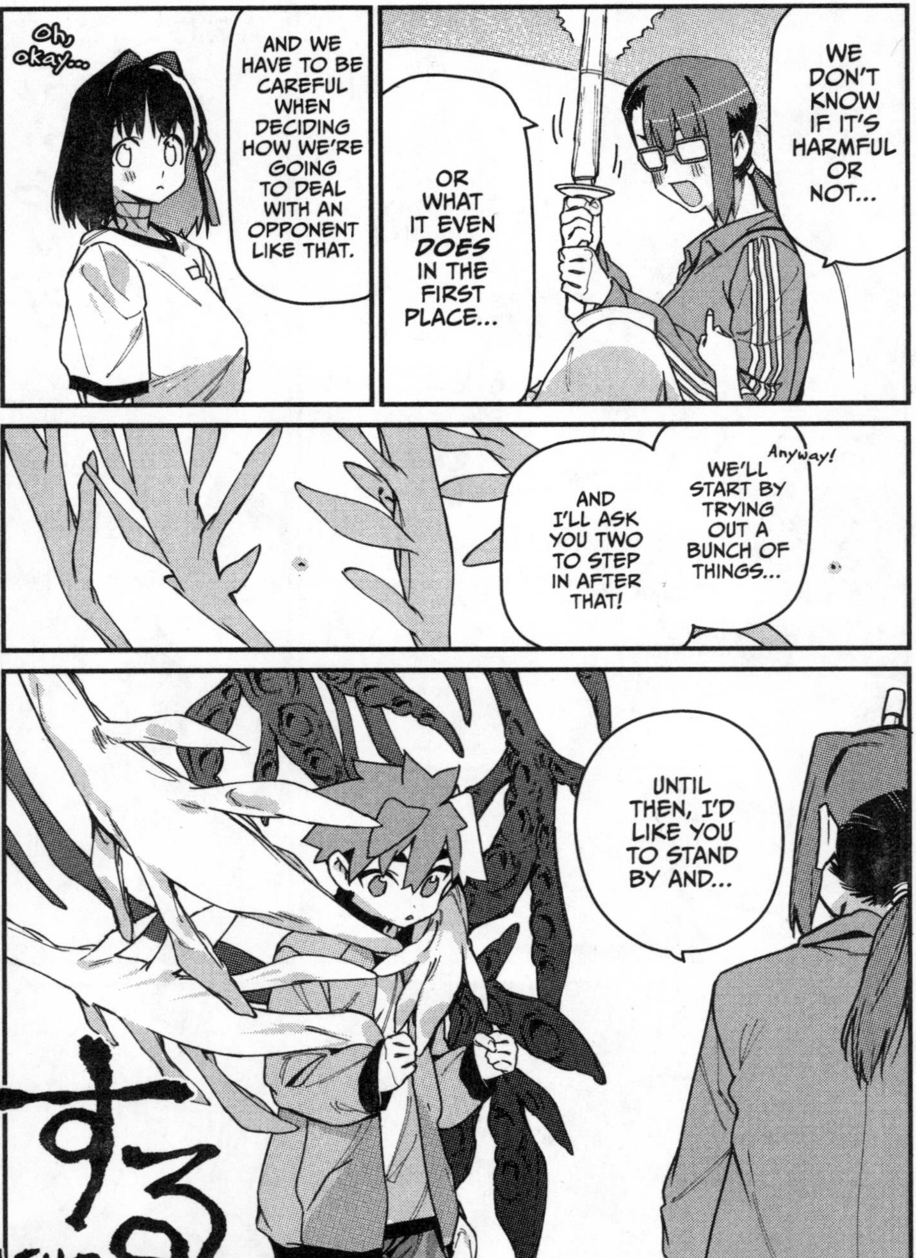
WE DON'T KNOW IF IT'S HARMFUL OR NOT...
OR WHAT IT EVEN ***DOES*** IN THE FIRST PLACE...
AND WE HAVE TO BE CAREFUL WHEN DECIDING HOW WE'RE GOING TO DEAL WITH AN OPPONENT LIKE THAT.
Oh, okay...
Anyway!
WE'LL START BY TRYING OUT A BUNCH OF THINGS...
AND I'LL ASK YOU TWO TO STEP IN AFTER THAT!
UNTIL THEN, I'D LIKE YOU TO STAND BY AND...
する
SLTHR

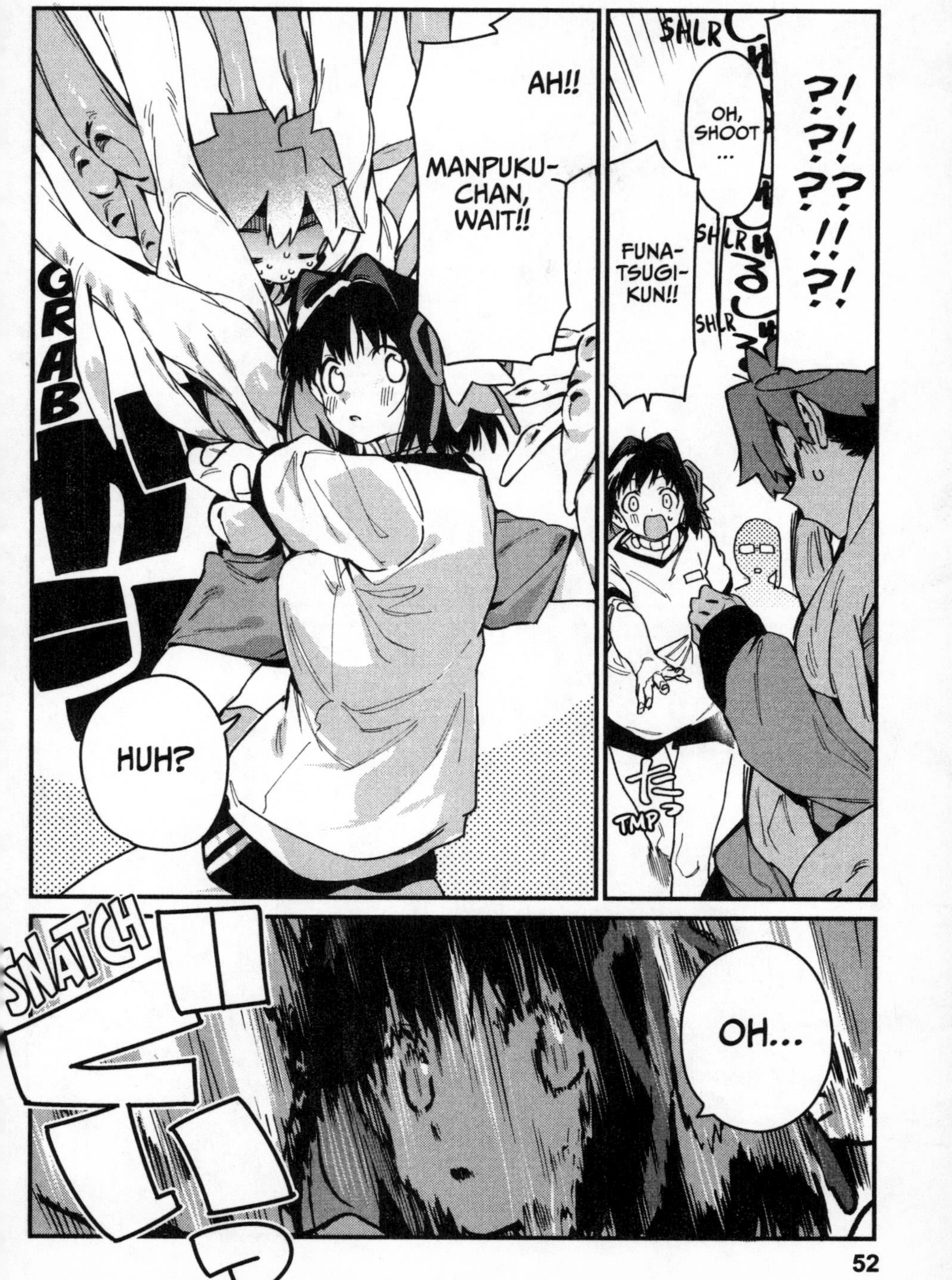
?!?!?!?!!?!
SHLR
OH, SHOOT...
SHLR
FUNA-TSUGI-KUN!!
SHLR
TMP
AH!!
MANPUKU-CHAN, WAIT!!
GRAB
HUH?
SNATCH
OH...

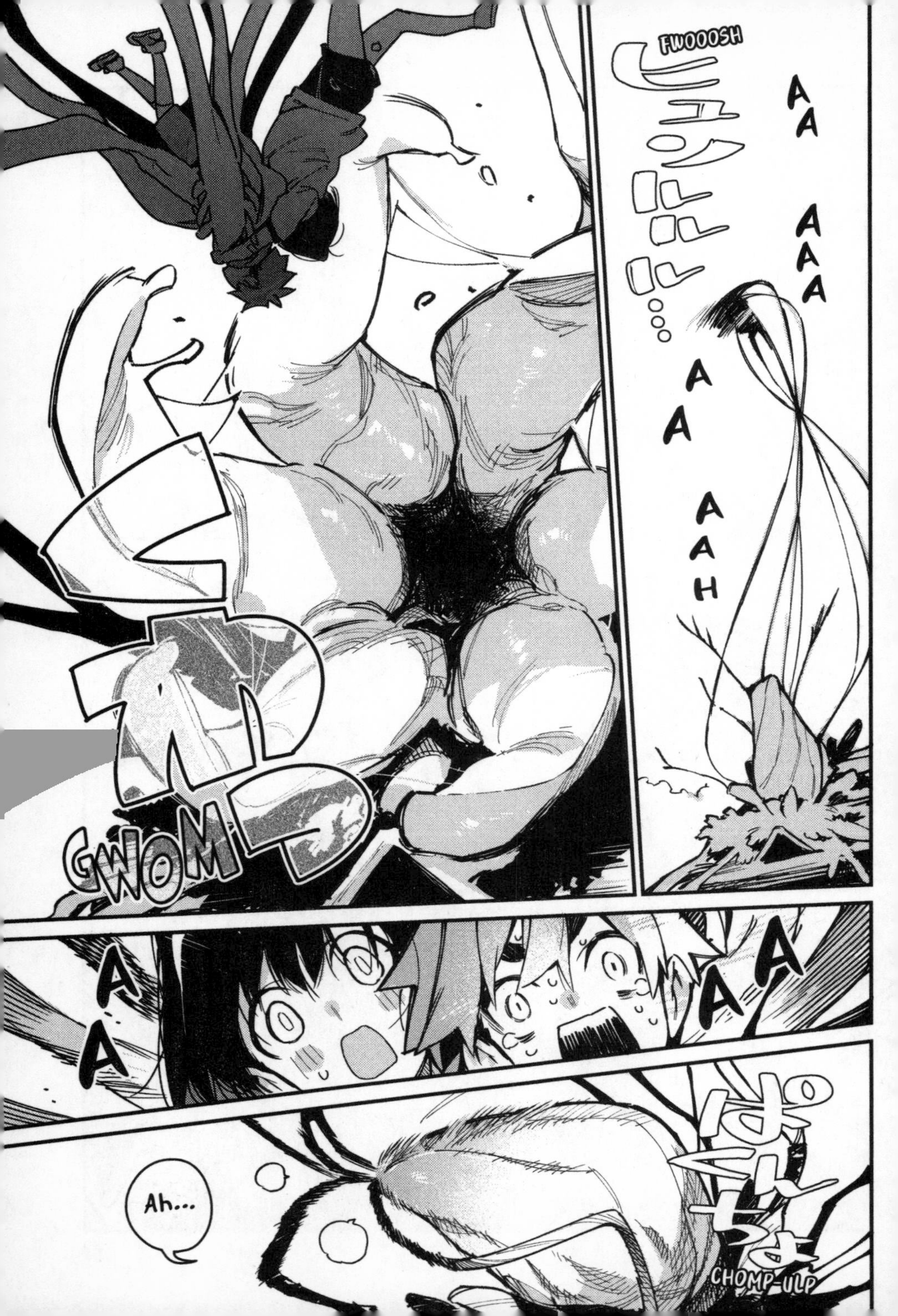
FWOOOSH
AA AAAAA A A AAAH
GWOM
AAA
AA
CHOMP-ULP
Ah...

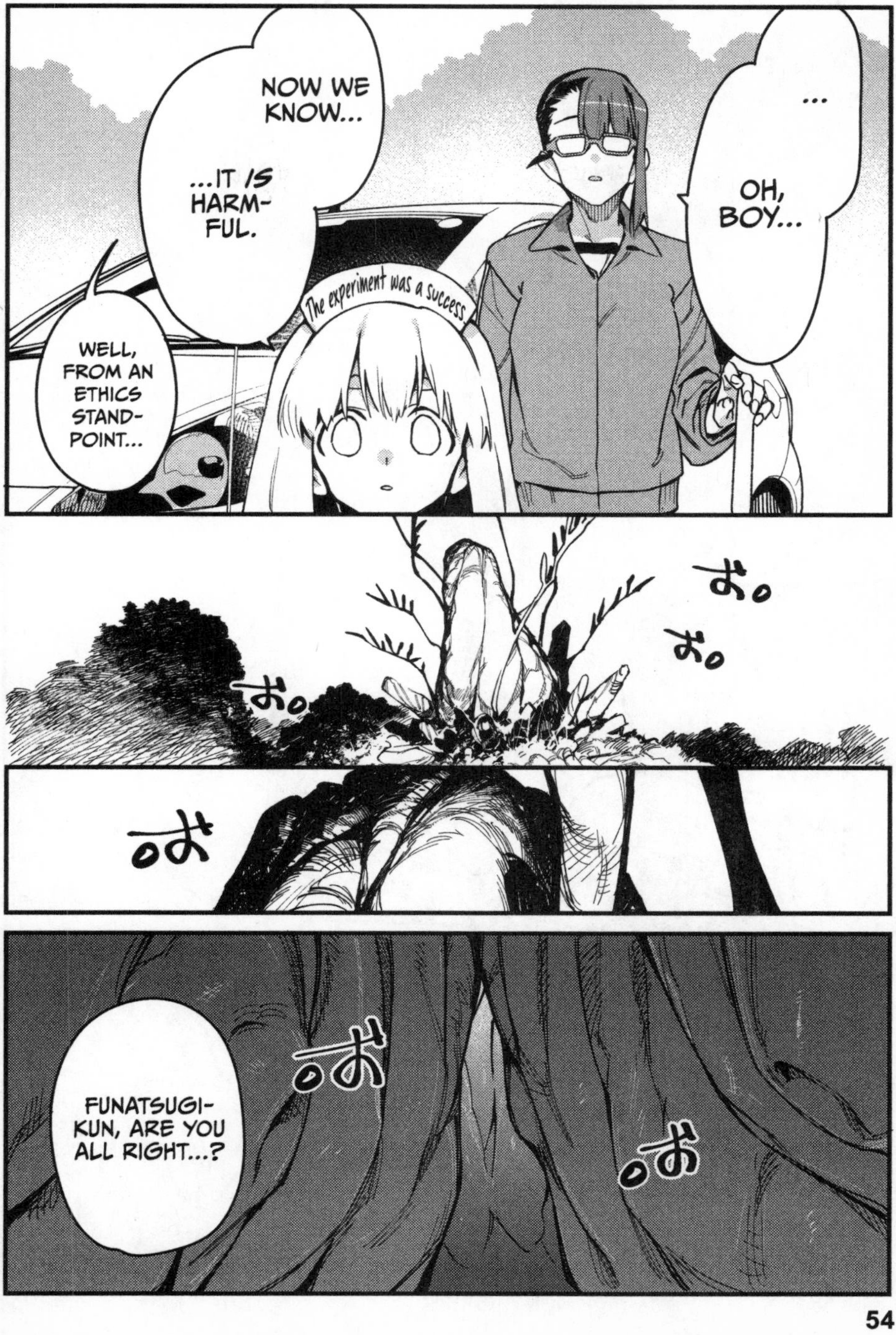
...
OH, BOY...
NOW WE KNOW...
...IT *IS* HARMFUL.
The experiment was a success
WELL, FROM AN ETHICS STANDPOINT...
お。
お。
お。
。お
。お
FUNATSUGI-KUN, ARE YOU ALL RIGHT...?
。お

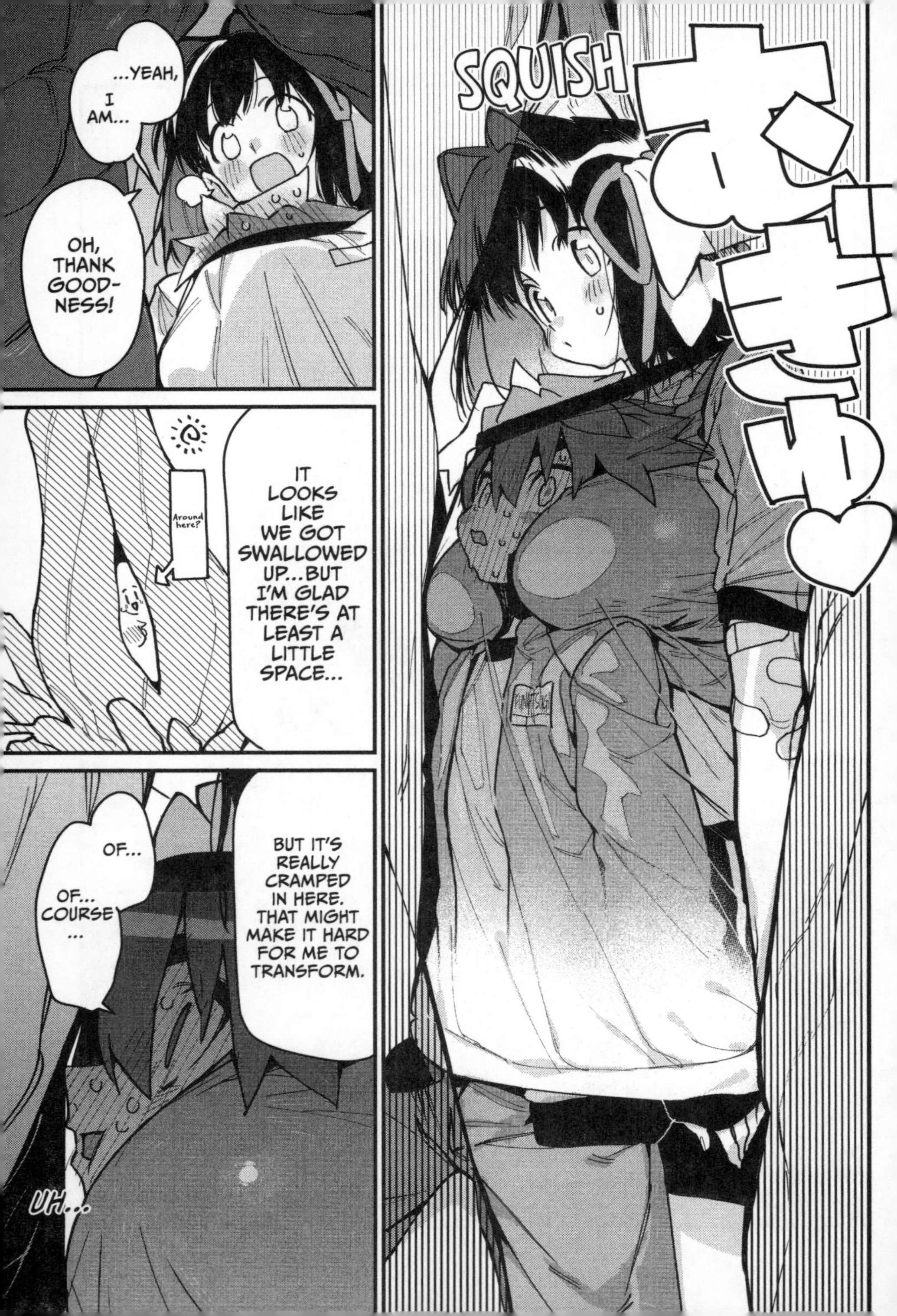
SQUISH
むぎゅ♡
...YEAH, I AM...
OH, THANK GOODNESS!
IT LOOKS LIKE WE GOT SWALLOWED UP...BUT I'M GLAD THERE'S AT LEAST A LITTLE SPACE...
Around here?
BUT IT'S REALLY CRAMPED IN HERE. THAT MIGHT MAKE IT HARD FOR ME TO TRANSFORM.
OF... OF... COURSE...
UH...

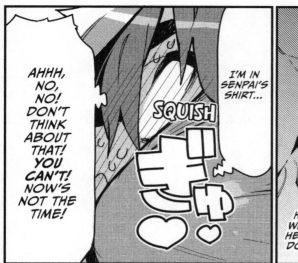

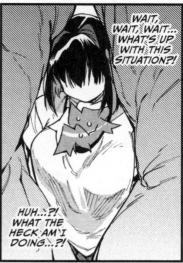

WAIT, WAIT, WAIT... WHAT'S UP WITH THIS SITUATION?!
HUH...?! WHAT THE HECK AM I DOING...?!
I'M IN SENPAI'S SHIRT...
AHHH, NO, NO! DON'T THINK ABOUT THAT! YOU CAN'T! NOW'S NOT THE TIME!
SQUISH
DUM-DA-DUM-DADDA-DA-DA-DUM-DA-DUM-DUM-DA-DUM-DA-DUM-DUM-DADDA-DUM-D
(RING TONE)
?!
MITSUHARA
OH... YOUR PHONE!
TIS I
URK...
BUT BOTH OF MY HANDS ARE STUCK...
Oh!!
THEN I'LL PICK IT UP!
HUH...?
-DUM-DUM-DA-DUM-DA-DUM-DUM-DUM-DUM-DA-DA-

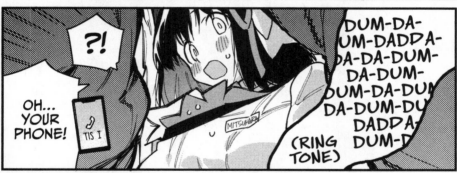

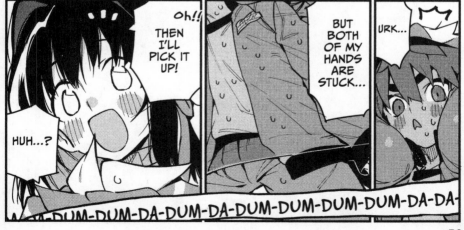

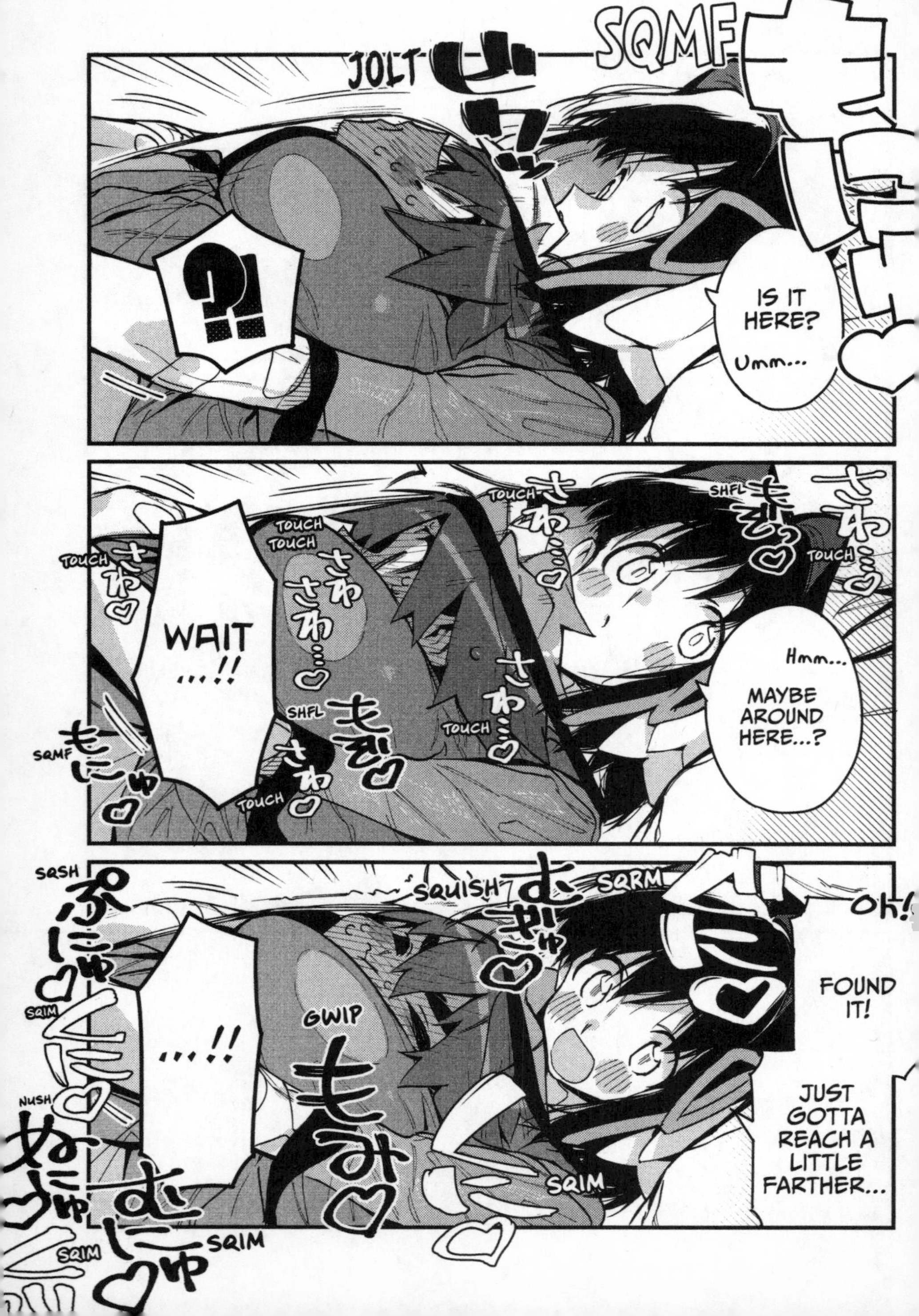
SQMF
IS IT HERE?
Umm...
JOLT
?!
TOUCH
SHFL
TOUCH
Hmm...
MAYBE AROUND HERE...?
TOUCH
TOUCH
TOUCH
TOUCH
WAIT ...!!
SHFL
TOUCH
TOUCH
SQMF
Oh!
FOUND IT!
JUST GOTTA REACH A LITTLE FARTHER...
SQRM
SQUISH
GWIP
...!!
SQIM
SQSH
SQIM
NUSH
SQIM
SQIM

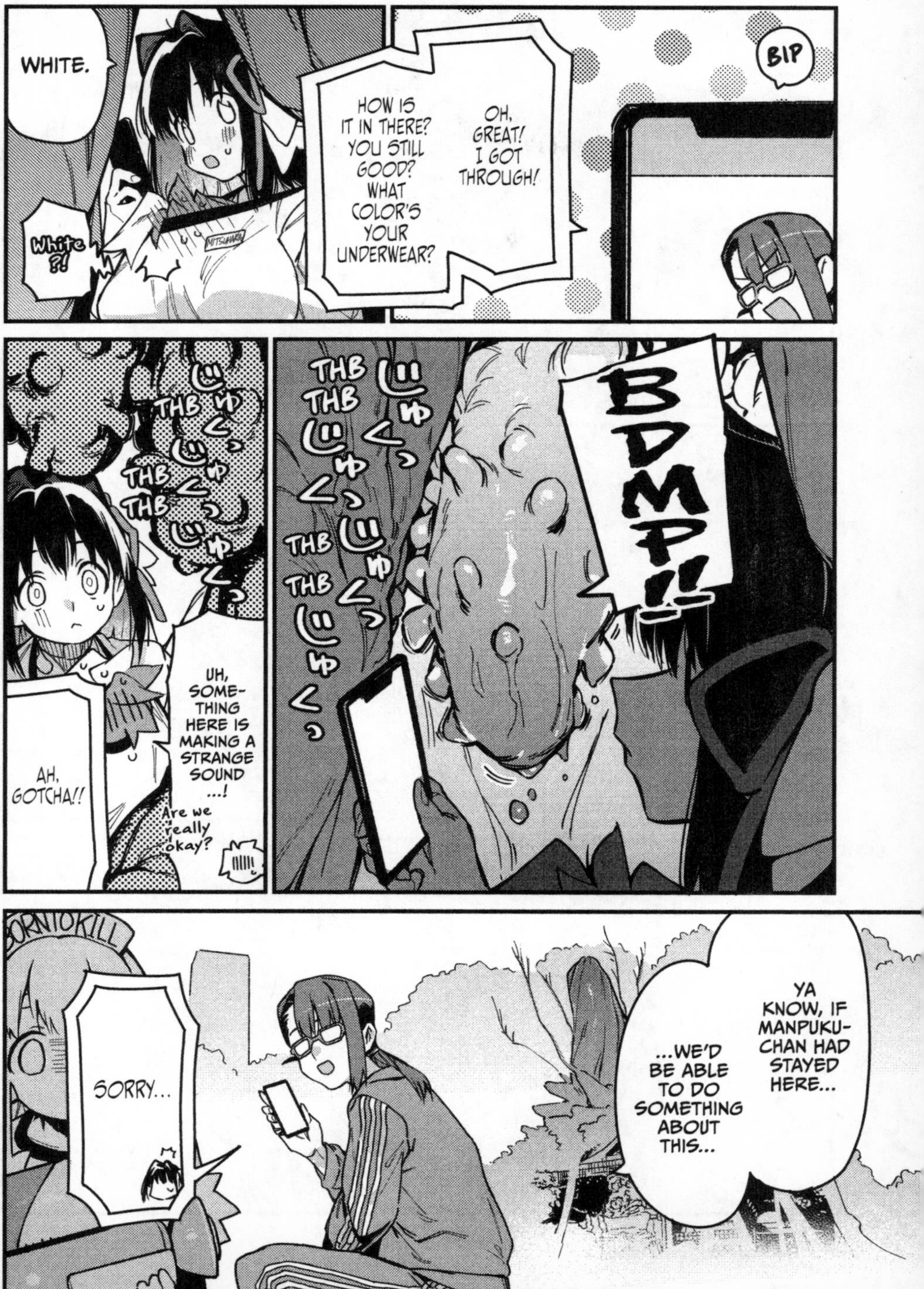
BIP
OH, GREAT! I GOT THROUGH!
HOW IS IT IN THERE? YOU STILL GOOD? WHAT COLOR'S YOUR UNDERWEAR?
WHITE.
White ?!
BDMP!!
THB THB じゅくっ じゅくっ
THB THB じゅくっ じゅくっ
THB THB じゅくっ じゅくっ
THB じゅくっ
THB THB じゅくっ じゅくっ
UH, SOME-THING HERE IS MAKING A STRANGE SOUND ...!
AH, GOTCHA!!
Are we really okay?
YA KNOW, IF MANPUKU-CHAN HAD STAYED HERE...
...WE'D BE ABLE TO DO SOMETHING ABOUT THIS...
SORRY...
BORNTOKILL

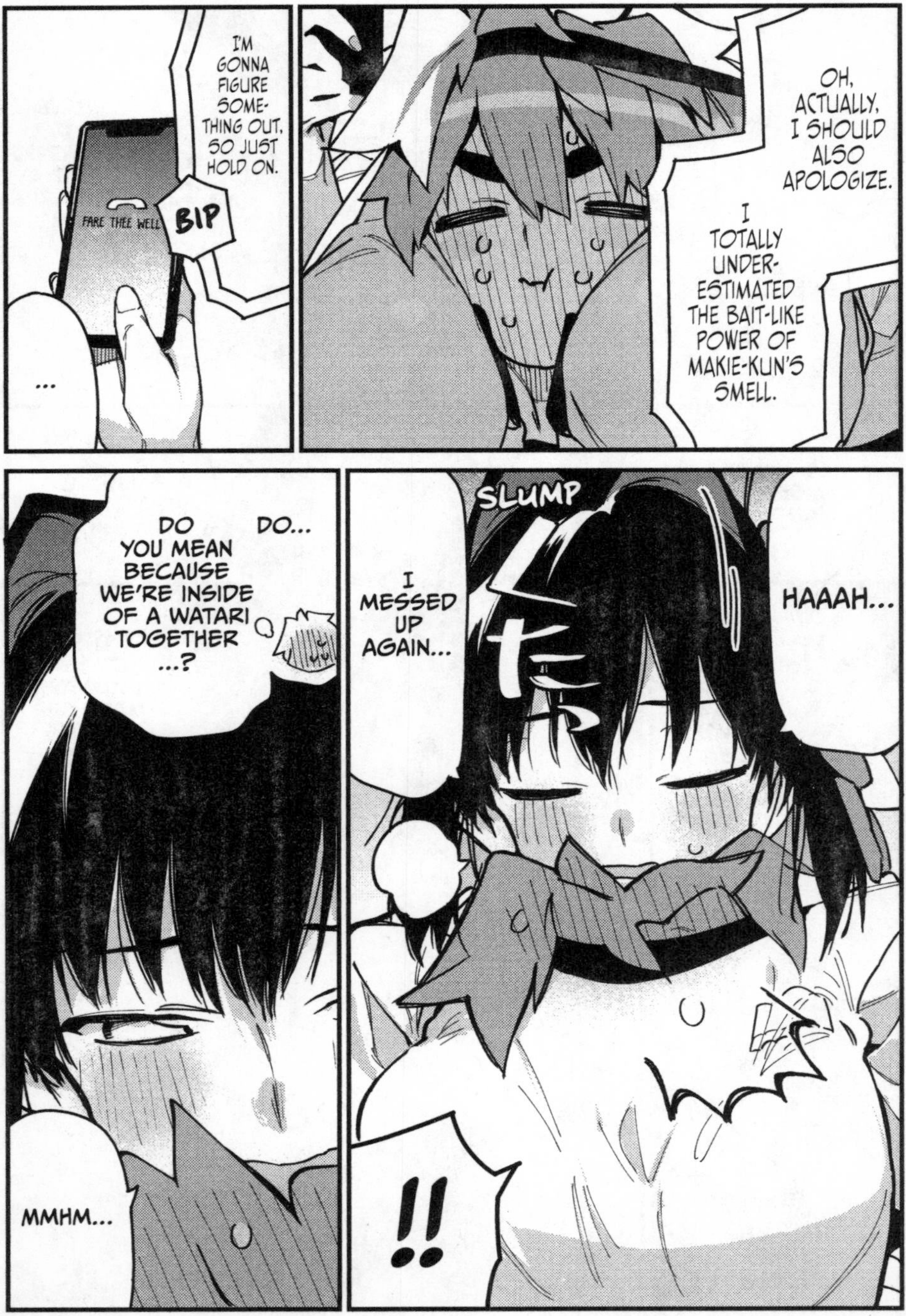
OH, ACTUALLY, I SHOULD ALSO APOLOGIZE.
I TOTALLY UNDER-ESTIMATED THE BAIT-LIKE POWER OF MAKIE-KUN'S SMELL.
I'M GONNA FIGURE SOME-THING OUT, SO JUST HOLD ON.
FARE THEE WELL
BIP
...
HAAAH...
SLUMP
I MESSED UP AGAIN...
!!
DO...
DO YOU MEAN BECAUSE WE'RE INSIDE OF A WATARI TOGETHER ...?
MMHM...

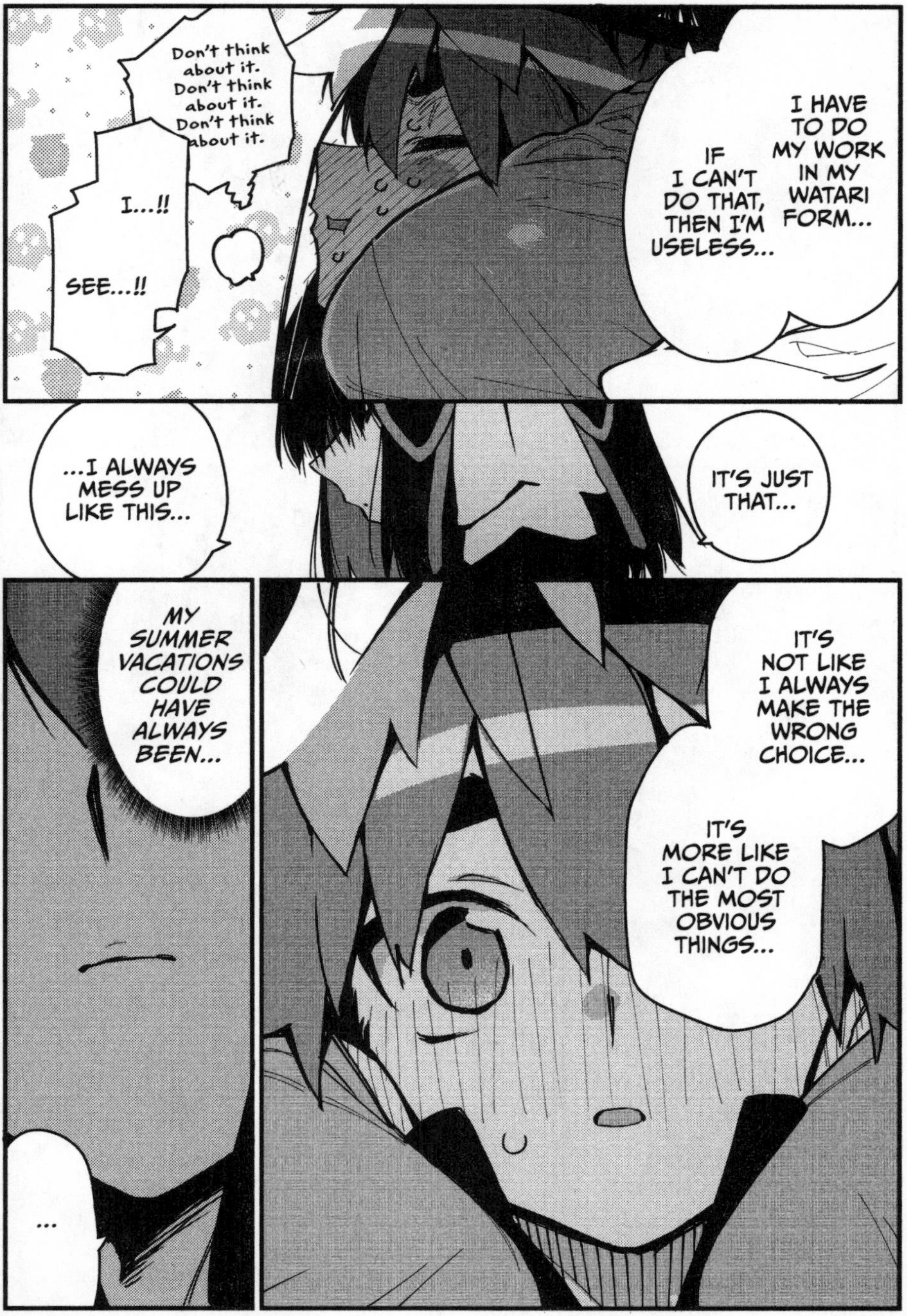
I HAVE TO DO MY WORK IN MY WATARI FORM...
IF I CAN'T DO THAT, THEN I'M USELESS...
Don't think about it. Don't think about it. Don't think about it.
I...!! SEE...!!
IT'S JUST THAT...
...I ALWAYS MESS UP LIKE THIS...
IT'S NOT LIKE I ALWAYS MAKE THE WRONG CHOICE...
IT'S MORE LIKE I CAN'T DO THE MOST OBVIOUS THINGS...
MY SUMMER VACATIONS COULD HAVE ALWAYS BEEN...
...

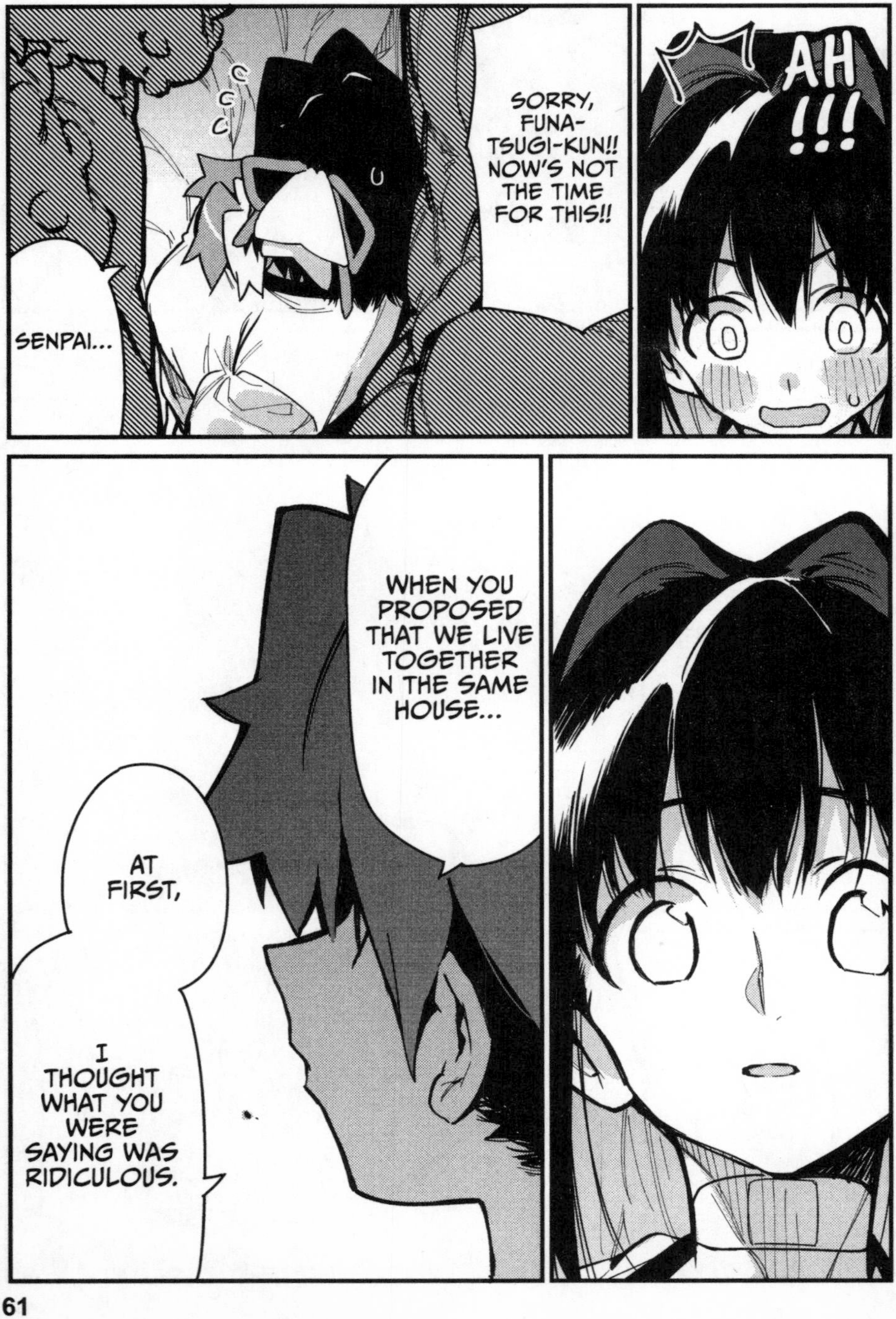
AH!!!
SORRY, FUNA-TSUGI-KUN!! NOW'S NOT THE TIME FOR THIS!!
SENPAI...
WHEN YOU PROPOSED THAT WE LIVE TOGETHER IN THE SAME HOUSE...
AT FIRST,
I THOUGHT WHAT YOU WERE SAYING WAS RIDICULOUS.

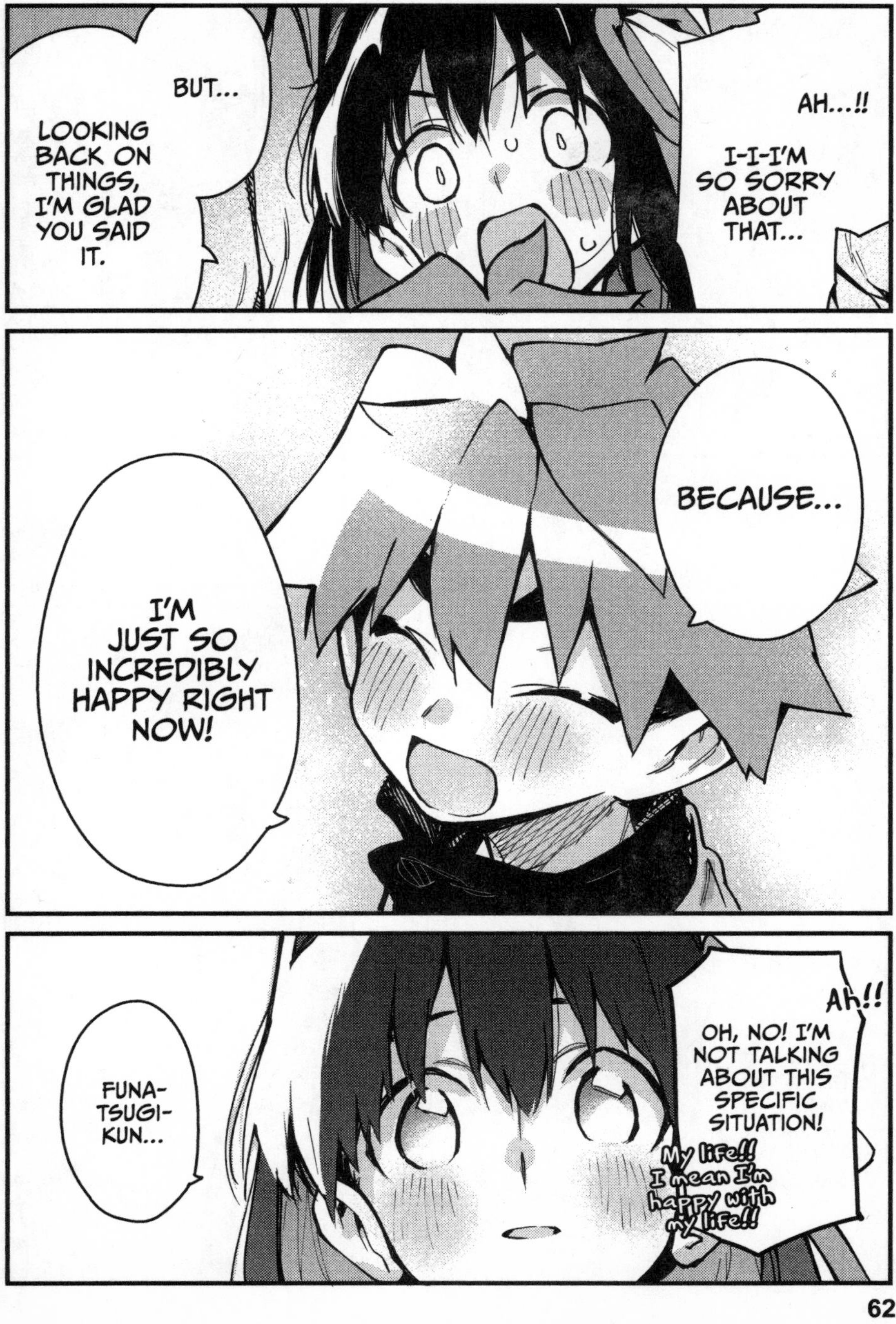
AH...!!
I-I-I'M SO SORRY ABOUT THAT...
BUT...
LOOKING BACK ON THINGS, I'M GLAD YOU SAID IT.
BECAUSE...
I'M JUST SO INCREDIBLY HAPPY RIGHT NOW!
Ah!!
OH, NO! I'M NOT TALKING ABOUT THIS SPECIFIC SITUATION!
My life!! I mean I'm happy with my life!!
FUNA-TSUGI-KUN...

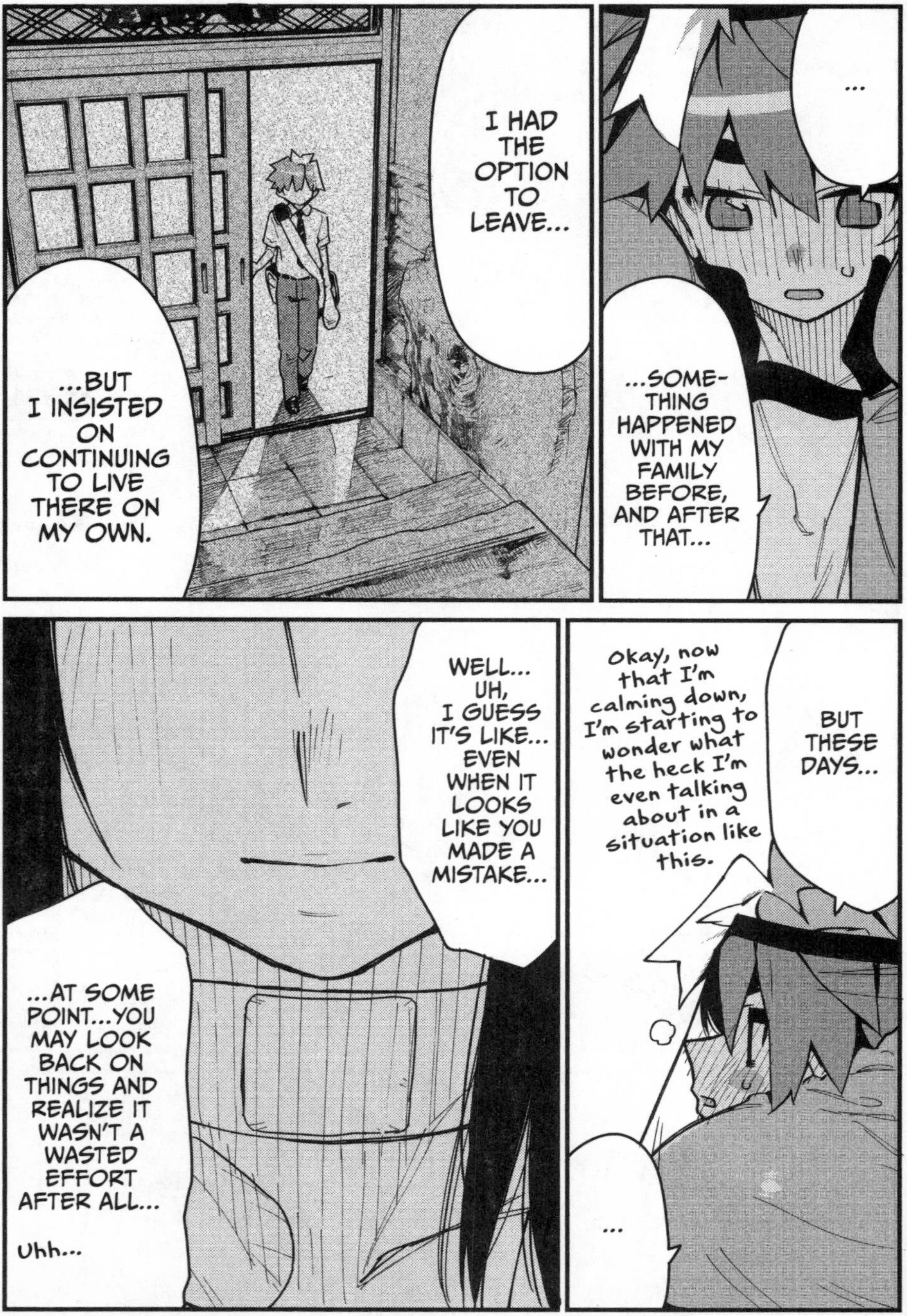
...
...SOMETHING HAPPENED WITH MY FAMILY BEFORE, AND AFTER THAT...
I HAD THE OPTION TO LEAVE...
...BUT I INSISTED ON CONTINUING TO LIVE THERE ON MY OWN.
BUT THESE DAYS...
Okay, now that I'm calming down, I'm starting to wonder what the heck I'm even talking about in a situation like this.
...
WELL... UH, I GUESS IT'S LIKE... EVEN WHEN IT LOOKS LIKE YOU MADE A MISTAKE...
...AT SOME POINT...YOU MAY LOOK BACK ON THINGS AND REALIZE IT WASN'T A WASTED EFFORT AFTER ALL...
Uhh...

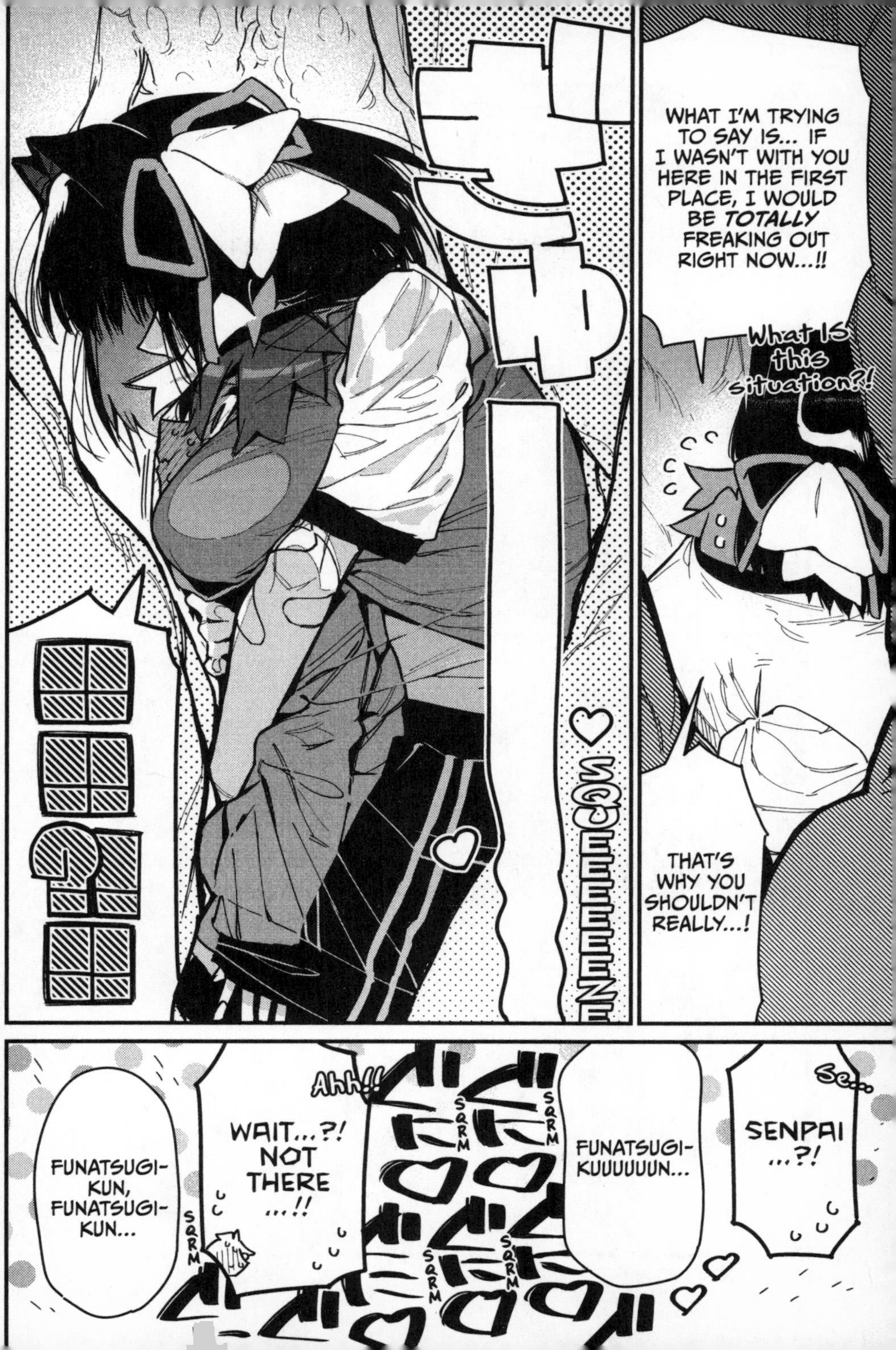
WHAT I'M TRYING TO SAY IS... IF I WASN'T WITH YOU HERE IN THE FIRST PLACE, I WOULD BE *TOTALLY* FREAKING OUT RIGHT NOW...!!
What IS this situation?!
THAT'S WHY YOU SHOULDN'T REALLY...!
SQUEEEEEZE
Se...
SENPAI ...?!
FUNATSUGI-KUUUUUUN...
SQRM
SQRM
Ahh!!
WAIT...?! NOT THERE ...!!
SQRM
SQRM
SQRM
FUNATSUGI-KUN, FUNATSUGI-KUN...

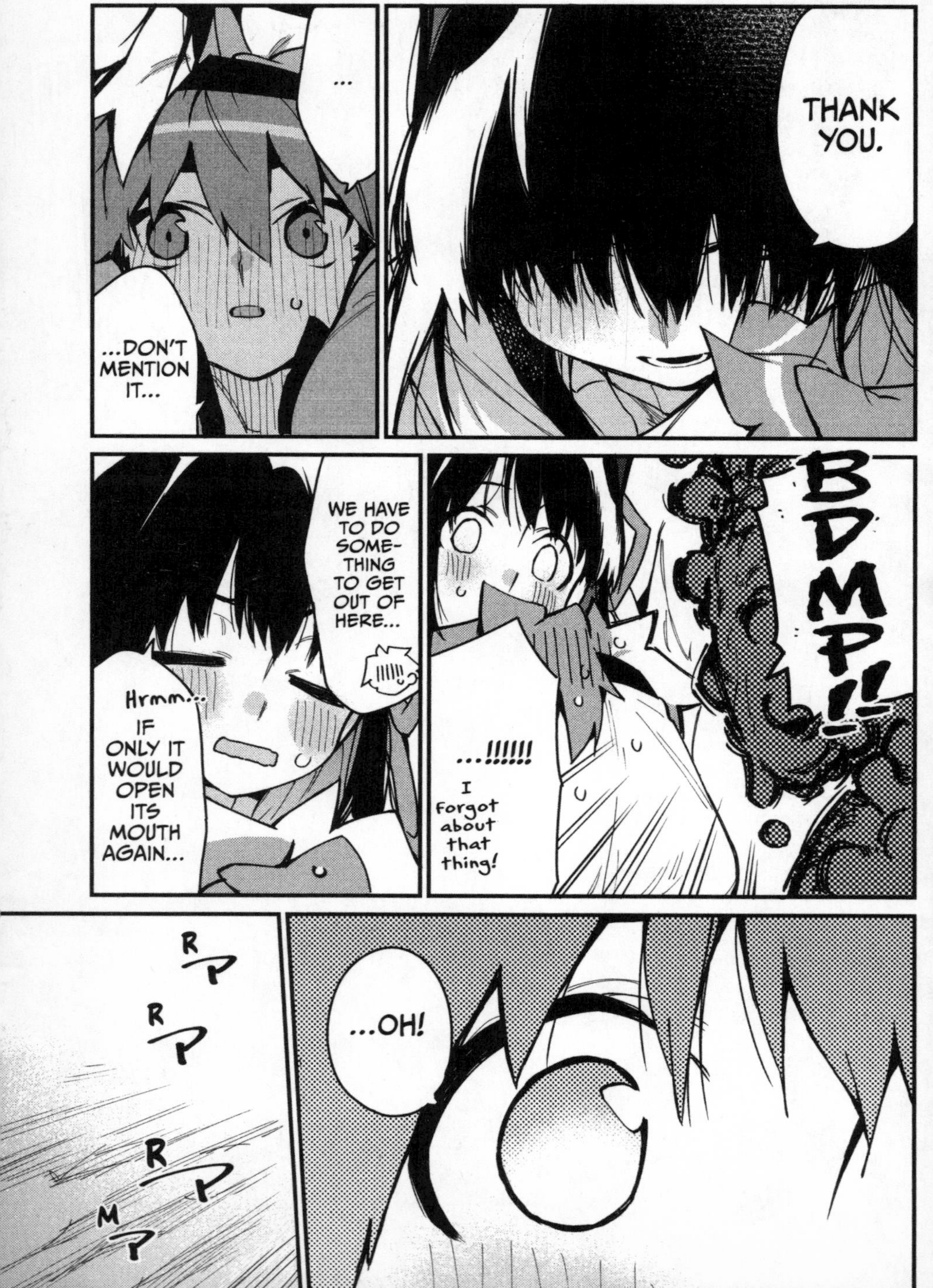
THANK YOU.
...
...DON'T MENTION IT...
BDMP!!
...!!!!!!
I forgot about that thing!
WE HAVE TO DO SOME-THING TO GET OUT OF HERE...
Hrmm...
IF ONLY IT WOULD OPEN ITS MOUTH AGAIN...
...OH!
RP
RP
RP
MP

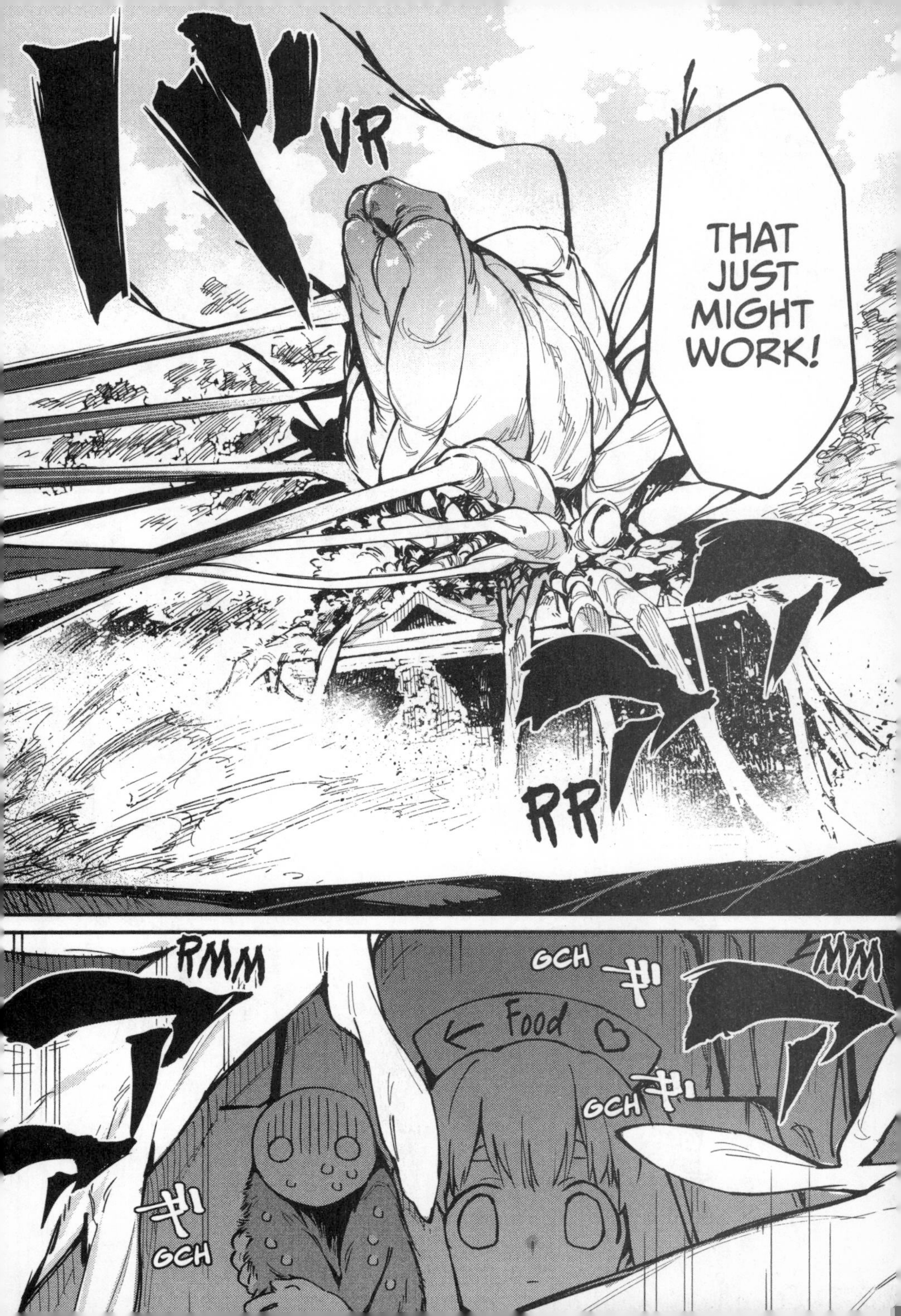
THAT JUST MIGHT WORK!
VR
RR
MM
GCH ギ
← Food
GCH ギ
RMM
ギ GCH

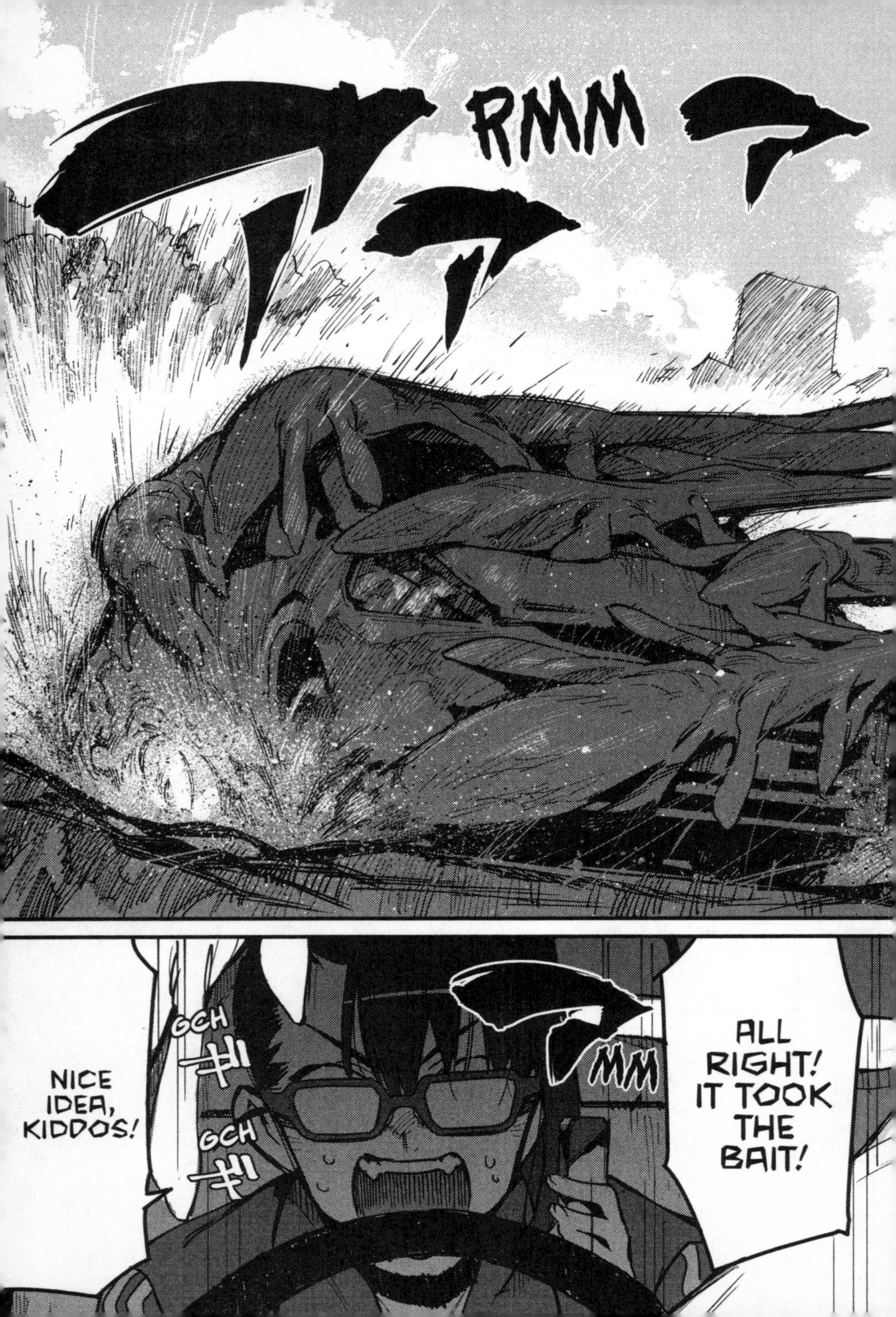
RMM
ALL RIGHT! IT TOOK THE BAIT!
MM
GCH
GCH
NICE IDEA, KIDDOS!

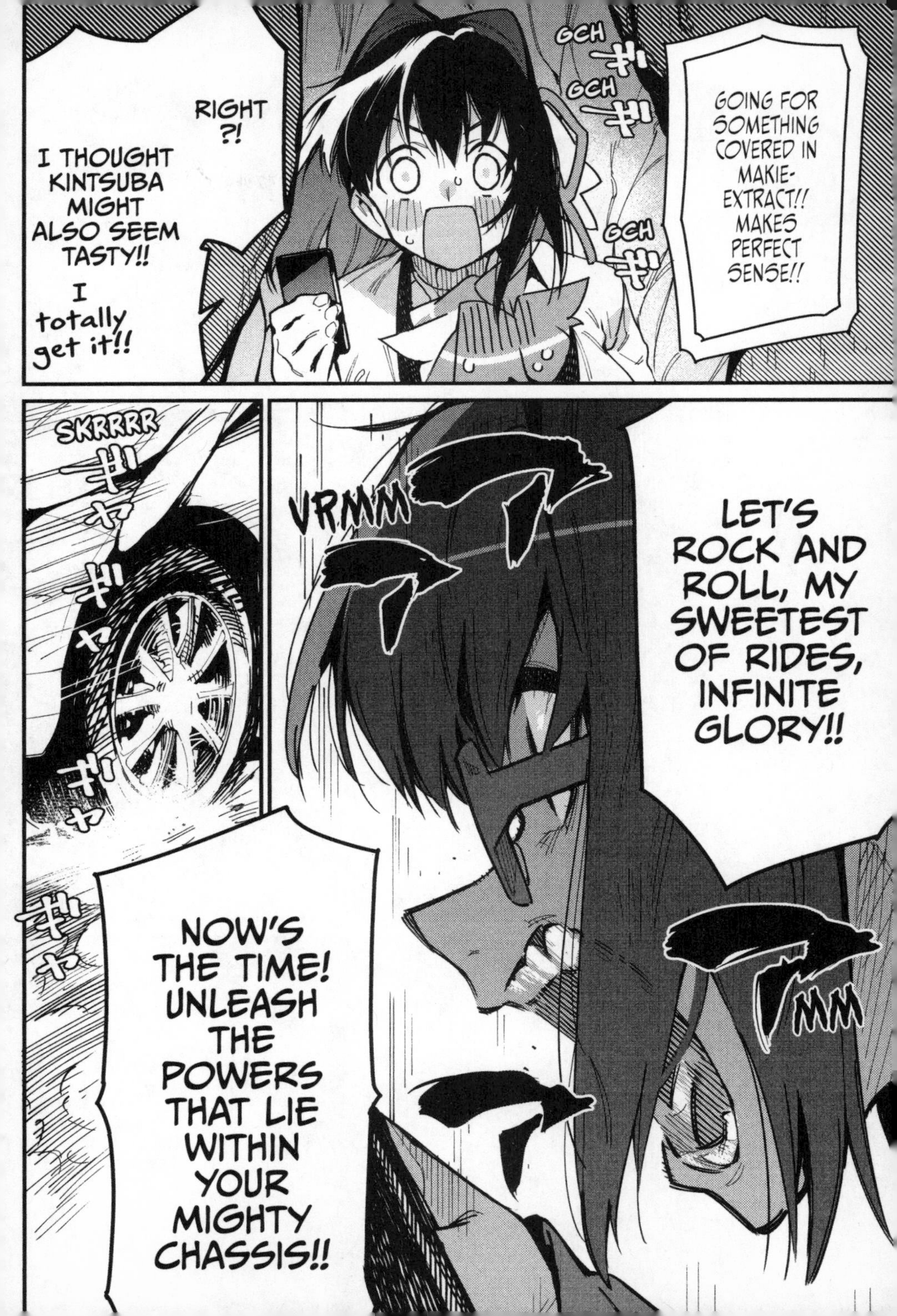
GOING FOR SOMETHING COVERED IN MAKIE-EXTRACT!! MAKES PERFECT SENSE!!
GCH
GCH
GCH
RIGHT ?!
I THOUGHT KINTSUBA MIGHT ALSO SEEM TASTY!!
I totally get it!!
LET'S ROCK AND ROLL, MY SWEETEST OF RIDES, INFINITE GLORY!!
VRMM
MM
NOW'S THE TIME! UNLEASH THE POWERS THAT LIE WITHIN YOUR MIGHTY CHASSIS!!
SKRRRR

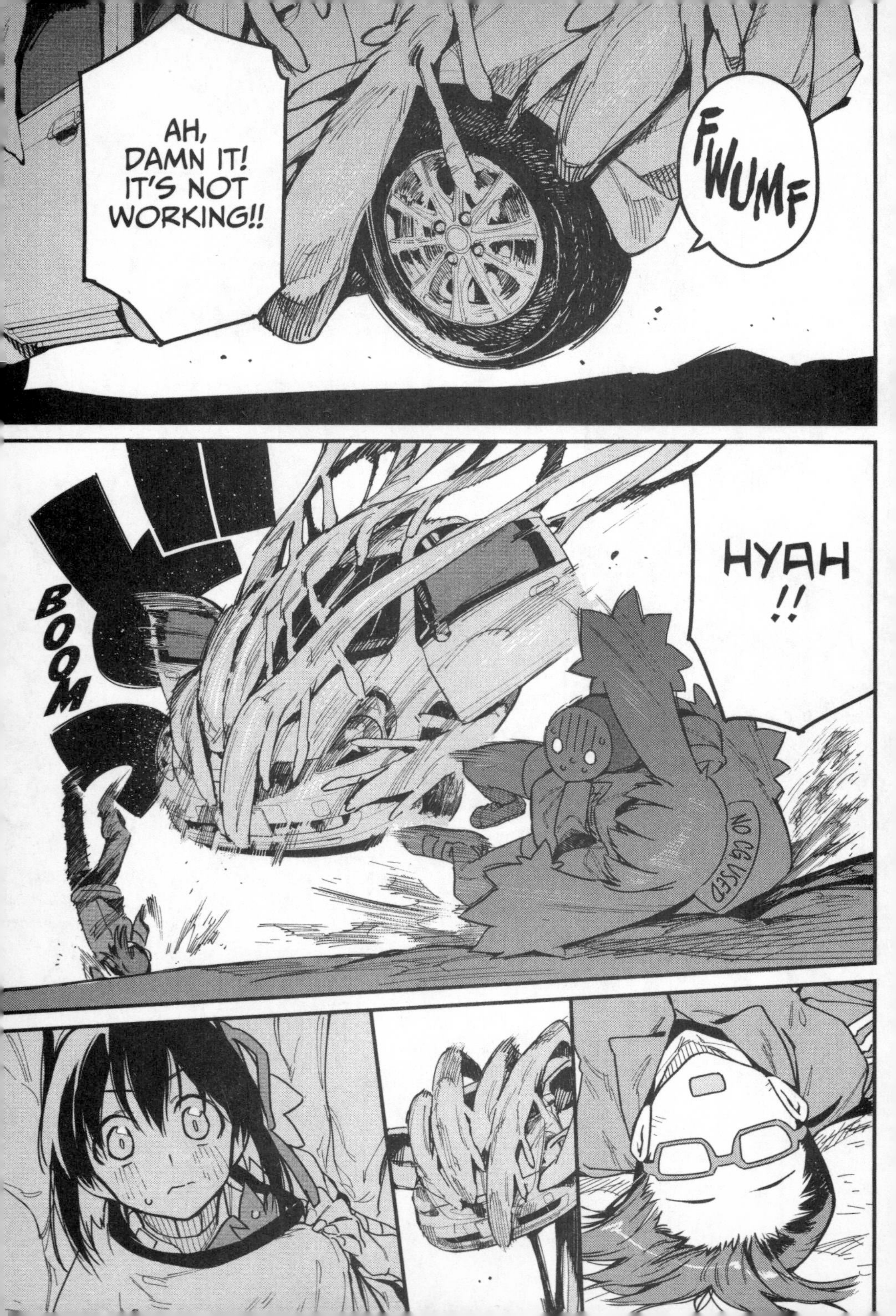
FWUMF
AH, DAMN IT! IT'S NOT WORKING!!
HYAH !!
BOOM
NO CG USED

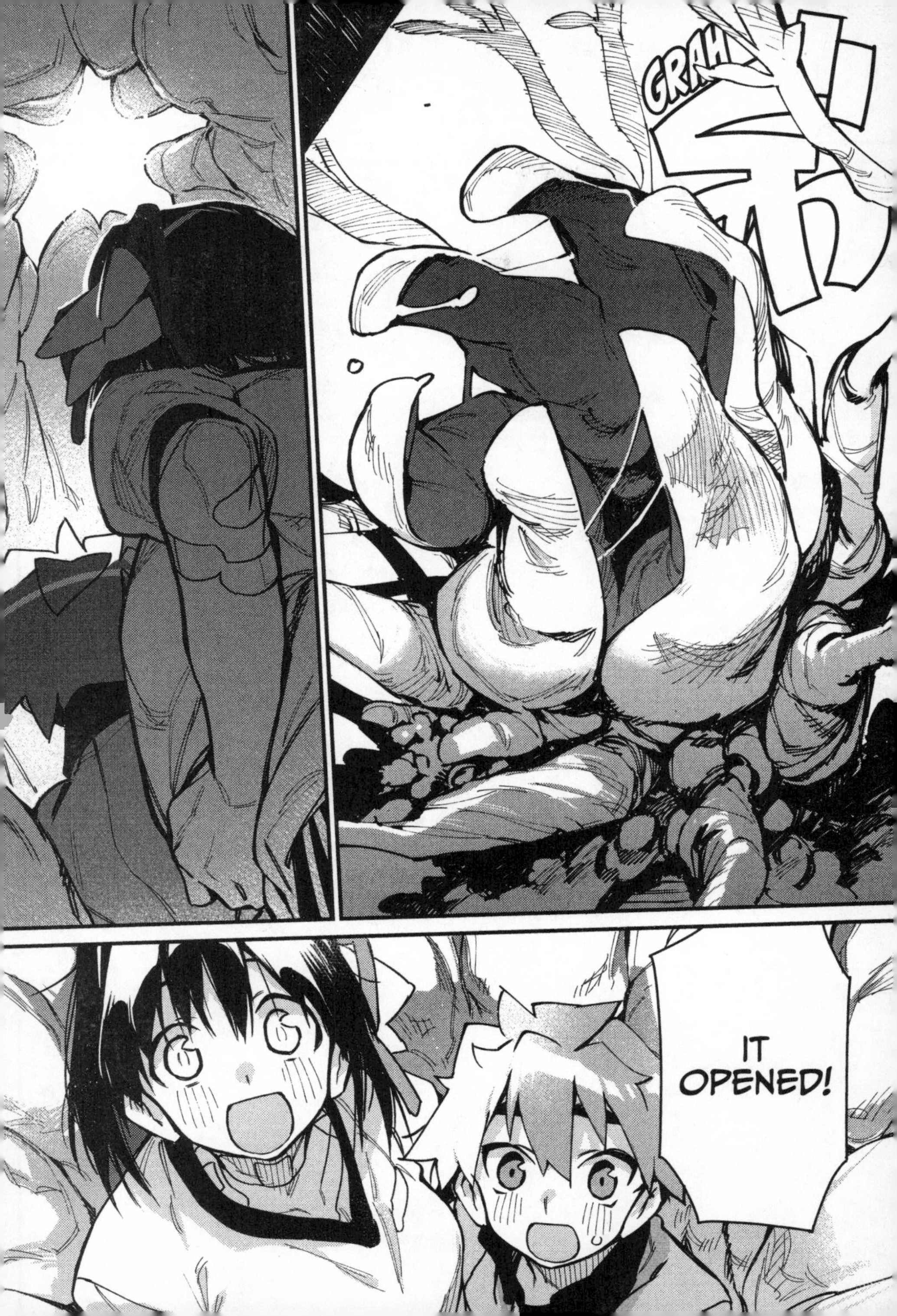
GRAH
IT OPENED!

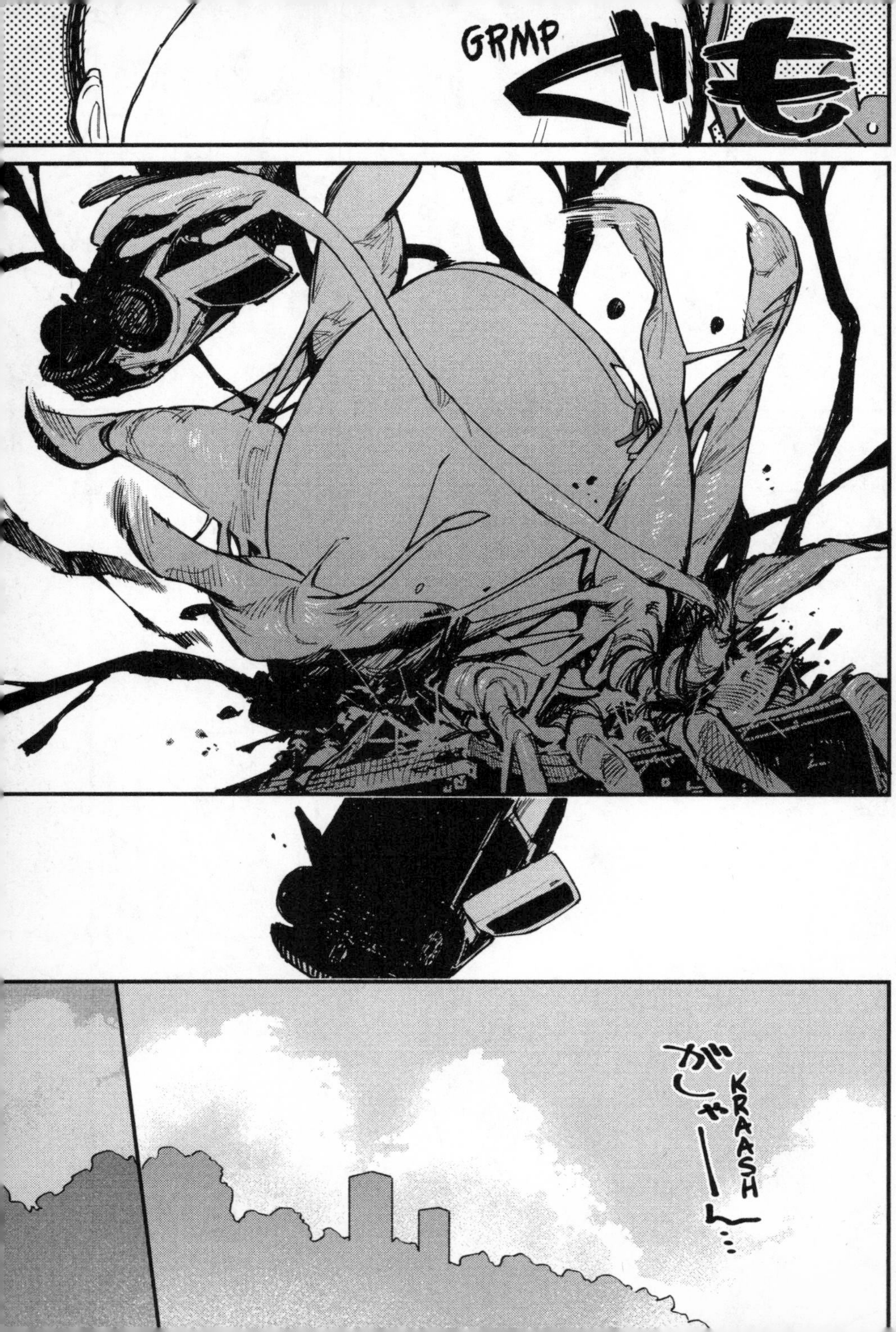
GRMP
ぐも
がしゃーん…
KRASH

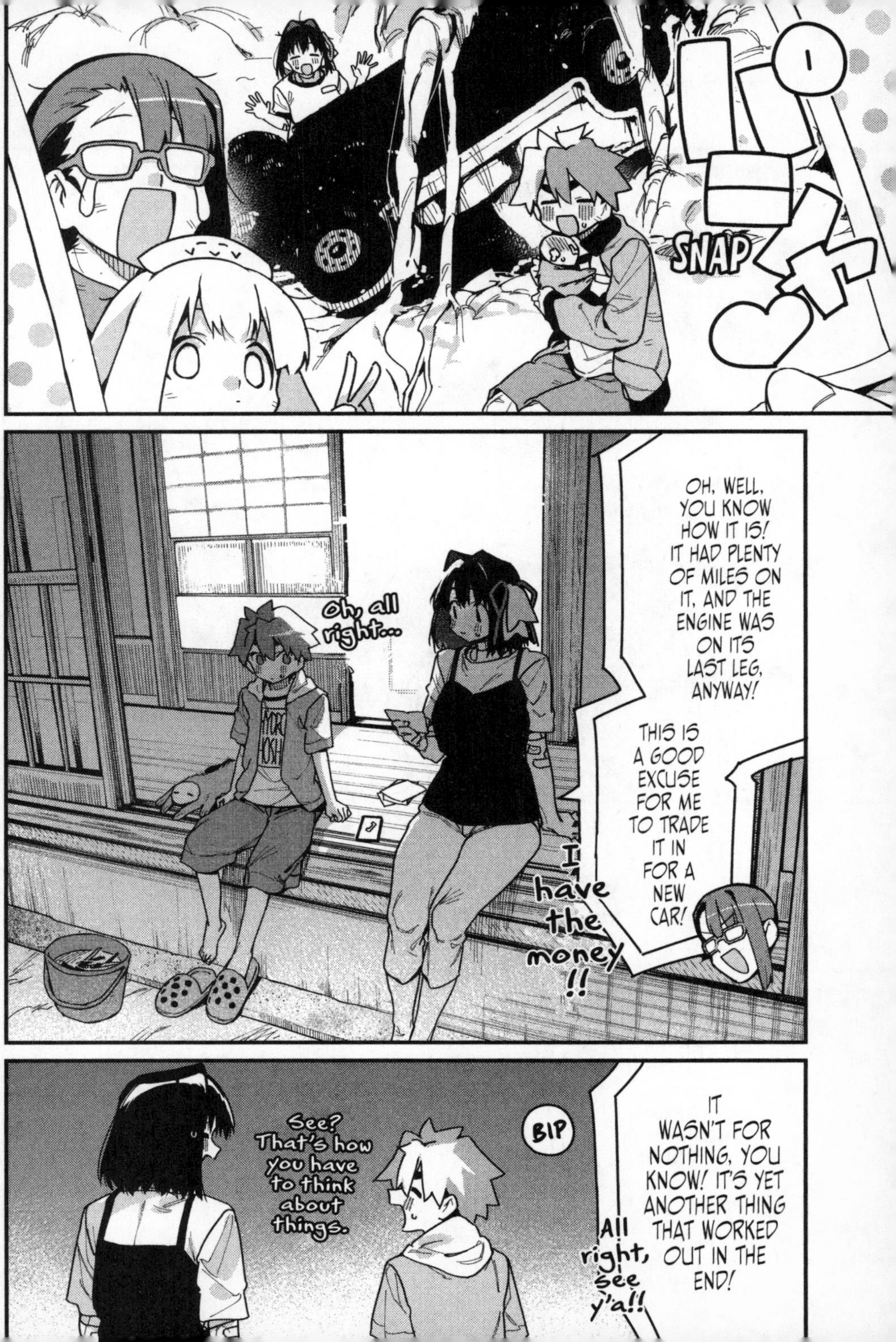
SNAP
OH, WELL, YOU KNOW HOW IT IS! IT HAD PLENTY OF MILES ON IT, AND THE ENGINE WAS ON ITS LAST LEG, ANYWAY!
THIS IS A GOOD EXCUSE FOR ME TO TRADE IT IN FOR A NEW CAR!
I have the money!!
Oh, all right...
IT WASN'T FOR NOTHING, YOU KNOW! IT'S YET ANOTHER THING THAT WORKED OUT IN THE END!
All right, see y'a!!
BIP
See? That's how you have to think about things.

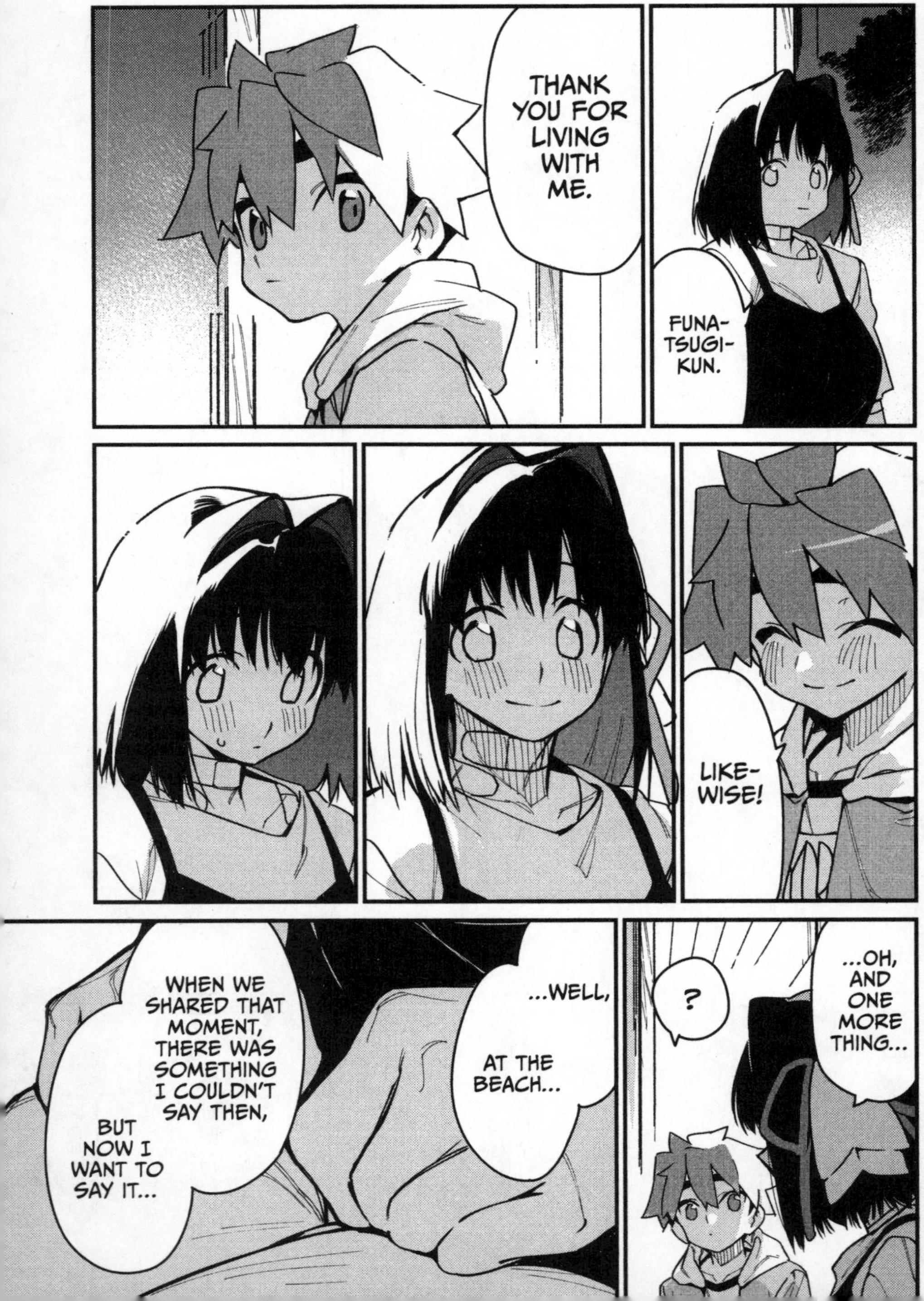
FUNA-TSUGI-KUN.
THANK YOU FOR LIVING WITH ME.
LIKE-WISE!
...OH, AND ONE MORE THING...
?
...WELL,
AT THE BEACH...
WHEN WE SHARED THAT MOMENT, THERE WAS SOMETHING I COULDN'T SAY THEN,
BUT NOW I WANT TO SAY IT...

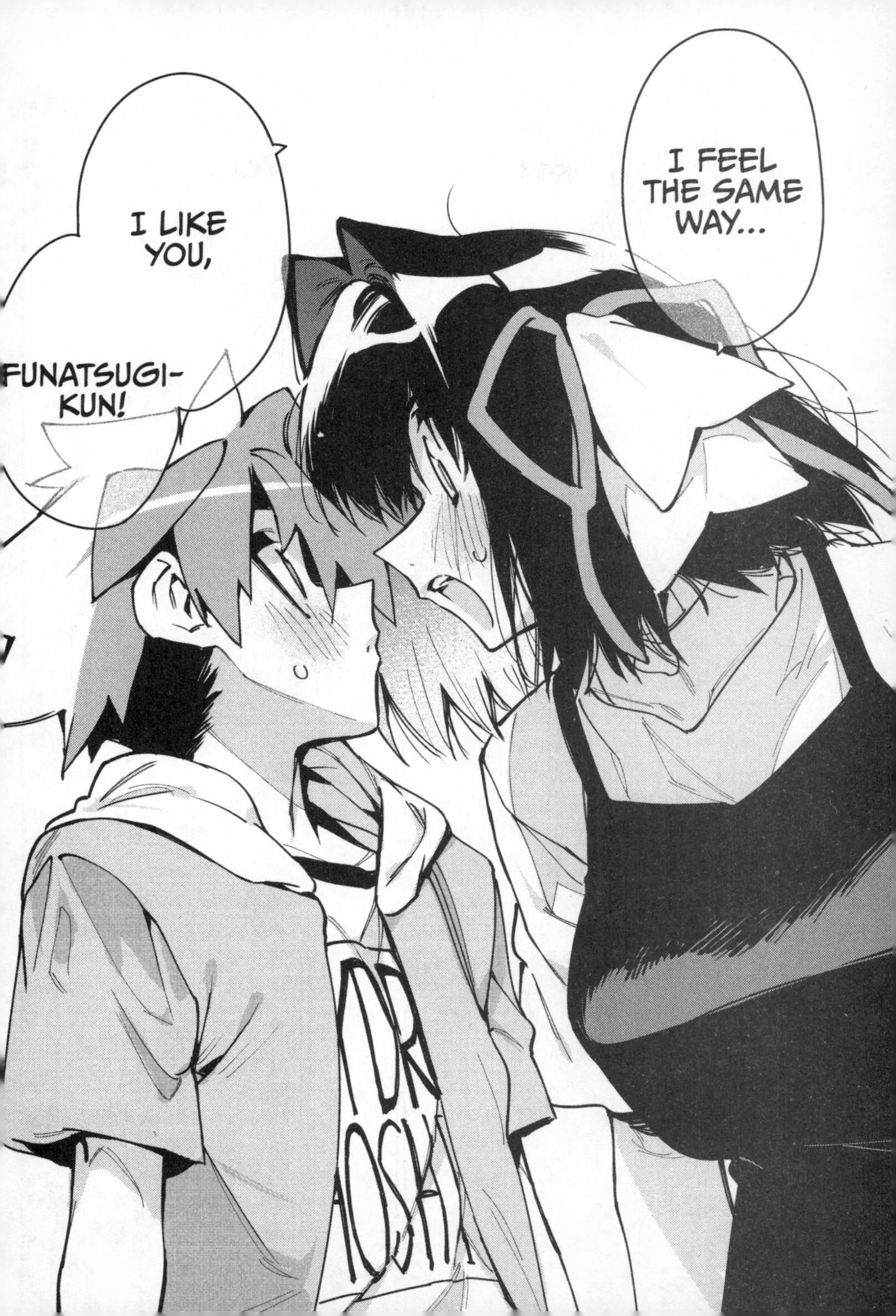
I FEEL THE SAME WAY...
I LIKE YOU, FUNATSUGI-KUN!

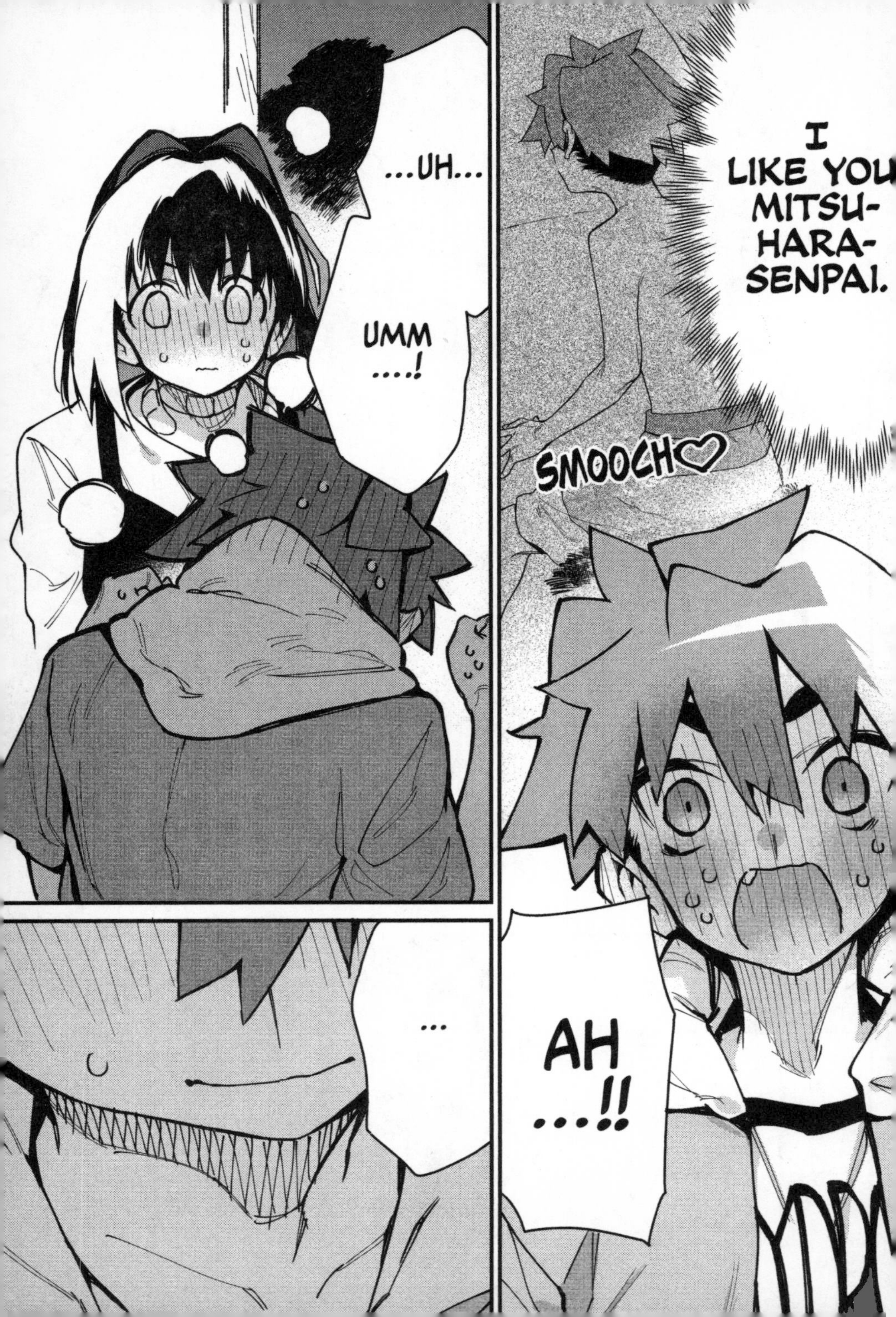
I LIKE YOU MITSUHARA-SENPAI.
SMOOCH♡
AH ...!!
...UH...
UMM ....!
...

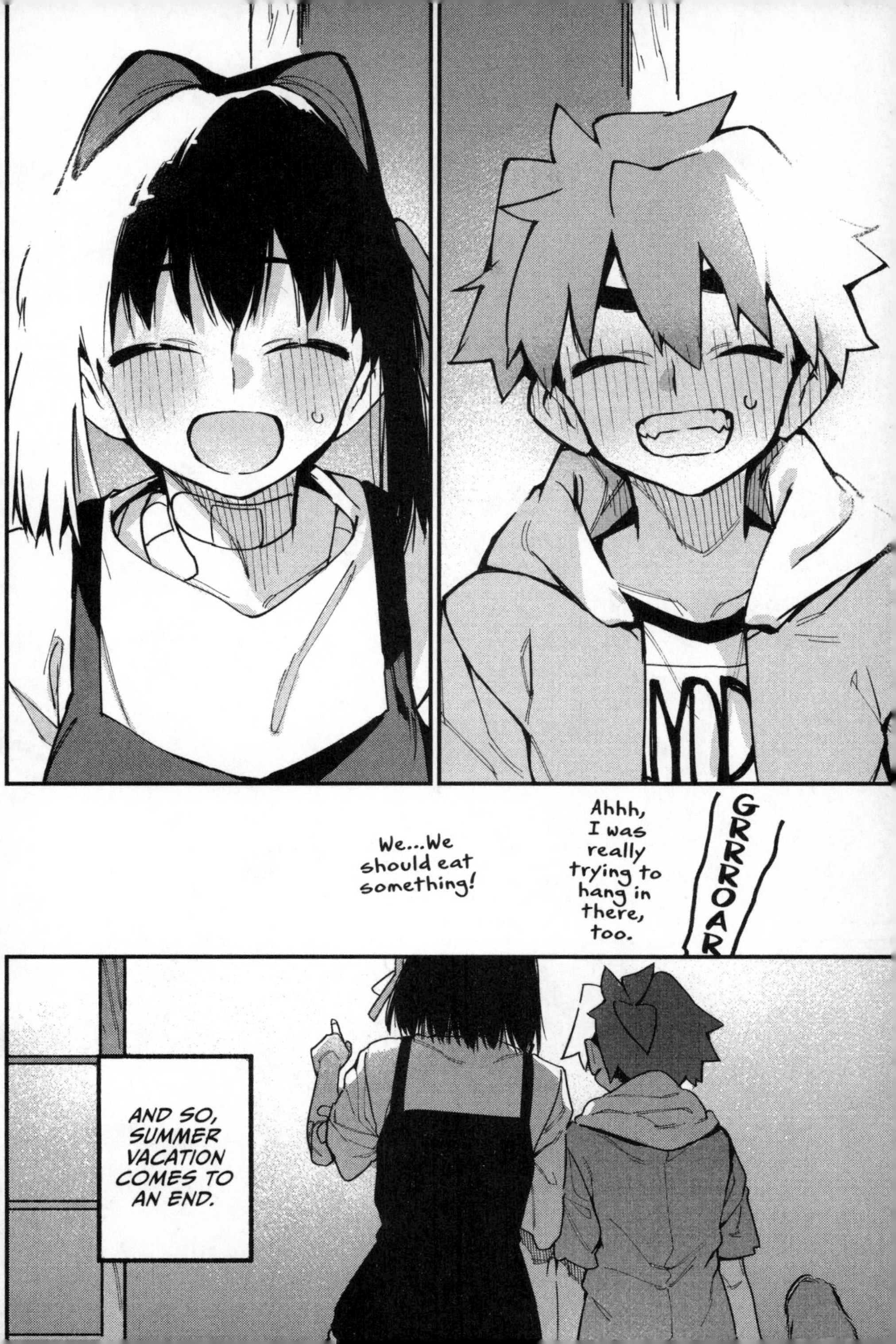
GRRROAR
Ahhh, I was really trying to hang in there, too.
We...We should eat something!
AND SO, SUMMER VACATION COMES TO AN END.

Sachi's
MONSTROUS
Appetite

It crossed my mind
that it would be super
awkward if she thought
she was being subtle by
doing this, but then
someone actually
pointed it out.
-Makie

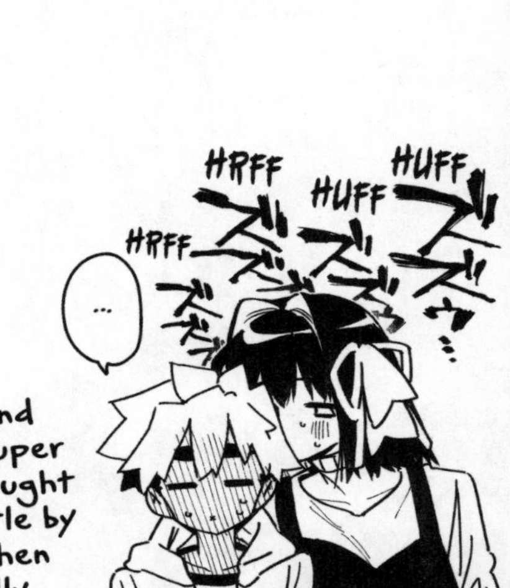
HUFF
HUFF
HRFF
HRFF
...

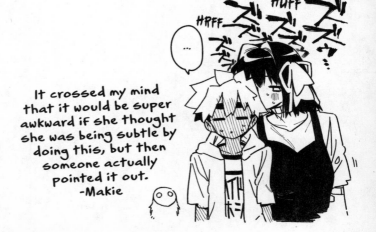

Chapter 13

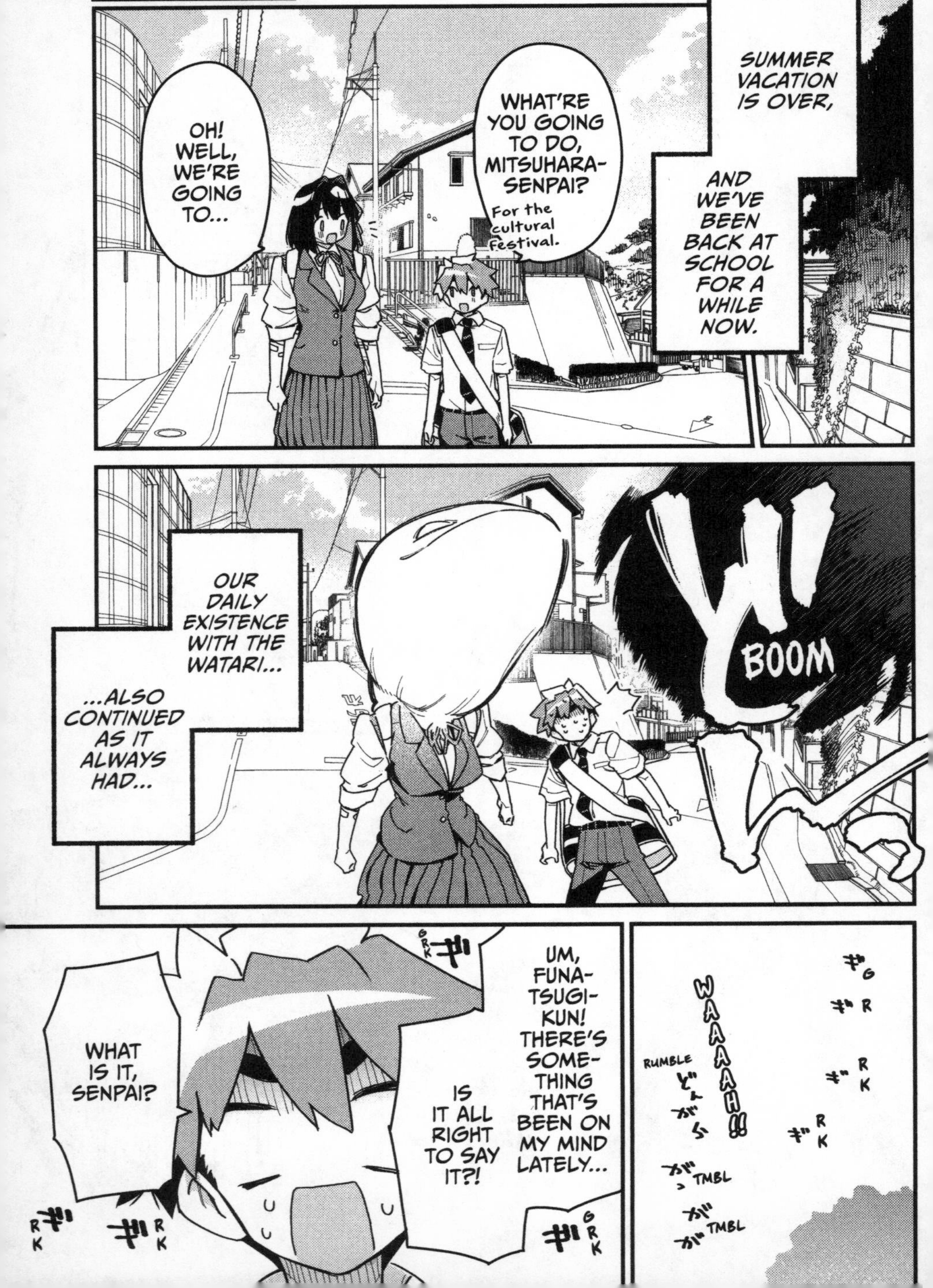
SUMMER VACATION IS OVER,
AND WE'VE BEEN BACK AT SCHOOL FOR A WHILE NOW.
WHAT'RE YOU GOING TO DO, MITSUHARA-SENPAI?
For the cultural festival.
OH! WELL, WE'RE GOING TO...
BOOM
OUR DAILY EXISTENCE WITH THE WATARI...
...ALSO CONTINUED AS IT ALWAYS HAD...
WAAAAAAH!!
G R R K R K
RUMBLE
TMBL
TMBL
UM, FUNATSUGI-KUN! THERE'S SOMETHING THAT'S BEEN ON MY MIND LATELY...
IS IT ALL RIGHT TO SAY IT?!
WHAT IS IT, SENPAI?
GRK
RK RK GRK

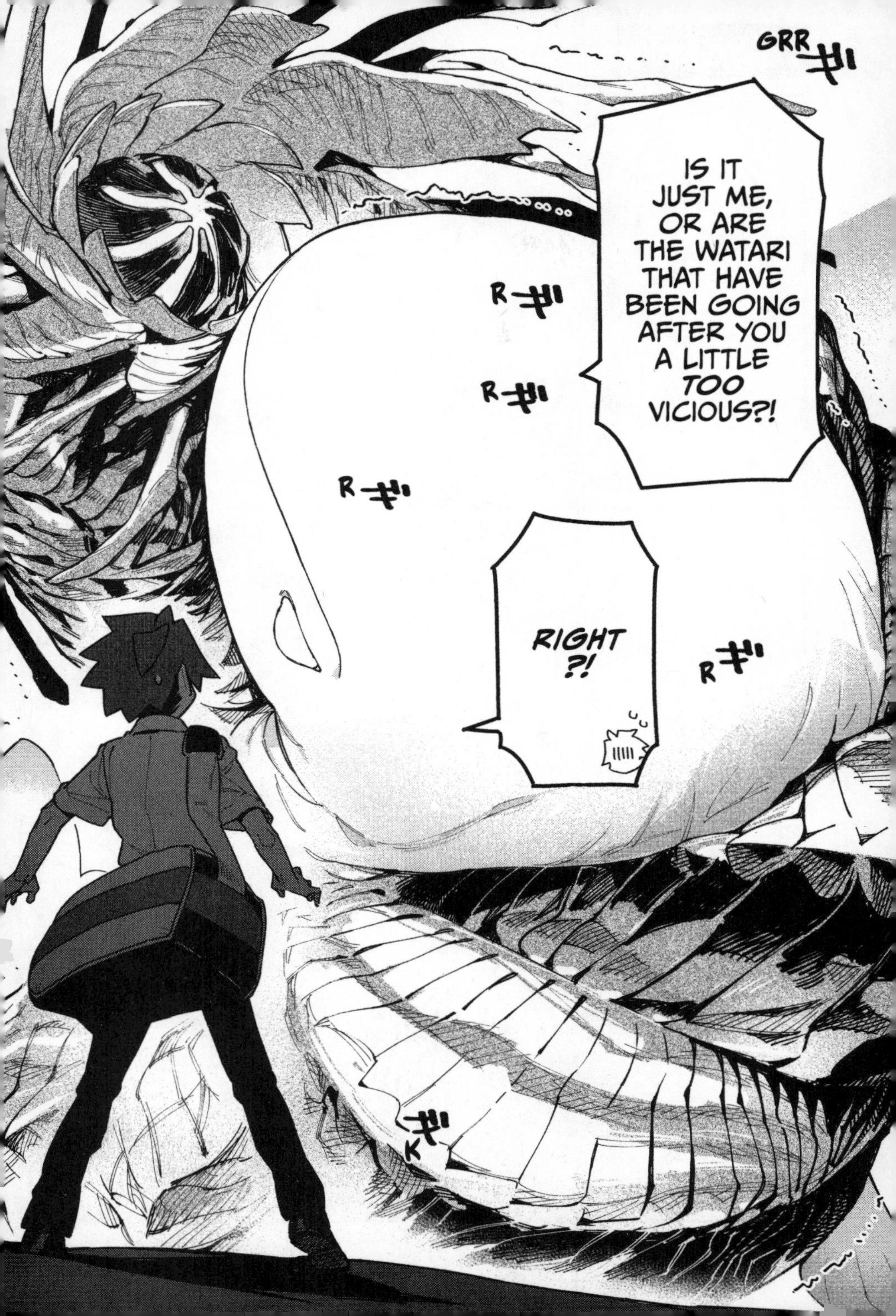
GRR ギ
IS IT JUST ME, OR ARE THE WATARI THAT HAVE BEEN GOING AFTER YOU A LITTLE *TOO* VICIOUS?!
R ギ
R ギ
R ギ
RIGHT ?!
R ギ
ギ K

Chapter 13: The Seedling Has a Purpose (1)

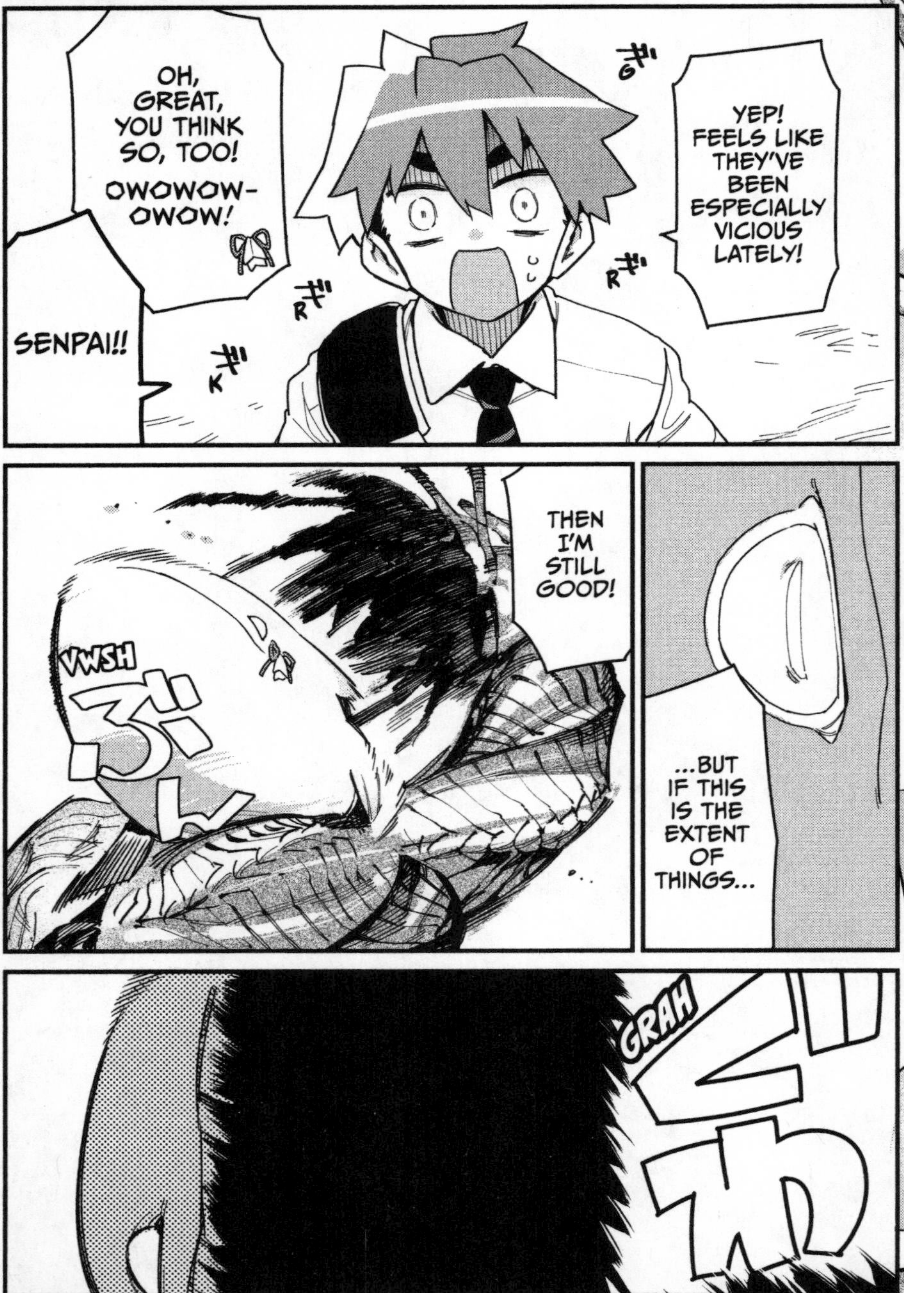
YEP! FEELS LIKE THEY'VE BEEN ESPECIALLY VICIOUS LATELY!
OH, GREAT, YOU THINK SO, TOO!
OWOWOW-OWOW!
SENPAI!!
...BUT IF THIS IS THE EXTENT OF THINGS...
THEN I'M STILL GOOD!
VWSH
GRAH

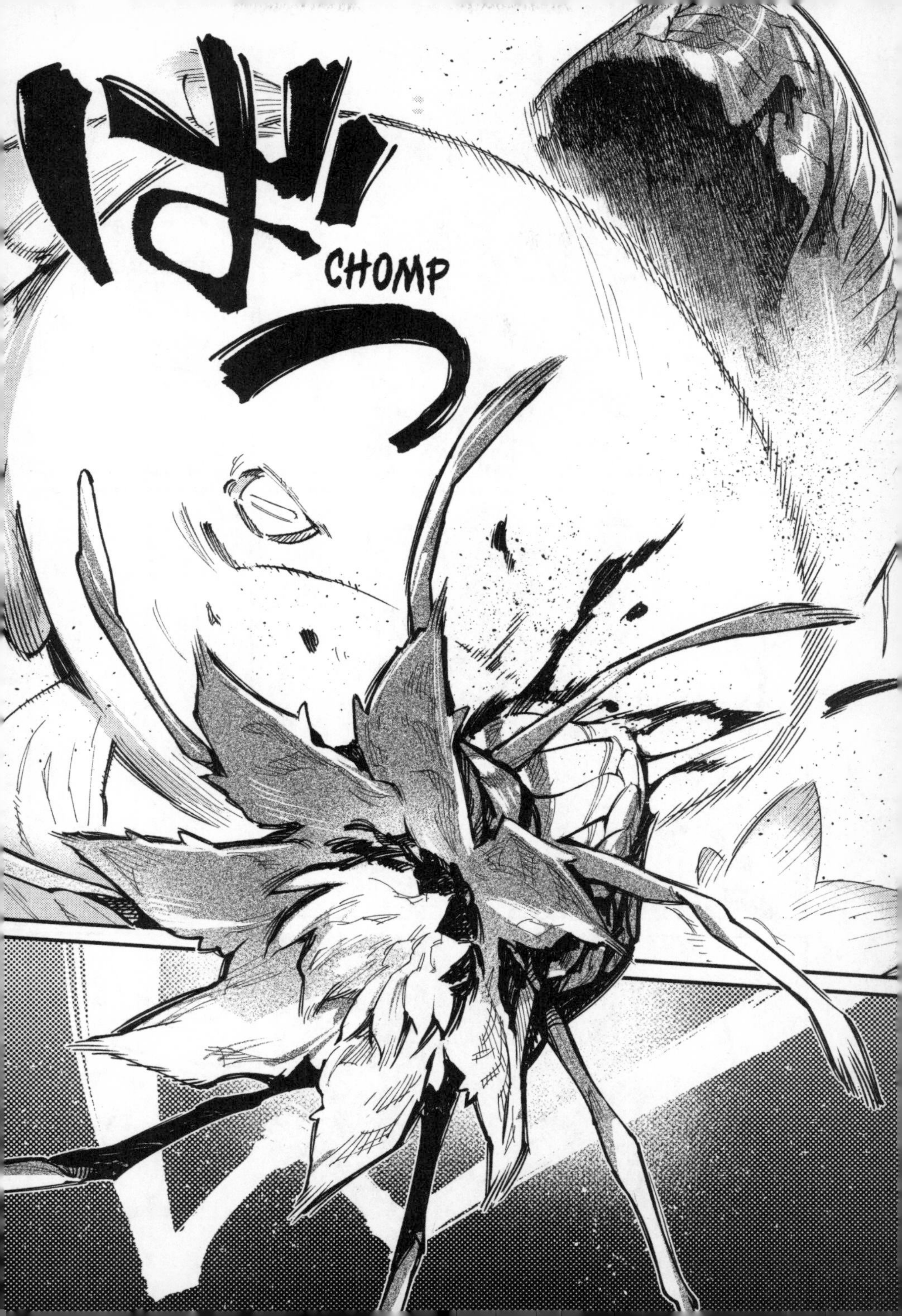
ばっ
CHOMP

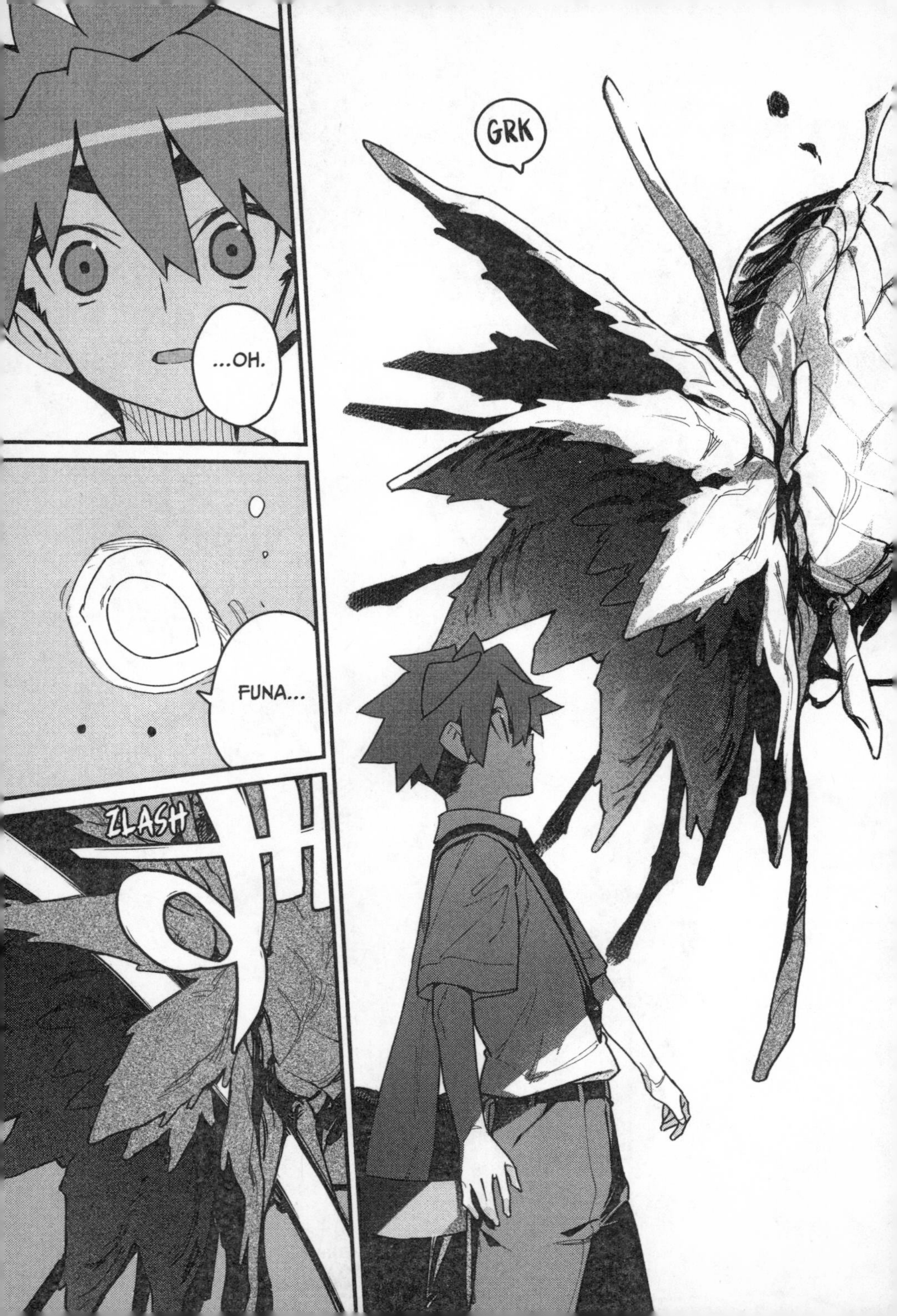
GRK
...OH.
FUNA...
ZLASH

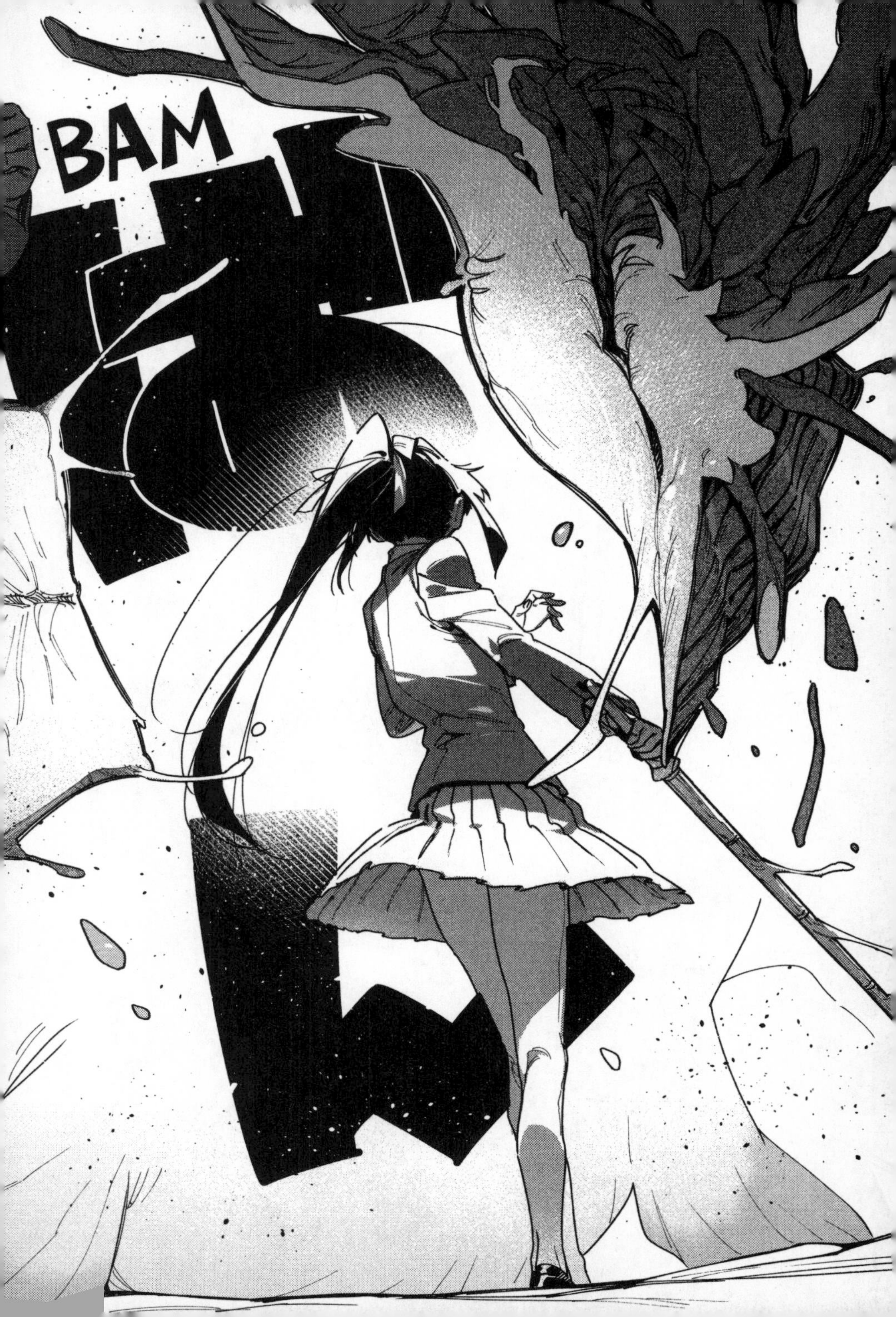
BAM

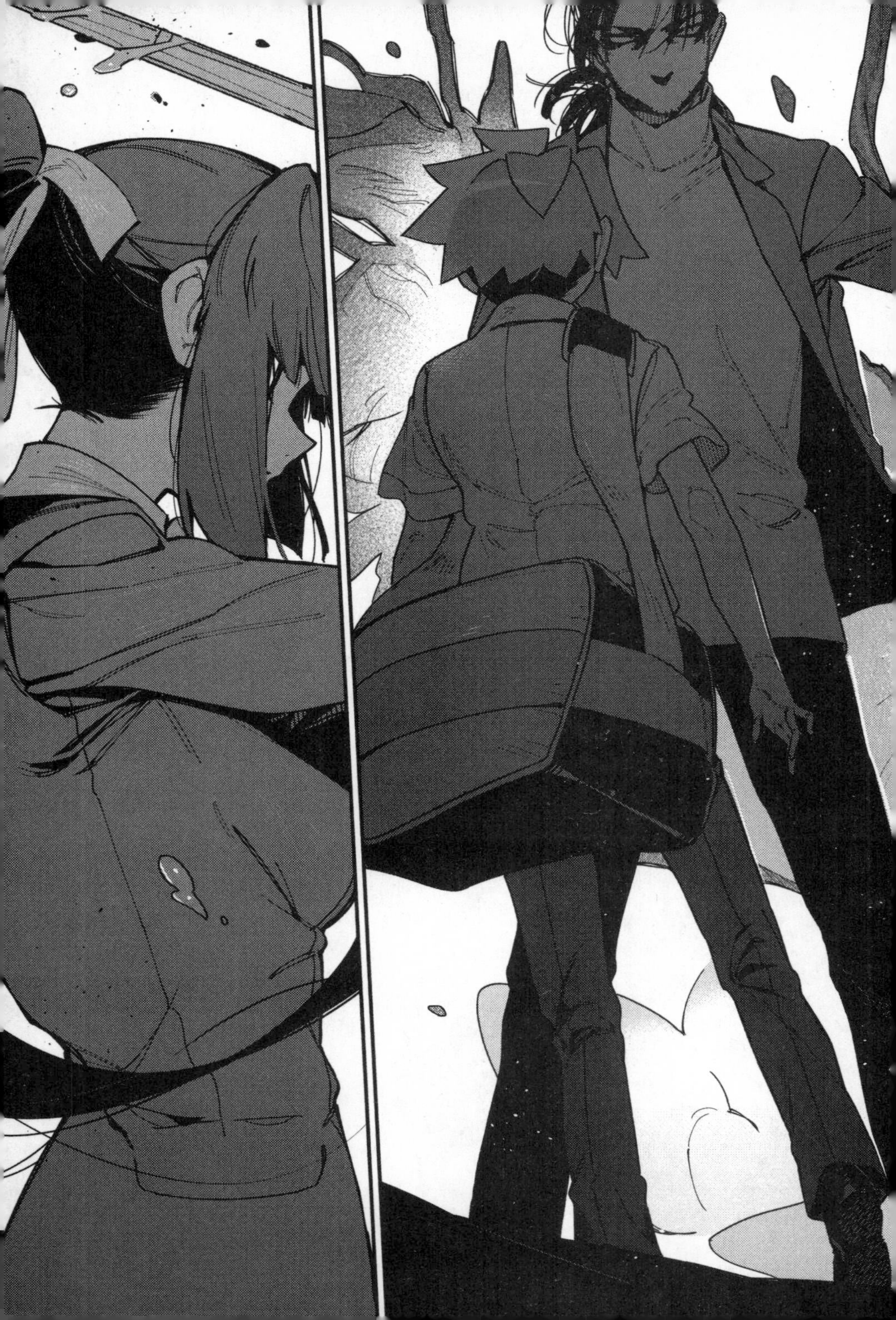

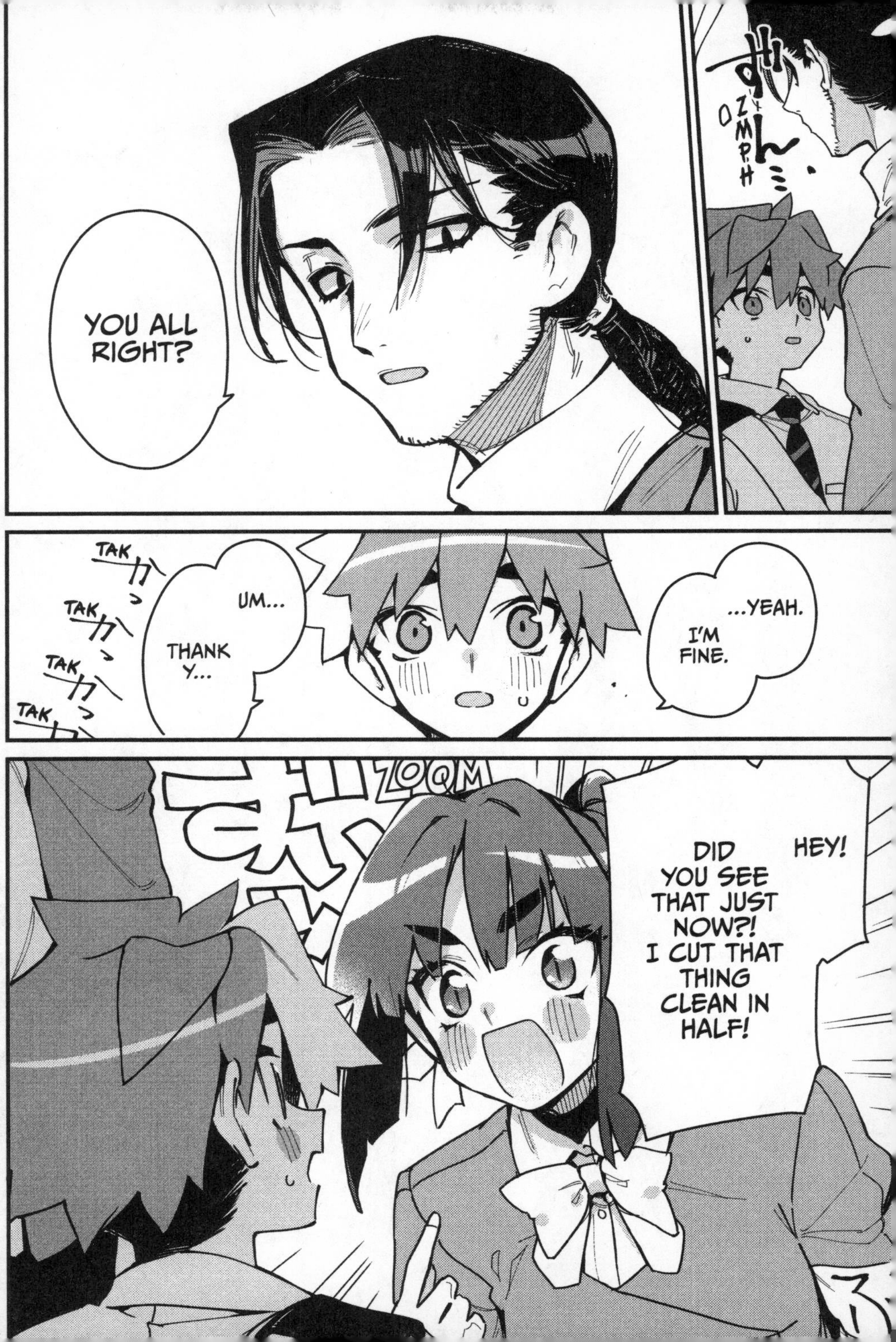
OZMPH
YOU ALL RIGHT?
...YEAH. I'M FINE.
UM... THANK Y...
TAK
TAK
TAK
TAK
ZOOM
HEY!
DID YOU SEE THAT JUST NOW?! I CUT THAT THING CLEAN IN HALF!

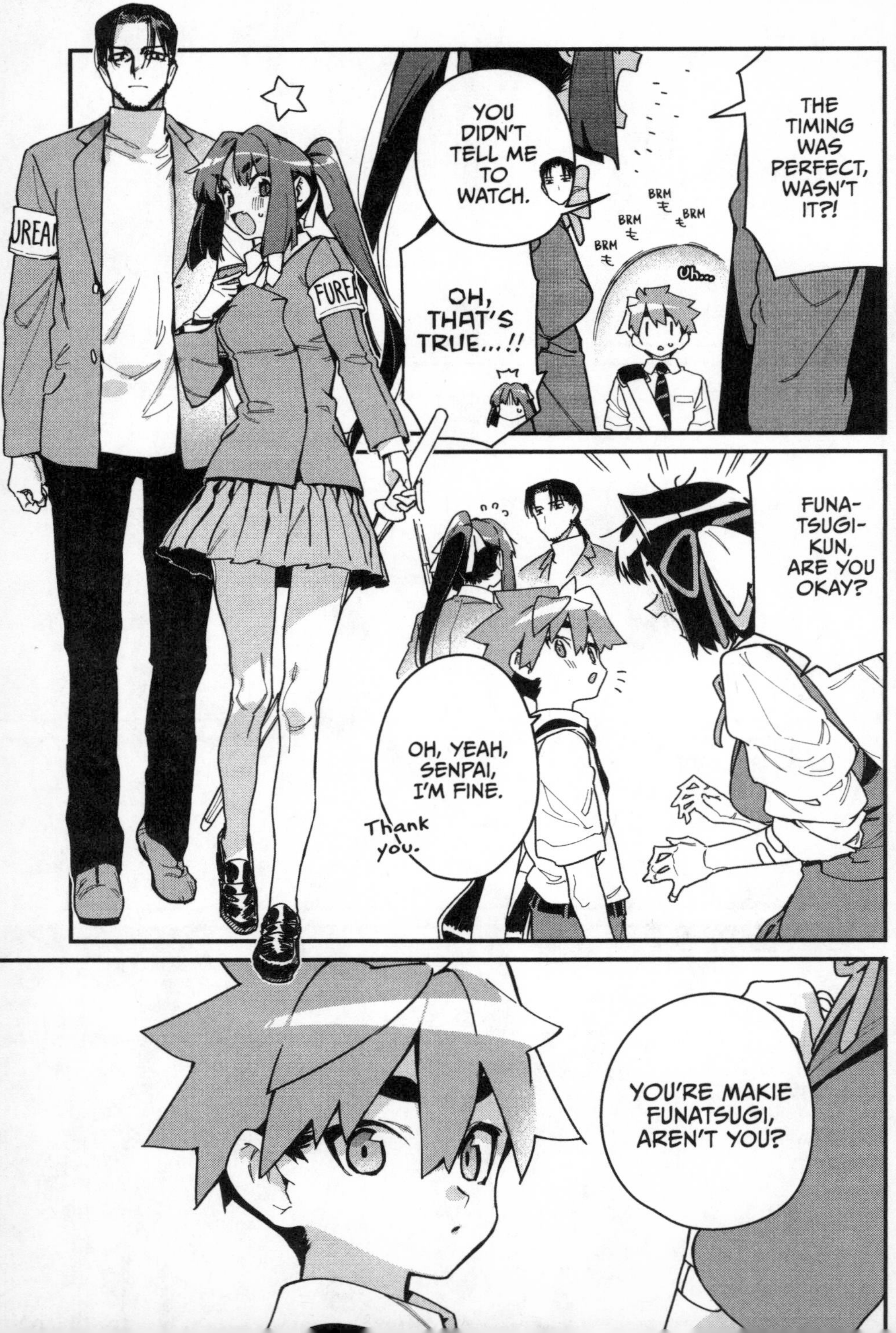
THE TIMING WAS PERFECT, WASN'T IT?!
YOU DIDN'T TELL ME TO WATCH.
BRM BRM BRM BRM
Uh...
OH, THAT'S TRUE...!!
FUNA-TSUGI-KUN, ARE YOU OKAY?
OH, YEAH, SENPAI, I'M FINE.
Thank you.
YOU'RE MAKIE FUNATSUGI, AREN'T YOU?

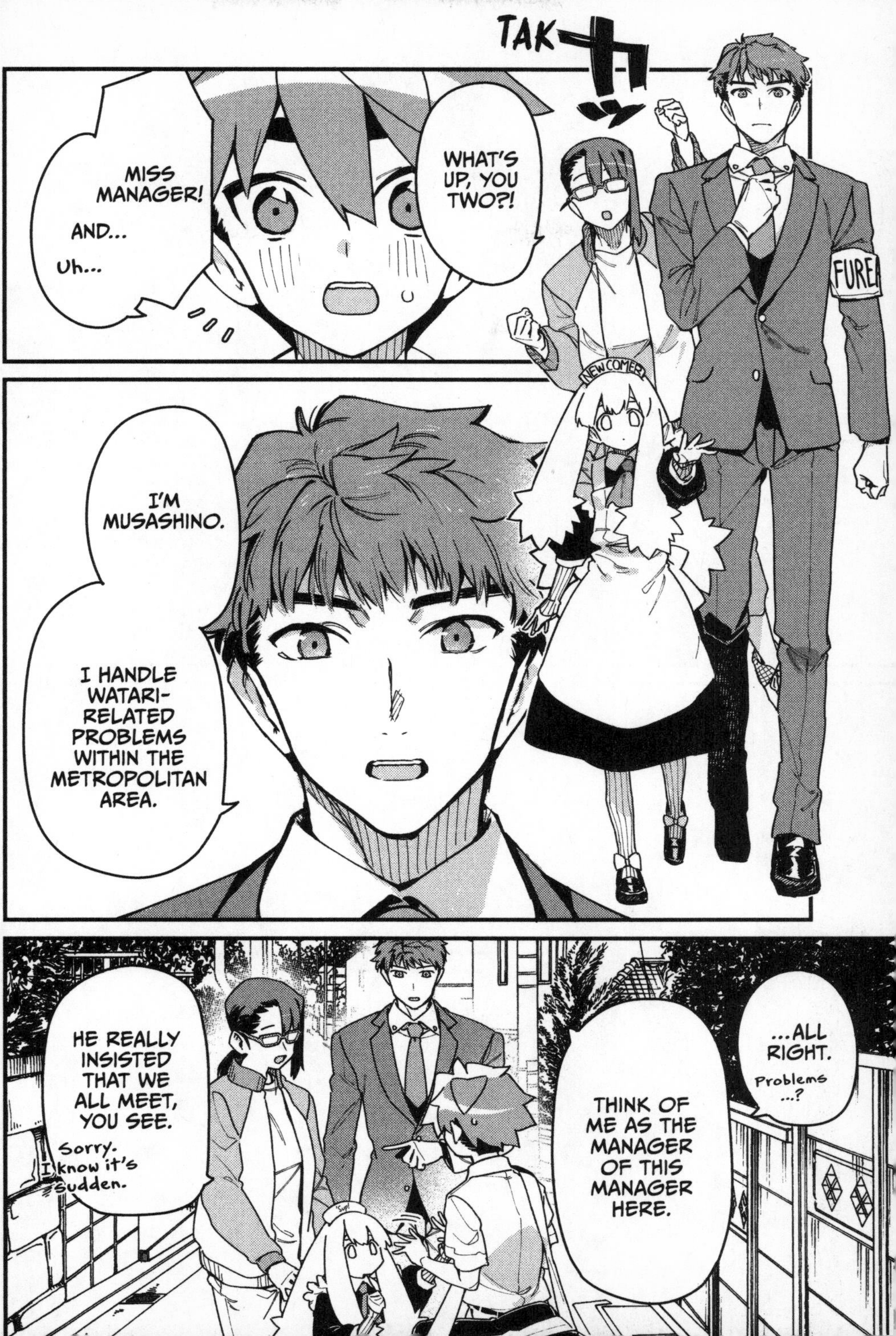
TAK
FUREA
NEW COMER
WHAT'S UP, YOU TWO?!
MISS MANAGER!
AND...
Uh...
I'M MUSASHINO.
I HANDLE WATARI-RELATED PROBLEMS WITHIN THE METROPOLITAN AREA.
...ALL RIGHT.
Problems...?
THINK OF ME AS THE MANAGER OF THIS MANAGER HERE.
HE REALLY INSISTED THAT WE ALL MEET, YOU SEE.
Sorry. I know it's sudden.
'Sup!

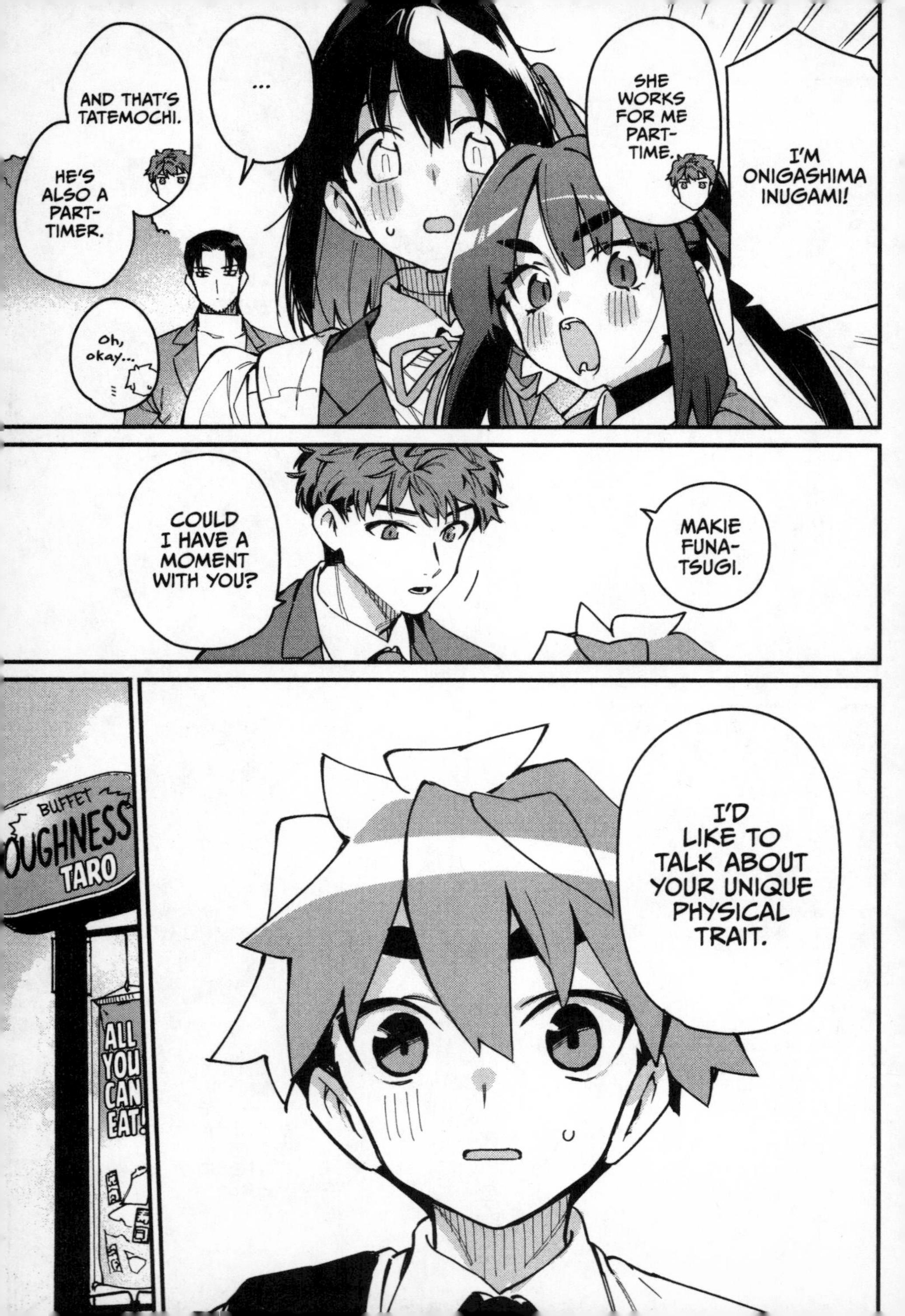
I'M ONIGASHIMA INUGAMI!
SHE WORKS FOR ME PART-TIME.
...
AND THAT'S TATEMOCHI.
HE'S ALSO A PART-TIMER.
Oh, okay...
MAKIE FUNATSUGI.
COULD I HAVE A MOMENT WITH YOU?
I'D LIKE TO TALK ABOUT YOUR UNIQUE PHYSICAL TRAIT.
BUFFET
OUGHNESS
TARO
ALL YOU CAN EAT!

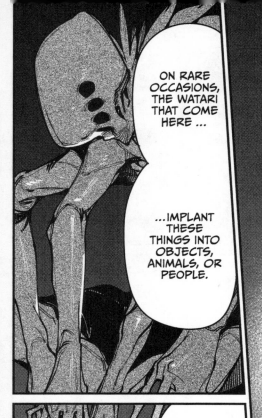

THIS IS SOMETHING CALLED...
...A SEEDLING.
ON RARE OCCASIONS, THE WATARI THAT COME HERE ...
...IMPLANT THESE THINGS INTO OBJECTS, ANIMALS, OR PEOPLE.
WHATEVER HAS THIS SEEDLING IMPLANTED IN THEM...
...EMITS A TYPE OF PHEROMONE THAT ATTRACTS WATARI.

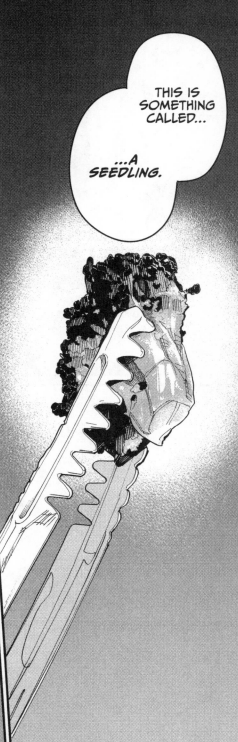

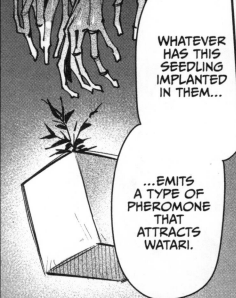

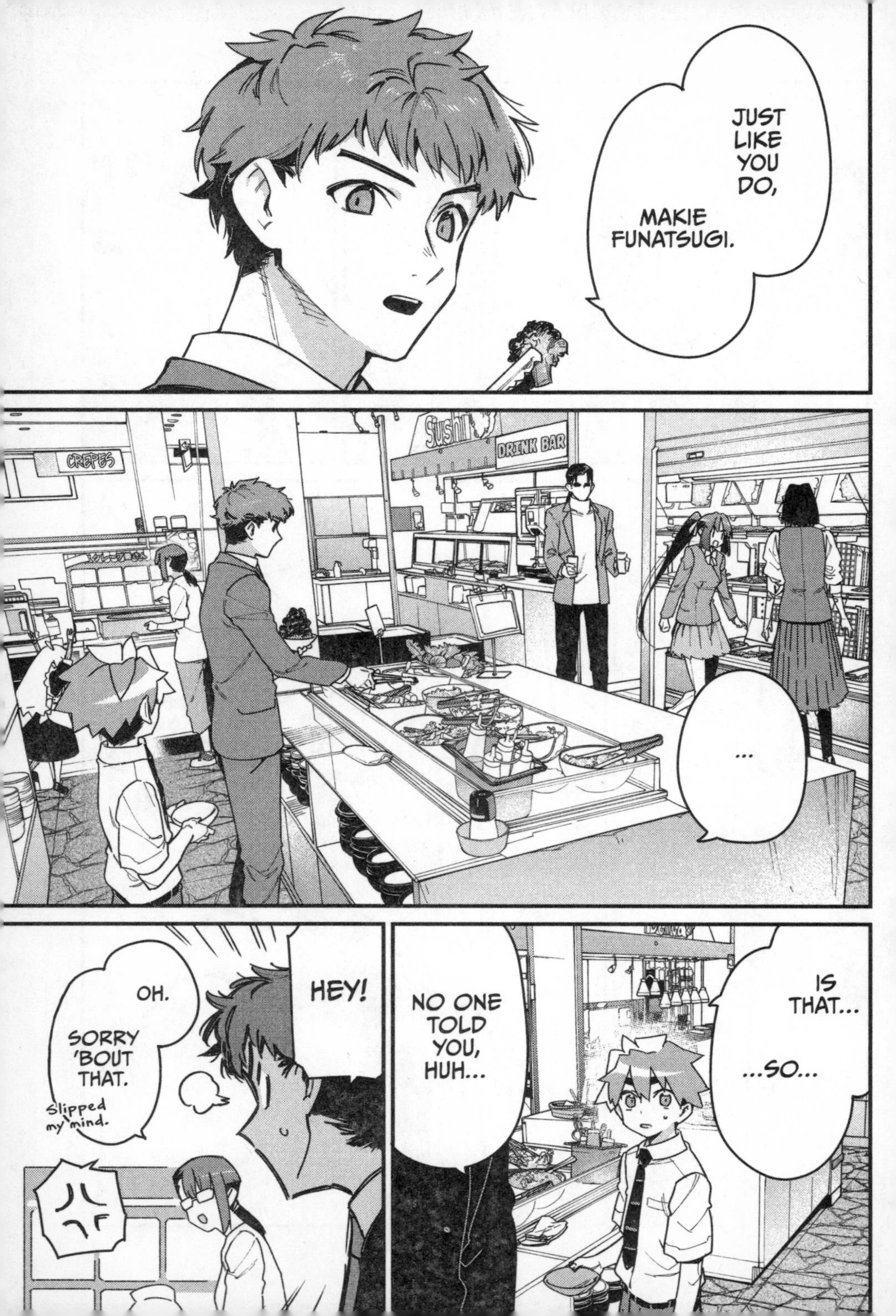
JUST LIKE YOU DO,
MAKIE FUNATSUGI.
SUSHI
DRINK BAR
CREPES
...
IS THAT...
...SO...
NO ONE TOLD YOU, HUH...
HEY!
OH.
SORRY 'BOUT THAT.
Slipped my mind.

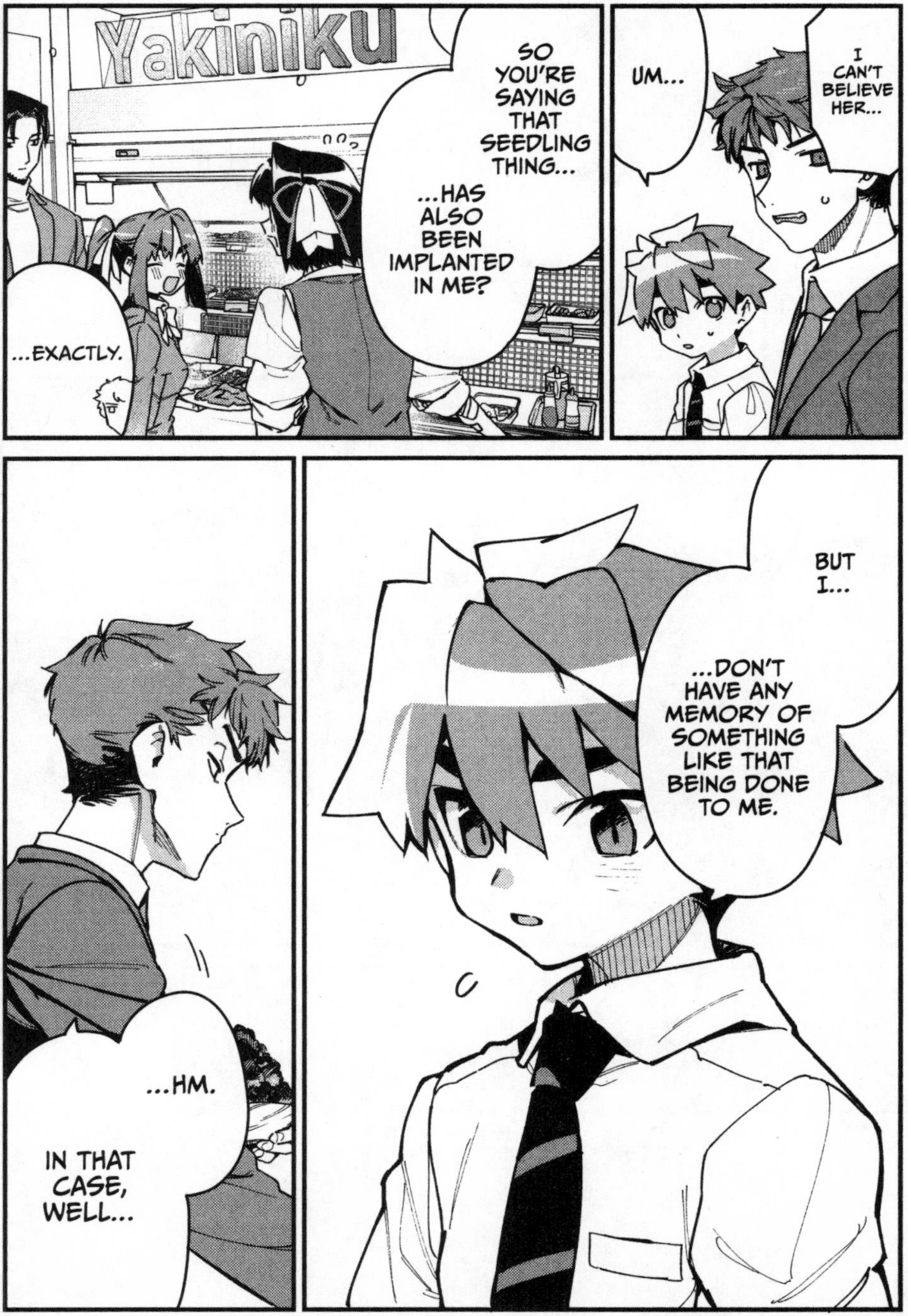
I CAN'T BELIEVE HER...
UM...
SO YOU'RE SAYING THAT SEEDLING THING...
...HAS ALSO BEEN IMPLANTED IN ME?
Yakiniku
...EXACTLY.
BUT I...
...DON'T HAVE ANY MEMORY OF SOMETHING LIKE THAT BEING DONE TO ME.
...HM.
IN THAT CASE, WELL...

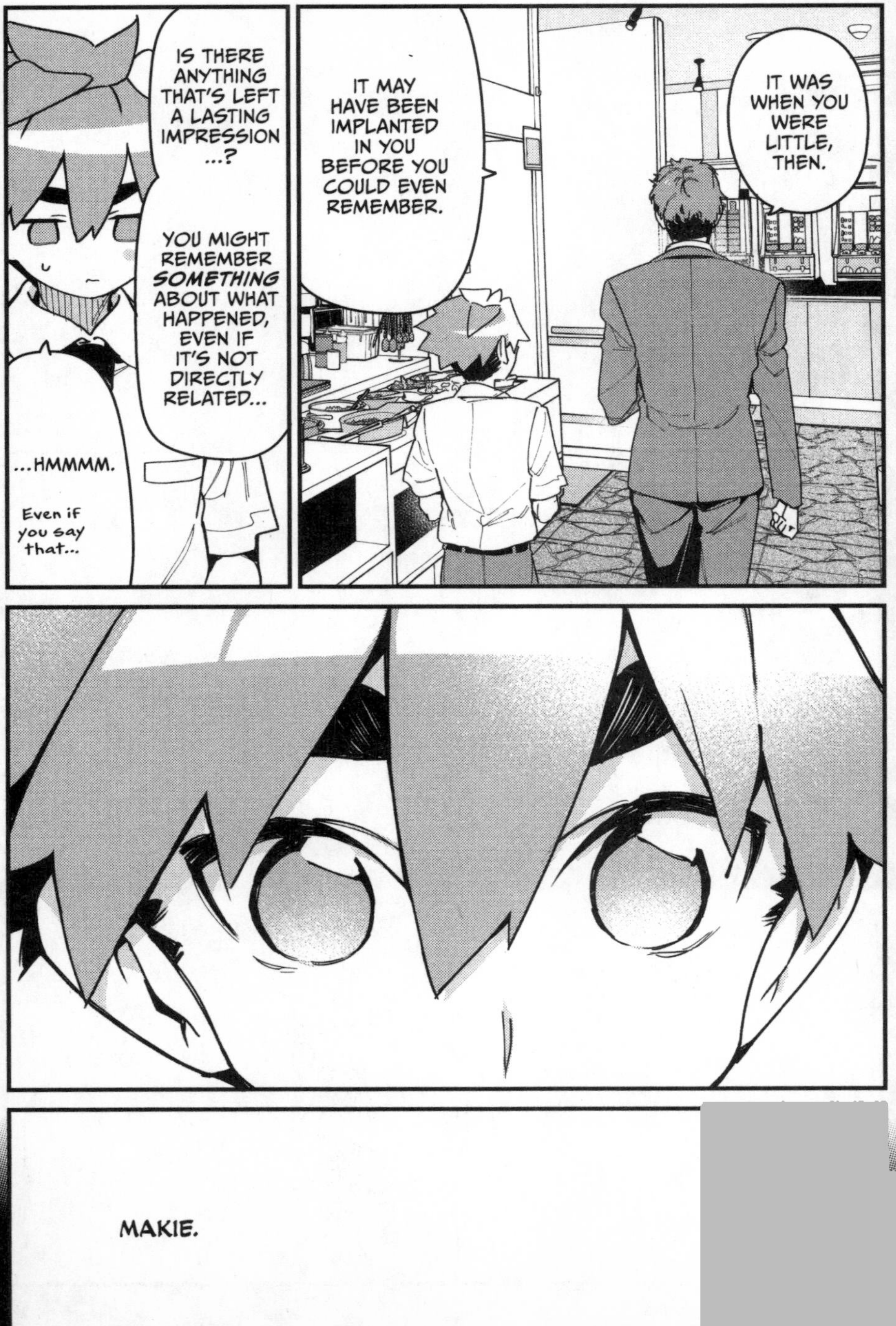
IT WAS WHEN YOU WERE LITTLE, THEN.
IT MAY HAVE BEEN IMPLANTED IN YOU BEFORE YOU COULD EVEN REMEMBER.
IS THERE ANYTHING THAT'S LEFT A LASTING IMPRESSION ...?
YOU MIGHT REMEMBER *SOMETHING* ABOUT WHAT HAPPENED, EVEN IF IT'S NOT DIRECTLY RELATED...
...HMMMM.
Even if you say that...
MAKIE.

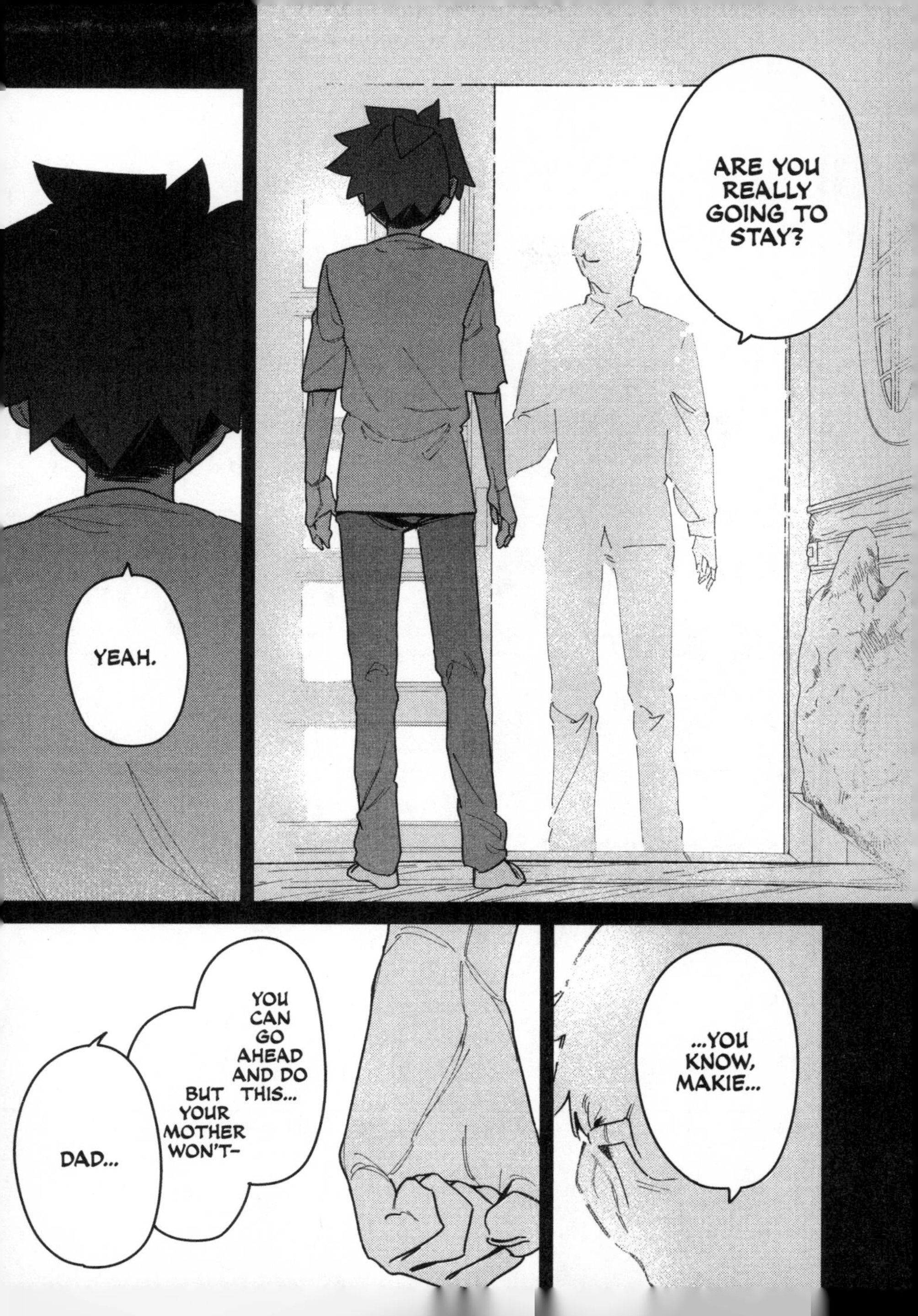
ARE YOU REALLY GOING TO STAY?
YEAH.
...YOU KNOW, MAKIE...
YOU CAN GO AHEAD AND DO THIS... BUT YOUR MOTHER WON'T-
DAD...

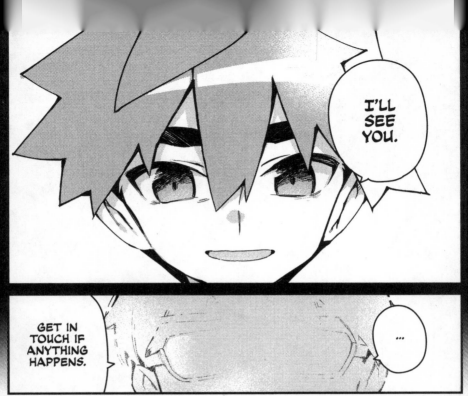

I'LL SEE YOU.
...
GET IN TOUCH IF ANYTHING HAPPENS.
NO... I DON'T THINK THAT'S IT.
THERE'S NOTHING THAT'S REALLY RINGING A BELL...
ALL RIGHT...
THEN LET'S CONSIDER THE PRESENT FOR NOW.

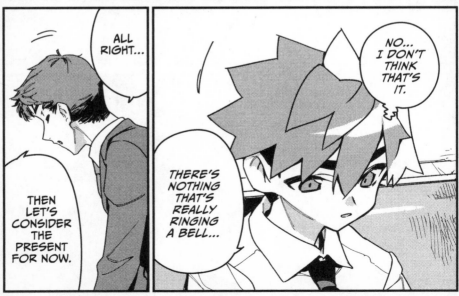

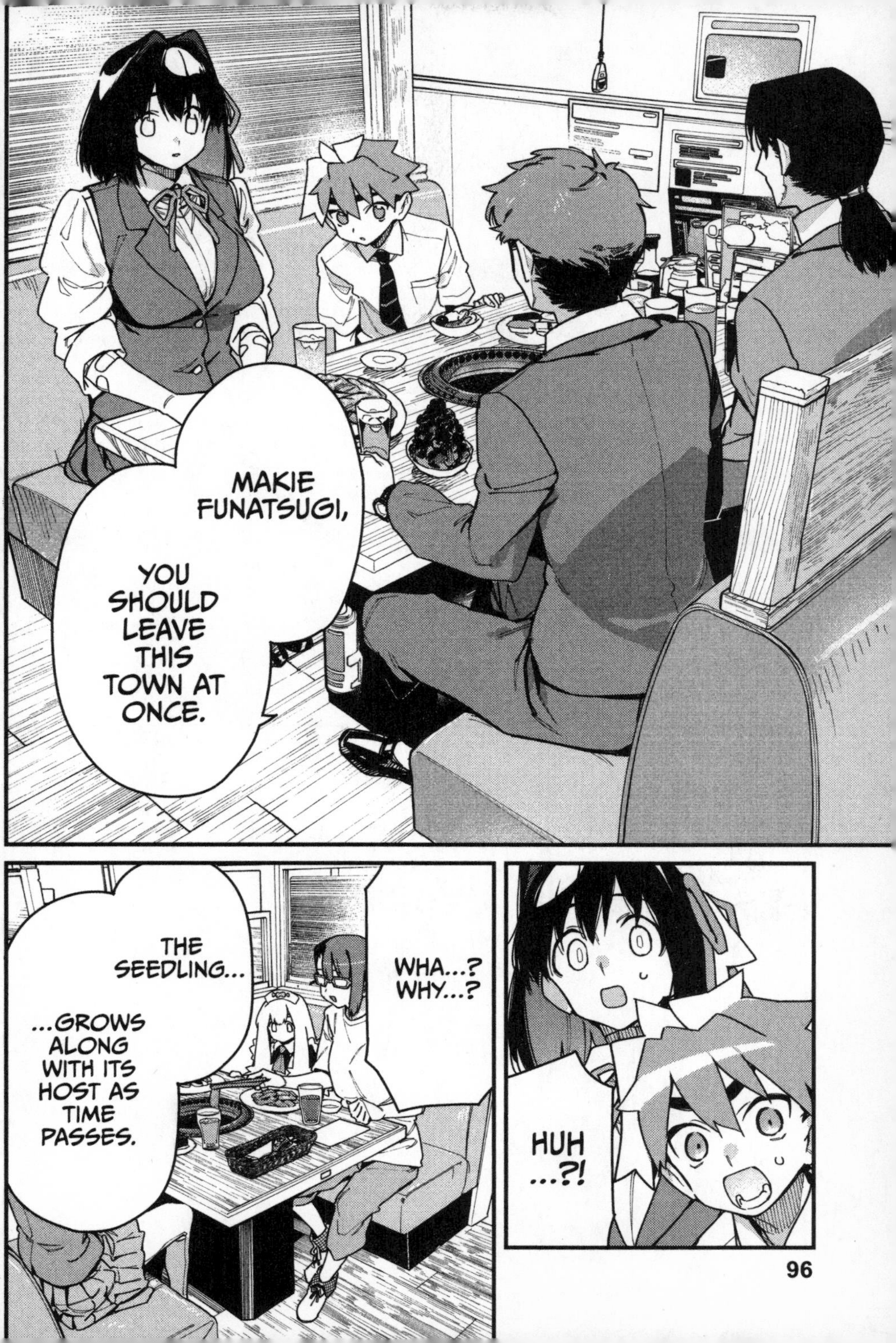
MAKIE FUNATSUGI,
YOU SHOULD LEAVE THIS TOWN AT ONCE.
HUH ...?!
WHA...? WHY...?
THE SEEDLING...
...GROWS ALONG WITH ITS HOST AS TIME PASSES.

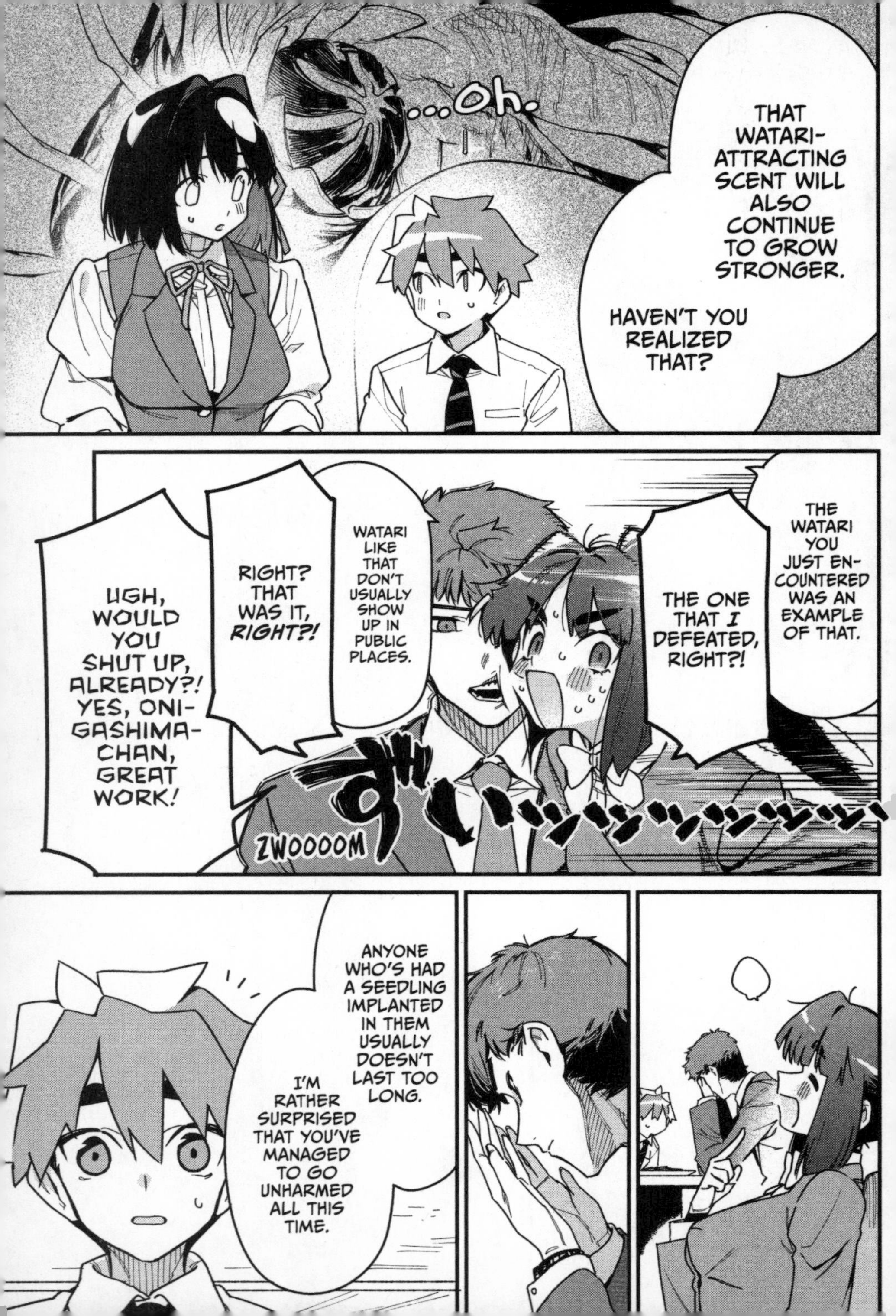
THAT WATARI-ATTRACTING SCENT WILL ALSO CONTINUE TO GROW STRONGER.
HAVEN'T YOU REALIZED THAT?
...Oh.
THE WATARI YOU JUST EN-COUNTERED WAS AN EXAMPLE OF THAT.
THE ONE THAT *I* DEFEATED, RIGHT?!
WATARI LIKE THAT DON'T USUALLY SHOW UP IN PUBLIC PLACES.
RIGHT? THAT WAS IT, ***RIGHT?!***
UGH, WOULD YOU SHUT UP, ALREADY?! YES, ONI-GASHIMA-CHAN, GREAT WORK!
ZWOOOOM
ANYONE WHO'S HAD A SEEDLING IMPLANTED IN THEM USUALLY DOESN'T LAST TOO LONG.
I'M RATHER SURPRISED THAT YOU'VE MANAGED TO GO UNHARMED ALL THIS TIME.

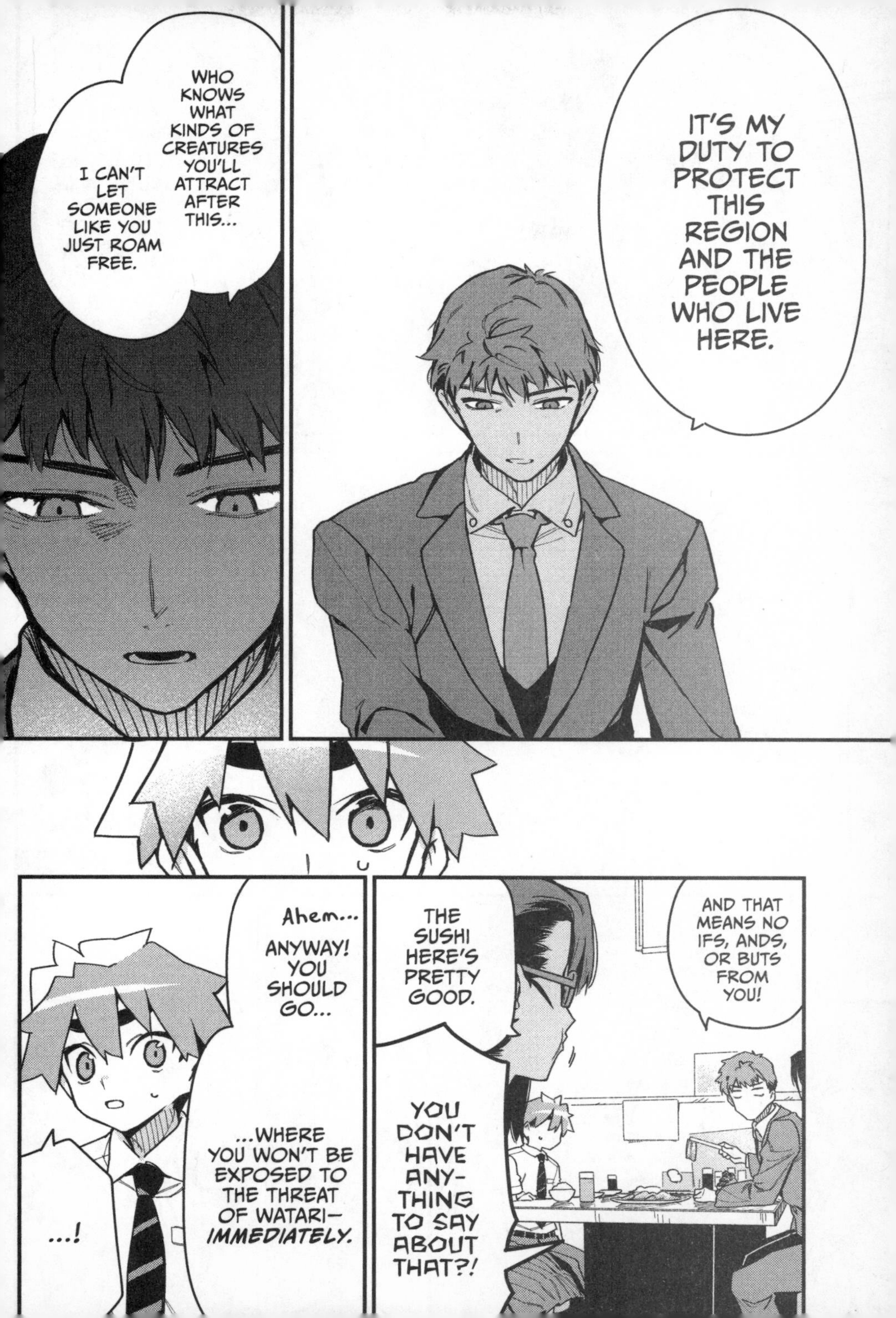
IT'S MY DUTY TO PROTECT THIS REGION AND THE PEOPLE WHO LIVE HERE.
WHO KNOWS WHAT KINDS OF CREATURES YOU'LL ATTRACT AFTER THIS...
I CAN'T LET SOMEONE LIKE YOU JUST ROAM FREE.
AND THAT MEANS NO IFS, ANDS, OR BUTS FROM YOU!
THE SUSHI HERE'S PRETTY GOOD.
YOU DON'T HAVE ANY-THING TO SAY ABOUT THAT?!
Ahem...
ANYWAY! YOU SHOULD GO...
...WHERE YOU WON'T BE EXPOSED TO THE THREAT OF WATARI—*IMMEDIATELY.*
...!

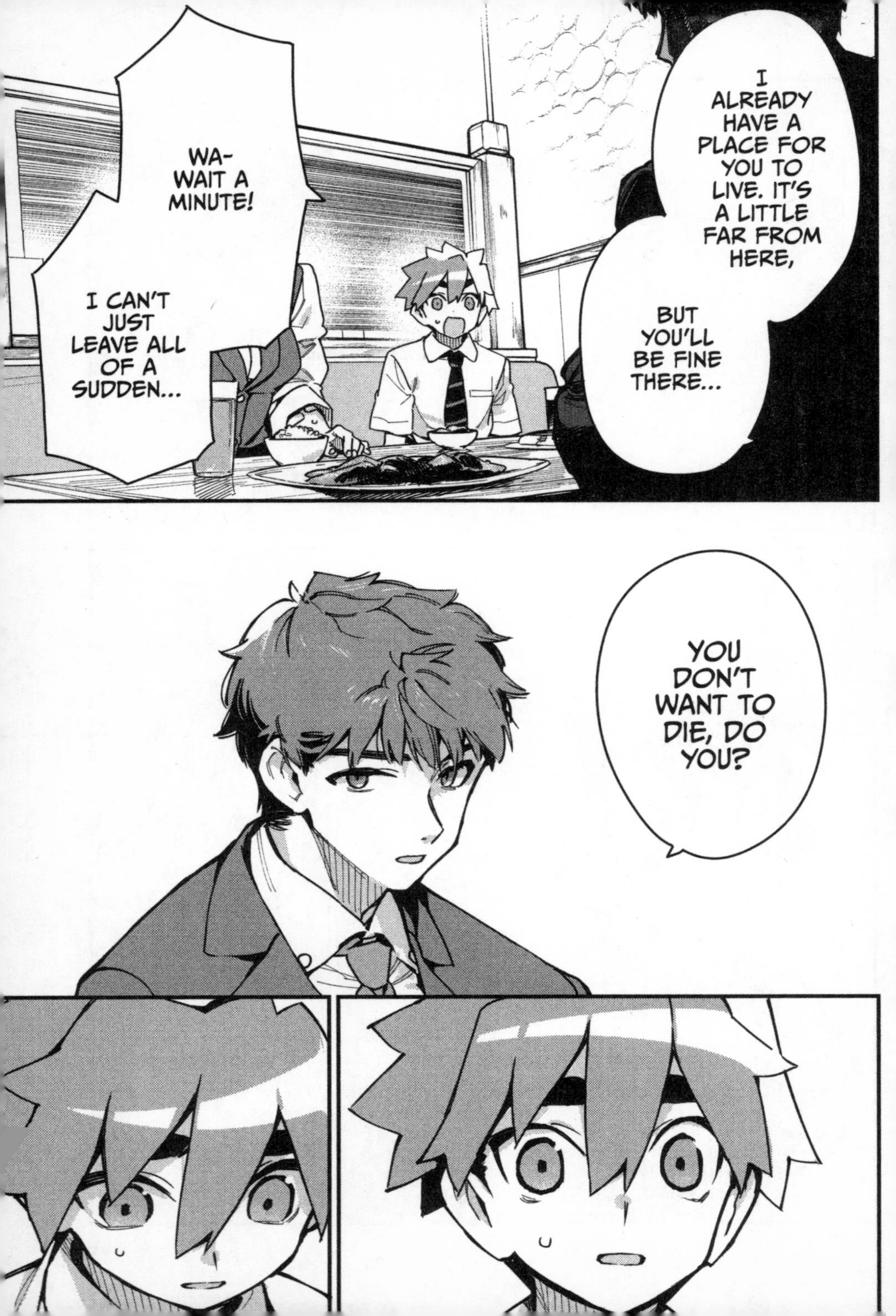
I ALREADY HAVE A PLACE FOR YOU TO LIVE. IT'S A LITTLE FAR FROM HERE,
BUT YOU'LL BE FINE THERE...
WA- WAIT A MINUTE!
I CAN'T JUST LEAVE ALL OF A SUDDEN...
YOU DON'T WANT TO DIE, DO YOU?

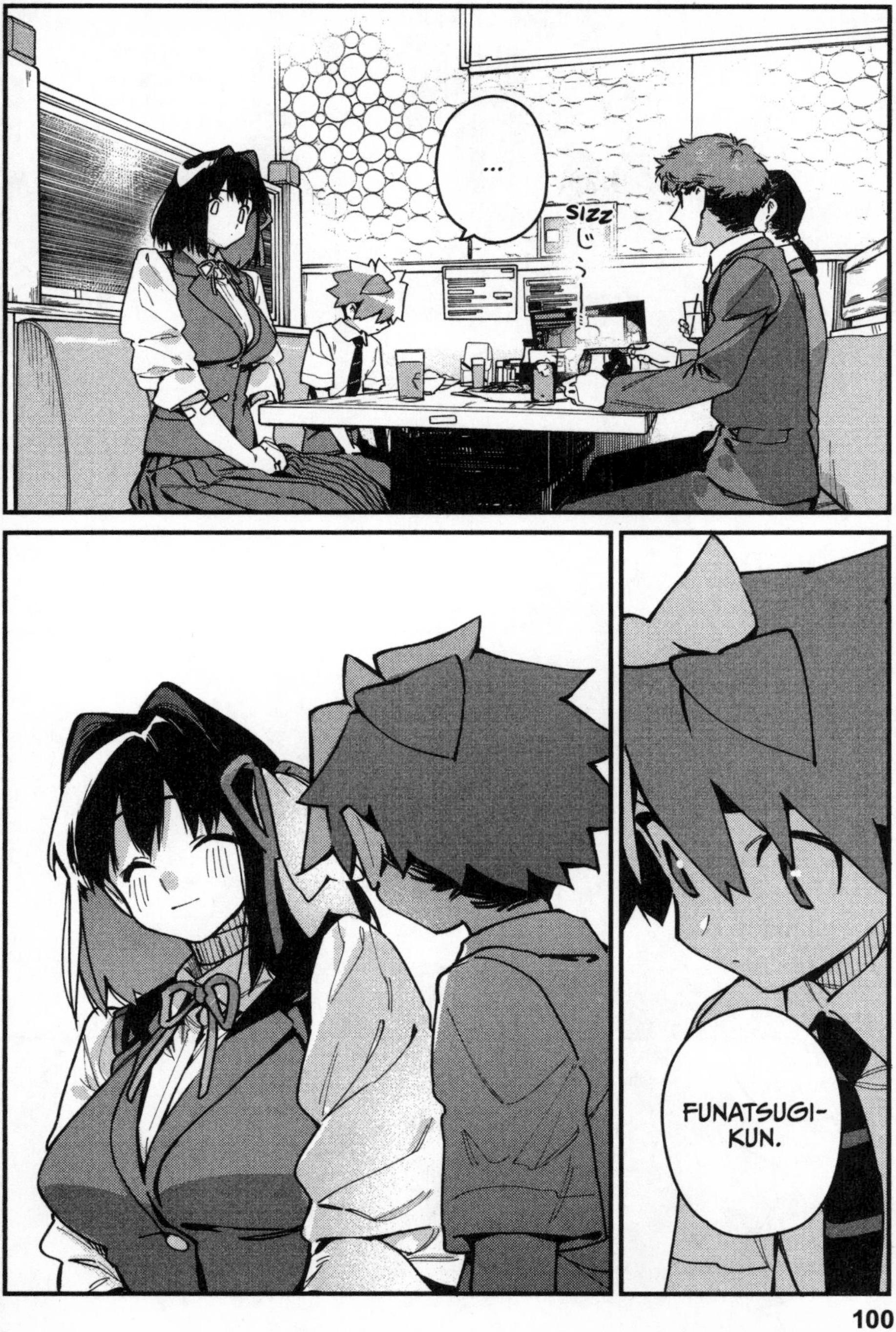
...
SIZZ
じう
FUNATSUGI-KUN.

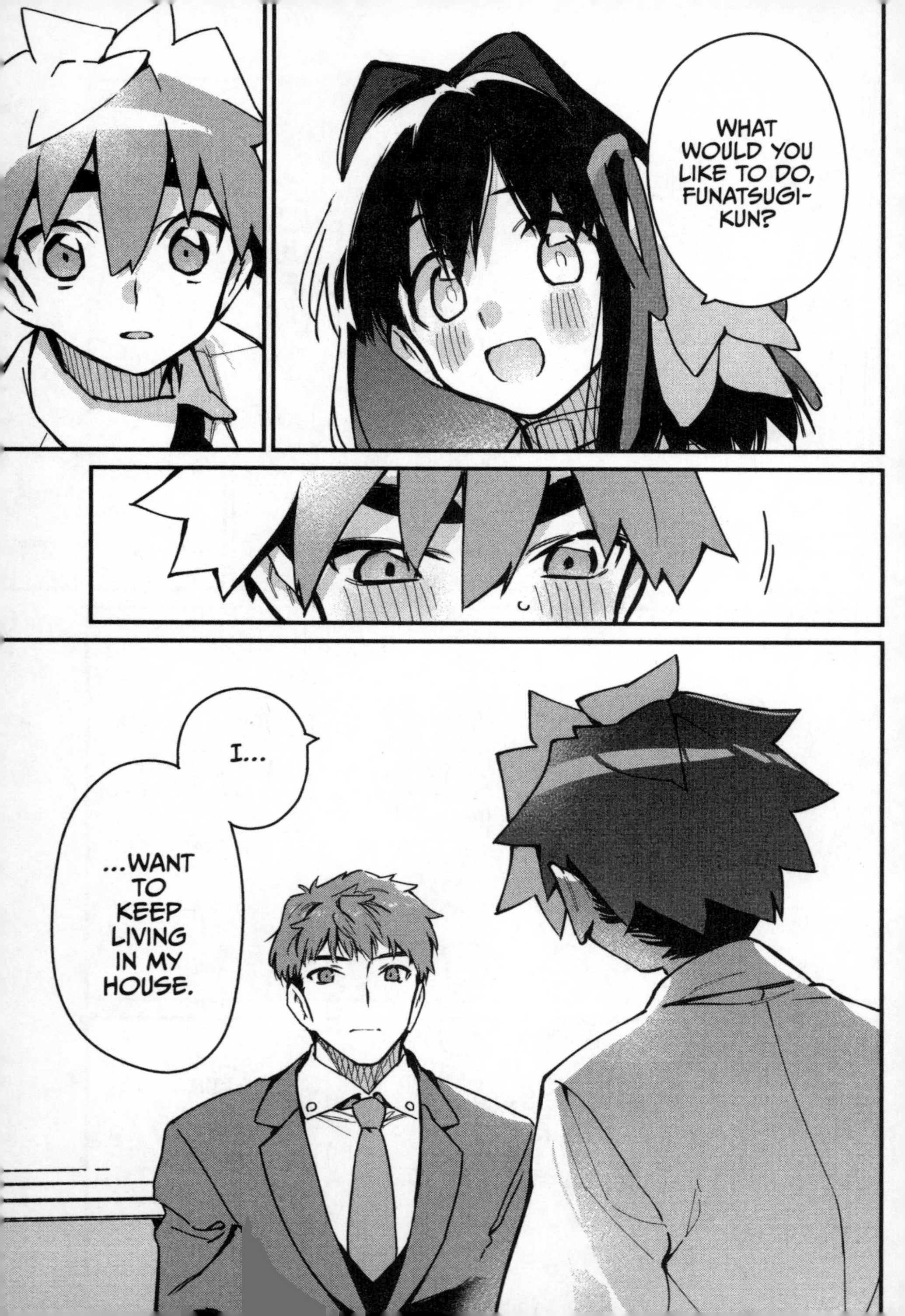
WHAT WOULD YOU LIKE TO DO, FUNATSUGI-KUN?
I...
...WANT TO KEEP LIVING IN MY HOUSE.

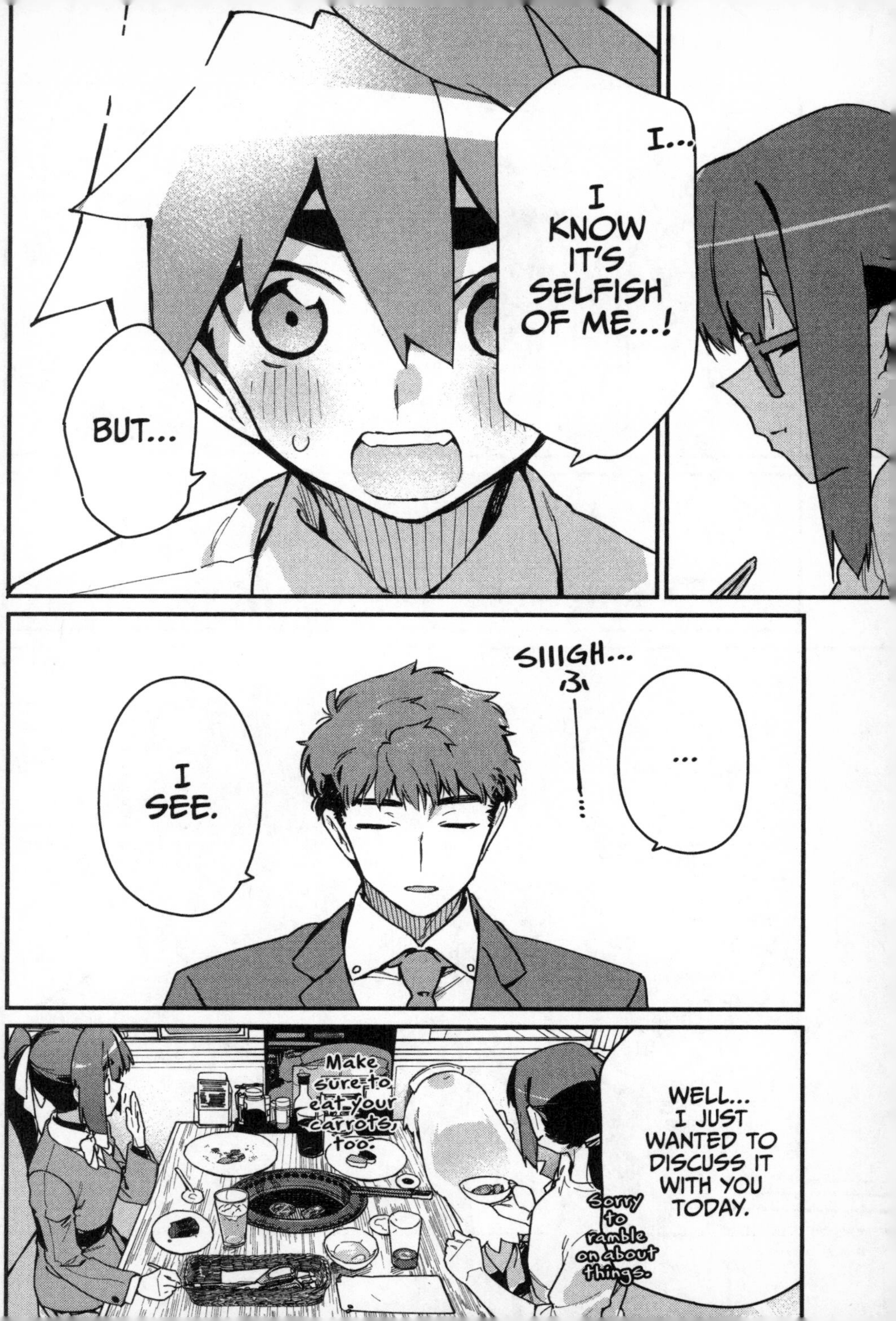
I...
I KNOW IT'S SELFISH OF ME...!
BUT...
SIIIGH... ふ
...
I SEE.
WELL... I JUST WANTED TO DISCUSS IT WITH YOU TODAY.
Sorry to ramble on about things.
Make sure to eat your carrots, too.

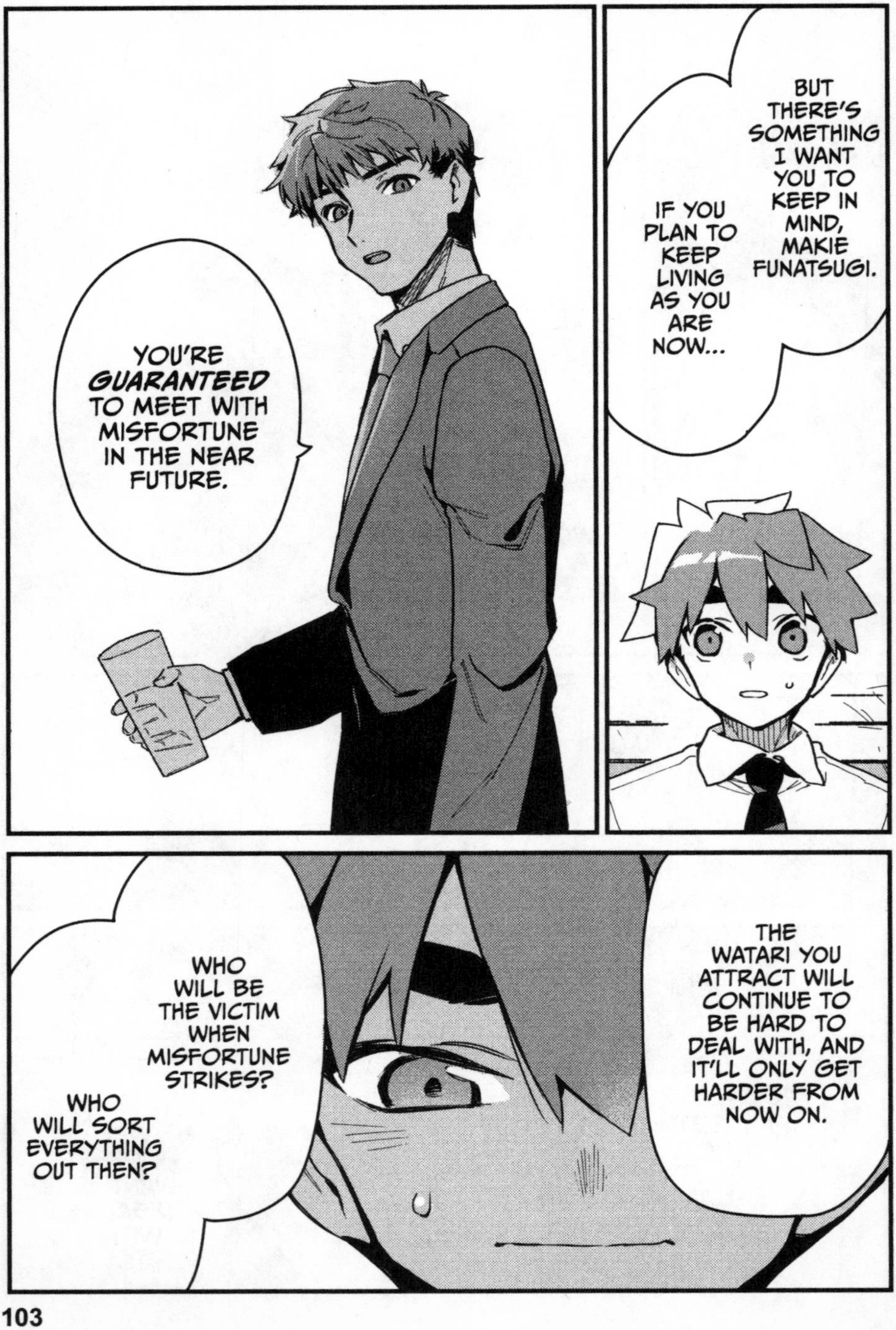
BUT THERE'S SOMETHING I WANT YOU TO KEEP IN MIND, MAKIE FUNATSUGI.
IF YOU PLAN TO KEEP LIVING AS YOU ARE NOW...
YOU'RE *GUARANTEED* TO MEET WITH MISFORTUNE IN THE NEAR FUTURE.
THE WATARI YOU ATTRACT WILL CONTINUE TO BE HARD TO DEAL WITH, AND IT'LL ONLY GET HARDER FROM NOW ON.
WHO WILL BE THE VICTIM WHEN MISFORTUNE STRIKES?
WHO WILL SORT EVERYTHING OUT THEN?

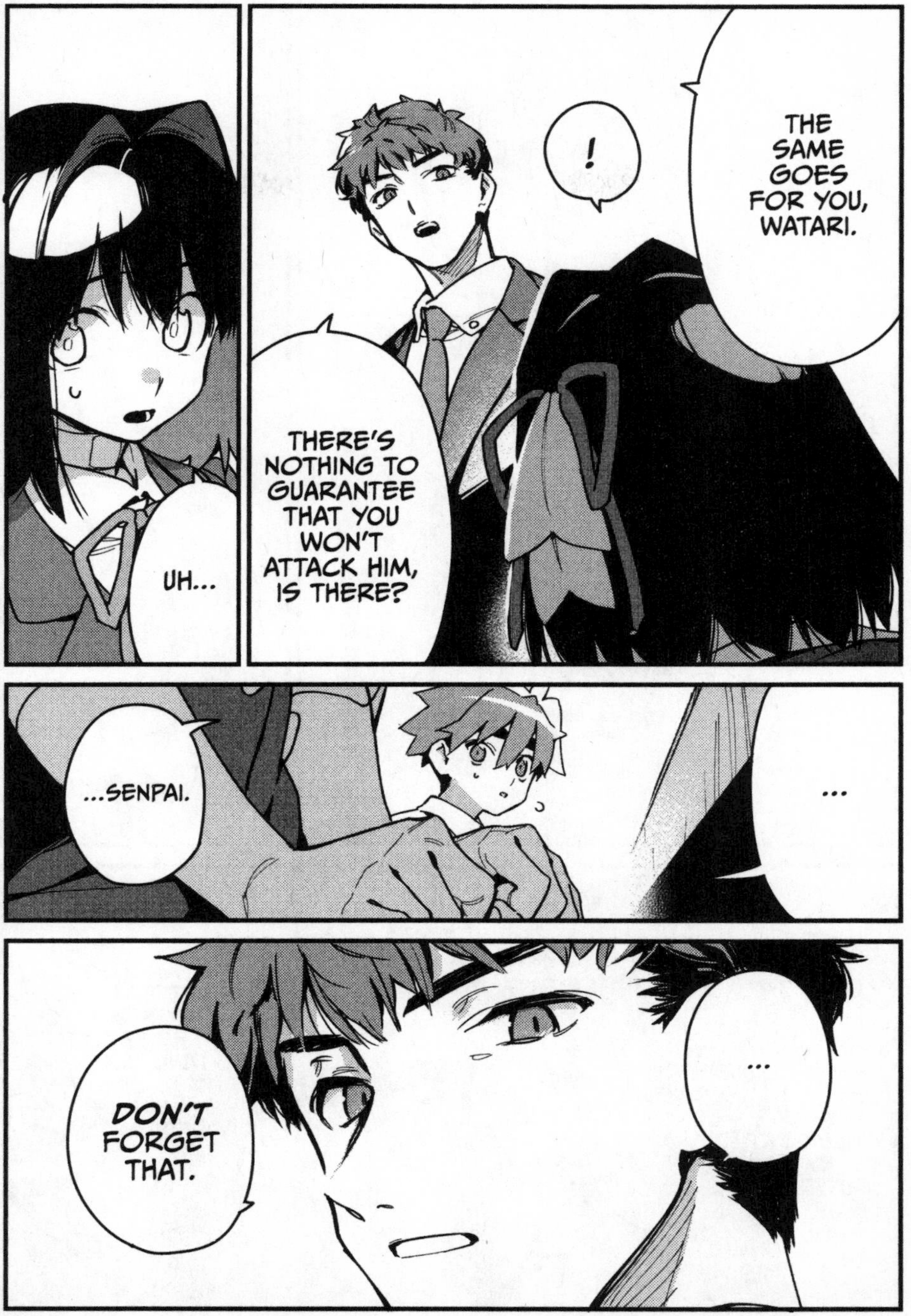
THE SAME GOES FOR YOU, WATARI.
!
THERE'S NOTHING TO GUARANTEE THAT YOU WON'T ATTACK HIM, IS THERE?
UH...
...
...SENPAI.
...
DON'T FORGET THAT.

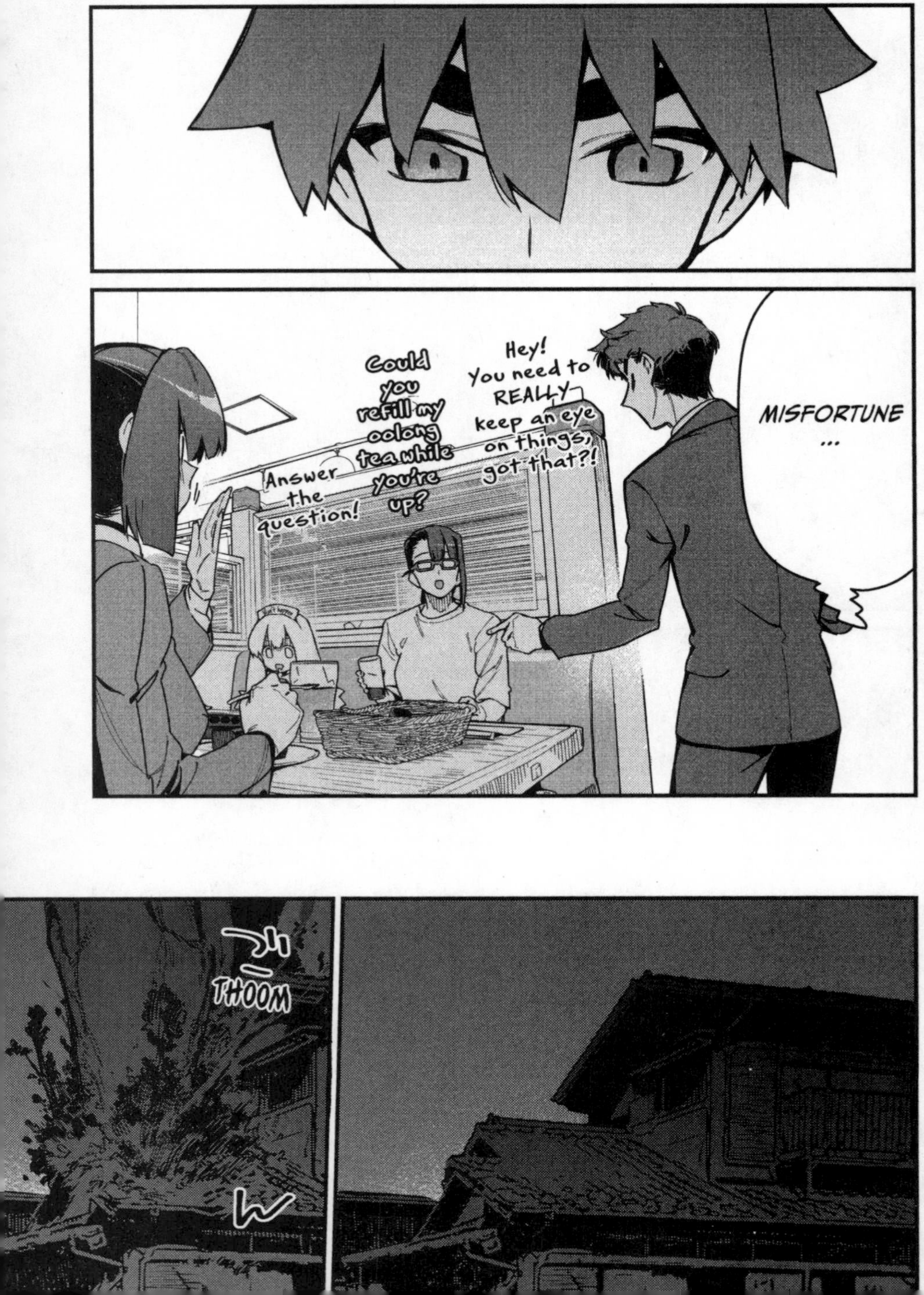
MISFORTUNE
...
Hey! You need to REALLY keep an eye on things, got that?!
Could you refill my oolong tea while you're up?
Answer the question!
THOOM

THOOOM
THOOOOM

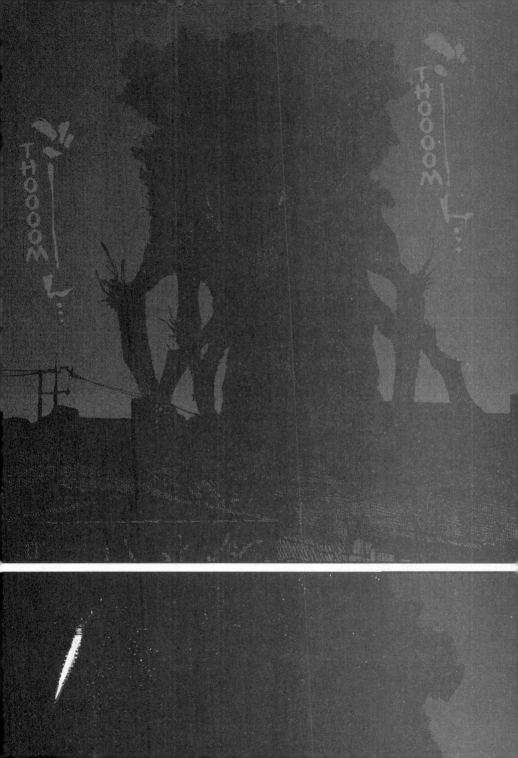

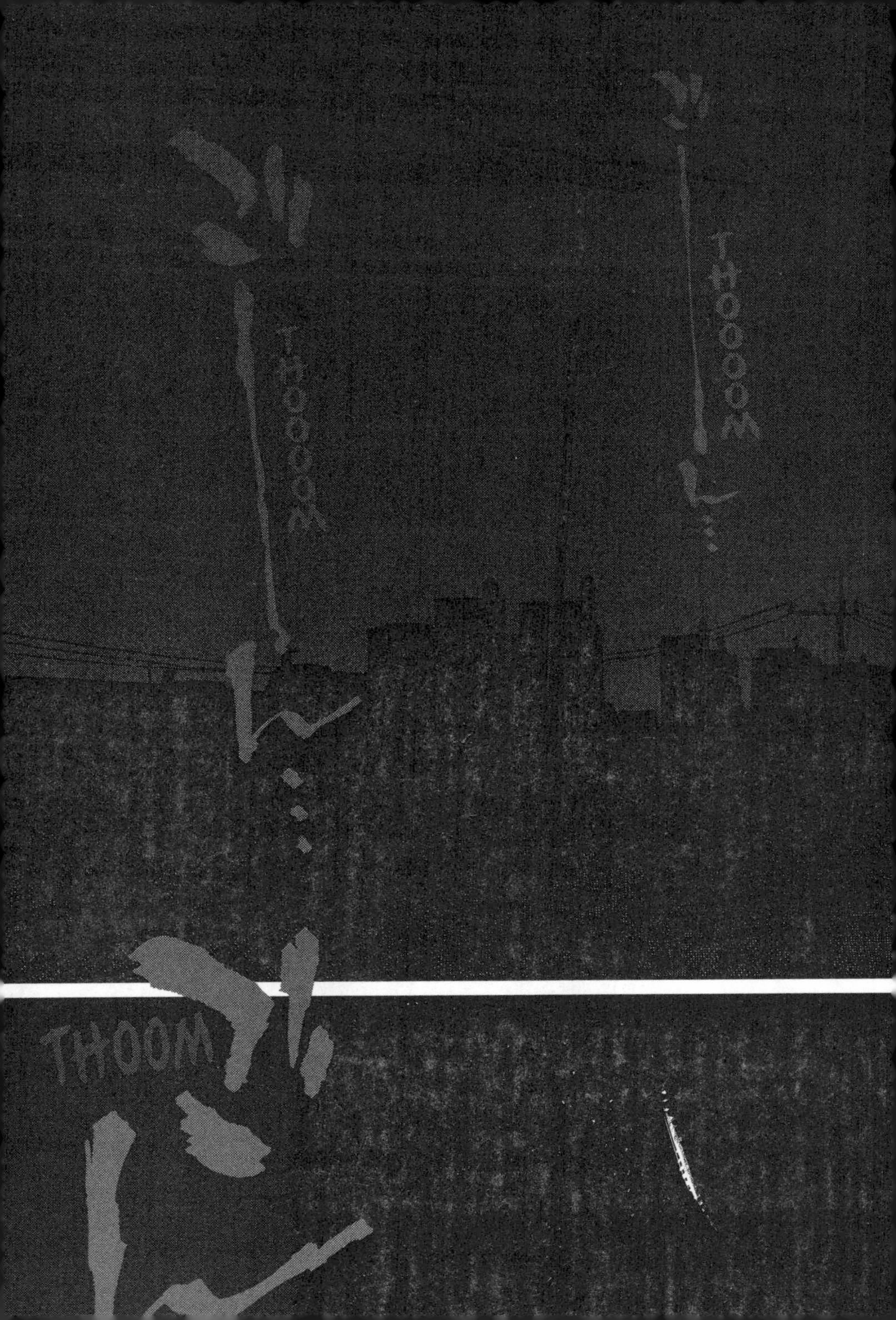
THOOOOM
THOOOOM
THOOM

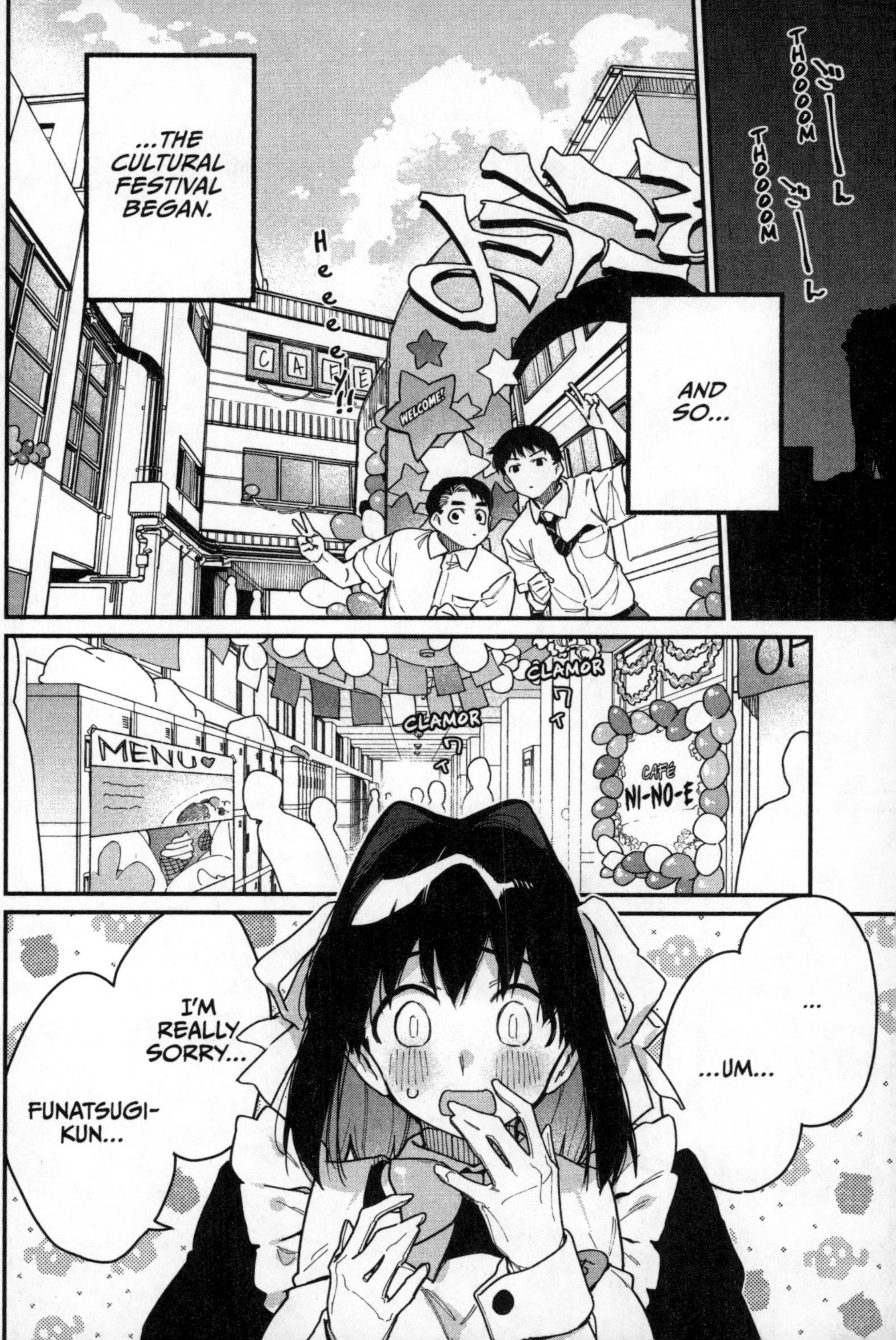
THOOOOM
THOOOOM
AND SO...
...THE CULTURAL FESTIVAL BEGAN.
Heeeeey!!
WELCOME!
CAFÉ
CLAMOR
CLAMOR
MENU
CAFÉ NI-NO-E
...
...UM...
I'M REALLY SORRY...
FUNATSUGI-KUN...

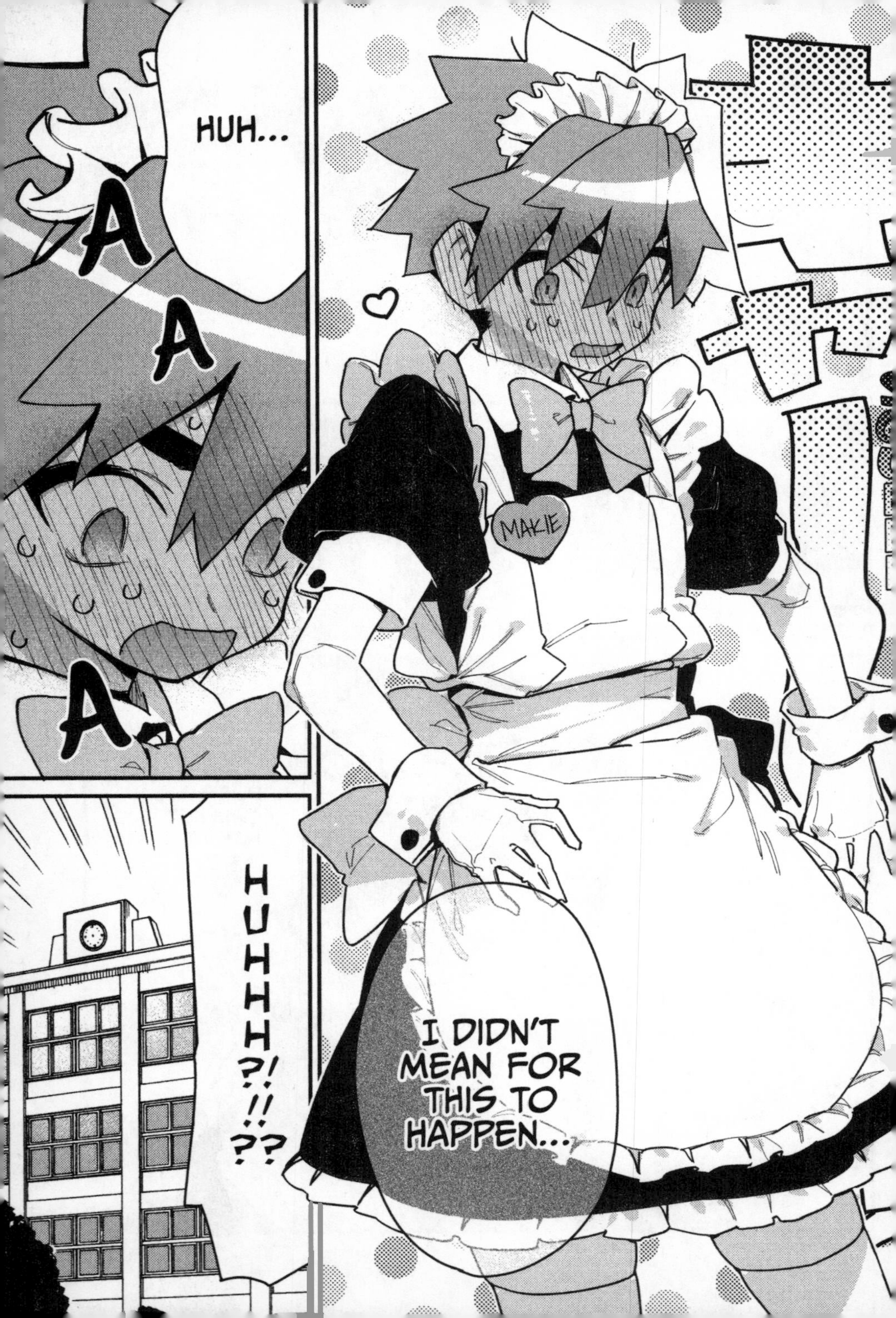
MAKIE
I DIDN'T MEAN FOR THIS TO HAPPEN...
HUH...
A A A
HUHHHH?!!!??

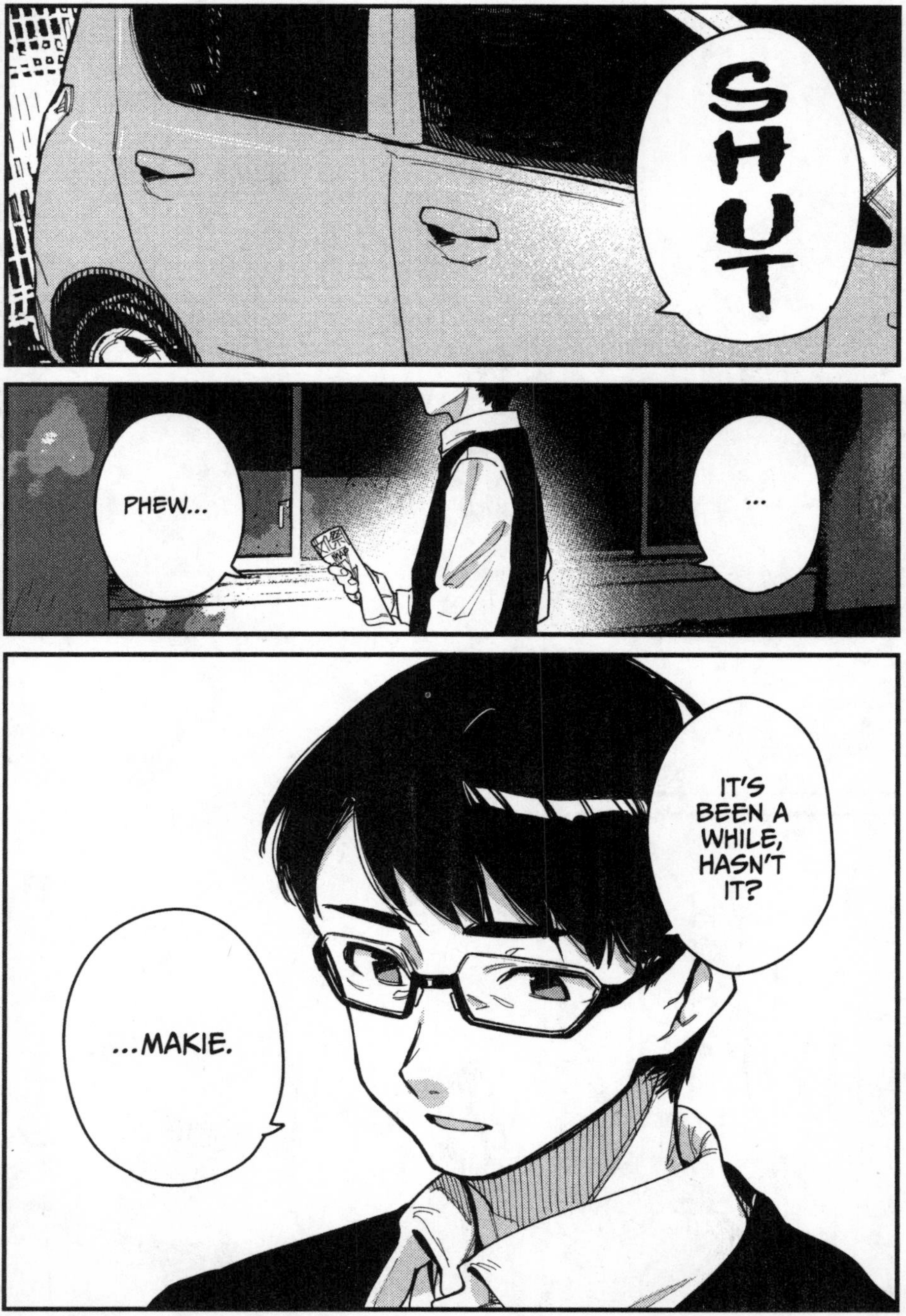
SHUT
...
PHEW...
IT'S BEEN A WHILE, HASN'T IT?
...MAKIE.

Chapter 14: The Seedling Has a Purpose (2)

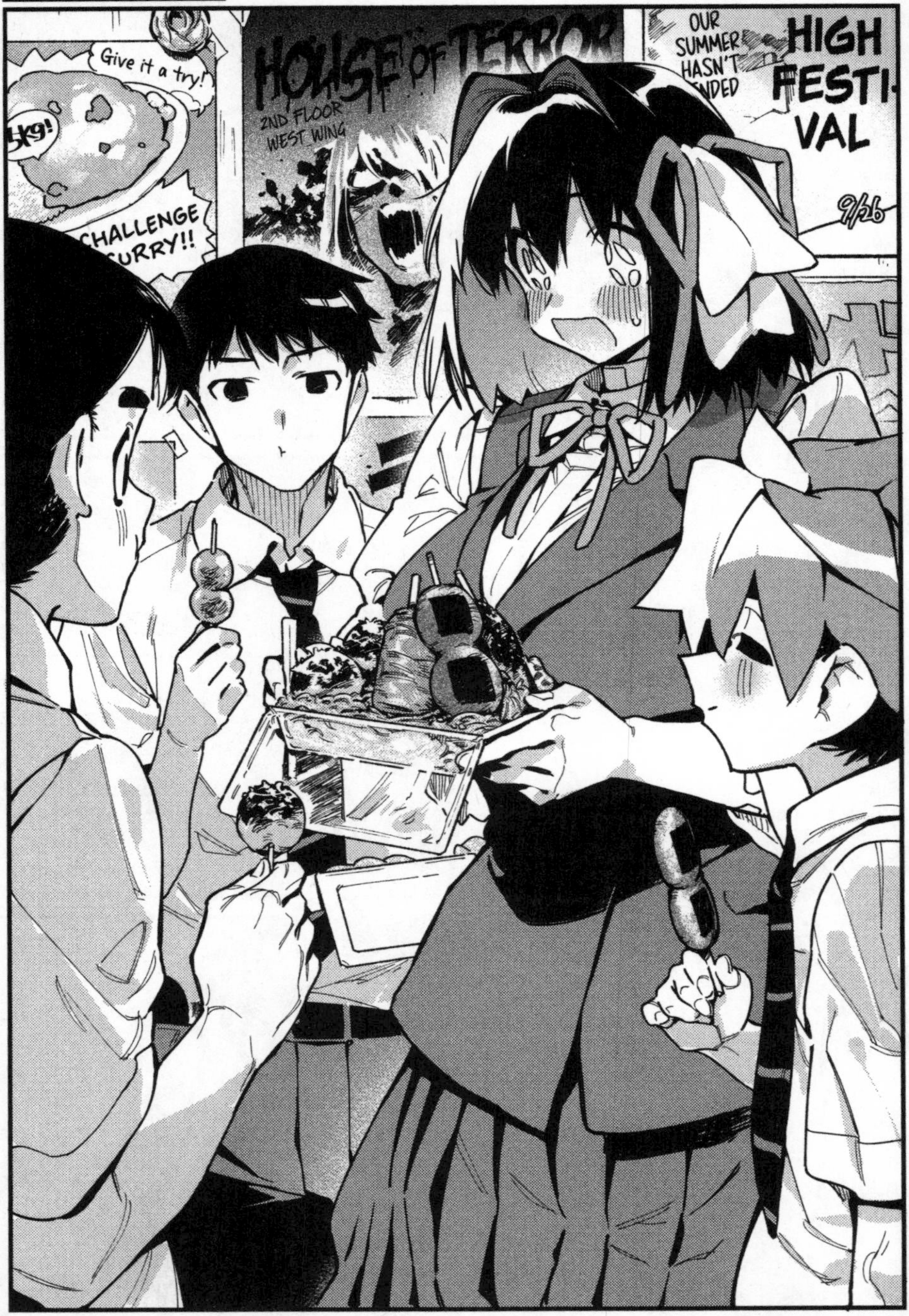
HIGH FESTIVAL
9/26
OUR SUMMER HASN'T ENDED
HOUSE OF TERROR
2ND FLOOR WEST WING
Give it a try!
5kg!
CHALLENGE CURRY!!

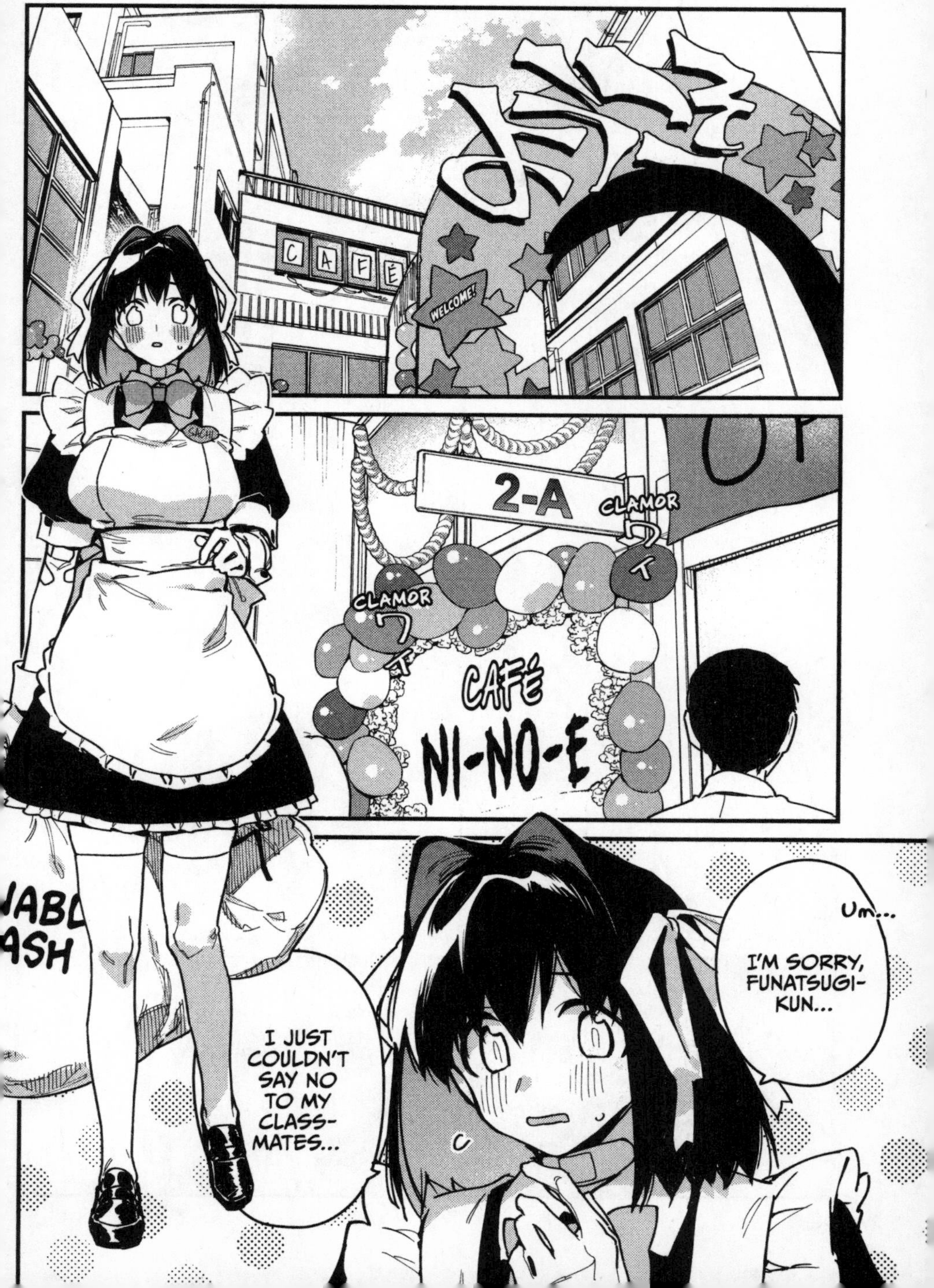
CAFÉ
WELCOME!
2-A
CLAMOR ワイ
CLAMOR ワイ
CAFÉ NI-NO-E
Um...
I'M SORRY, FUNATSUGI-KUN...
I JUST COULDN'T SAY NO TO MY CLASSMATES...

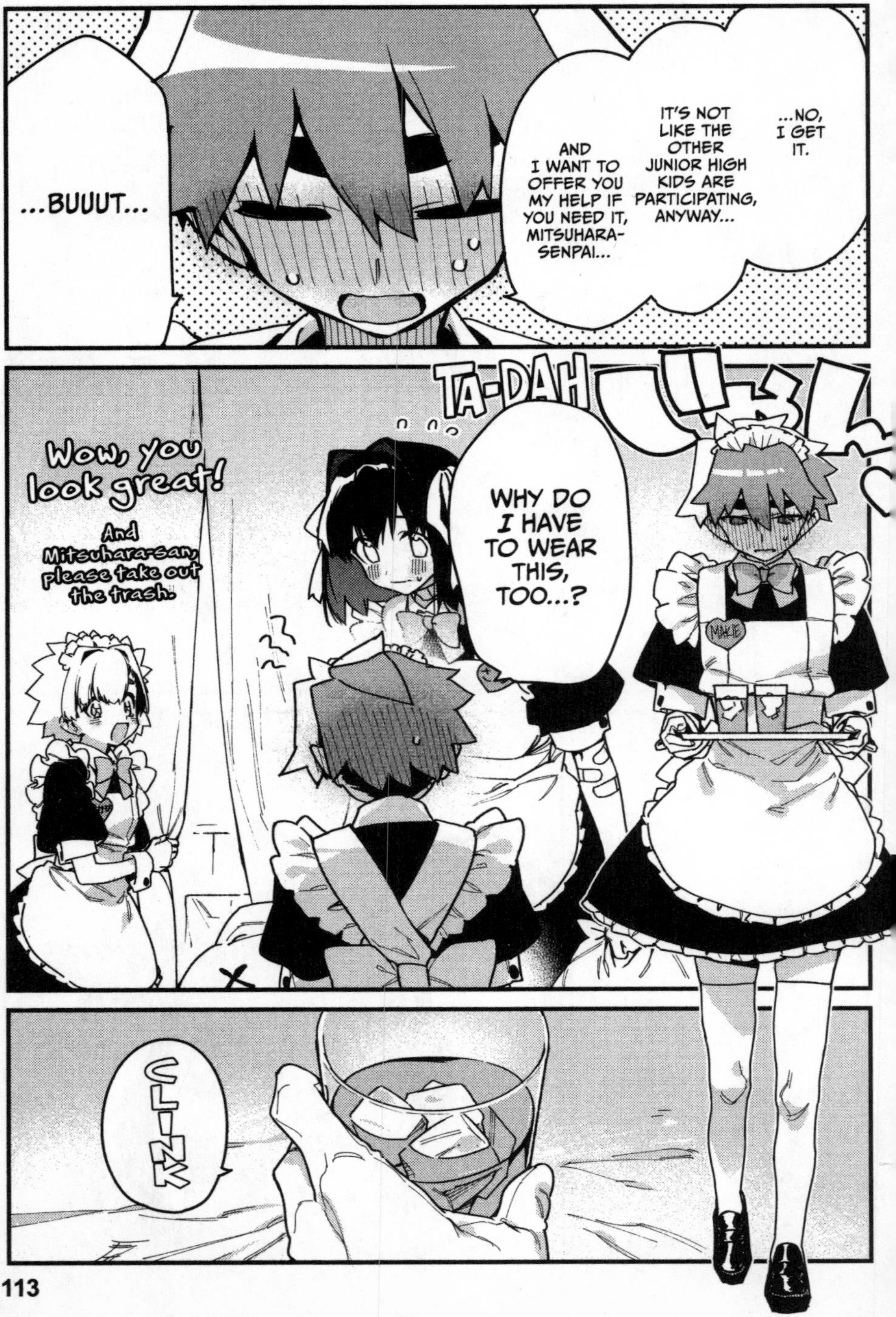
...NO, I GET IT.
IT'S NOT LIKE THE OTHER JUNIOR HIGH KIDS ARE PARTICIPATING, ANYWAY...
AND I WANT TO OFFER YOU MY HELP IF YOU NEED IT, MITSUHARA-SENPAI...
...BUUUT...
TA-DAH
WHY DO I HAVE TO WEAR THIS, TOO...?
Wow, you look great!
And Mitsuhara-san, please take out the trash.
CLINK

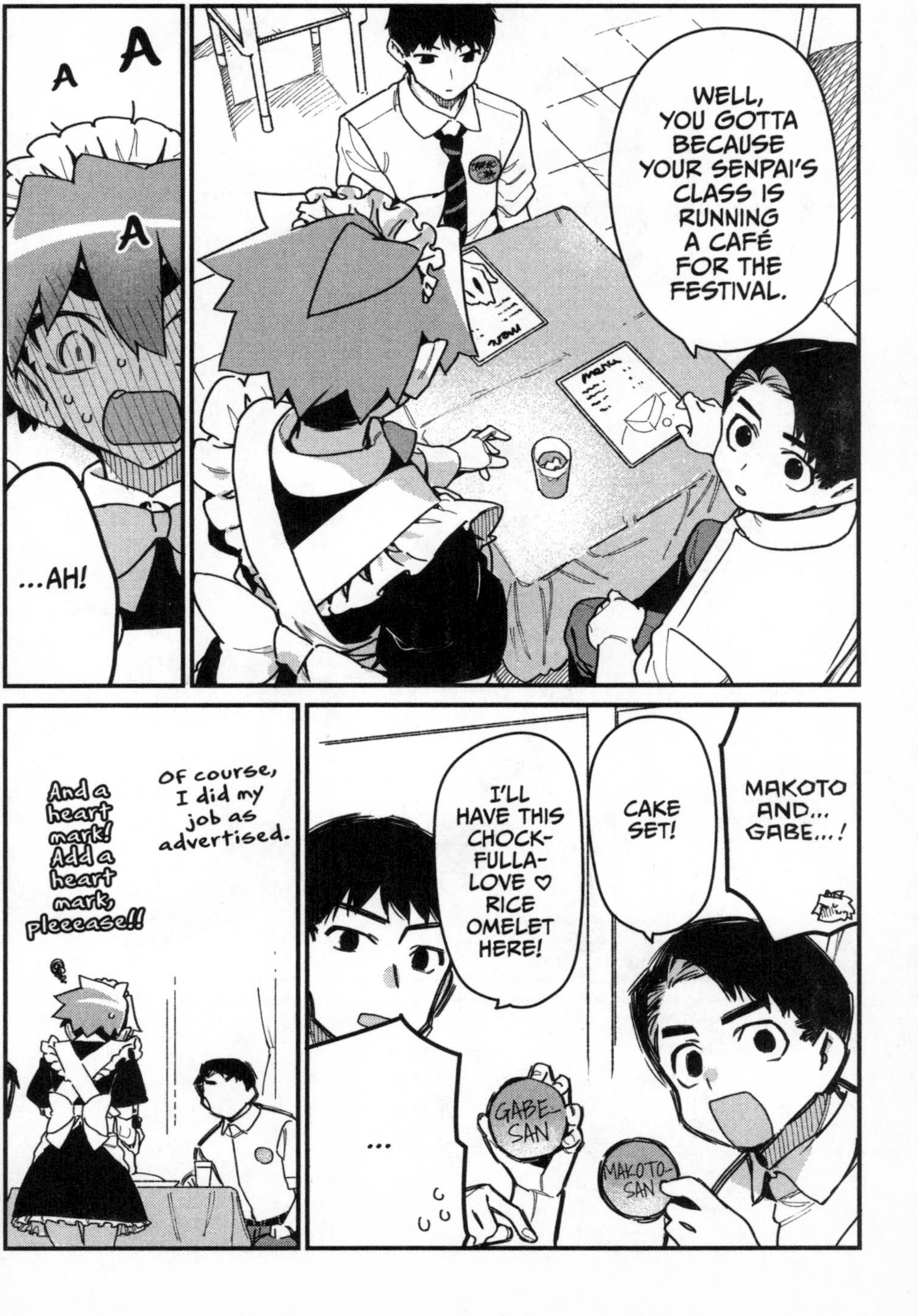
WELL, YOU GOTTA BECAUSE YOUR SENPAI'S CLASS IS RUNNING A CAFÉ FOR THE FESTIVAL.
A A A
...AH!
MAKOTO AND... GABE...!
CAKE SET!
I'LL HAVE THIS CHOCK-FULLA-LOVE ♡ RICE OMELET HERE!
...
GABE-SAN
MAKOTO-SAN
Of course, I did my job as advertised.
And a heart mark! Add a heart mark! Add a heart mark, pleeease!!

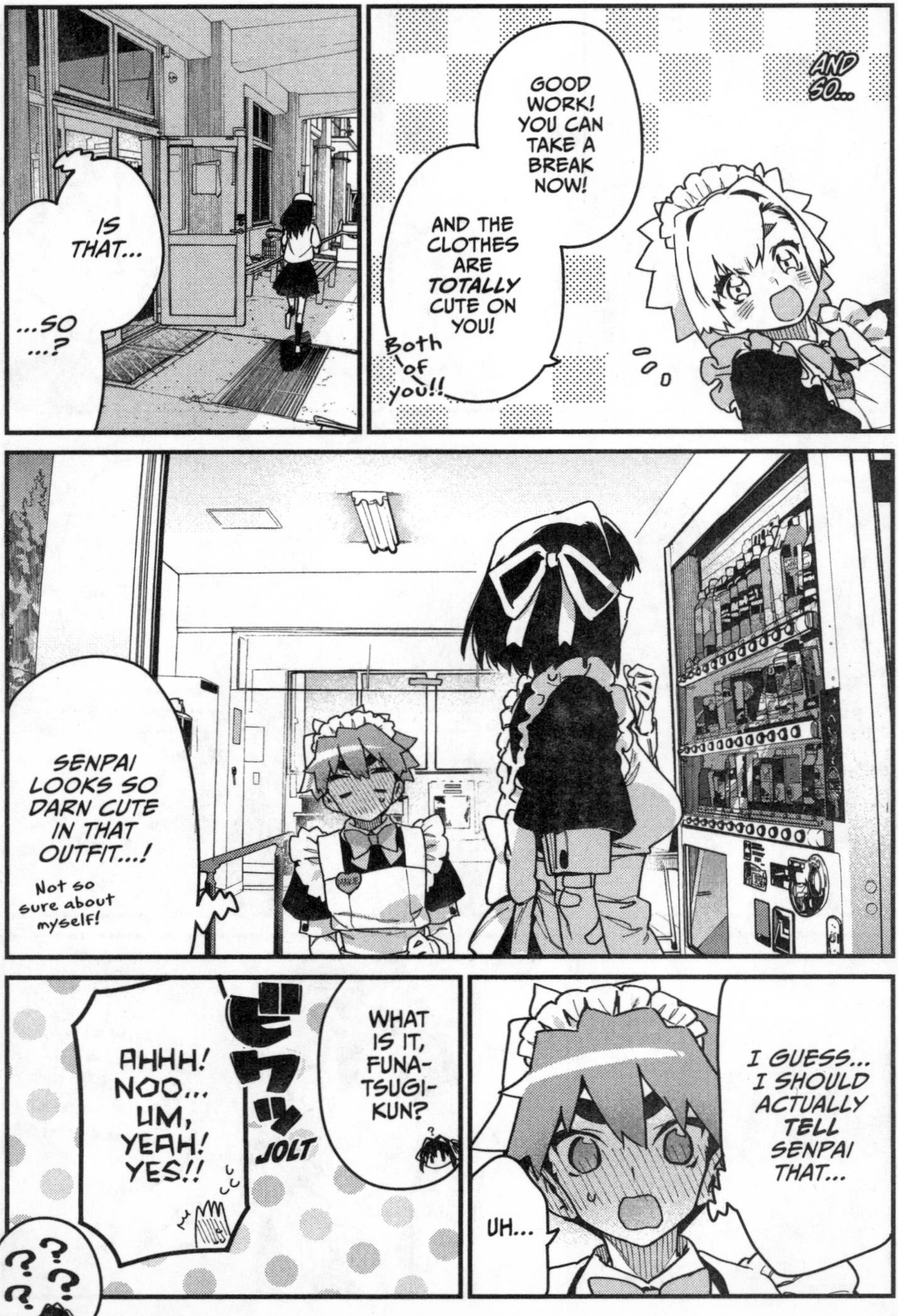
AND SO...
GOOD WORK! YOU CAN TAKE A BREAK NOW!
AND THE CLOTHES ARE TOTALLY CUTE ON YOU!
Both of you!!
IS THAT...
...SO ...?
SENPAI LOOKS SO DARN CUTE IN THAT OUTFIT...!
Not so sure about myself!
I GUESS... I SHOULD ACTUALLY TELL SENPAI THAT...
UH...
WHAT IS IT, FUNA-TSUGI-KUN?
JOLT
AHHH! NOO... UM, YEAH! YES!!
????

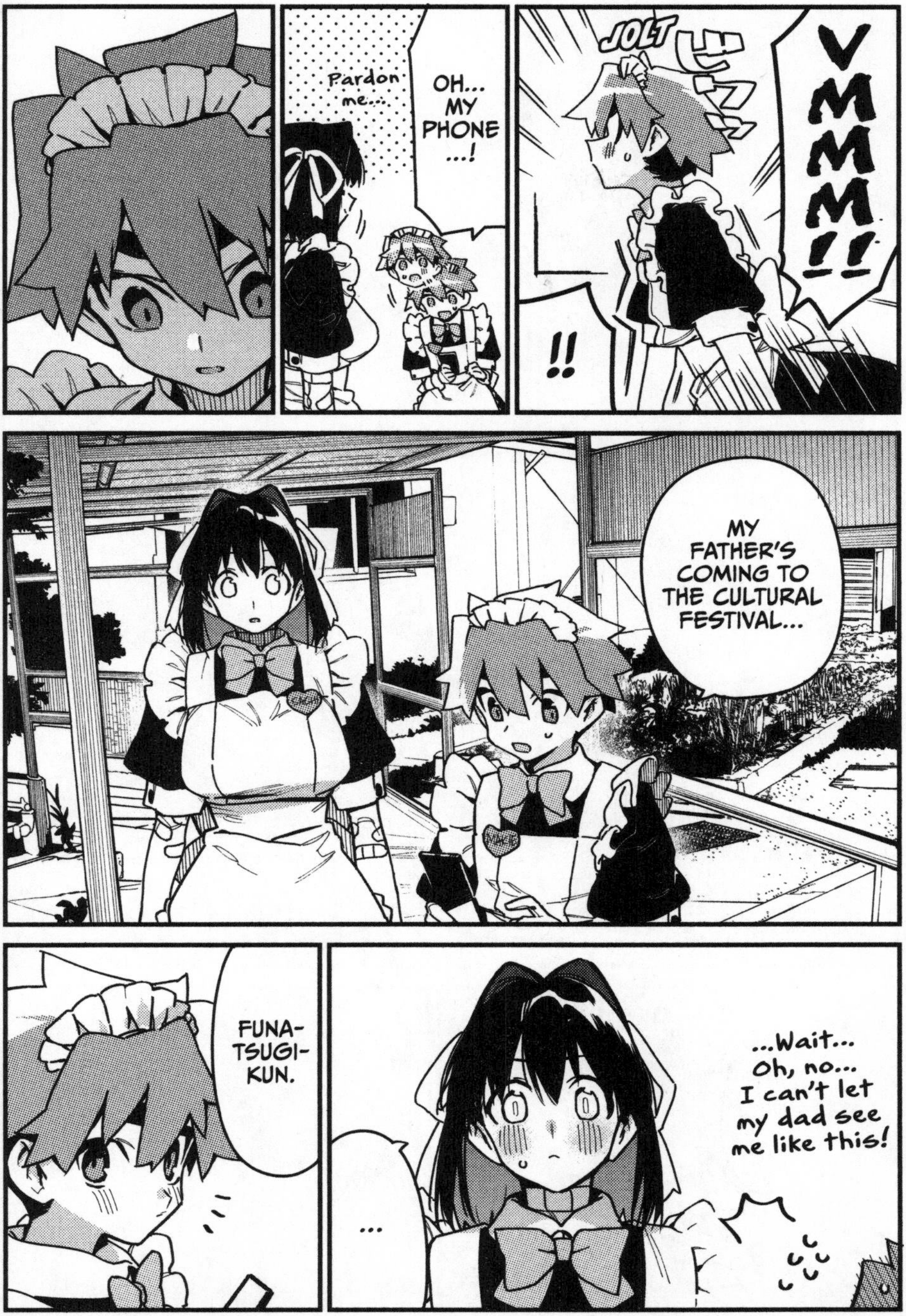
JOLT
VMMM!!
!!
OH... MY PHONE ...!
Pardon me...
MY FATHER'S COMING TO THE CULTURAL FESTIVAL...
...Wait... Oh, no... I can't let my dad see me like this!
...
FUNA-TSUGI-KUN.

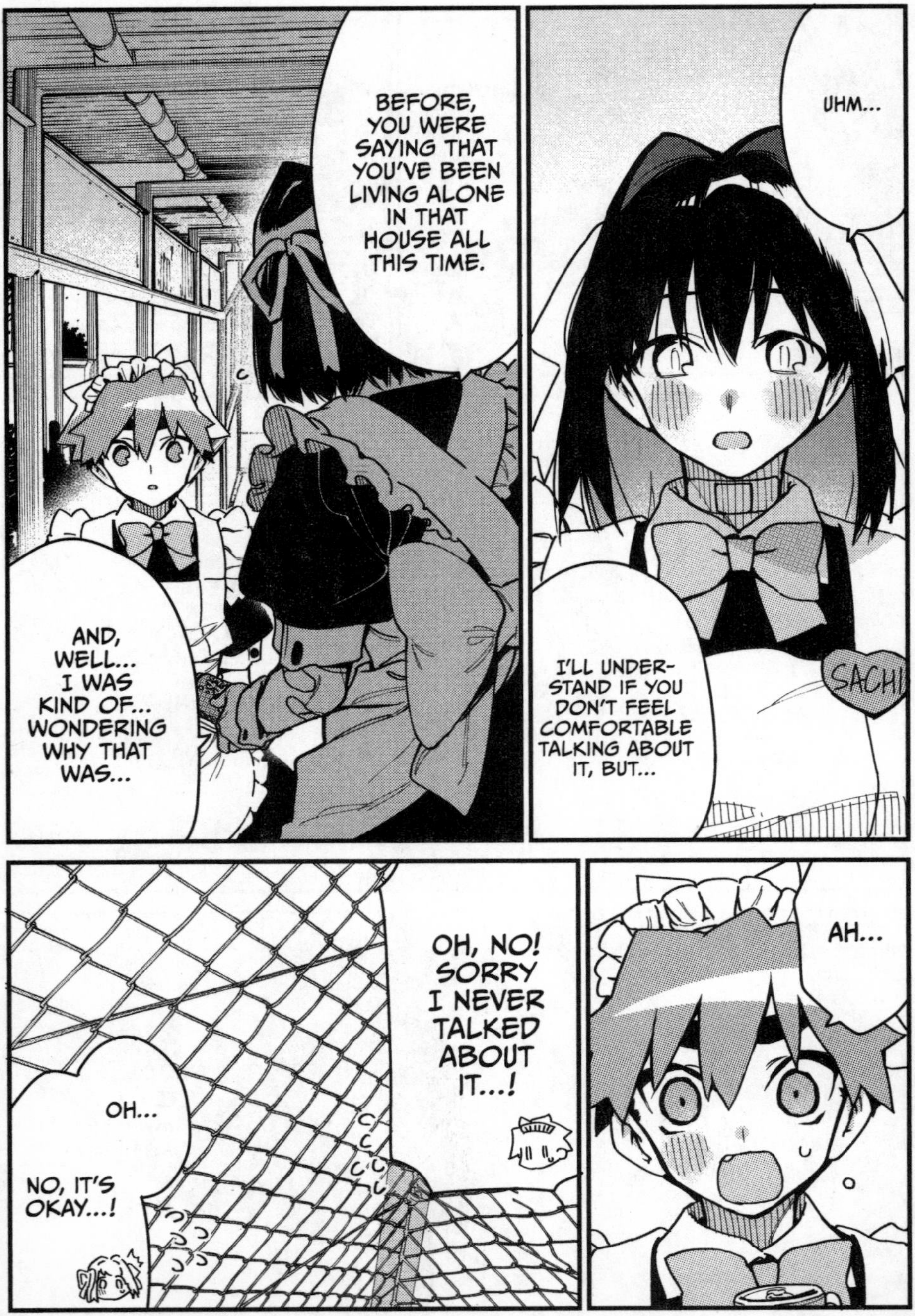
UHM...
I'LL UNDER-STAND IF YOU DON'T FEEL COMFORTABLE TALKING ABOUT IT, BUT...
SACHI
BEFORE, YOU WERE SAYING THAT YOU'VE BEEN LIVING ALONE IN THAT HOUSE ALL THIS TIME.
AND, WELL... I WAS KIND OF... WONDERING WHY THAT WAS...
AH...
OH, NO! SORRY I NEVER TALKED ABOUT IT...!
OH...
NO, IT'S OKAY...!

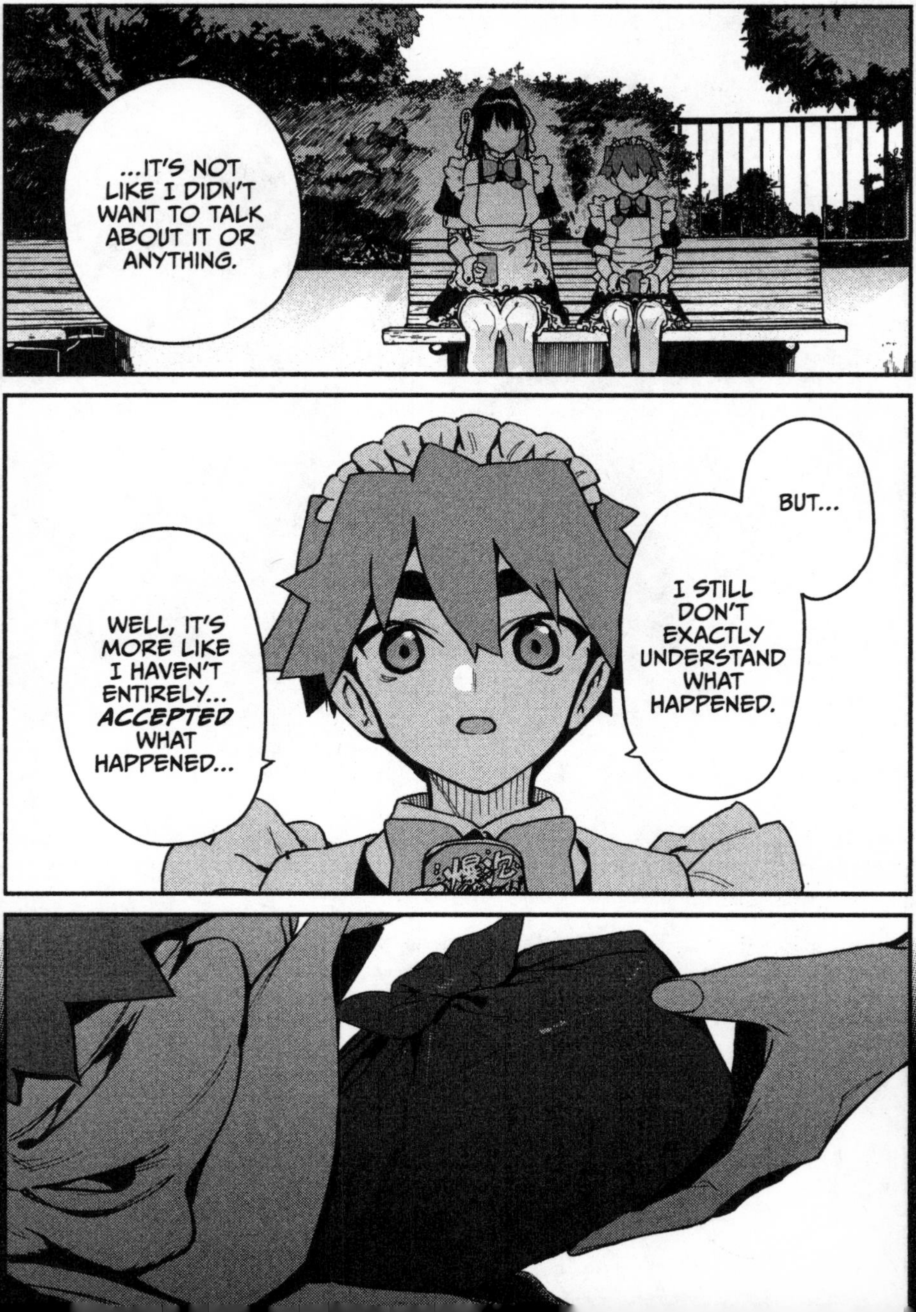
...IT'S NOT LIKE I DIDN'T WANT TO TALK ABOUT IT OR ANYTHING.
BUT...
I STILL DON'T EXACTLY UNDERSTAND WHAT HAPPENED.
WELL, IT'S MORE LIKE I HAVEN'T ENTIRELY... *ACCEPTED* WHAT HAPPENED...

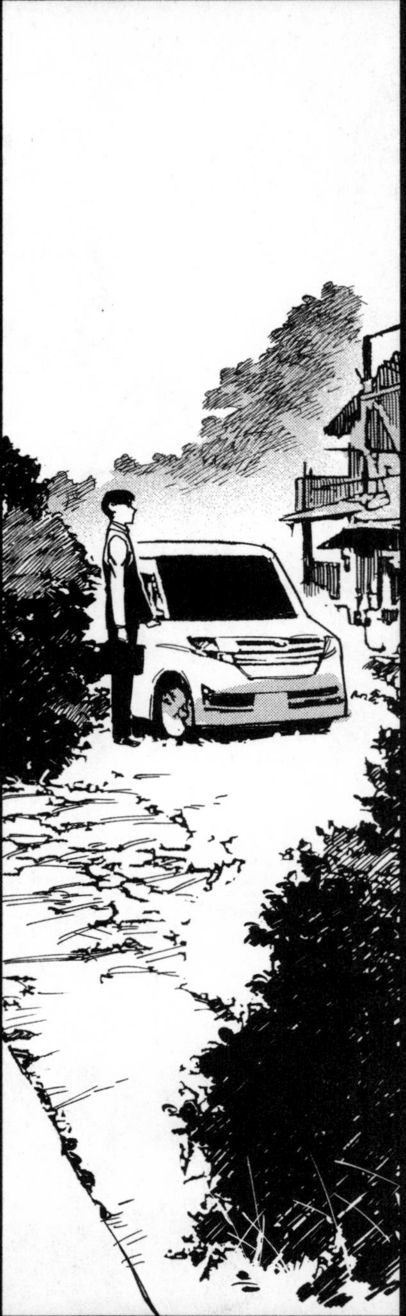

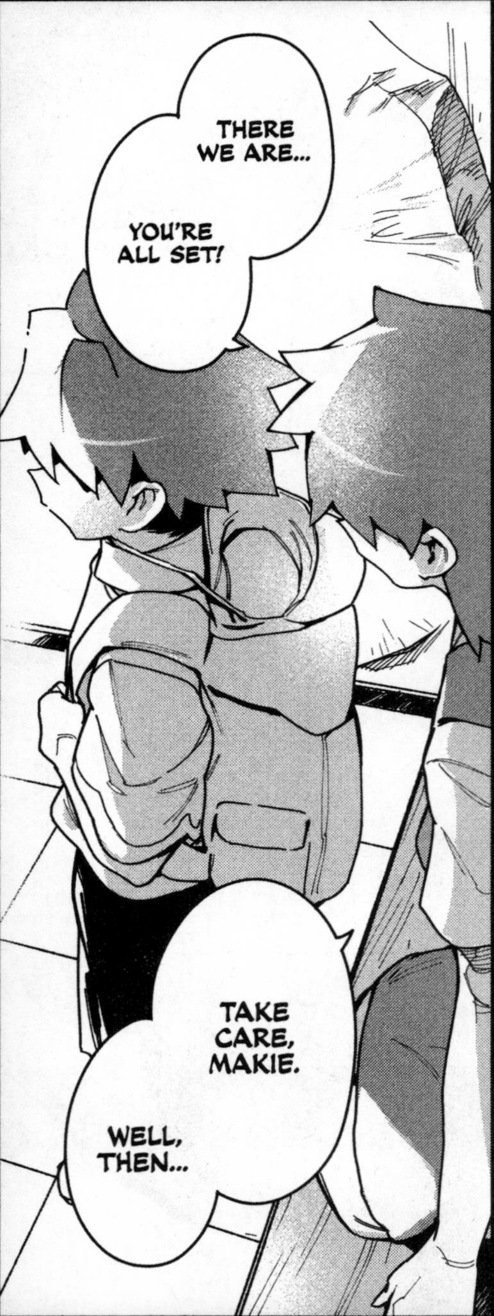
THERE WE ARE... YOU'RE ALL SET!
TAKE CARE, MAKIE. WELL, THEN...

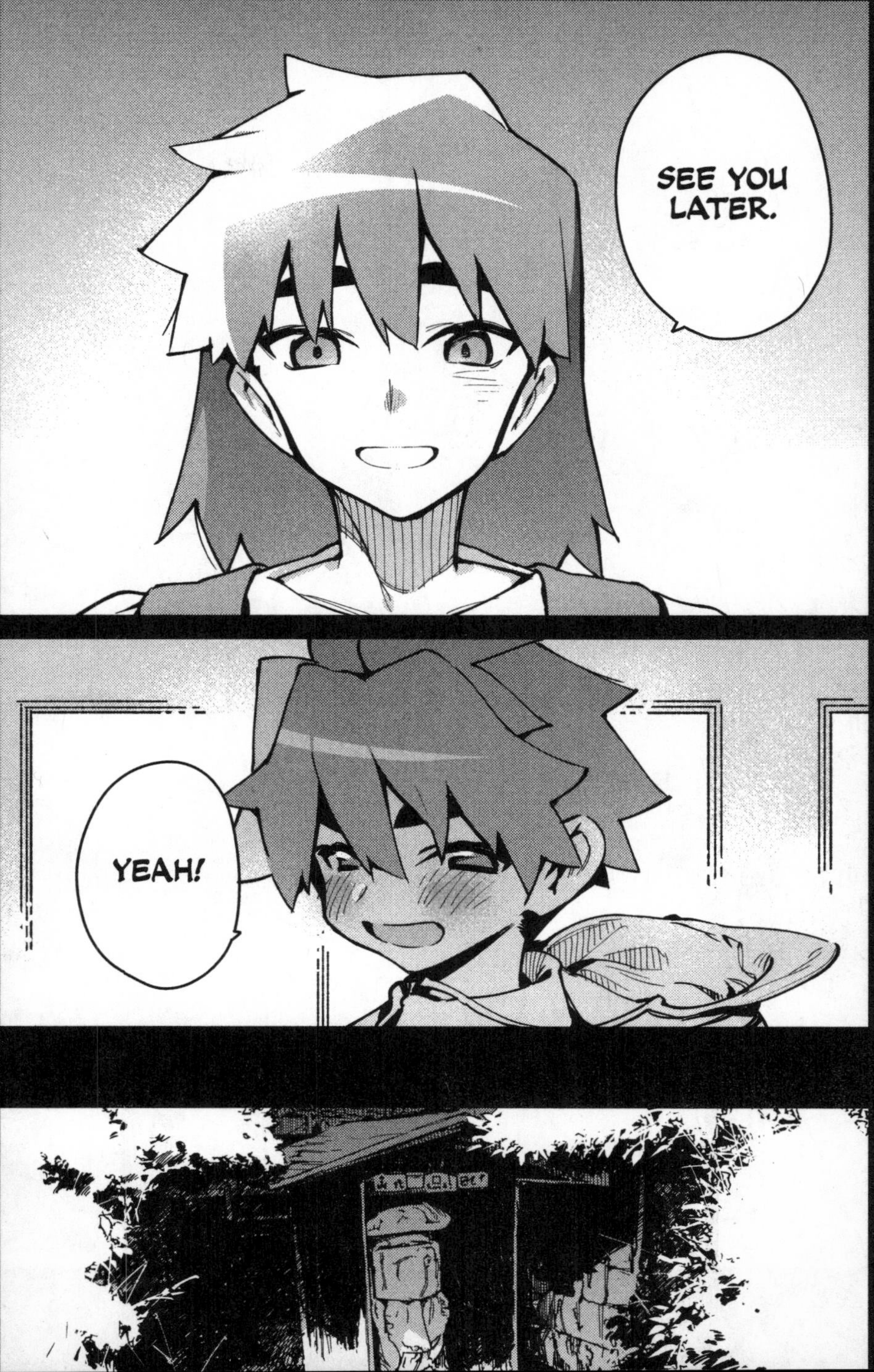
SEE YOU LATER.
YEAH!

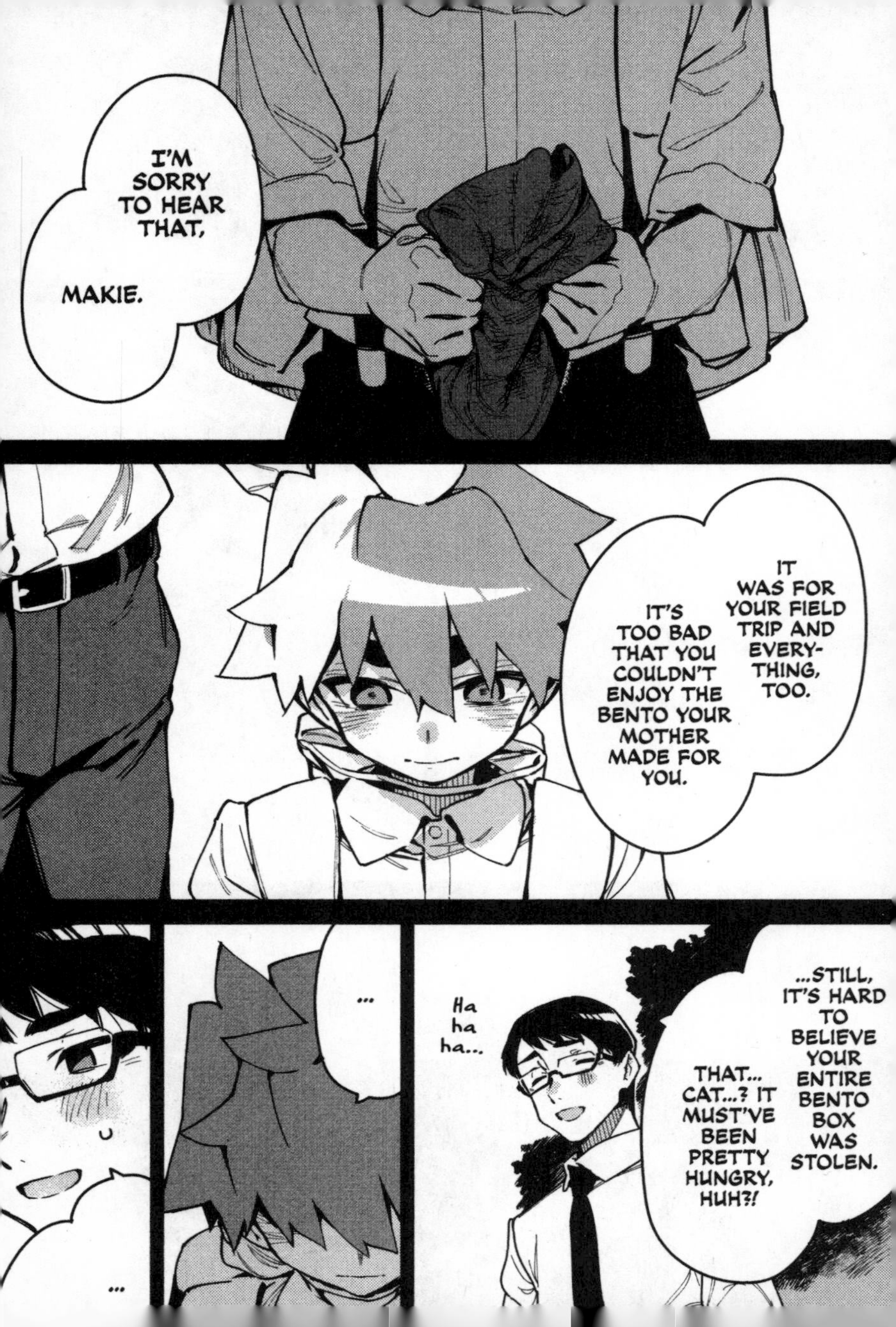
I'M SORRY TO HEAR THAT,
MAKIE.
IT WAS FOR YOUR FIELD TRIP AND EVERY-THING, TOO.
IT'S TOO BAD THAT YOU COULDN'T ENJOY THE BENTO YOUR MOTHER MADE FOR YOU.
...STILL, IT'S HARD TO BELIEVE YOUR ENTIRE BENTO BOX WAS STOLEN.
THAT... CAT...? IT MUST'VE BEEN PRETTY HUNGRY, HUH?!
Ha ha ha...
...
...

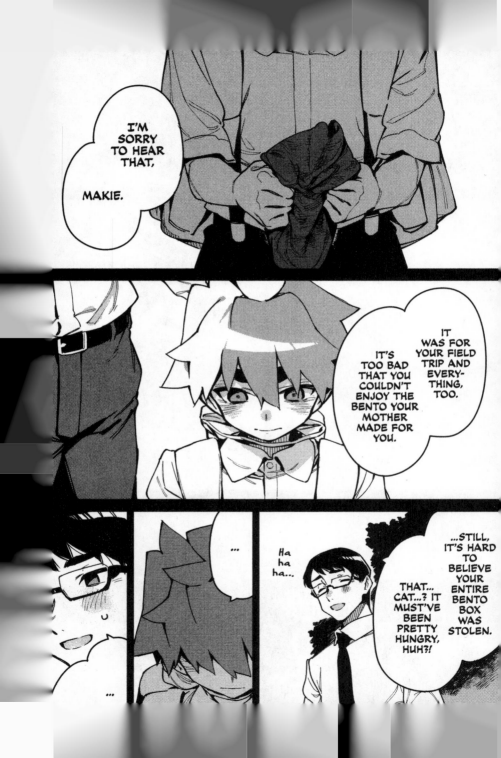

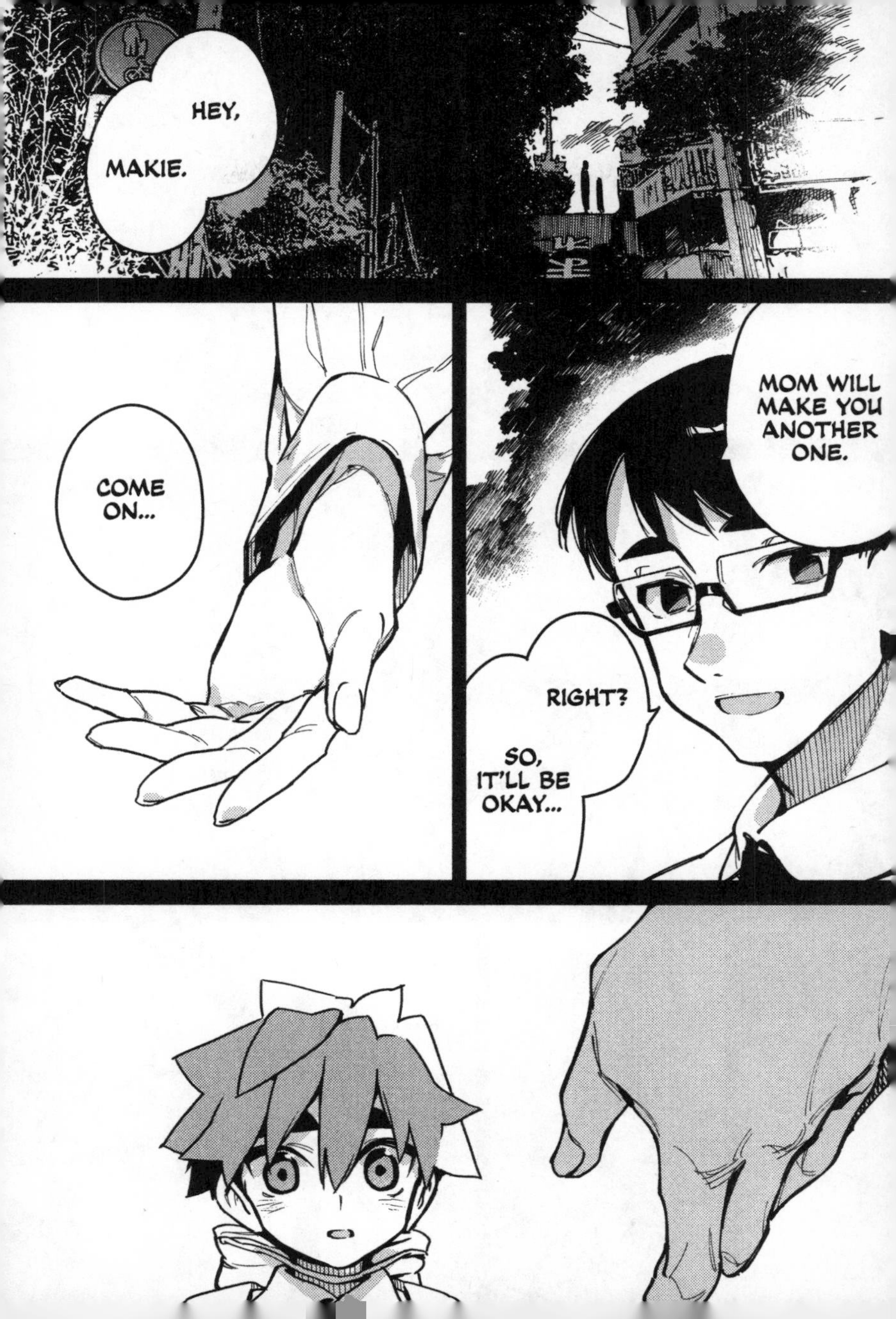
HEY, MAKIE.
MOM WILL MAKE YOU ANOTHER ONE.
RIGHT?
SO, IT'LL BE OKAY...
COME ON...

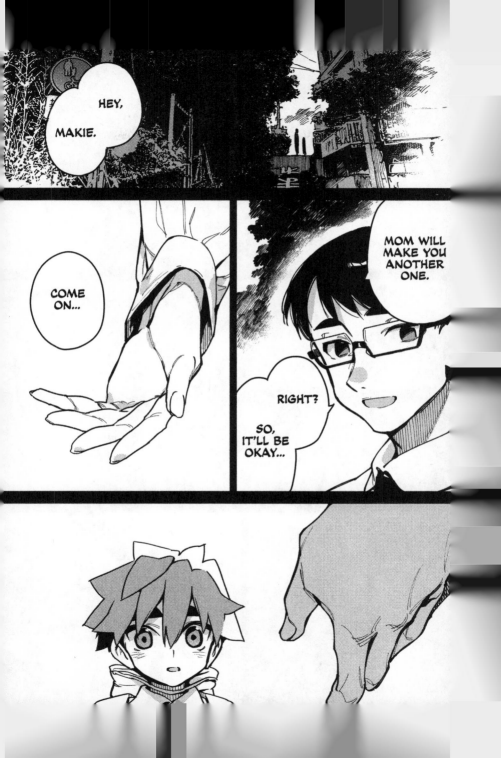

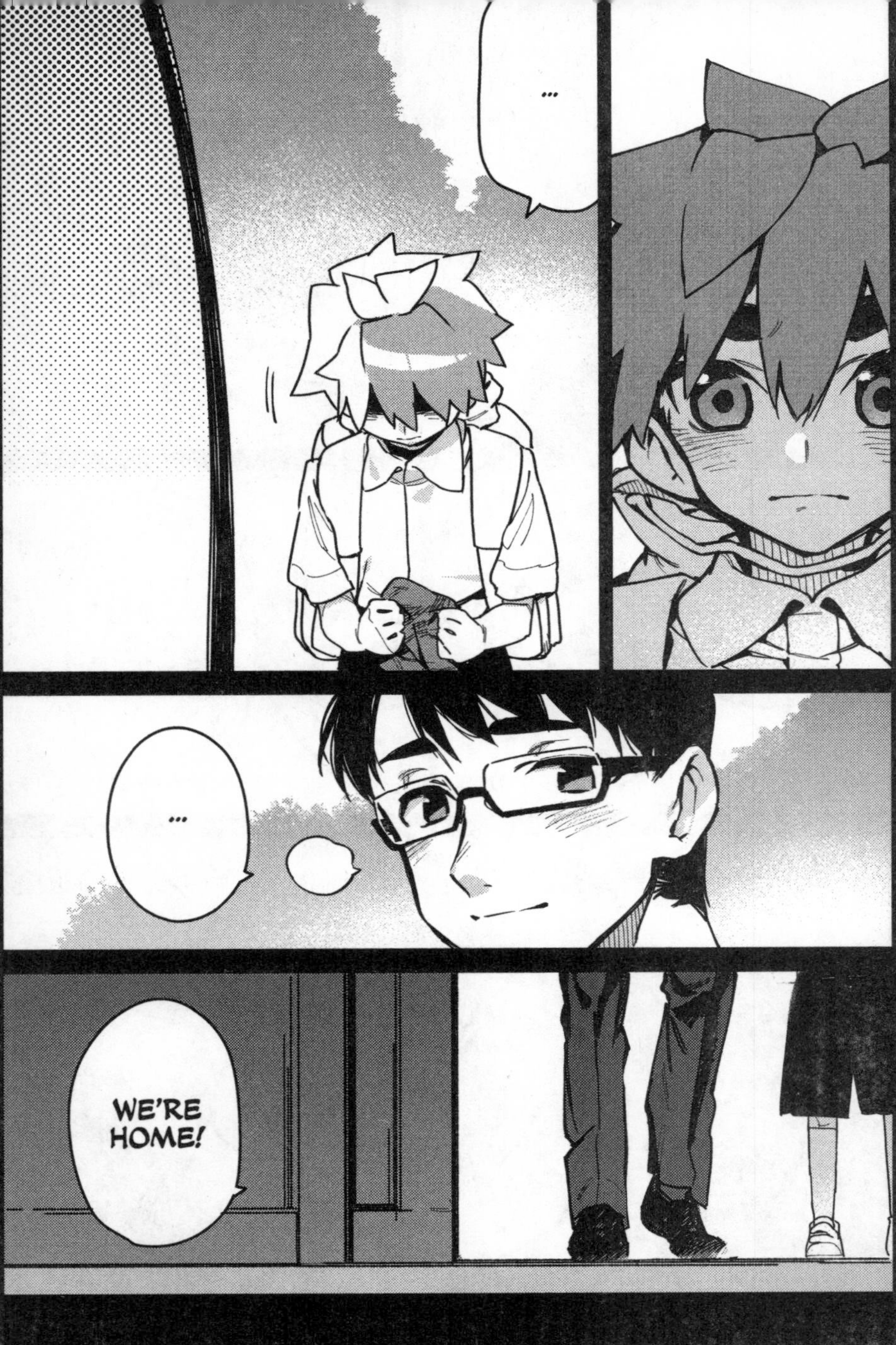
...
...
WE'RE HOME!

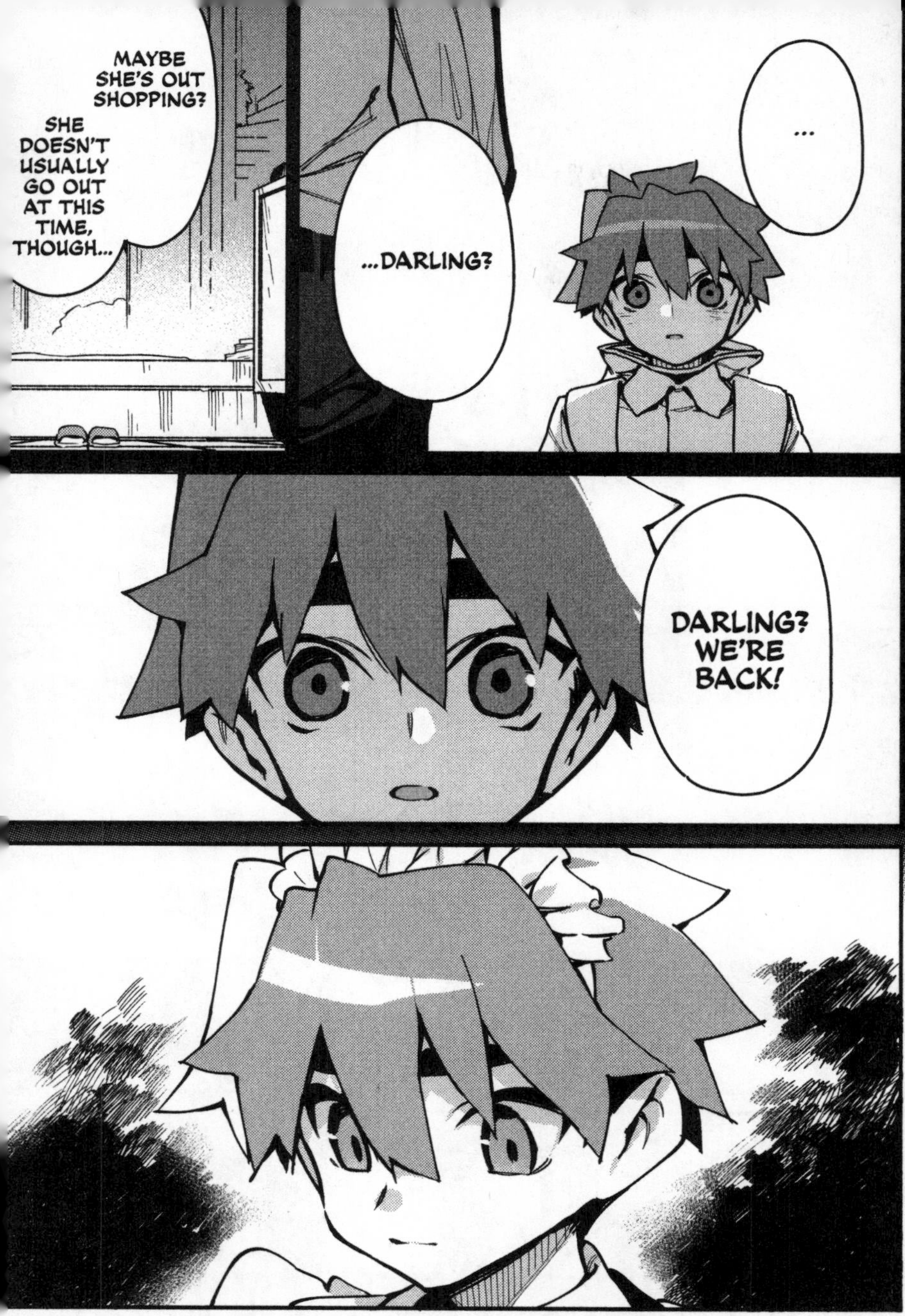
...
...DARLING?
MAYBE SHE'S OUT SHOPPING?
SHE DOESN'T USUALLY GO OUT AT THIS TIME, THOUGH...
DARLING? WE'RE BACK!

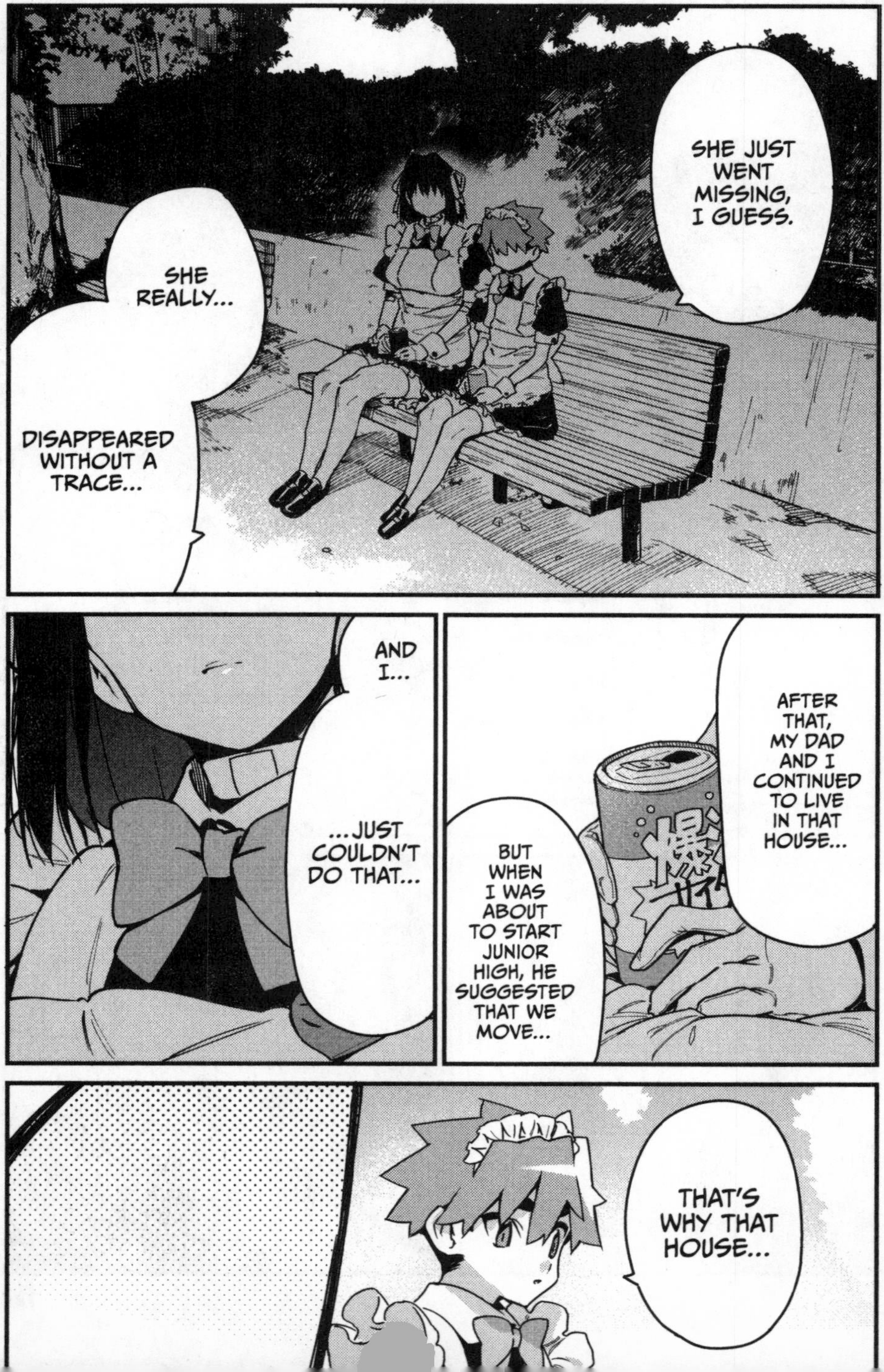
SHE JUST WENT MISSING, I GUESS.
SHE REALLY...
DISAPPEARED WITHOUT A TRACE...
AFTER THAT, MY DAD AND I CONTINUED TO LIVE IN THAT HOUSE...
BUT WHEN I WAS ABOUT TO START JUNIOR HIGH, HE SUGGESTED THAT WE MOVE...
AND I...
...JUST COULDN'T DO THAT...
THAT'S WHY THAT HOUSE...

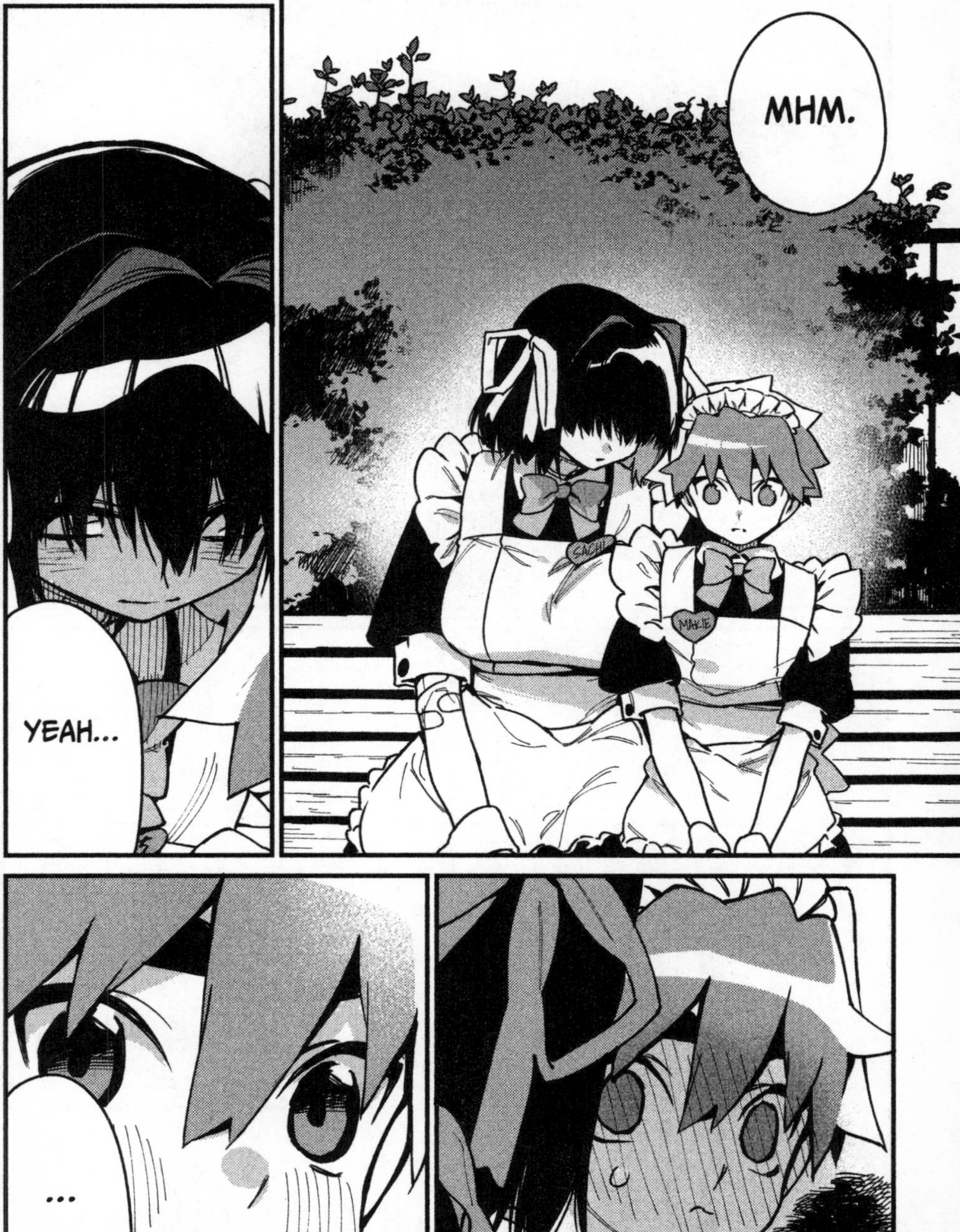
MHM.
SACHI
MAKIE
YEAH...
...

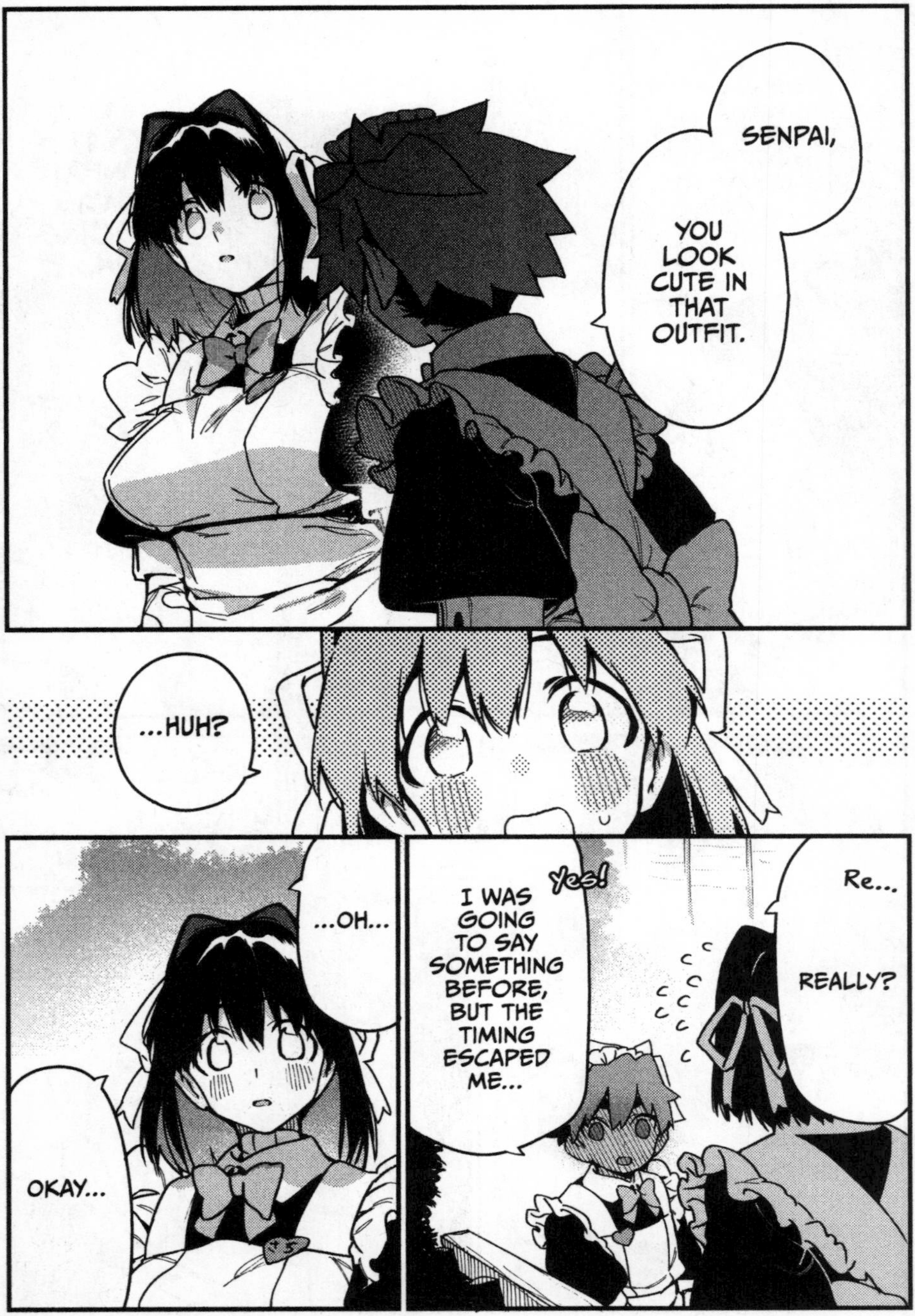
SENPAI,
YOU LOOK CUTE IN THAT OUTFIT.
...HUH?
Re...
REALLY?
Yes!
I WAS GOING TO SAY SOMETHING BEFORE, BUT THE TIMING ESCAPED ME...
...OH...
OKAY...

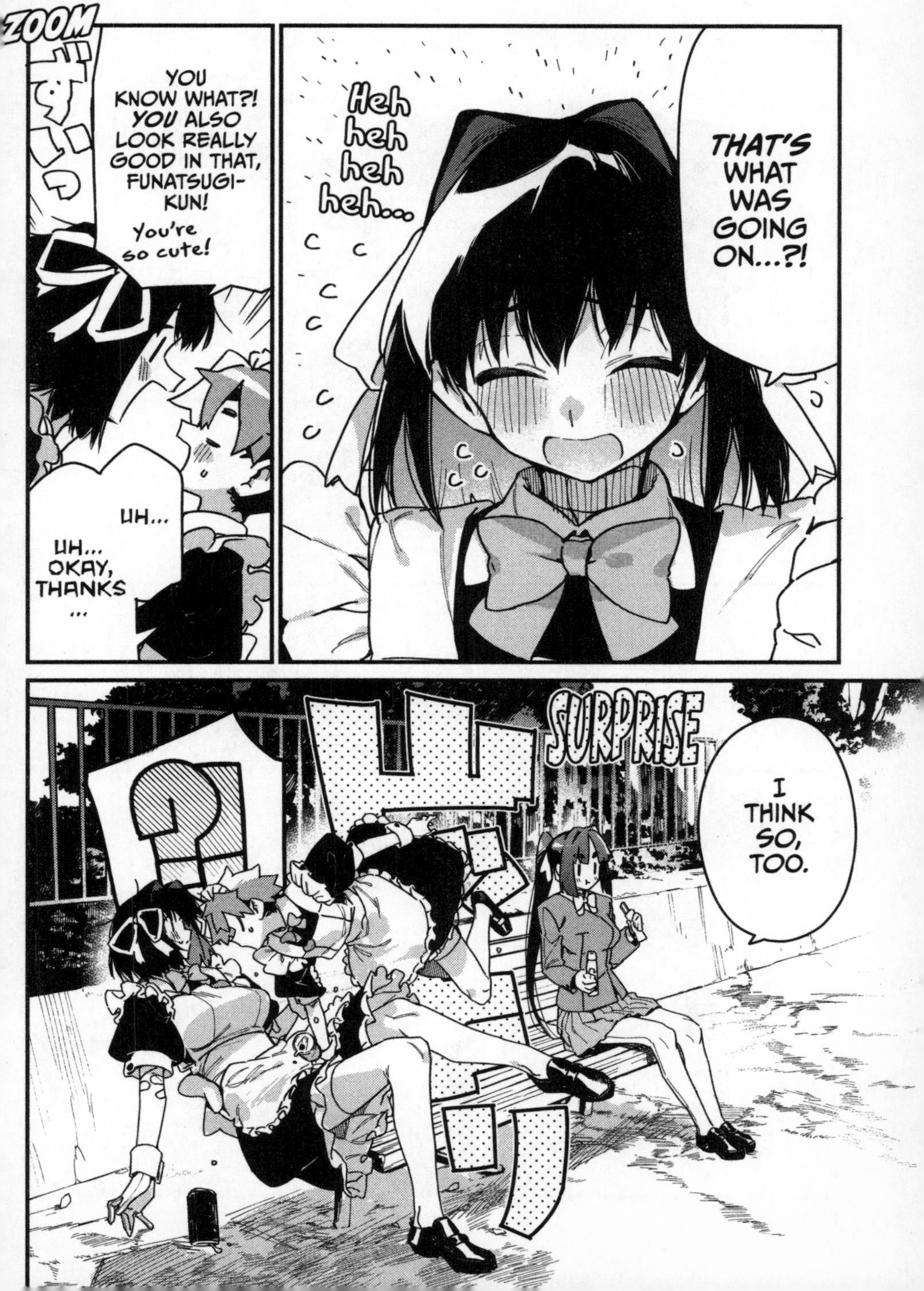
THAT'S WHAT WAS GOING ON...?!
Heh heh heh heh...
ZOOM
YOU KNOW WHAT?! YOU ALSO LOOK REALLY GOOD IN THAT, FUNATSUGI-KUN!
You're so cute!
UH...
UH... OKAY, THANKS...
I THINK SO, TOO.
SURPRISE

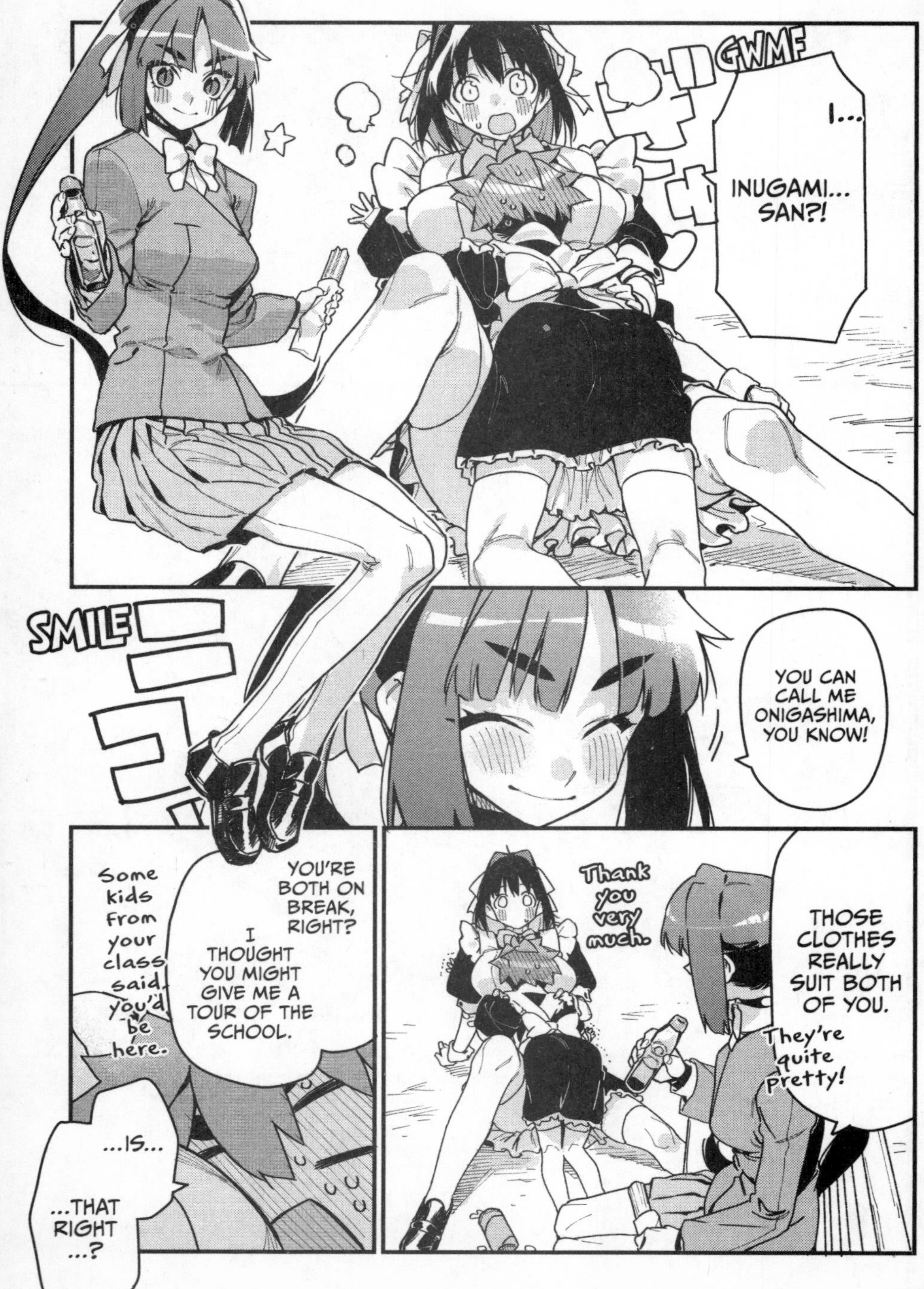
GWMF
I... INUGAMI... SAN?!
YOU CAN CALL ME ONIGASHIMA, YOU KNOW!
SMILE
THOSE CLOTHES REALLY SUIT BOTH OF YOU.
They're quite pretty!
Thank you very much.
YOU'RE BOTH ON BREAK, RIGHT?
I THOUGHT YOU MIGHT GIVE ME A TOUR OF THE SCHOOL.
Some kids from your class said you'd be here.
...IS...
...THAT RIGHT ...?

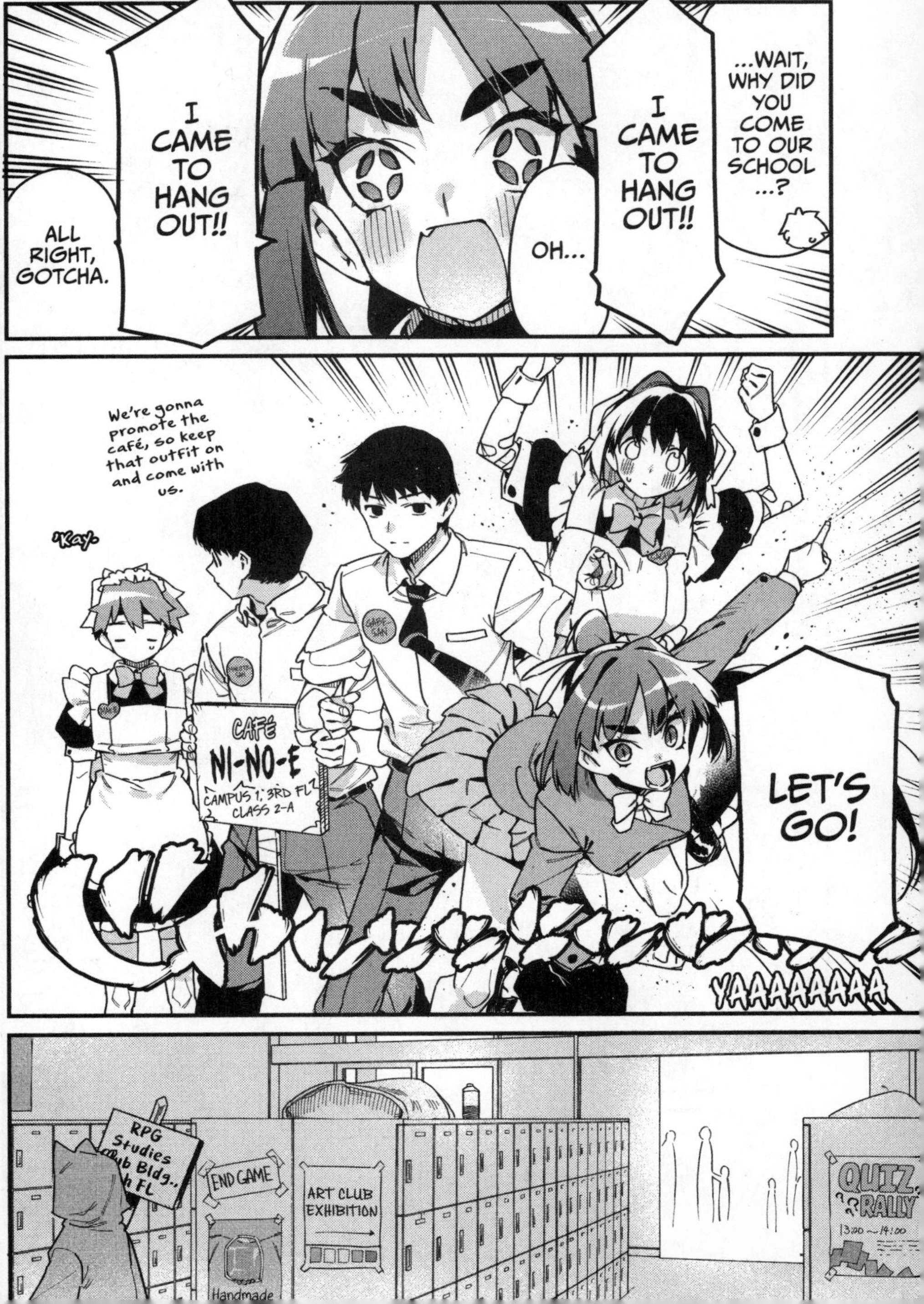
...WAIT, WHY DID YOU COME TO OUR SCHOOL ...?
I CAME TO HANG OUT!!
OH...
I CAME TO HANG OUT!!
ALL RIGHT, GOTCHA.
LET'S GO!
We're gonna promote the café, so keep that outfit on and come with us.
'Kay.
CAFÉ
NI-NO-E
CAMPUS 1, 3RD FL
CLASS 2-A
YAAAAAAAA
QUIZ RALLY
13:00 ~ 14:00
ART CLUB EXHIBITION
END GAME
RPG Studies
Handmade

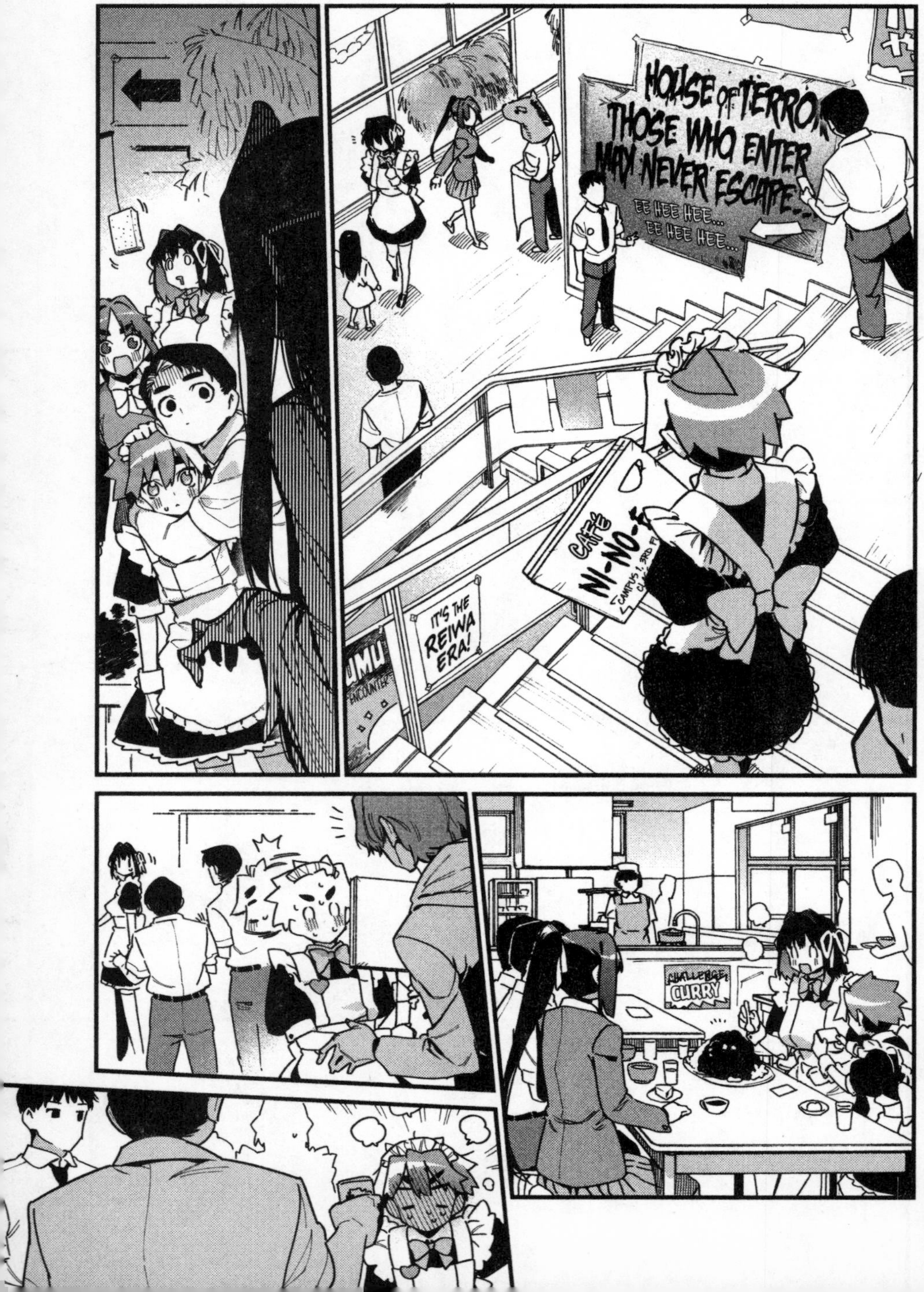
HOUSE OF TERRO
THOSE WHO ENTER
MAY NEVER ESCAPE...
EE HEE HEE... EE HEE HEE...
CAFÉ NI-NO-
CAMPUS 1, 3RD FL
IT'S THE REIWA ERA!
ENCOUNTER
CHALLENGE CURRY

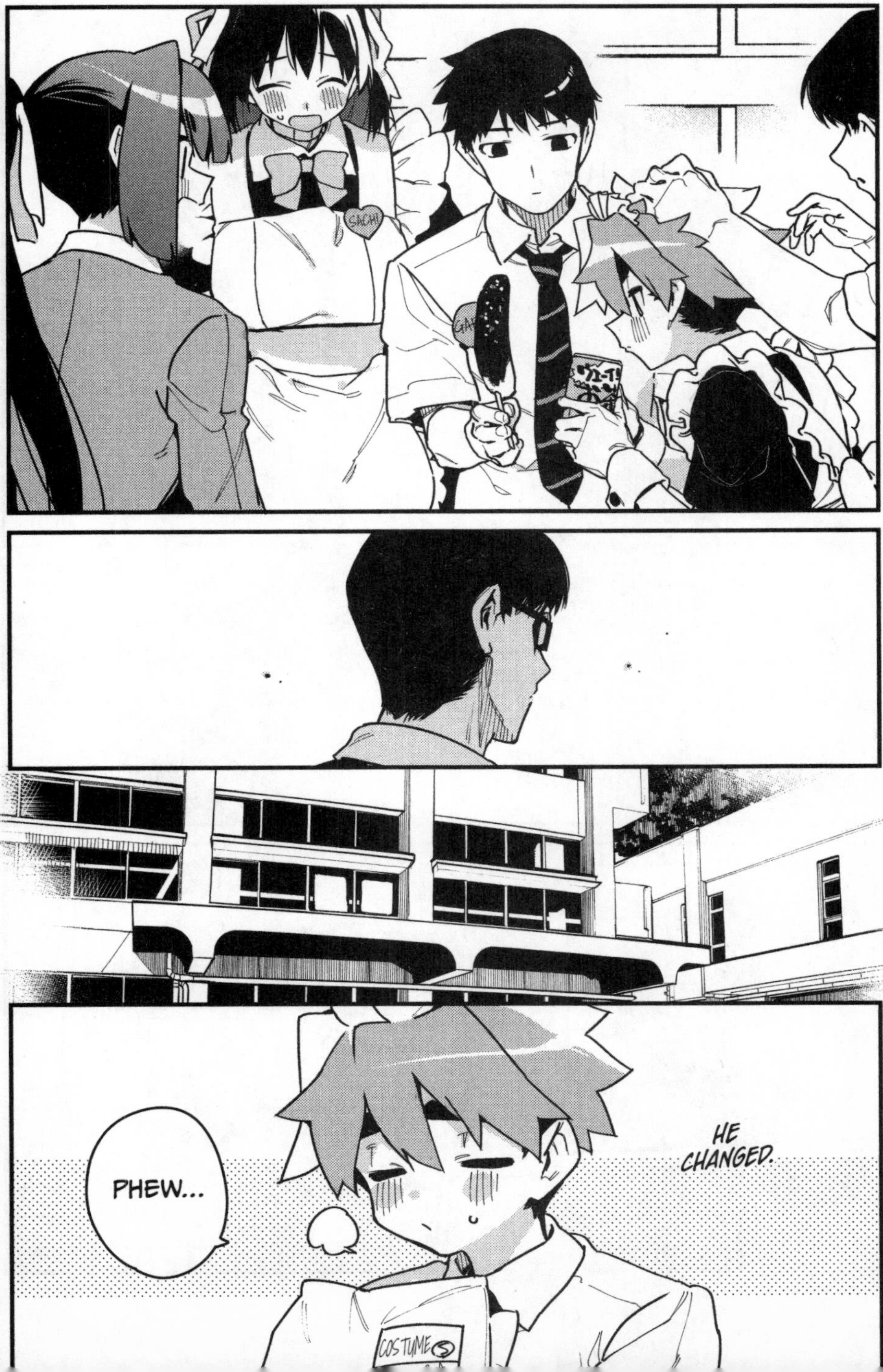
GACHI
HE CHANGED.
PHEW...
COSTUME

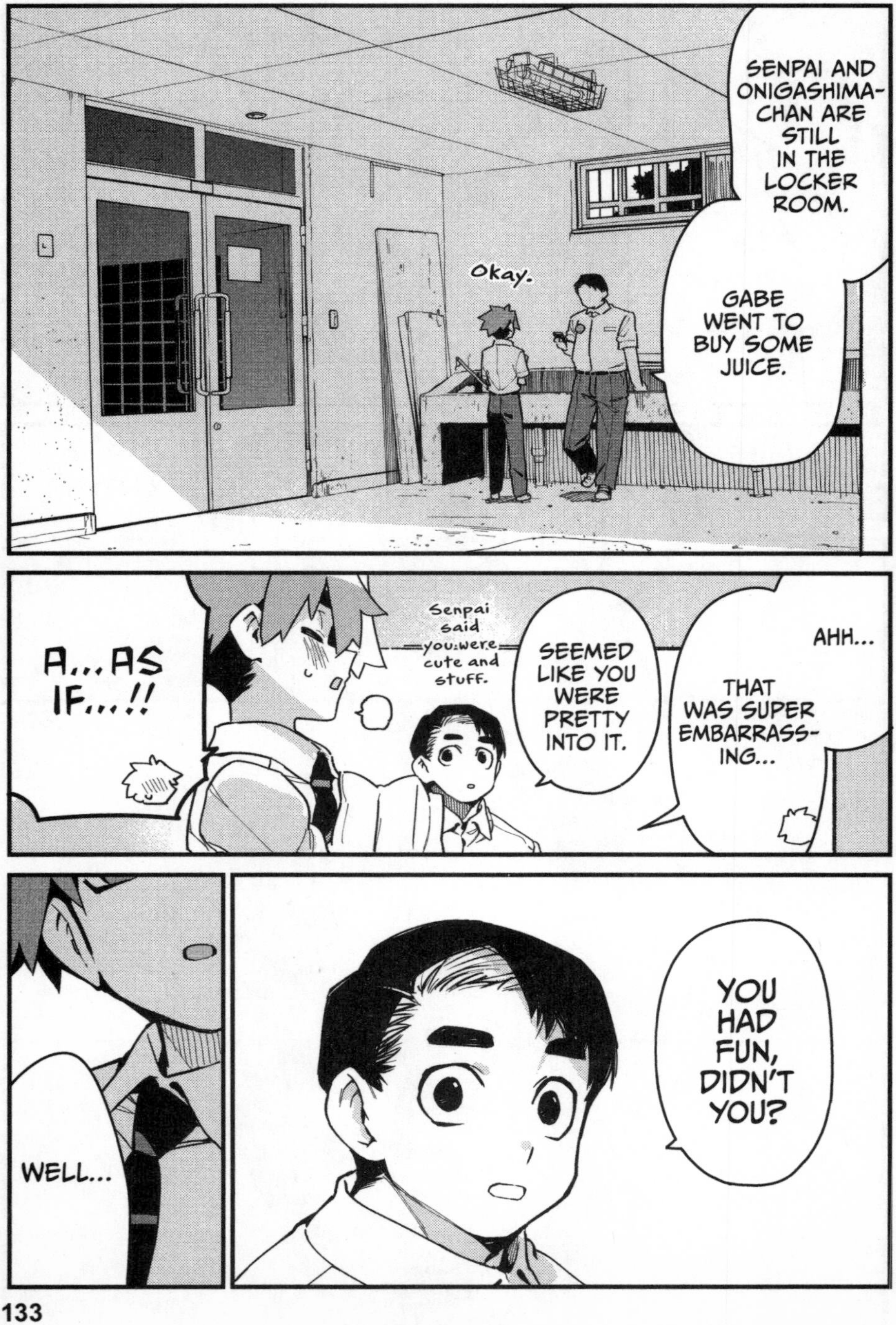
SENPAI AND ONIGASHIMA-CHAN ARE STILL IN THE LOCKER ROOM.
GABE WENT TO BUY SOME JUICE.
Okay.
AHH...
THAT WAS SUPER EMBARRASS-ING...
SEEMED LIKE YOU WERE PRETTY INTO IT.
Senpai said you were cute and stuff.
A...AS IF...!!
YOU HAD FUN, DIDN'T YOU?
WELL...

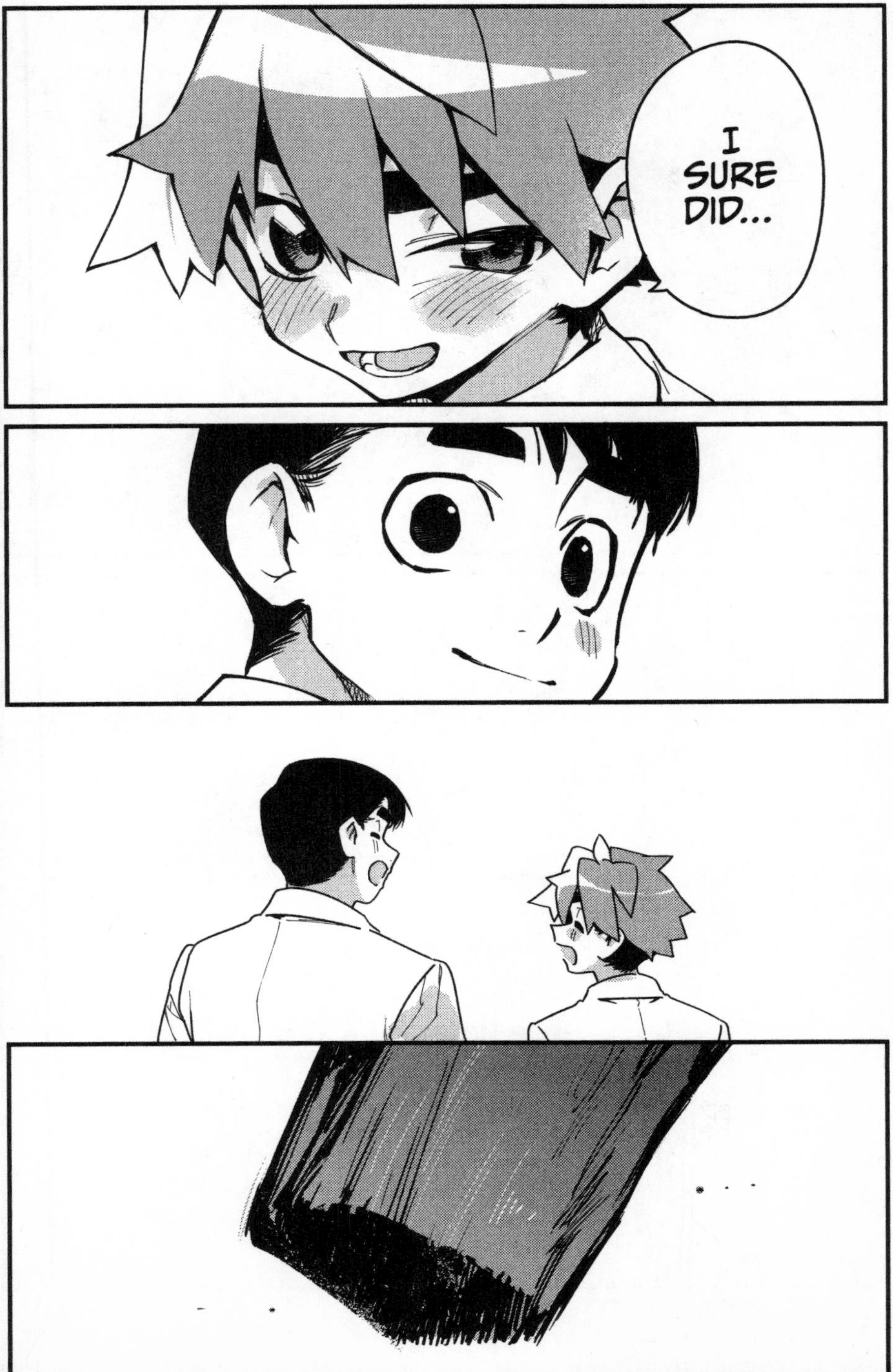
I SURE DID...

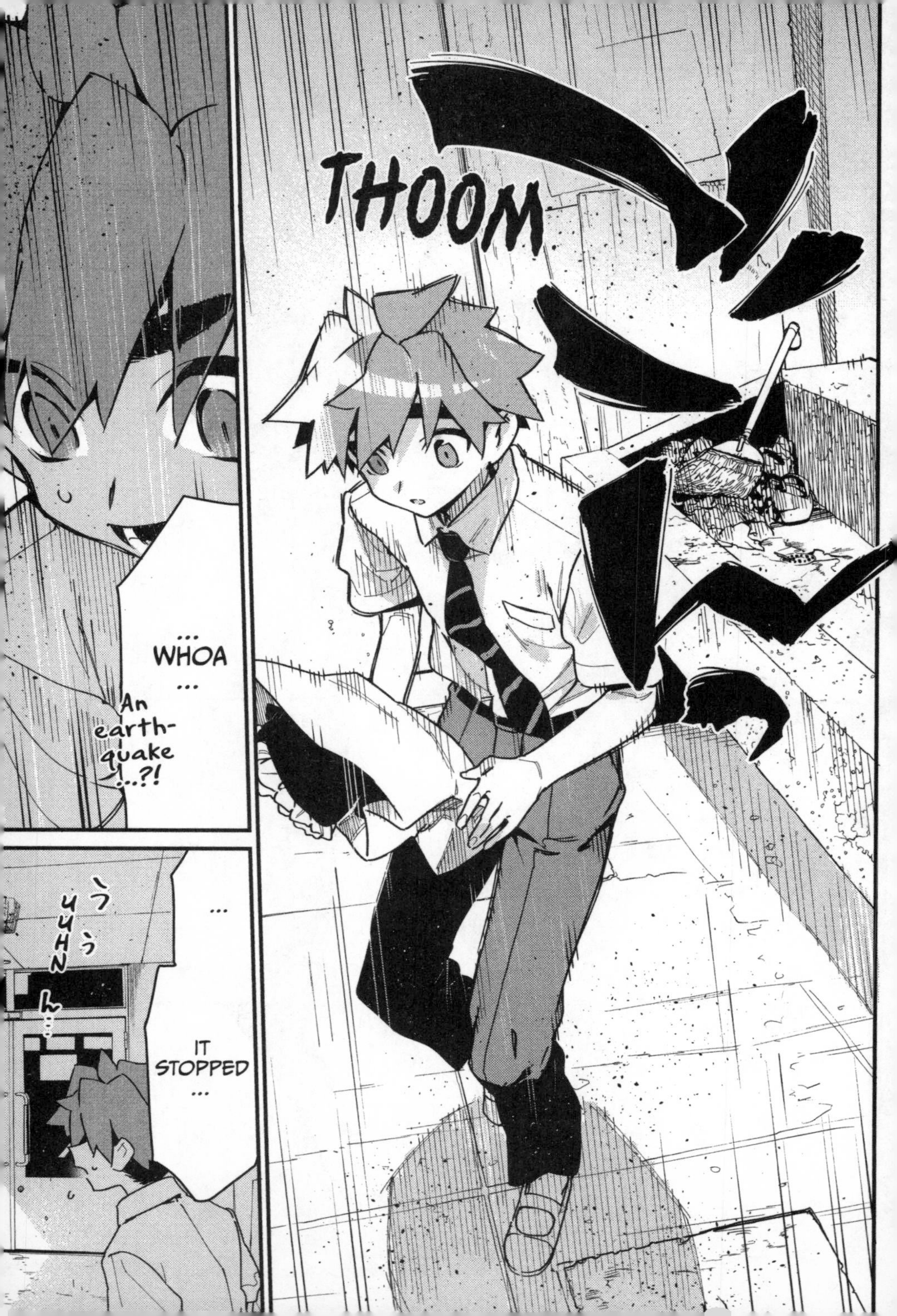
THOOM
... WHOA ...
An earthquake ...?!
... IT STOPPED ...
UUHN

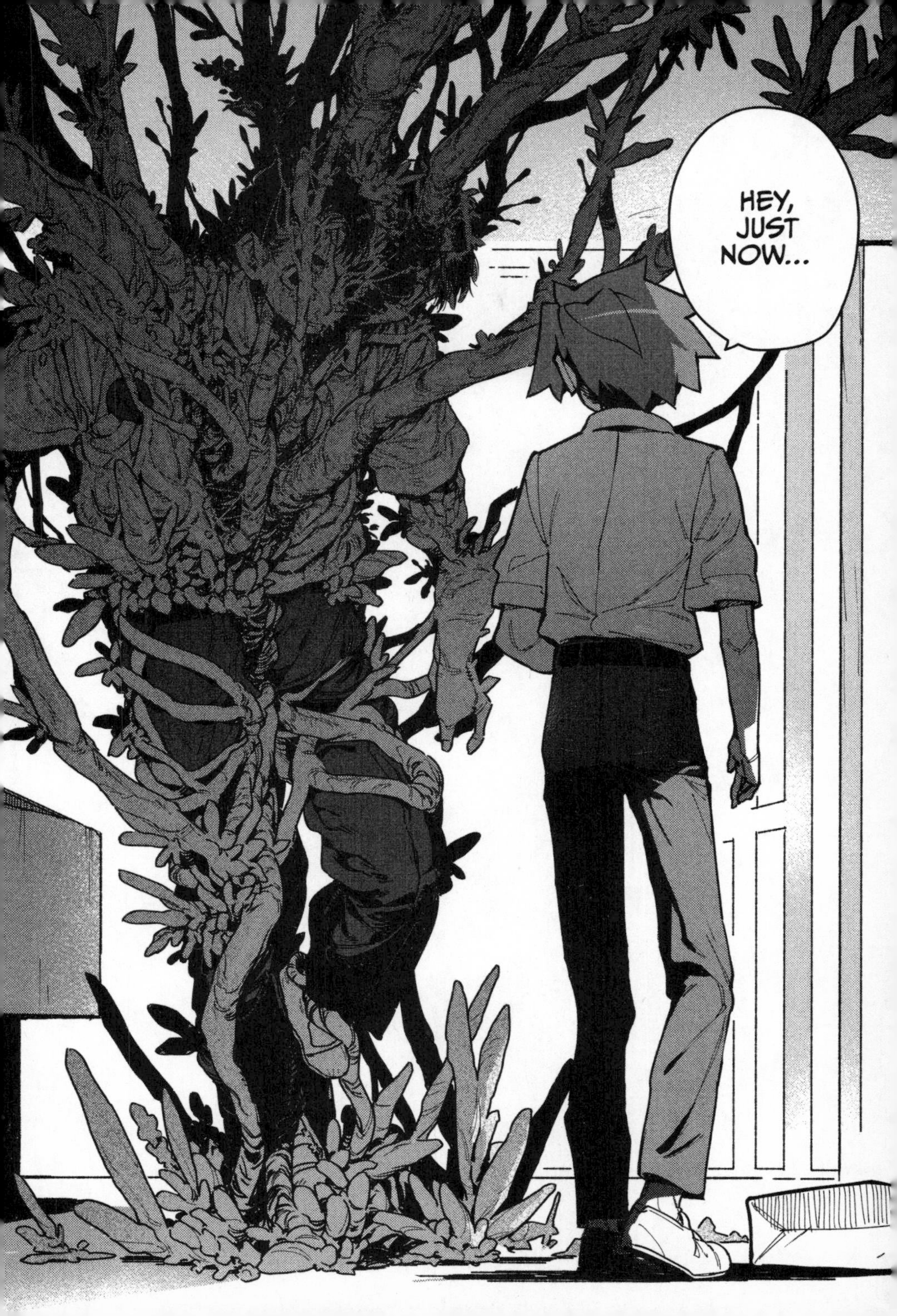
HEY, JUST NOW...

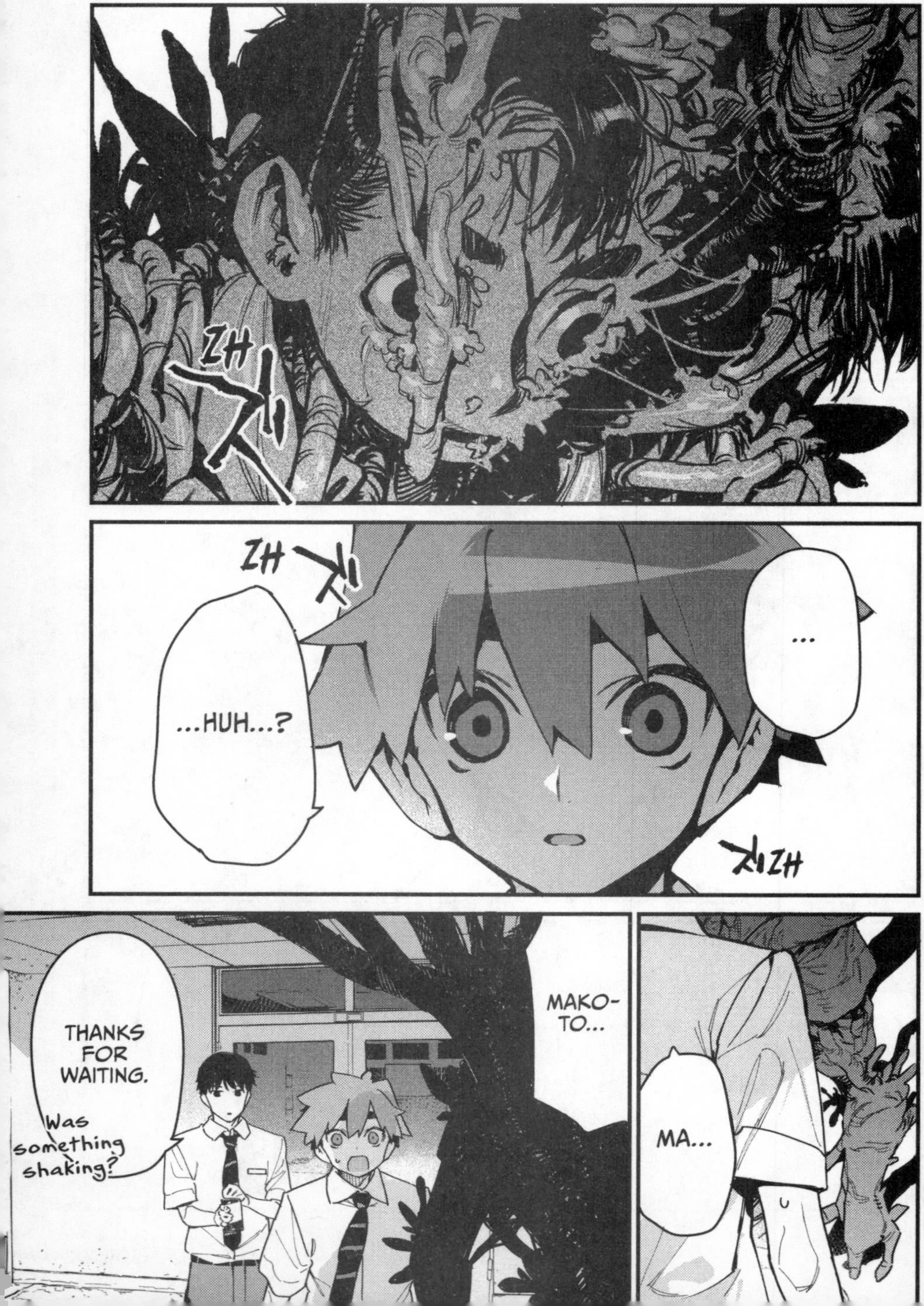
ZH
ZH
...
...HUH...?
ZH
MA...
MAKO-TO...
THANKS FOR WAITING.
Was something shaking?

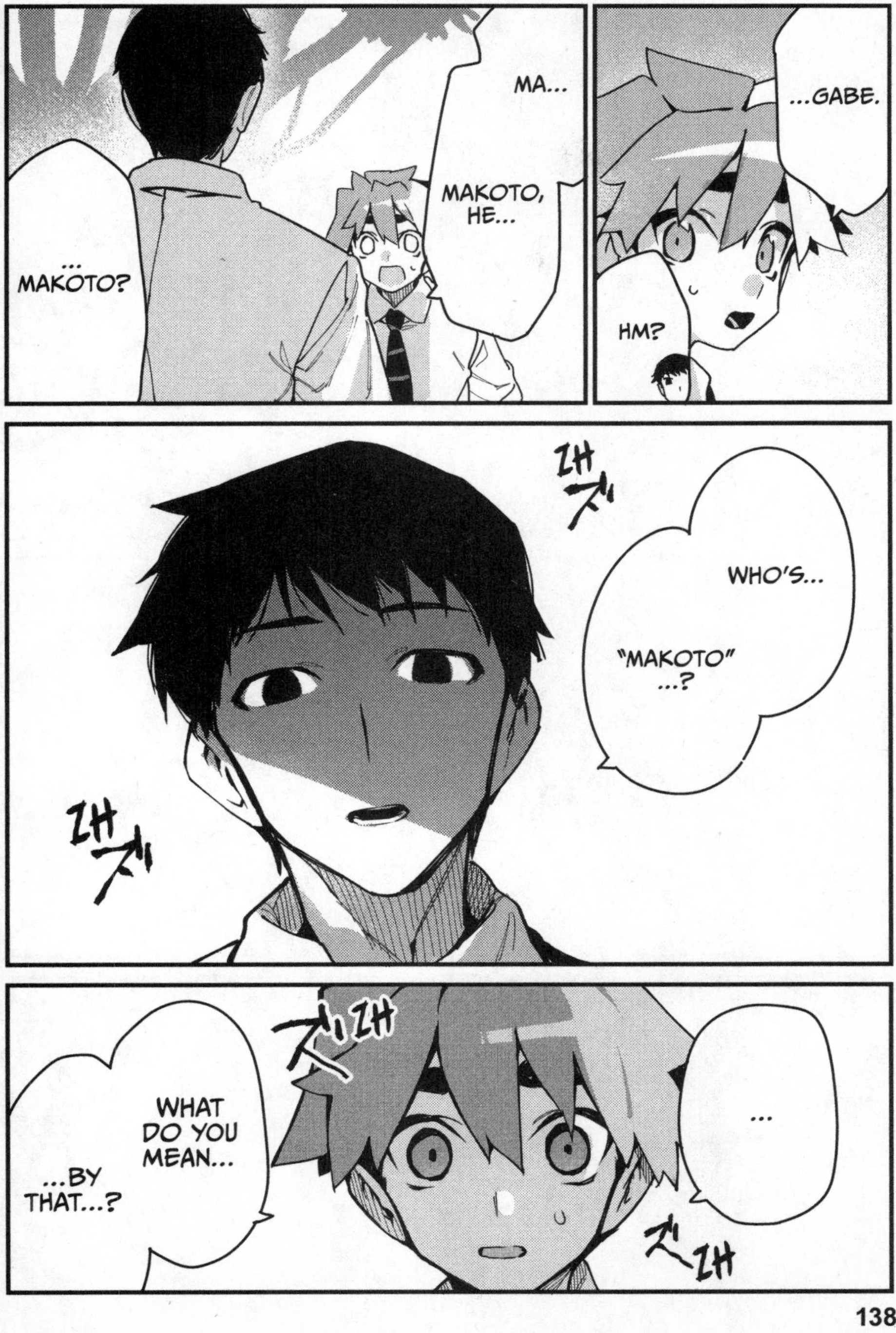
...GABE.
HM?
MA...
MAKOTO, HE...
... MAKOTO?
ZH
WHO'S...
"MAKOTO" ...?
ZH
...
ZH
WHAT DO YOU MEAN...
...BY THAT...?
ZH

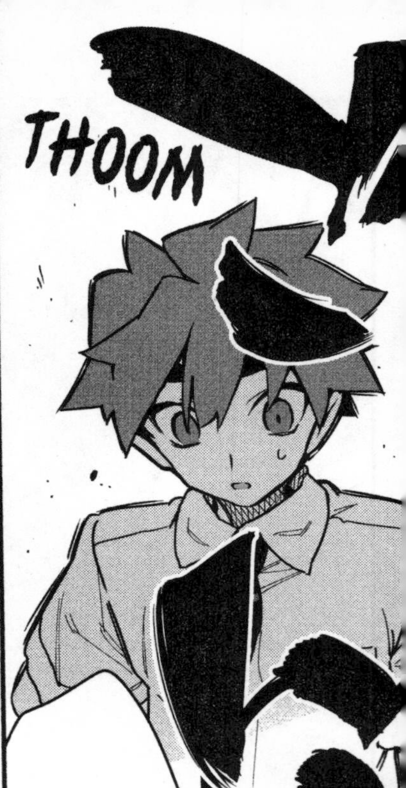
THOOM
...!!
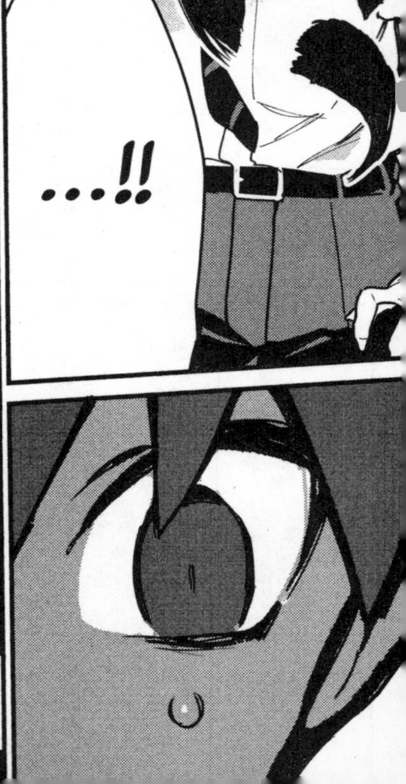
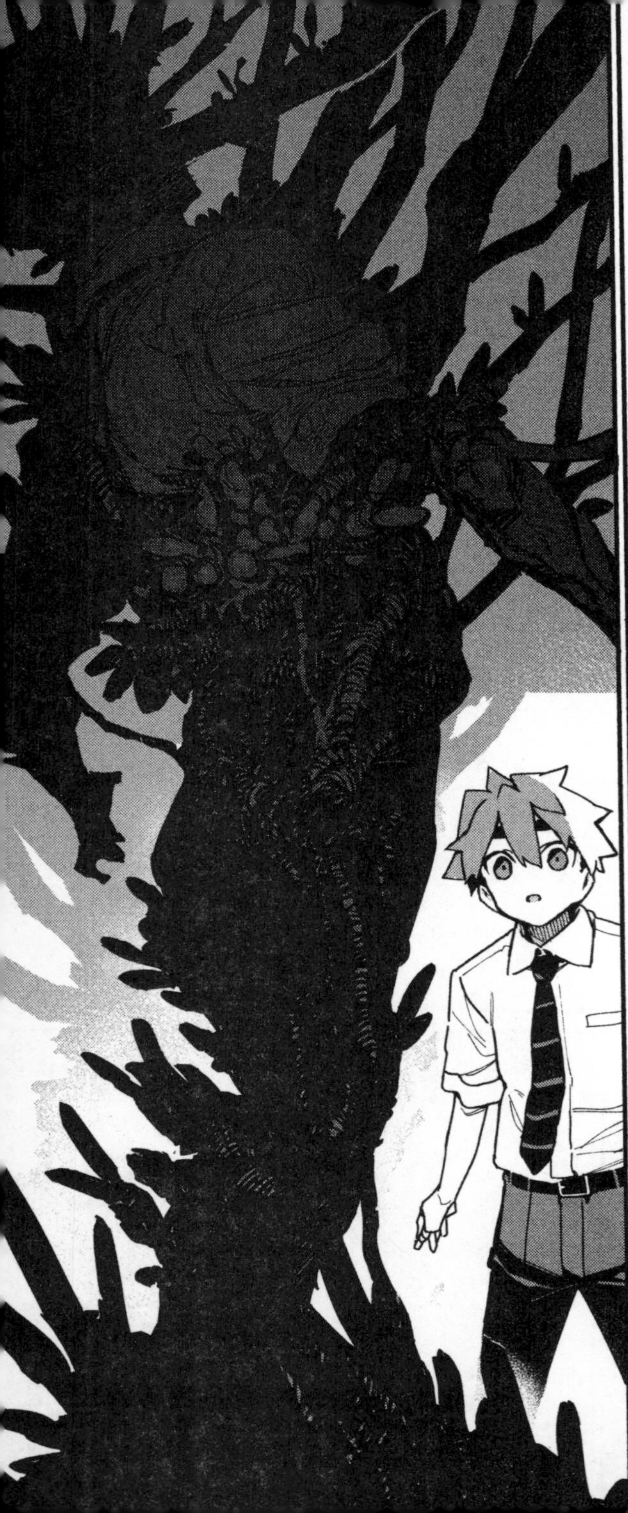

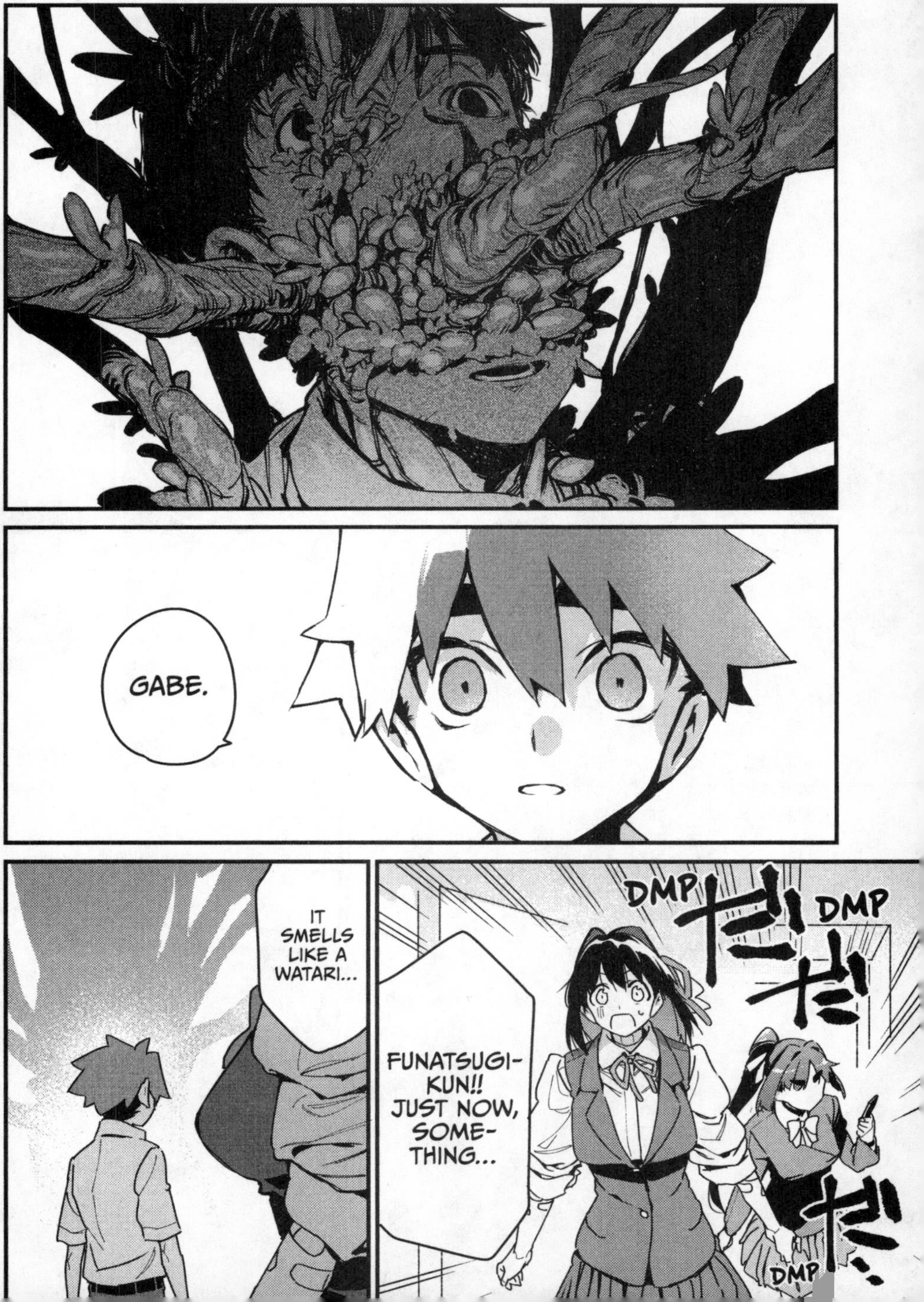
GABE.
DMP
DMP
FUNATSUGI-KUN!! JUST NOW, SOMETHING...
DMP
IT SMELLS LIKE A WATARI...

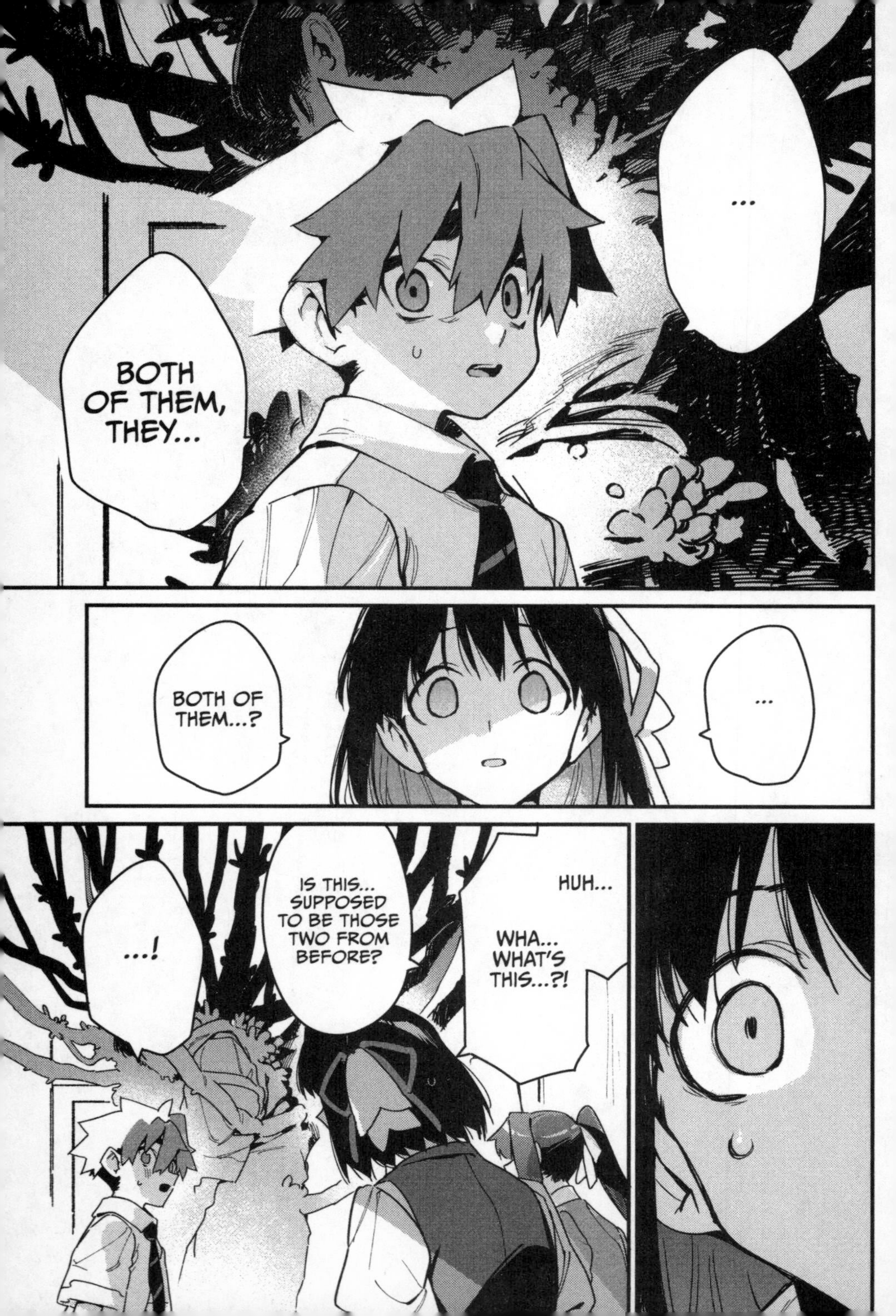
...
BOTH OF THEM, THEY...
...
BOTH OF THEM...?
HUH...
WHA... WHAT'S THIS...?!
IS THIS... SUPPOSED TO BE THOSE TWO FROM BEFORE?
...!

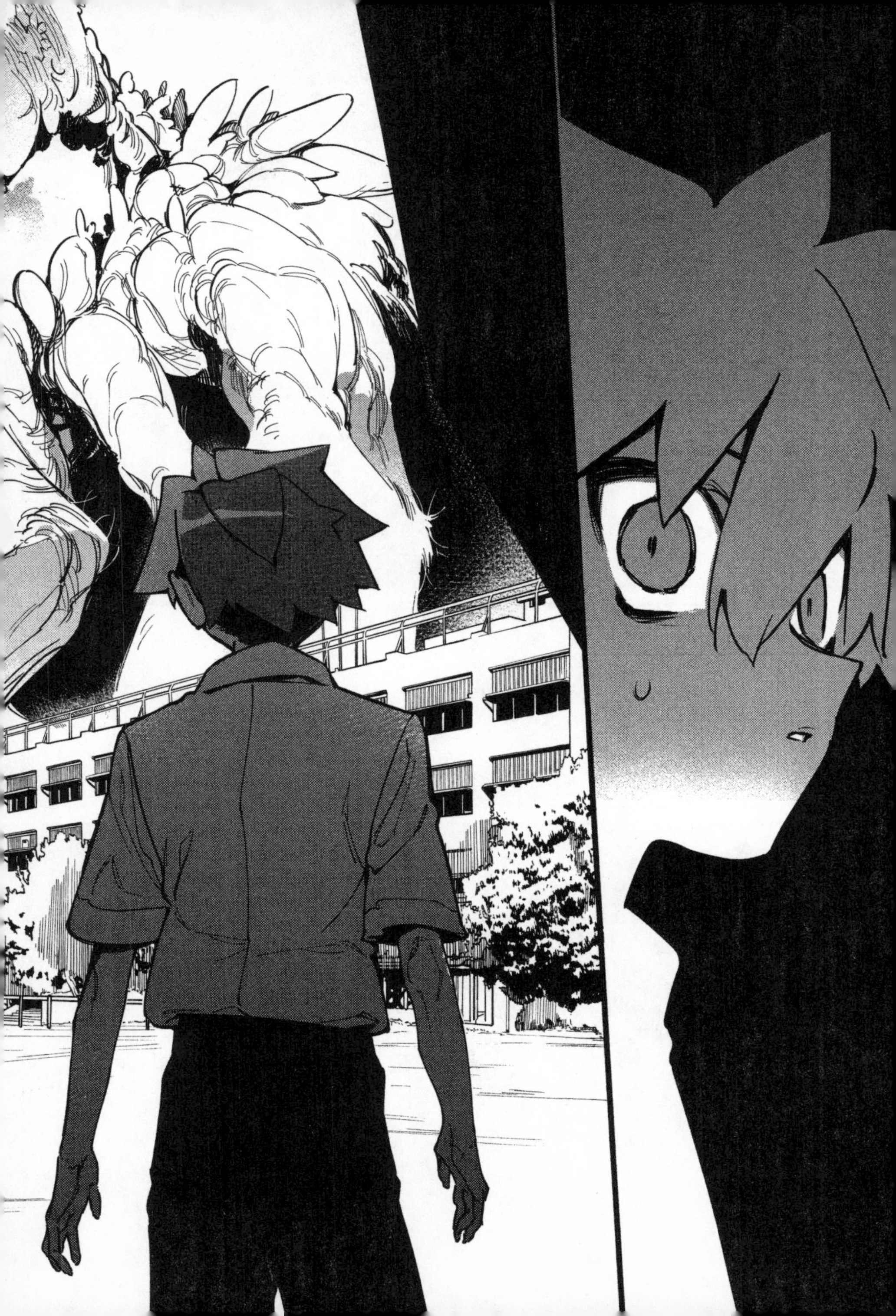

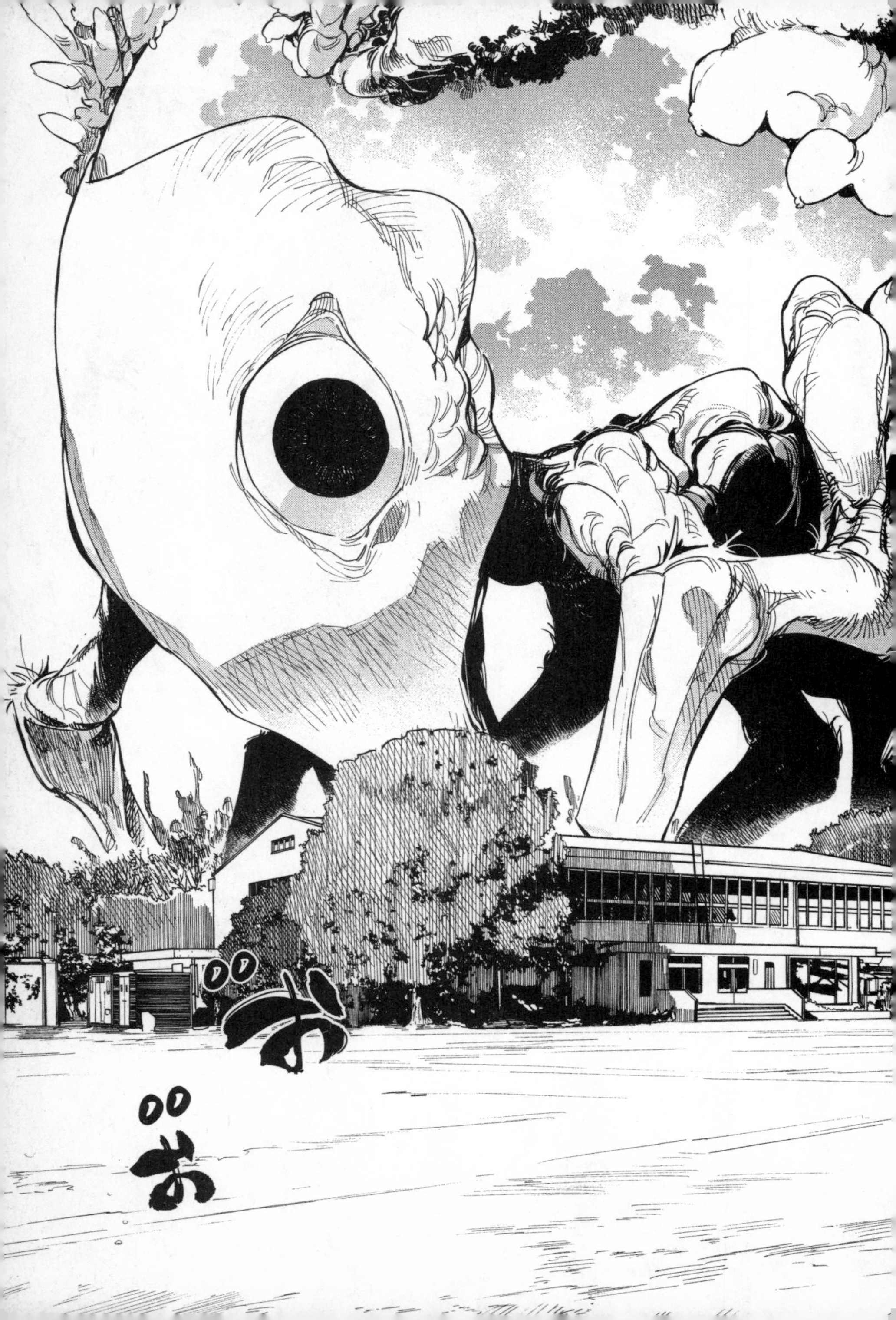
お゙
お゙

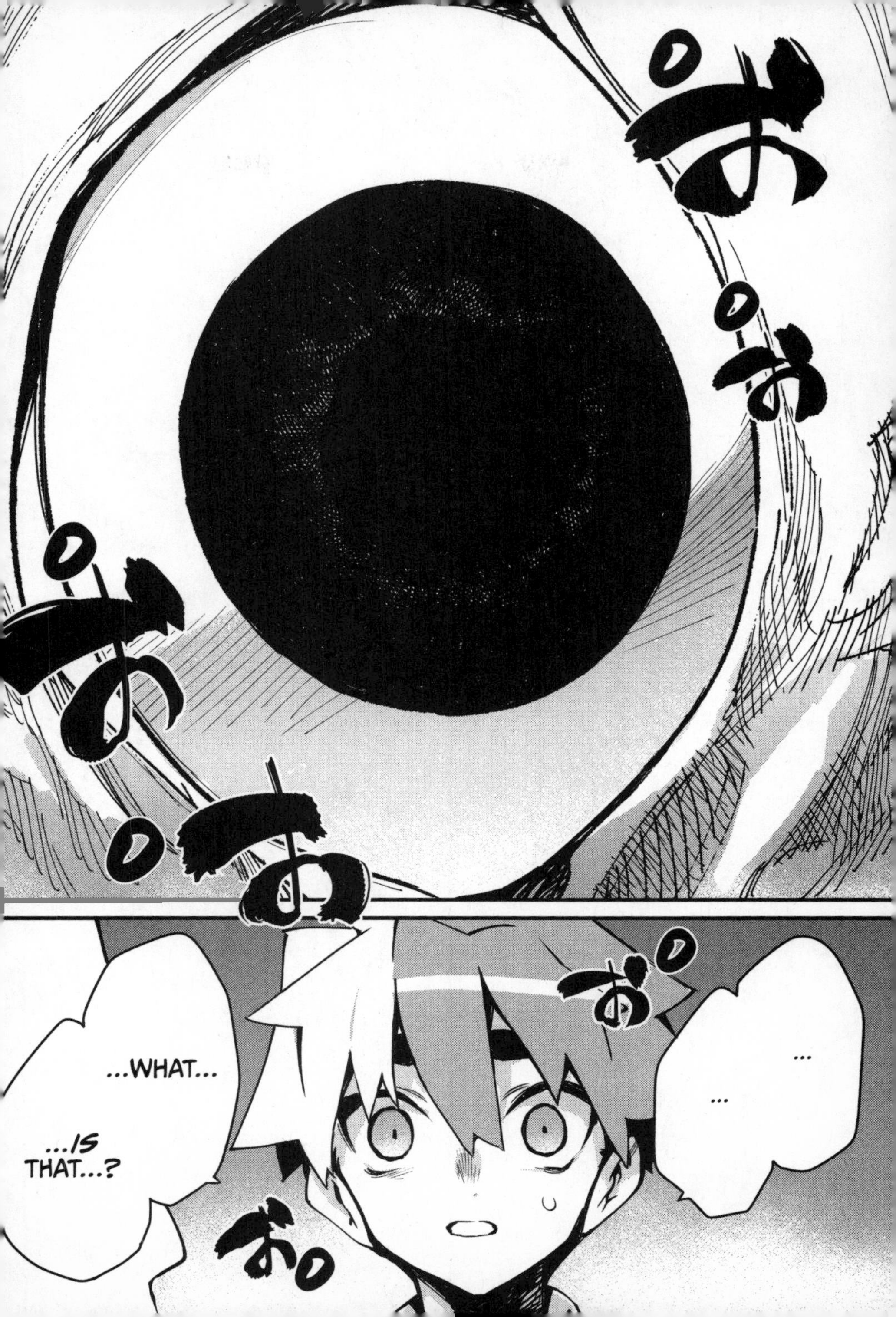
... ...
...WHAT... ...IS THAT...?

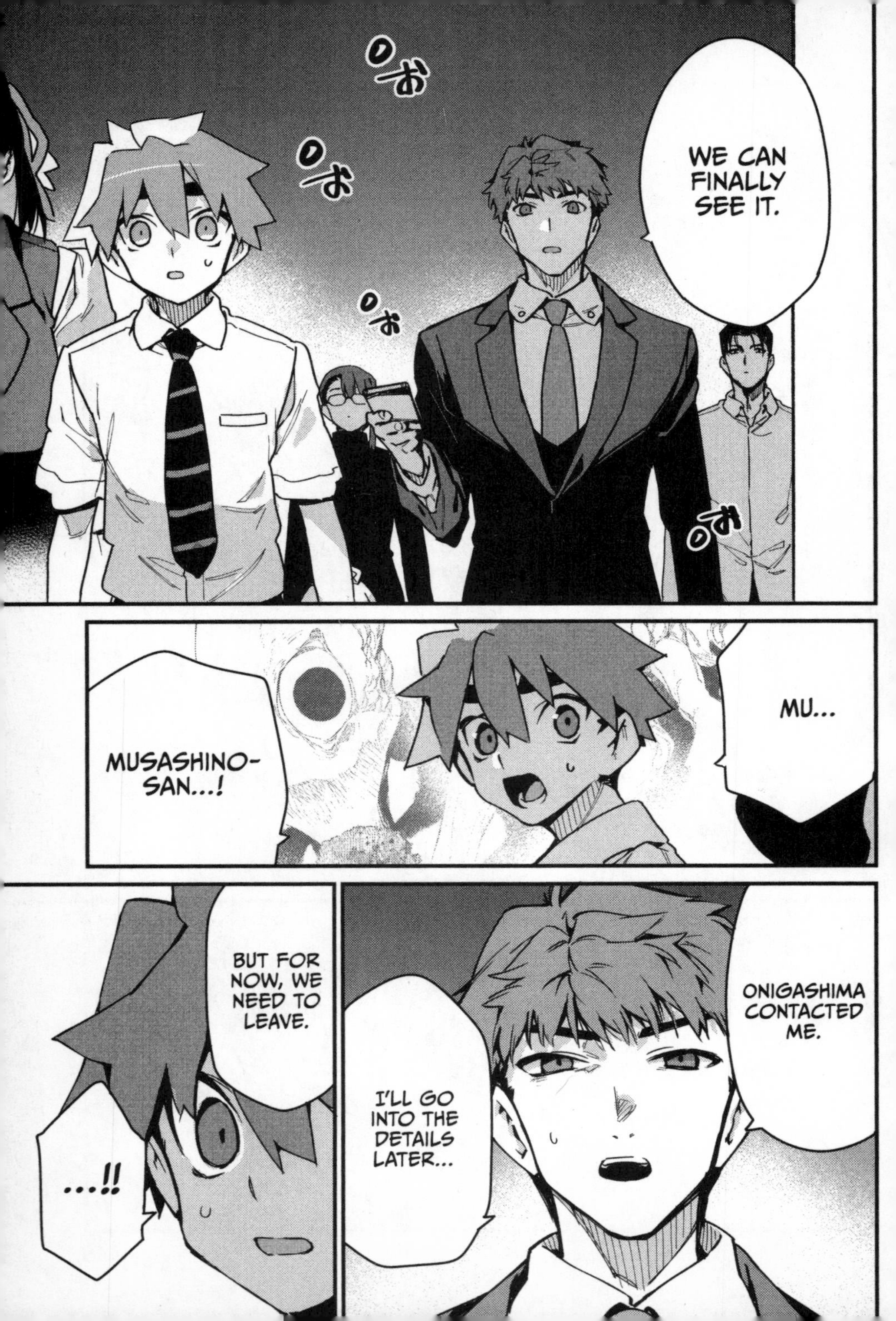
WE CAN FINALLY SEE IT.
MU...
MUSASHINO-SAN...!
ONIGASHIMA CONTACTED ME.
I'LL GO INTO THE DETAILS LATER...
BUT FOR NOW, WE NEED TO LEAVE.
...!!

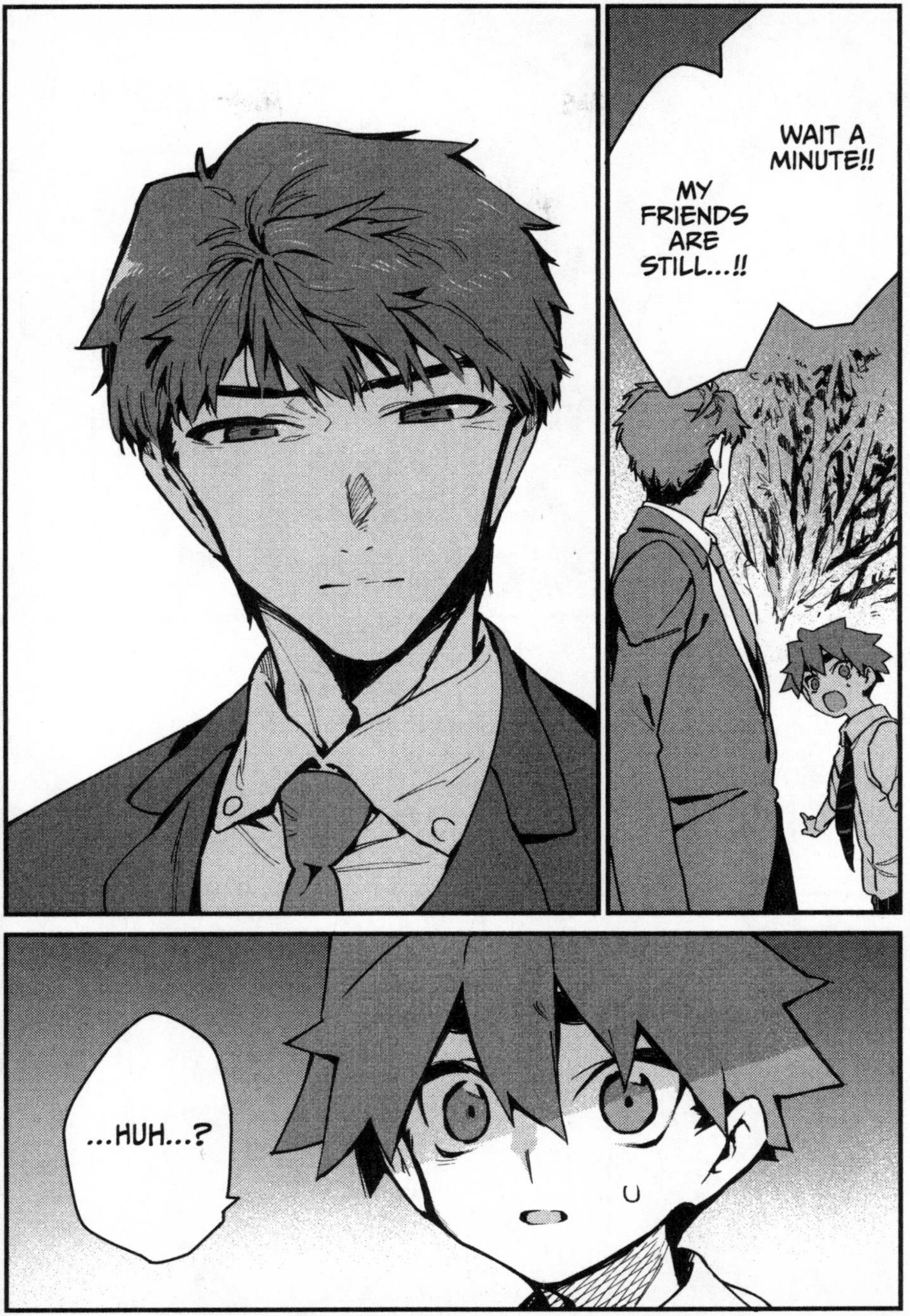
WAIT A MINUTE!!
MY FRIENDS ARE STILL...!!
...HUH...?

Sachi's MONSTROUS Appetite

Sachi's MONSTROUS Appetite

Chapter 15: The Seedling Has a Purpose (3)

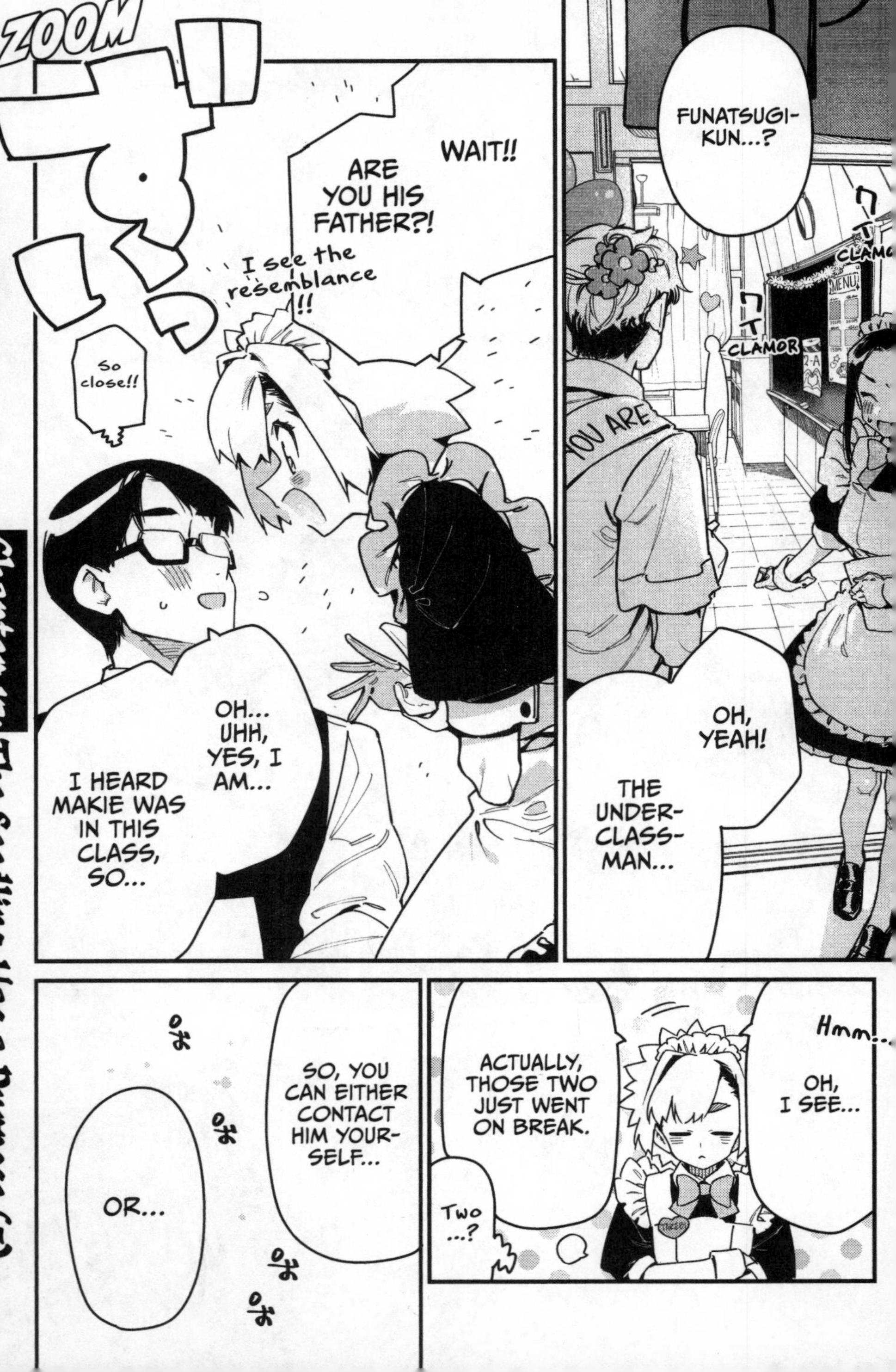
FUNATSUGI-KUN...?
CLAMOR
CLAMOR
YOU ARE
OH, YEAH!
THE UNDER-CLASS-MAN...
ZOOM
WAIT!!
ARE YOU HIS FATHER?!
I see the resemblance!!
So close!!
OH... UHH, YES, I AM...
I HEARD MAKIE WAS IN THIS CLASS, SO...
Hmm...
OH, I SEE...
ACTUALLY, THOSE TWO JUST WENT ON BREAK.
Two ...?
SO, YOU CAN EITHER CONTACT HIM YOUR-SELF...
OR...

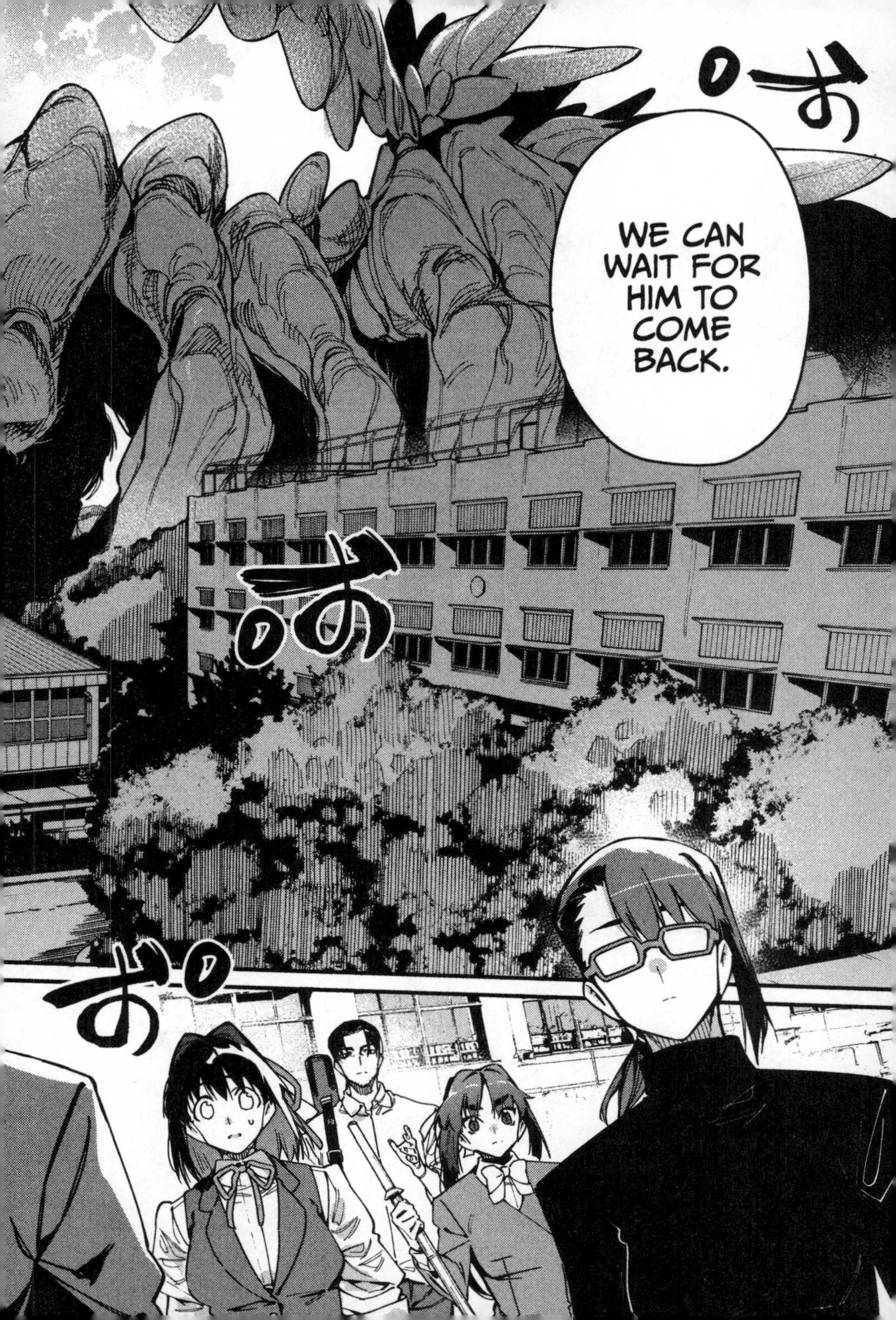

WE CAN WAIT FOR HIM TO COME BACK.
おぉ
あぉ
おぉ

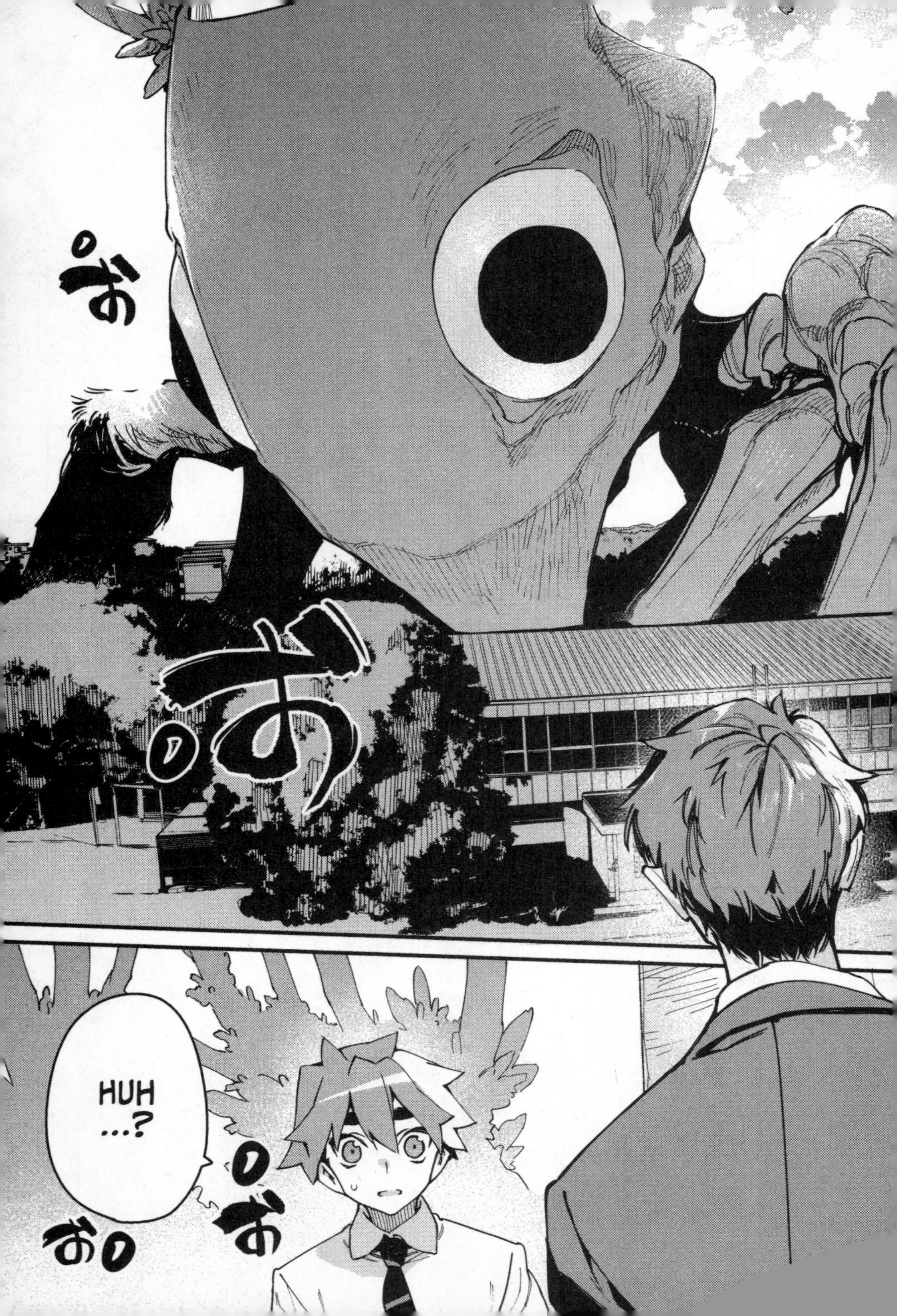
HUH ...?

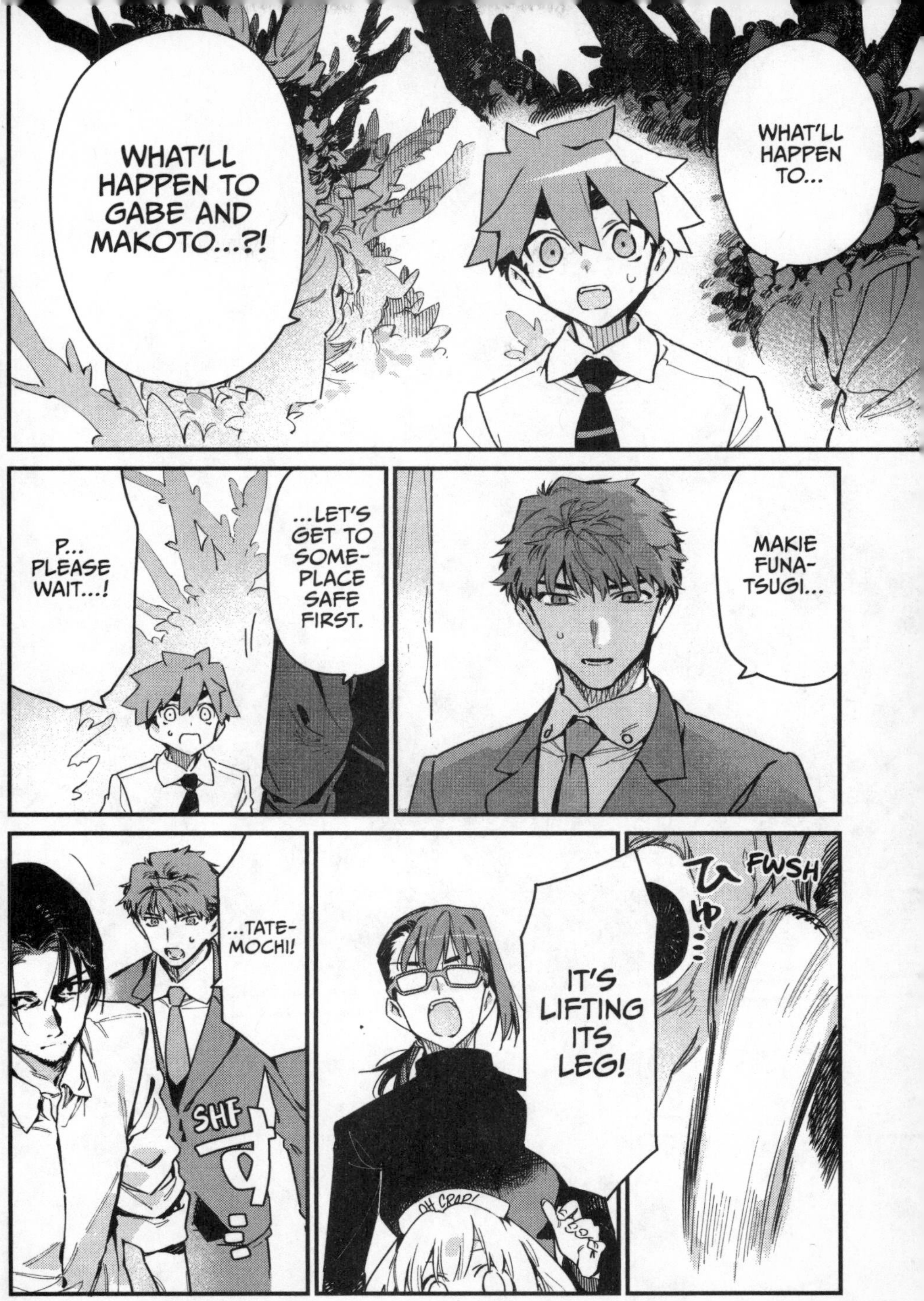
WHAT'LL HAPPEN TO...
WHAT'LL HAPPEN TO GABE AND MAKOTO...?!
MAKIE FUNA-TSUGI...
...LET'S GET TO SOME-PLACE SAFE FIRST.
P... PLEASE WAIT...!
ひゅ FWSH
IT'S LIFTING ITS LEG!
OH CRAP!
...TATE-MOCHI!
SHF す

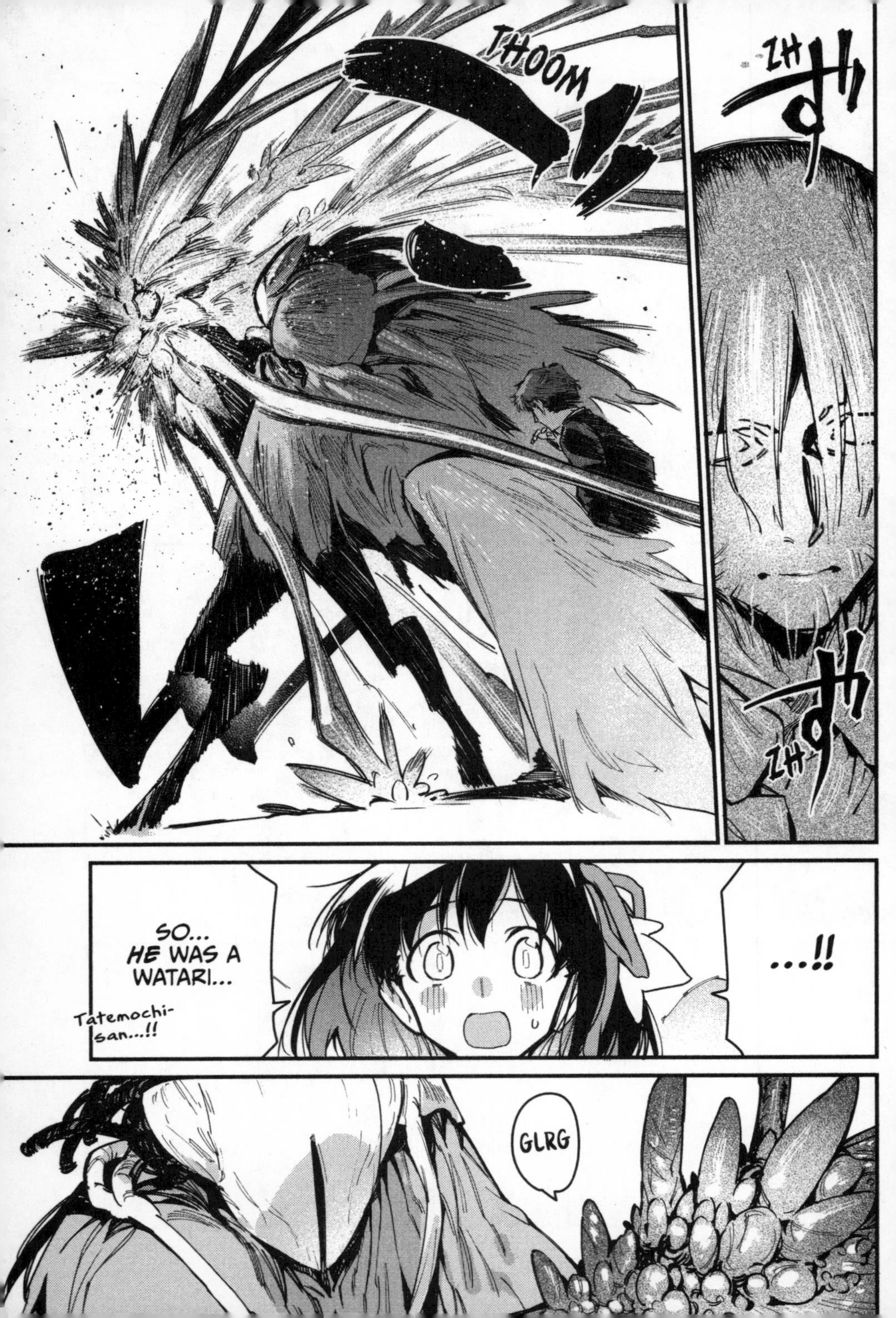
ZH
ZH
THOOM
...!!
SO... HE WAS A WATARI...
Tatemochi-san...!!
GLRG

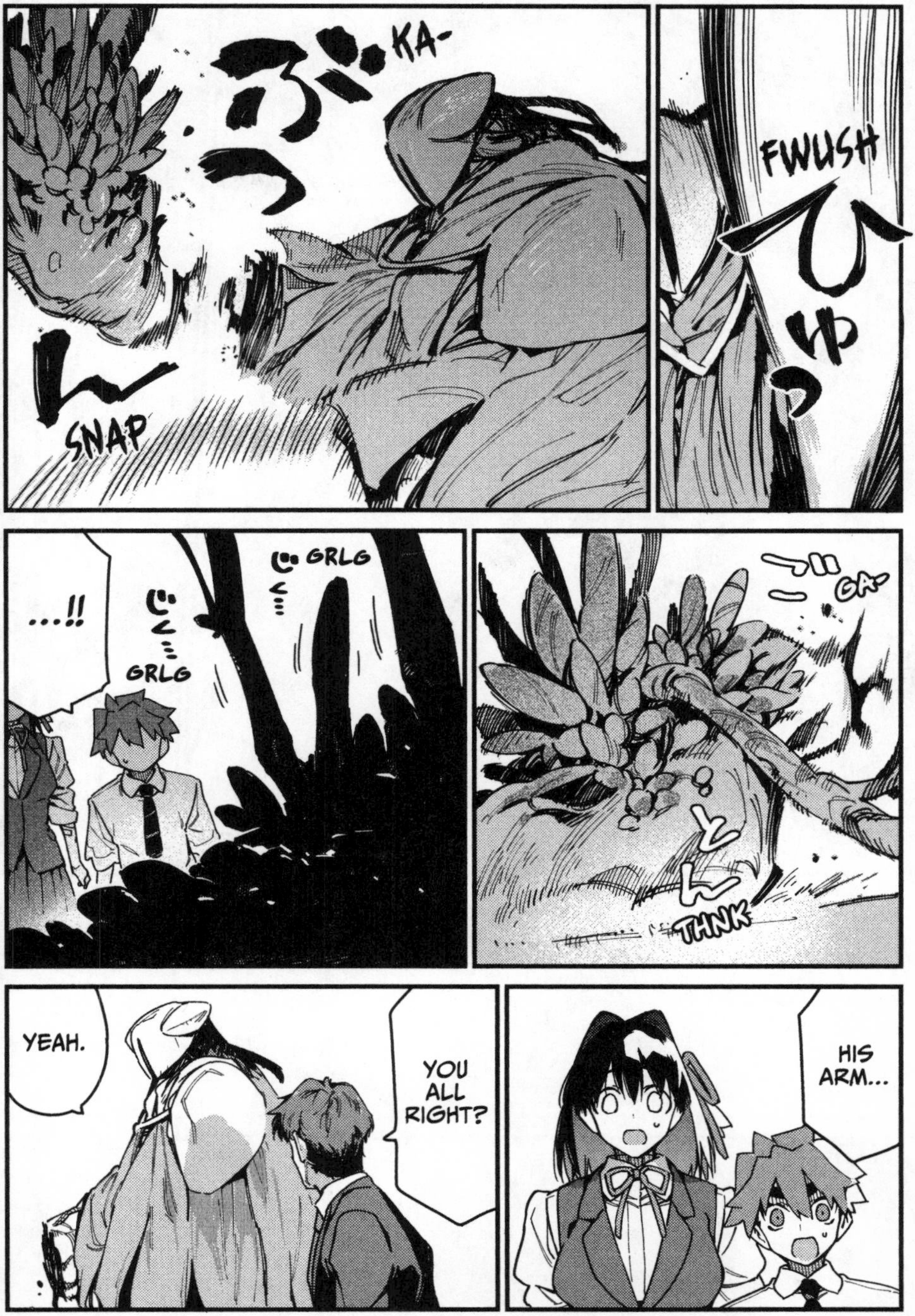
ひゅっ
FWUSH
ぶつん
KA-
SNAP
ゴッ
GA-
とん
THNK
じく…
GRLG
じく…
GRLG
...!!
HIS ARM...
YOU ALL RIGHT?
YEAH.

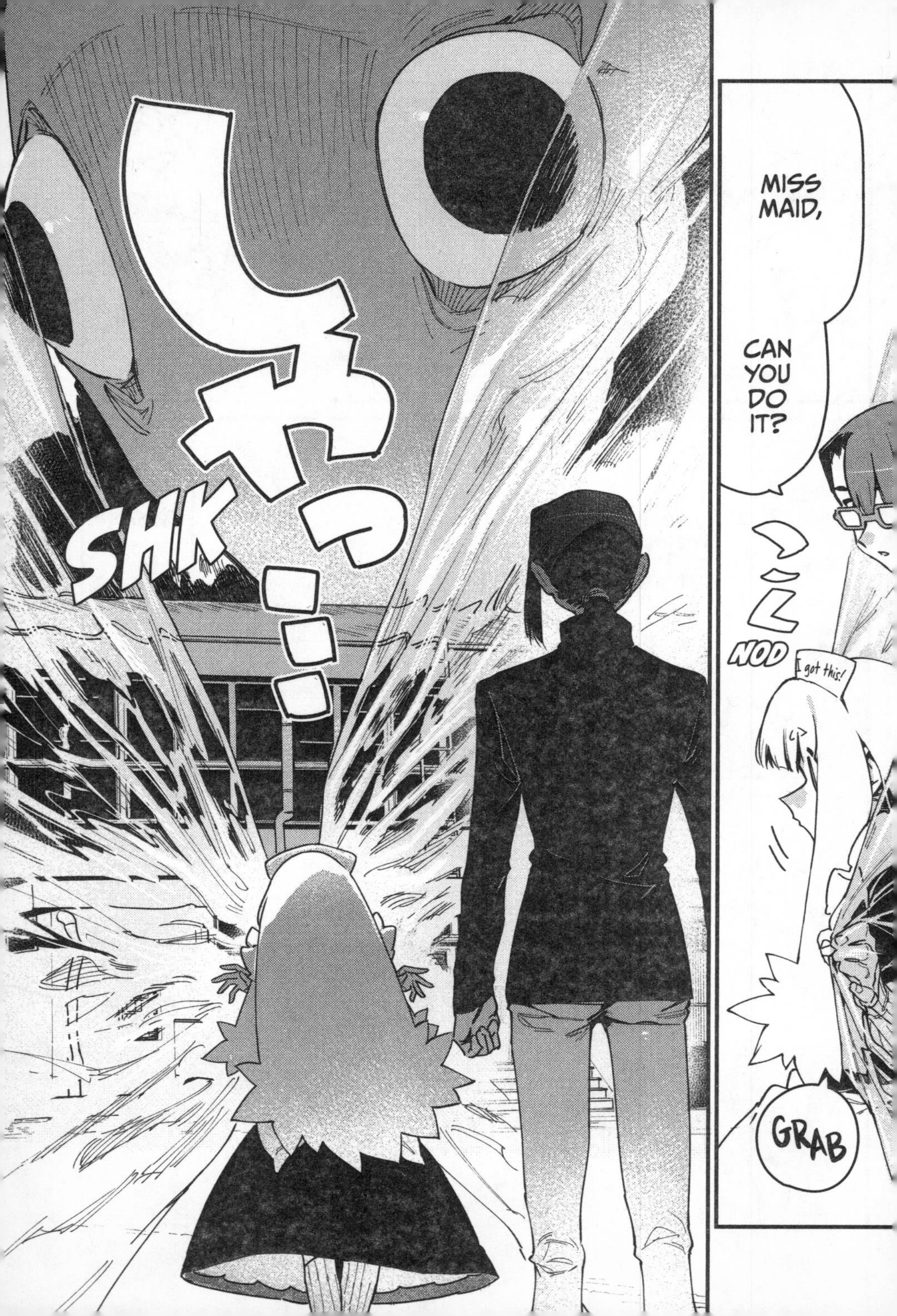
MISS MAID,
CAN YOU DO IT?
NOD
I got this!
GRAB
SHK

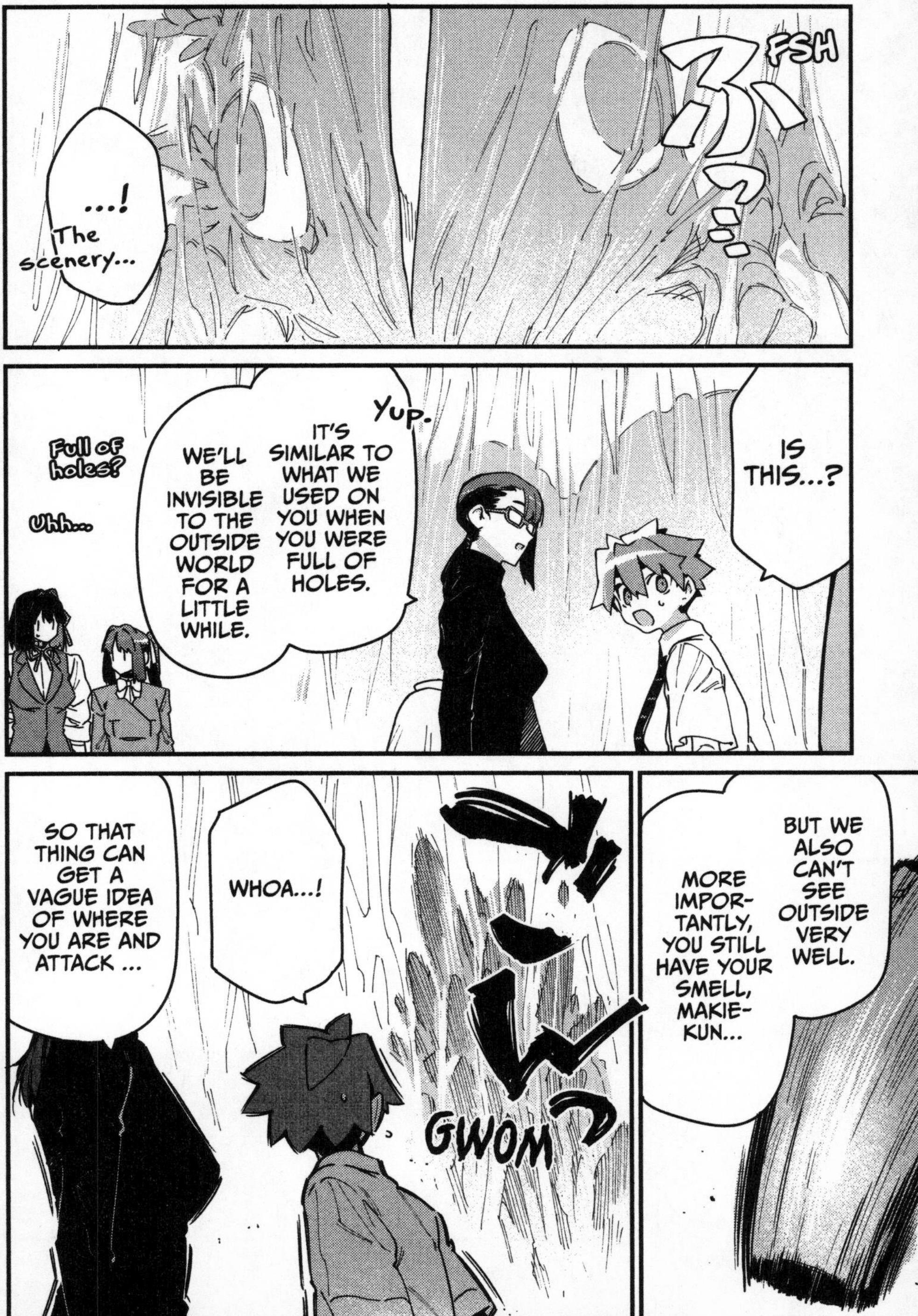
FSH
...! The scenery...
IS THIS...?
Yup.
IT'S SIMILAR TO WHAT WE USED ON YOU WHEN YOU WERE FULL OF HOLES.
WE'LL BE INVISIBLE TO THE OUTSIDE WORLD FOR A LITTLE WHILE.
Full of holes?
Uhh...
BUT WE ALSO CAN'T SEE OUTSIDE VERY WELL.
MORE IMPORTANTLY, YOU STILL HAVE YOUR SMELL, MAKIE-KUN...
GWOM
WHOA...!
SO THAT THING CAN GET A VAGUE IDEA OF WHERE YOU ARE AND ATTACK ...

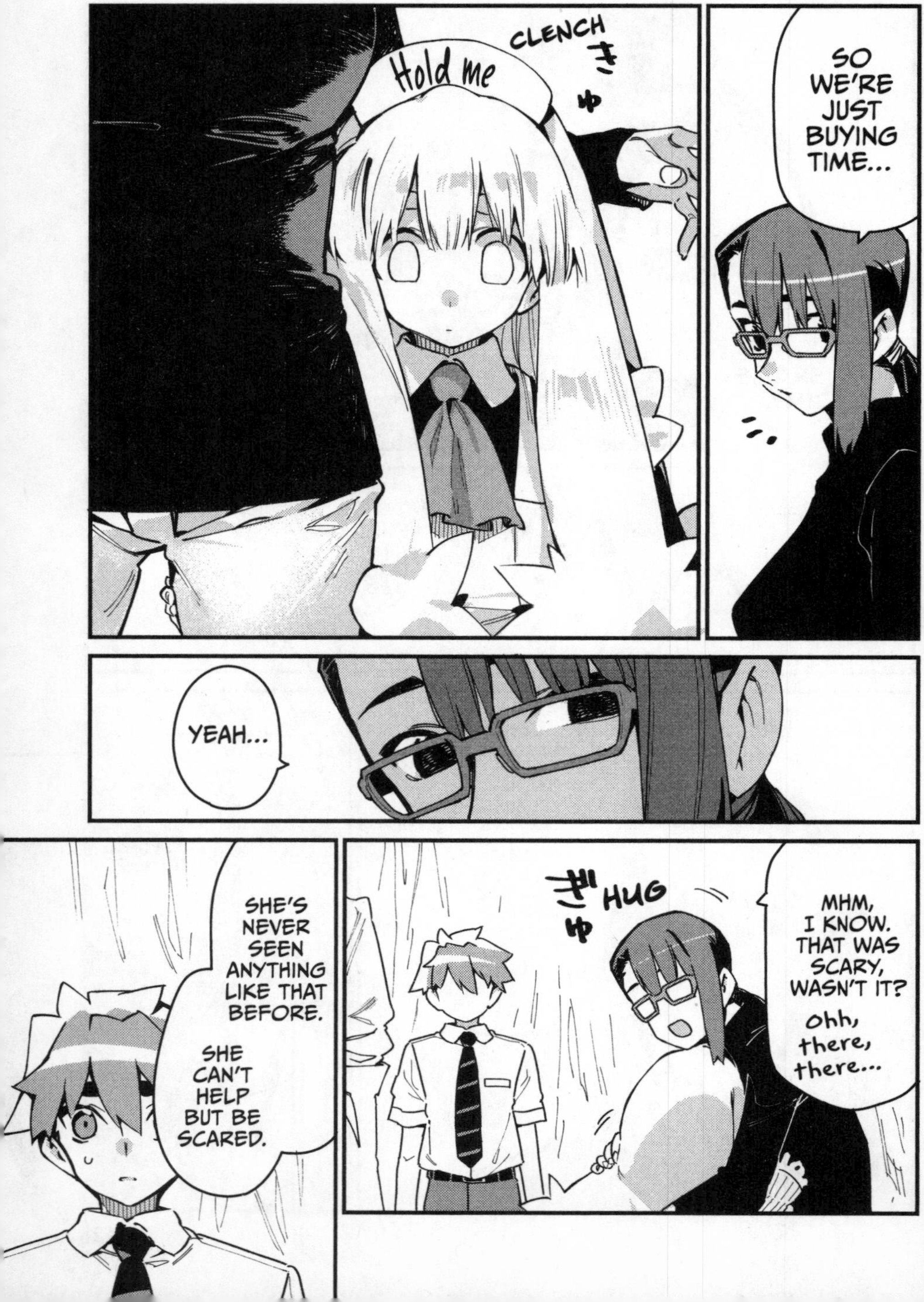
SO WE'RE JUST BUYING TIME...
Hold me
きゅ
CLENCH
YEAH...
MHM, I KNOW. THAT WAS SCARY, WASN'T IT?
Ohh, there, there...
ぎゅ
HUG
SHE'S NEVER SEEN ANYTHING LIKE THAT BEFORE.
SHE CAN'T HELP BUT BE SCARED.

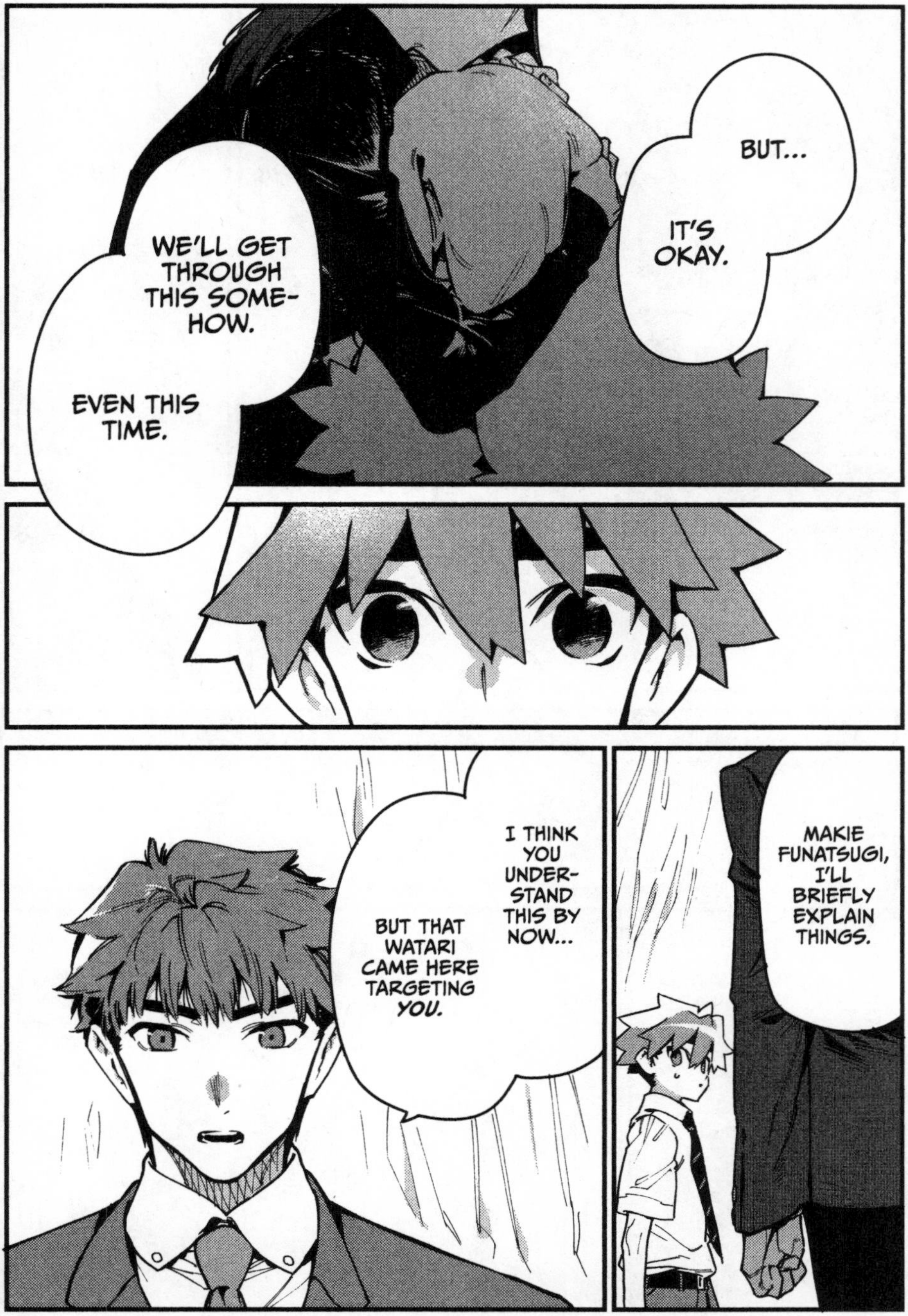
BUT...
IT'S OKAY.
WE'LL GET THROUGH THIS SOME-HOW.
EVEN THIS TIME.
MAKIE FUNATSUGI, I'LL BRIEFLY EXPLAIN THINGS.
I THINK YOU UNDER-STAND THIS BY NOW...
BUT THAT WATARI CAME HERE TARGETING *YOU.*

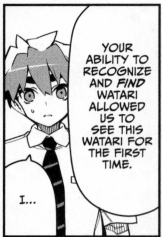

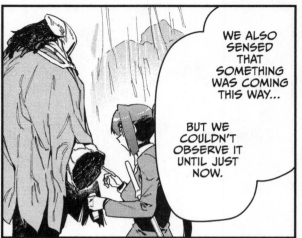

WE ALSO SENSED THAT SOMETHING WAS COMING THIS WAY...
BUT WE COULDN'T OBSERVE IT UNTIL JUST NOW.
YOUR ABILITY TO RECOGNIZE AND *FIND* WATARI ALLOWED US TO SEE THIS WATARI FOR THE FIRST TIME.
I...
THOOM
...!
... IT'S SEARCHING AROUND...
THAT WATARI'S KNOWN AS A "KANETSUKI" OR "MIDORI-MAKI."
IT WAS CONFIRMED A LONG TIME AGO, BUT NO ONE'S SEEN ONE FOR QUITE SOME TIME.
Had no idea it could get that huge.
I THINK YOU CAN TELL FROM LOOKING AT IT,
BUT ANYTHING THAT WATARI MEDDLES WITH TURNS INTO VEGETATION.

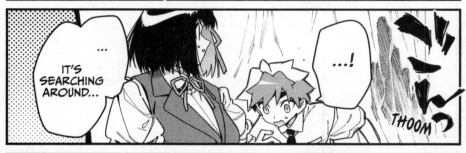

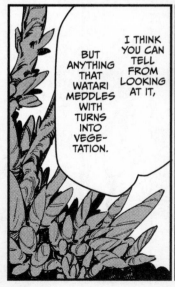

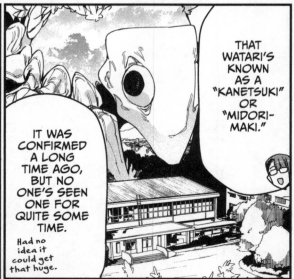

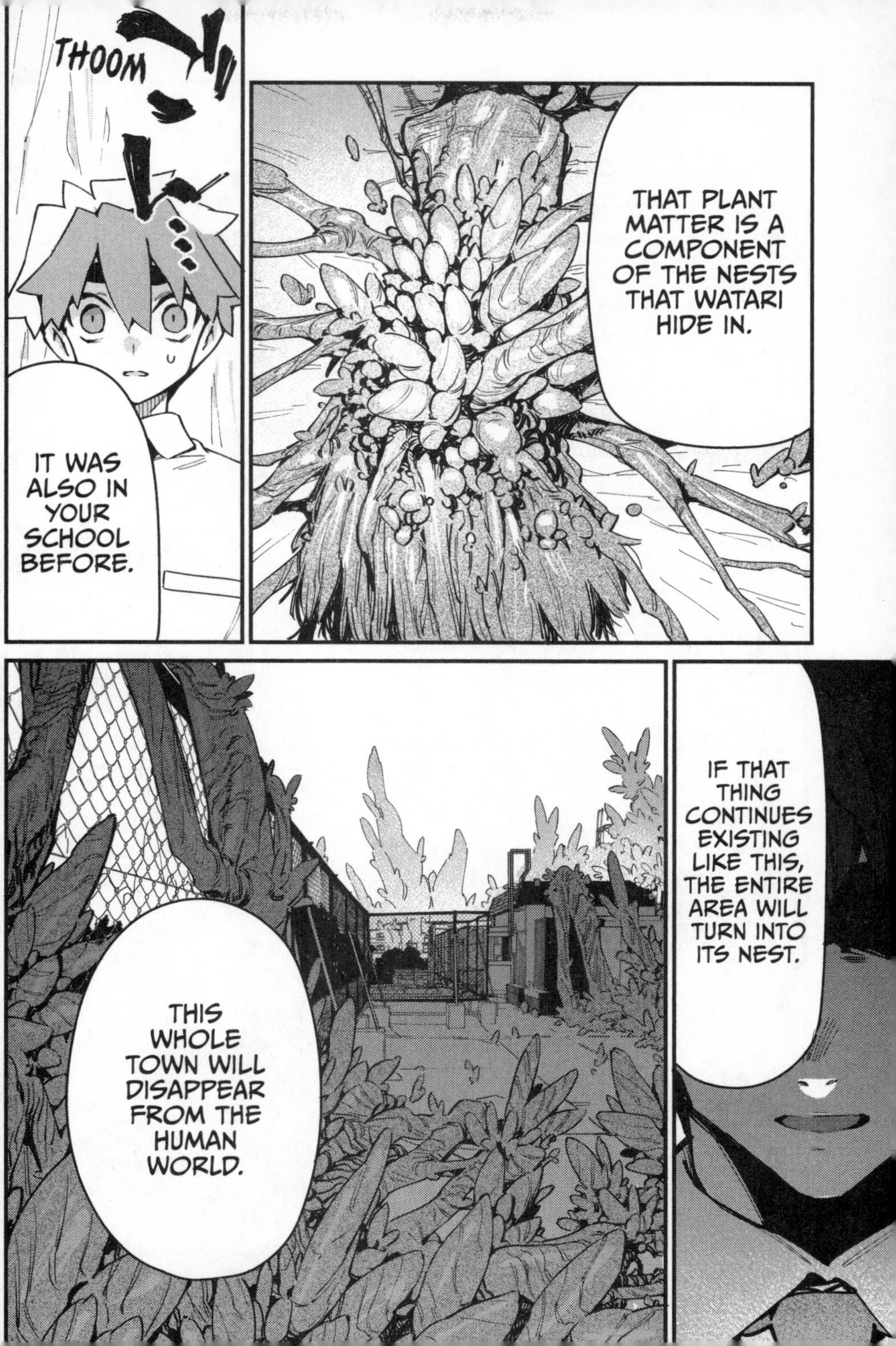
THAT PLANT MATTER IS A COMPONENT OF THE NESTS THAT WATARI HIDE IN.
THOOM
IT WAS ALSO IN YOUR SCHOOL BEFORE.
IF THAT THING CONTINUES EXISTING LIKE THIS, THE ENTIRE AREA WILL TURN INTO ITS NEST.
THIS WHOLE TOWN WILL DISAPPEAR FROM THE HUMAN WORLD.

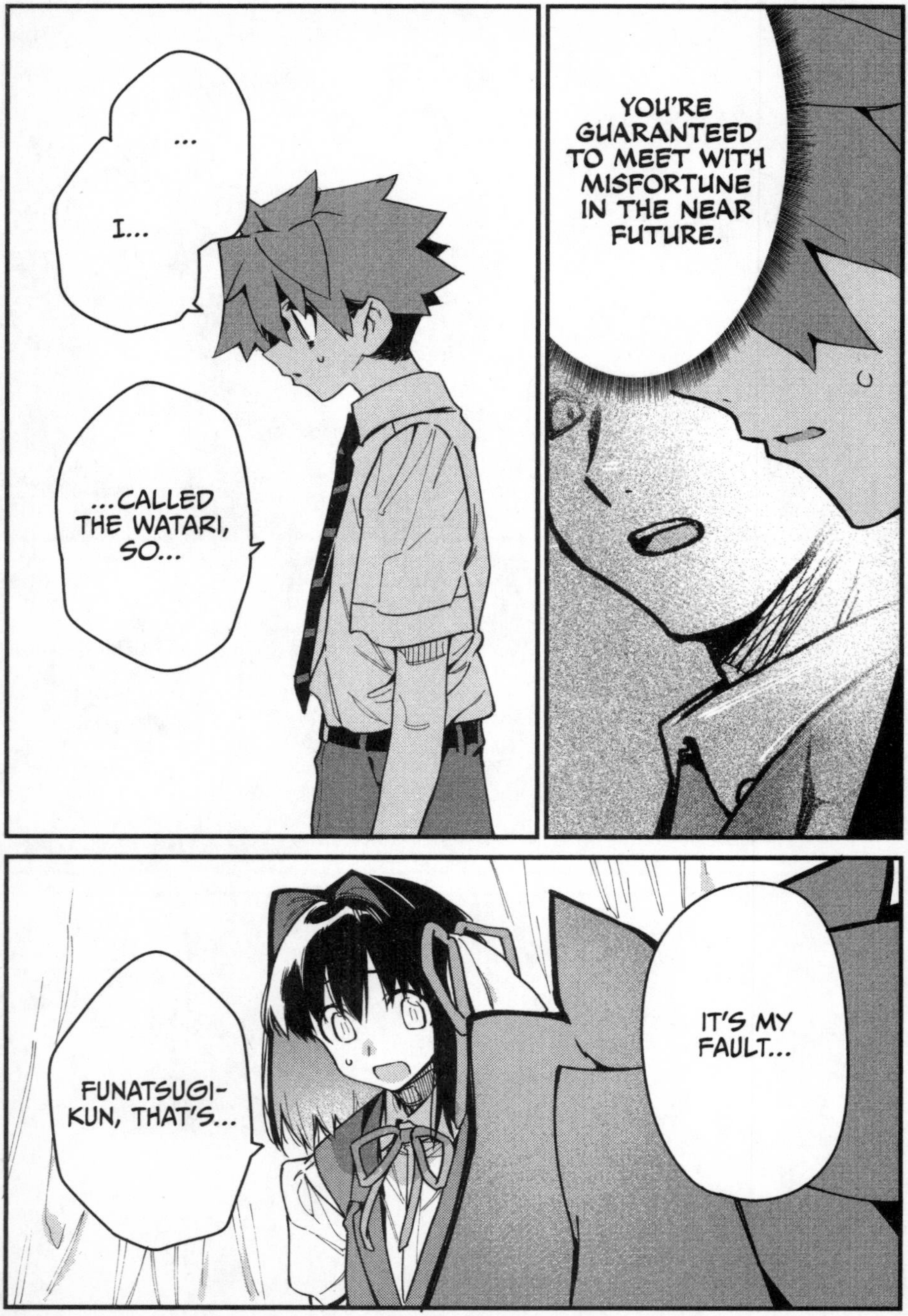
YOU'RE GUARANTEED TO MEET WITH MISFORTUNE IN THE NEAR FUTURE.
...
I...
...CALLED THE WATARI, SO...
IT'S MY FAULT...
FUNATSUGI-KUN, THAT'S...

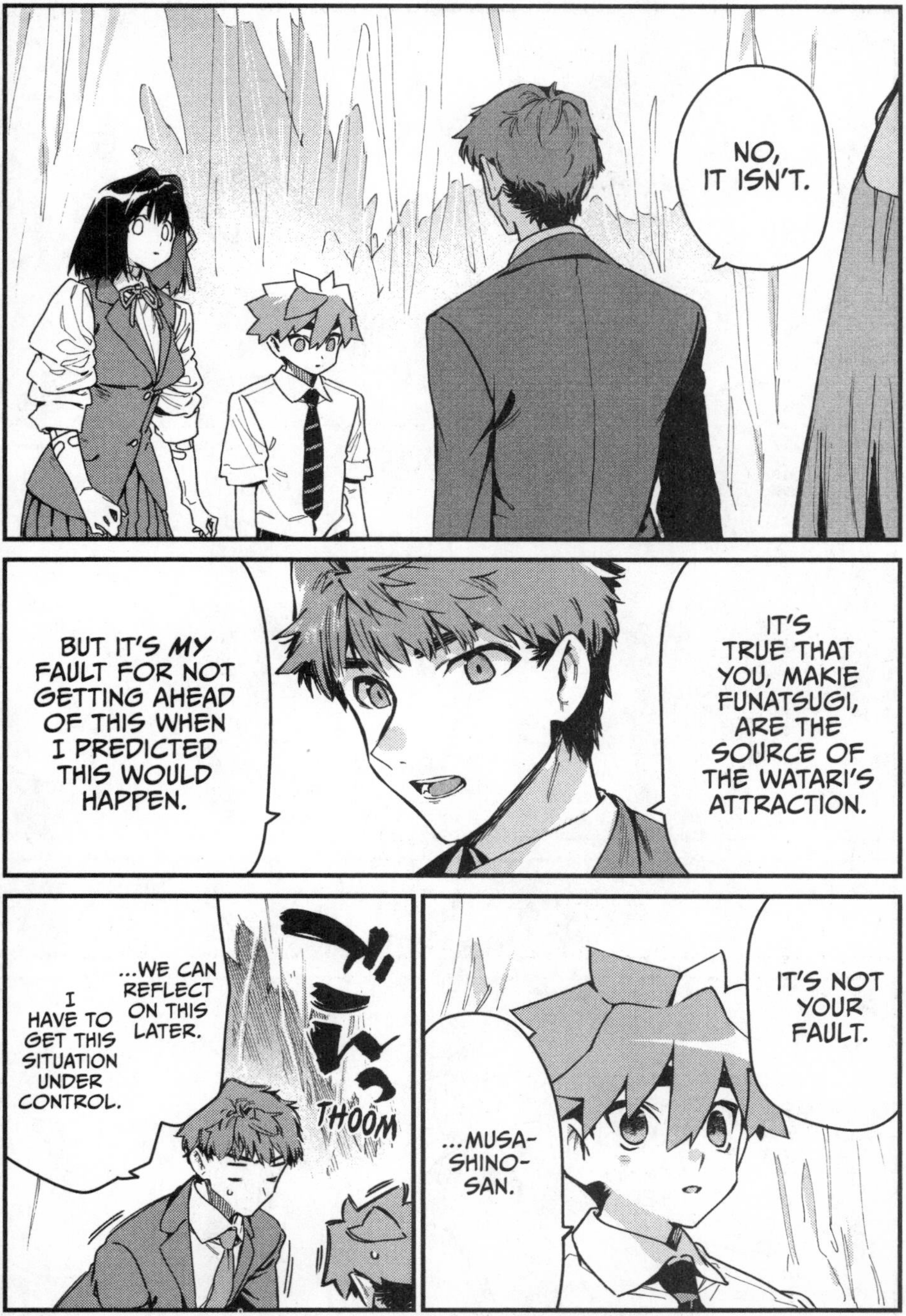
NO, IT ISN'T.
IT'S TRUE THAT YOU, MAKIE FUNATSUGI, ARE THE SOURCE OF THE WATARI'S ATTRACTION.
BUT IT'S *MY* FAULT FOR NOT GETTING AHEAD OF THIS WHEN I PREDICTED THIS WOULD HAPPEN.
IT'S NOT YOUR FAULT.
...MUSA-SHINO-SAN.
...WE CAN REFLECT ON THIS LATER.
I HAVE TO GET THIS SITUATION UNDER CONTROL.
THOOM

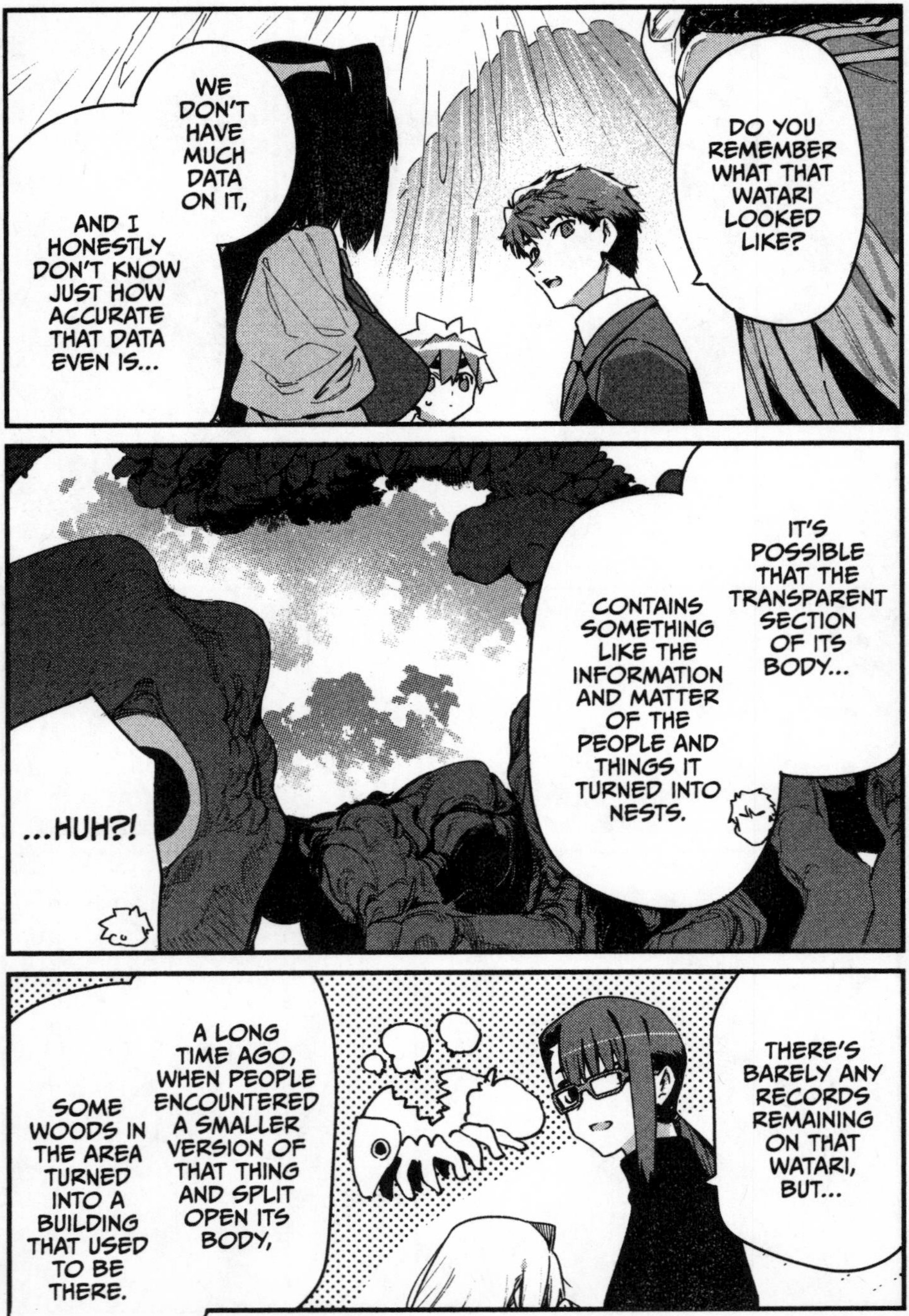
DO YOU REMEMBER WHAT THAT WATARI LOOKED LIKE?
WE DON'T HAVE MUCH DATA ON IT,
AND I HONESTLY DON'T KNOW JUST HOW ACCURATE THAT DATA EVEN IS...
IT'S POSSIBLE THAT THE TRANSPARENT SECTION OF ITS BODY...
CONTAINS SOMETHING LIKE THE INFORMATION AND MATTER OF THE PEOPLE AND THINGS IT TURNED INTO NESTS.
...HUH?!
THERE'S BARELY ANY RECORDS REMAINING ON THAT WATARI, BUT...
A LONG TIME AGO, WHEN PEOPLE ENCOUNTERED A SMALLER VERSION OF THAT THING AND SPLIT OPEN ITS BODY,
SOME WOODS IN THE AREA TURNED INTO A BUILDING THAT USED TO BE THERE.

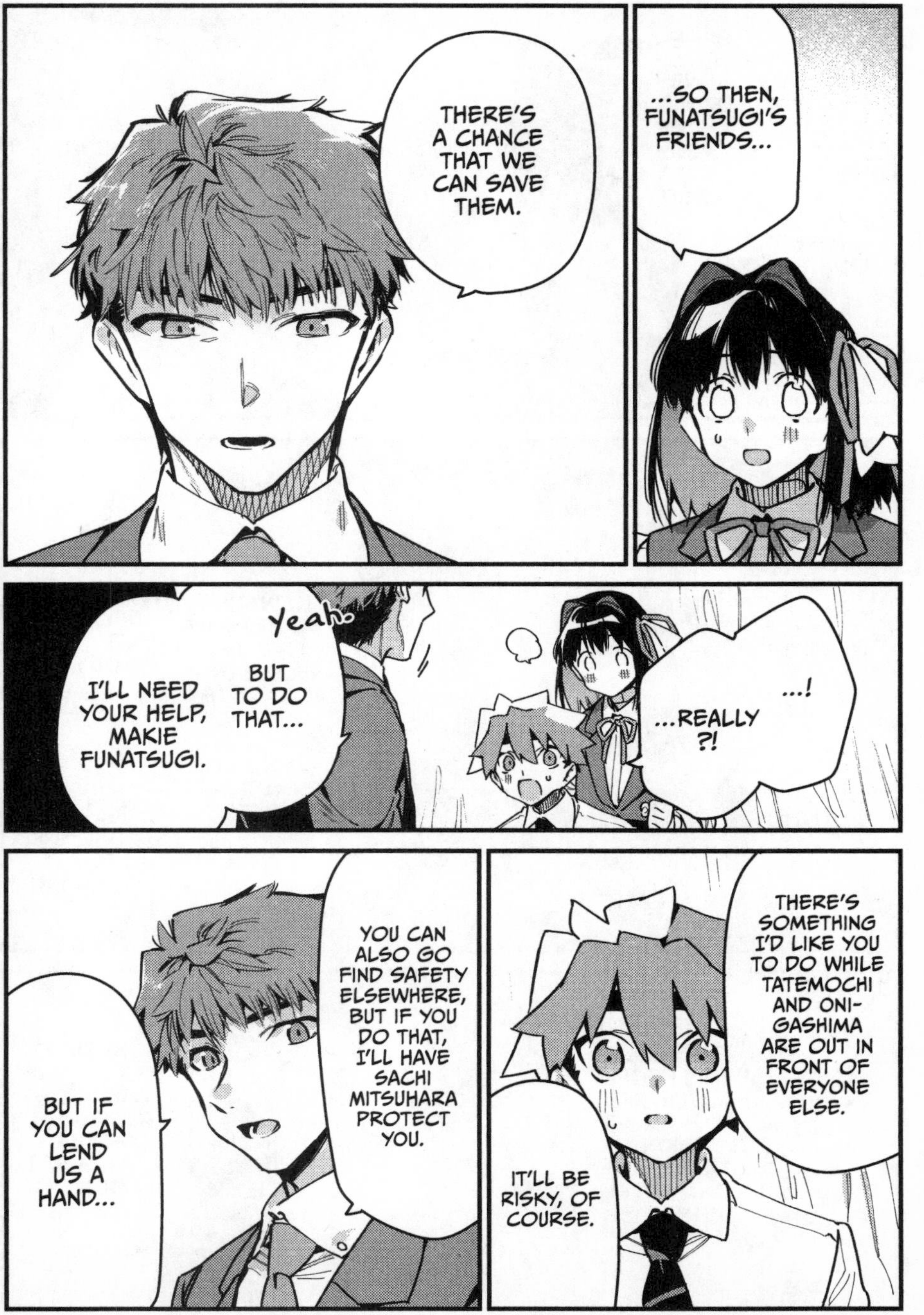
...SO THEN, FUNATSUGI'S FRIENDS...
THERE'S A CHANCE THAT WE CAN SAVE THEM.
...!
...REALLY ?!
Yeah.
BUT TO DO THAT...
I'LL NEED YOUR HELP, MAKIE FUNATSUGI.
THERE'S SOMETHING I'D LIKE YOU TO DO WHILE TATEMOCHI AND ONI-GASHIMA ARE OUT IN FRONT OF EVERYONE ELSE.
IT'LL BE RISKY, OF COURSE.
YOU CAN ALSO GO FIND SAFETY ELSEWHERE, BUT IF YOU DO THAT, I'LL HAVE SACHI MITSUHARA PROTECT YOU.
BUT IF YOU CAN LEND US A HAND...

...
...I...
Now
WA...

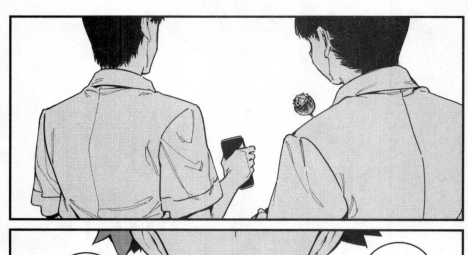

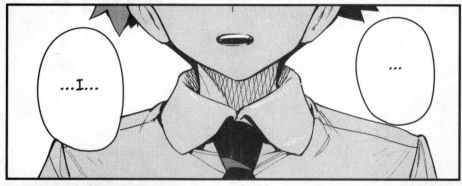

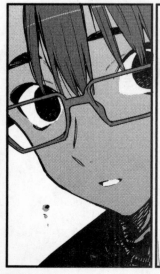

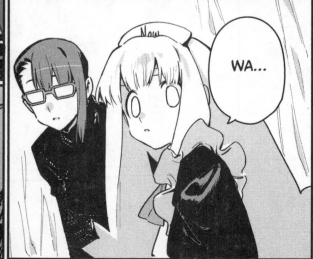

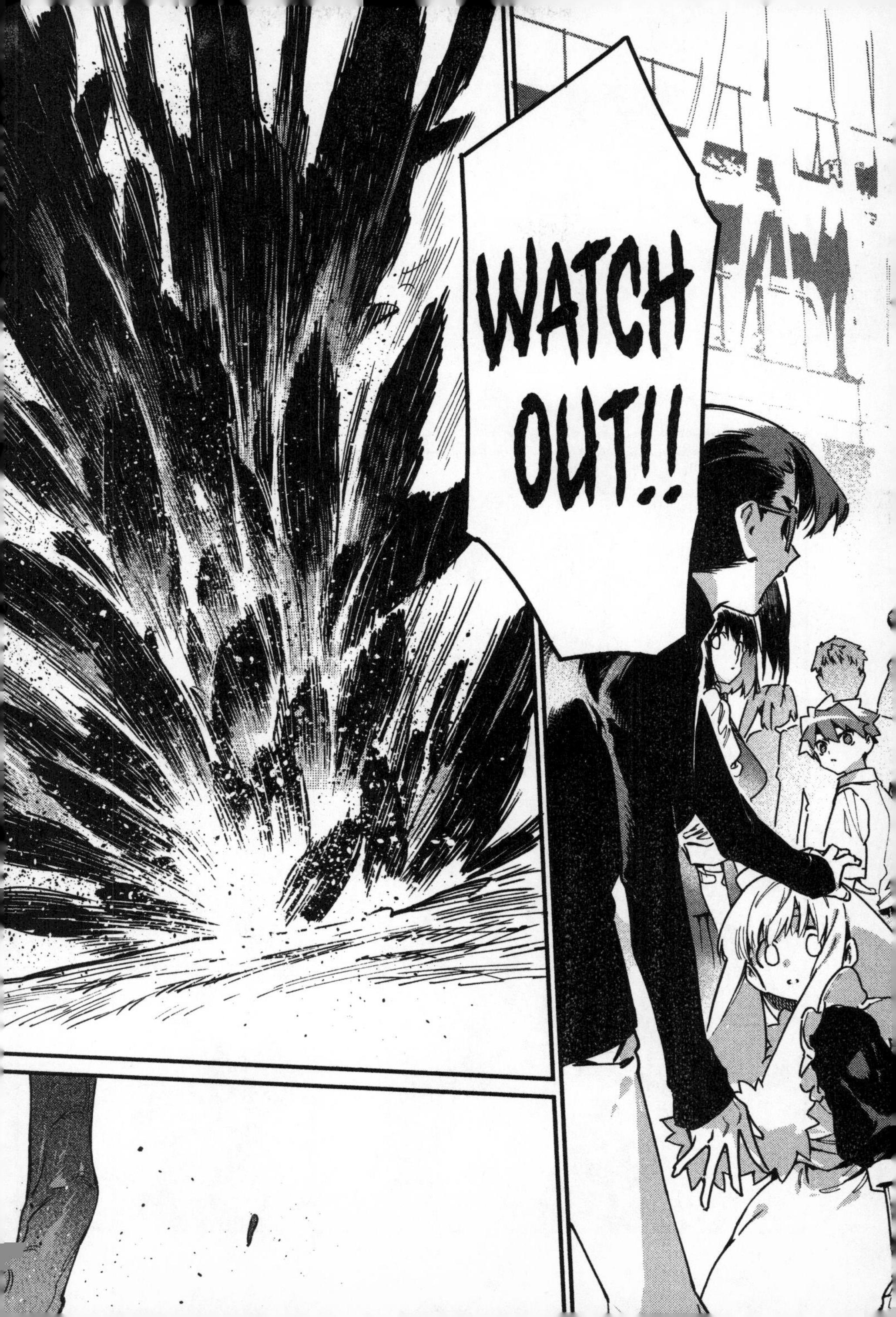
WATCH OUT!!

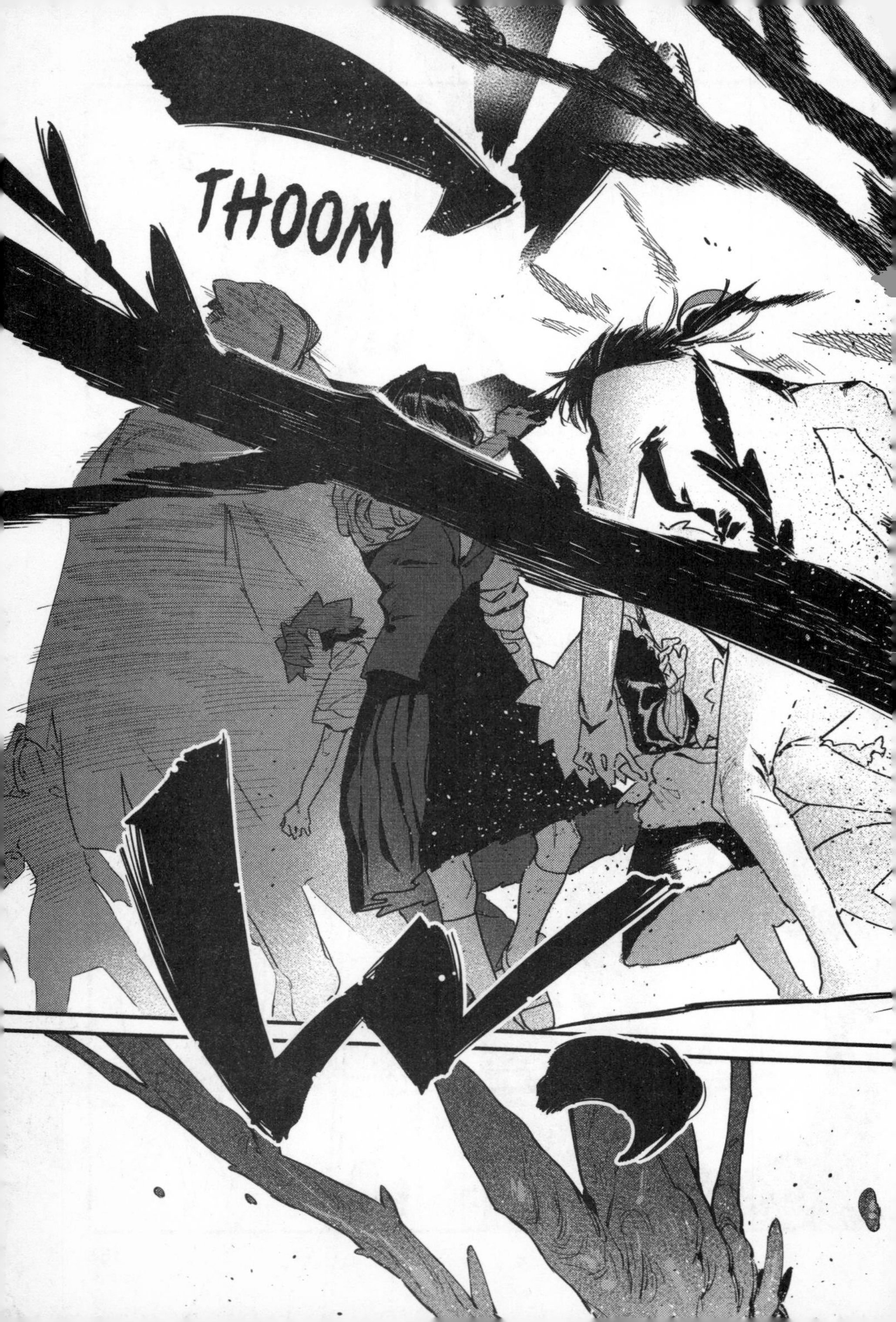
THOOM

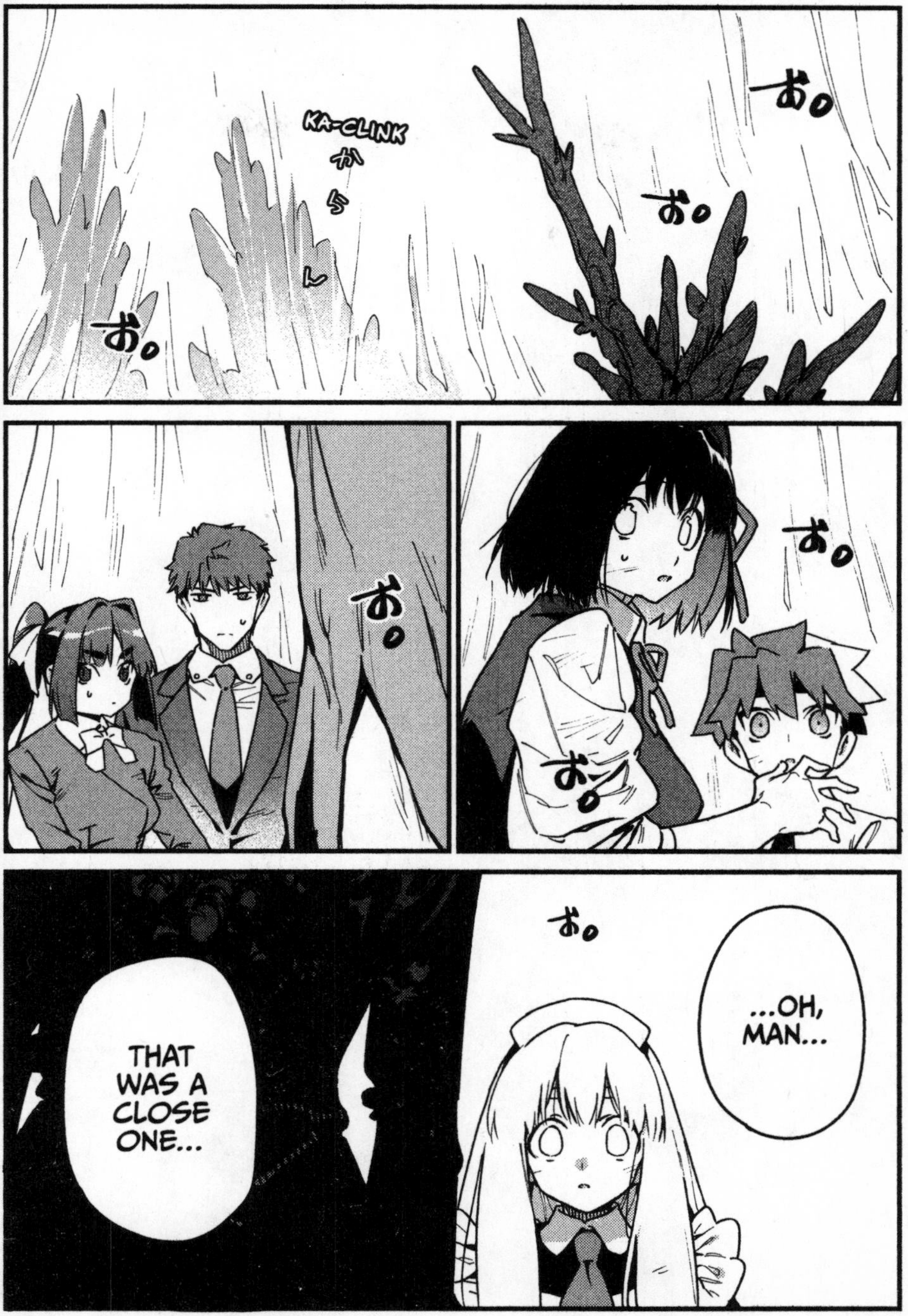
お。
お。
KA-CLINK
からん
お。
お。
お。
お。
お。
...OH, MAN...
THAT WAS A CLOSE ONE...

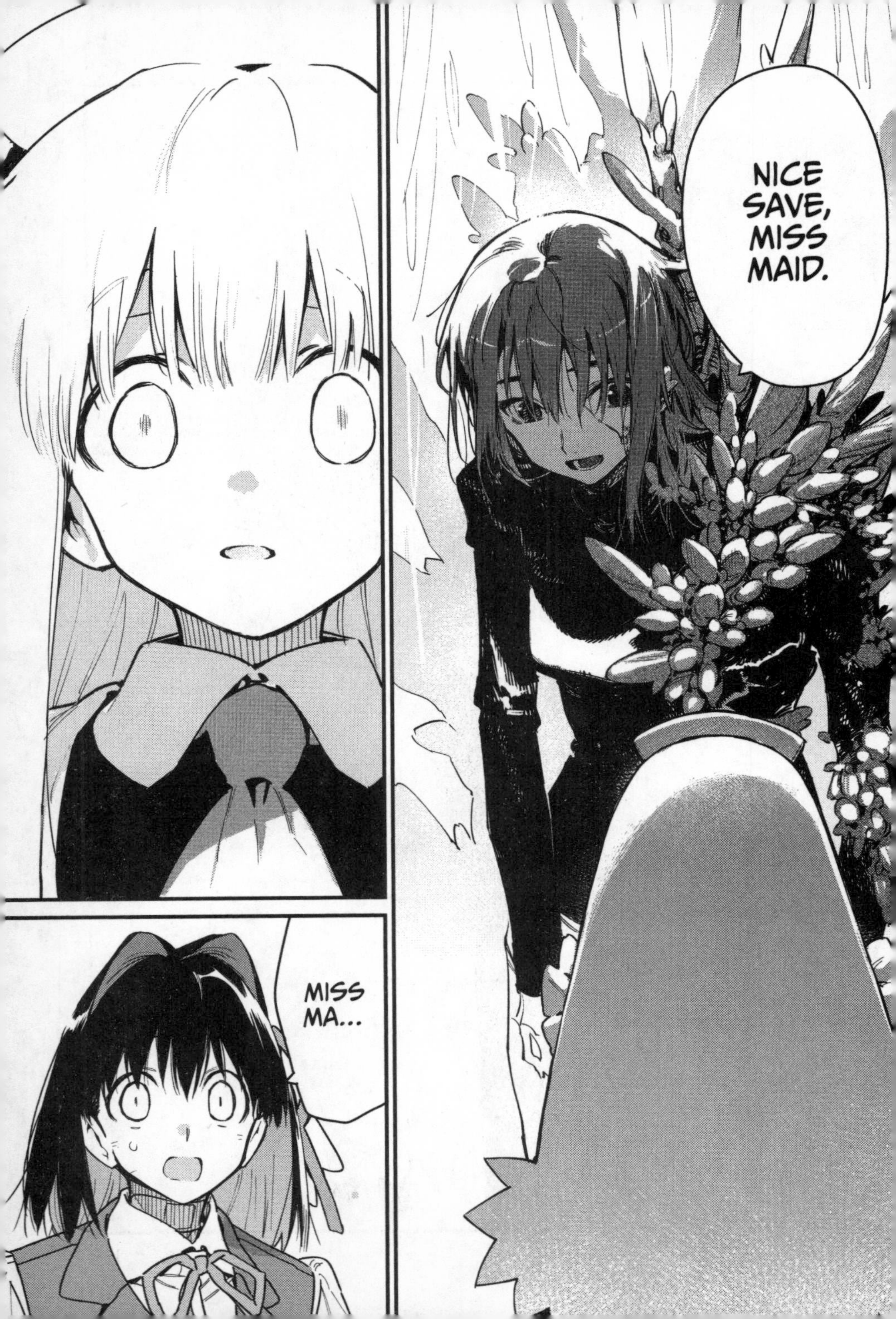
NICE SAVE, MISS MAID.
MISS MA...

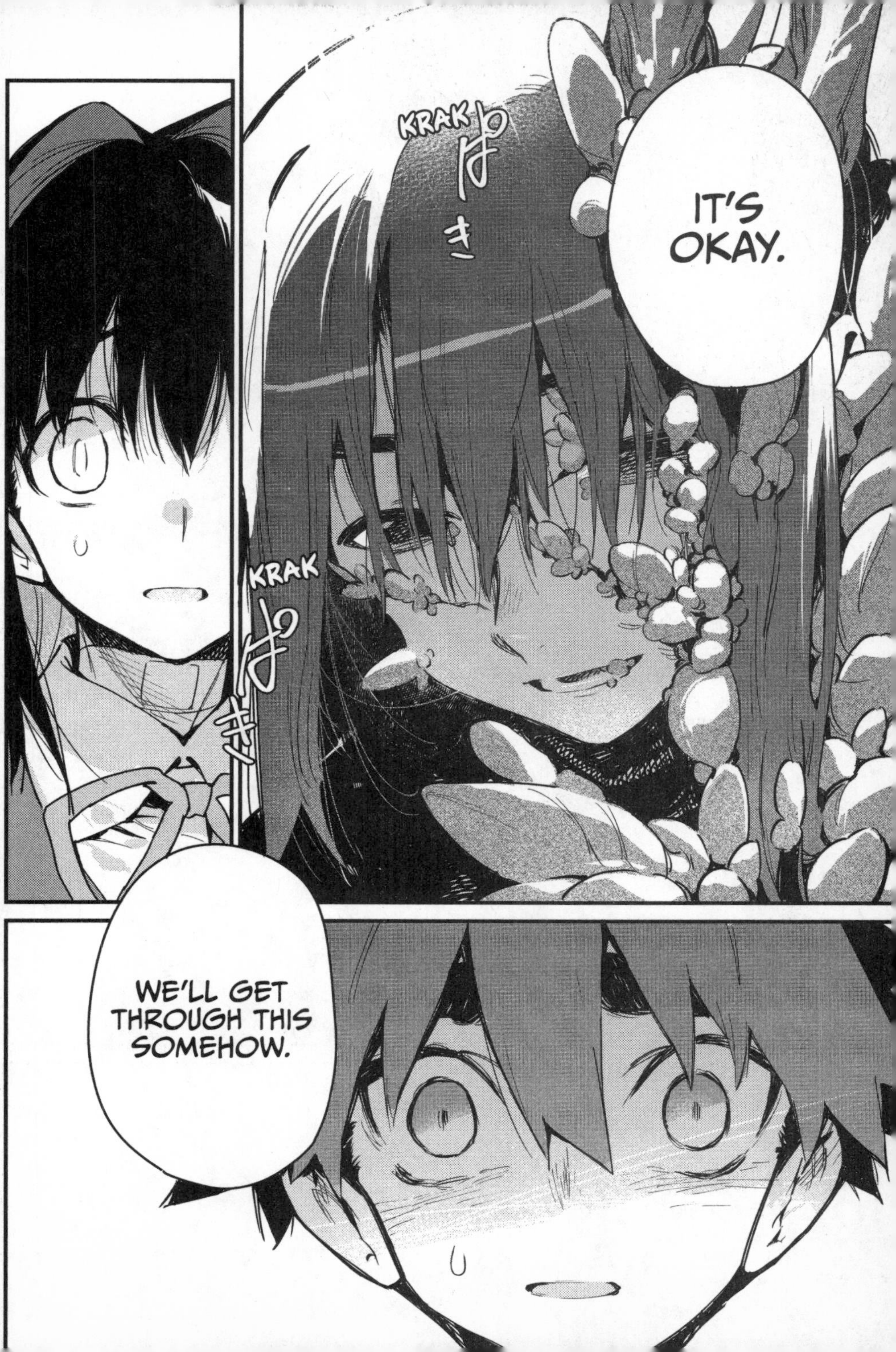
KRAK ぱき
IT'S OKAY.
KRAK ぱき
WE'LL GET THROUGH THIS SOMEHOW.

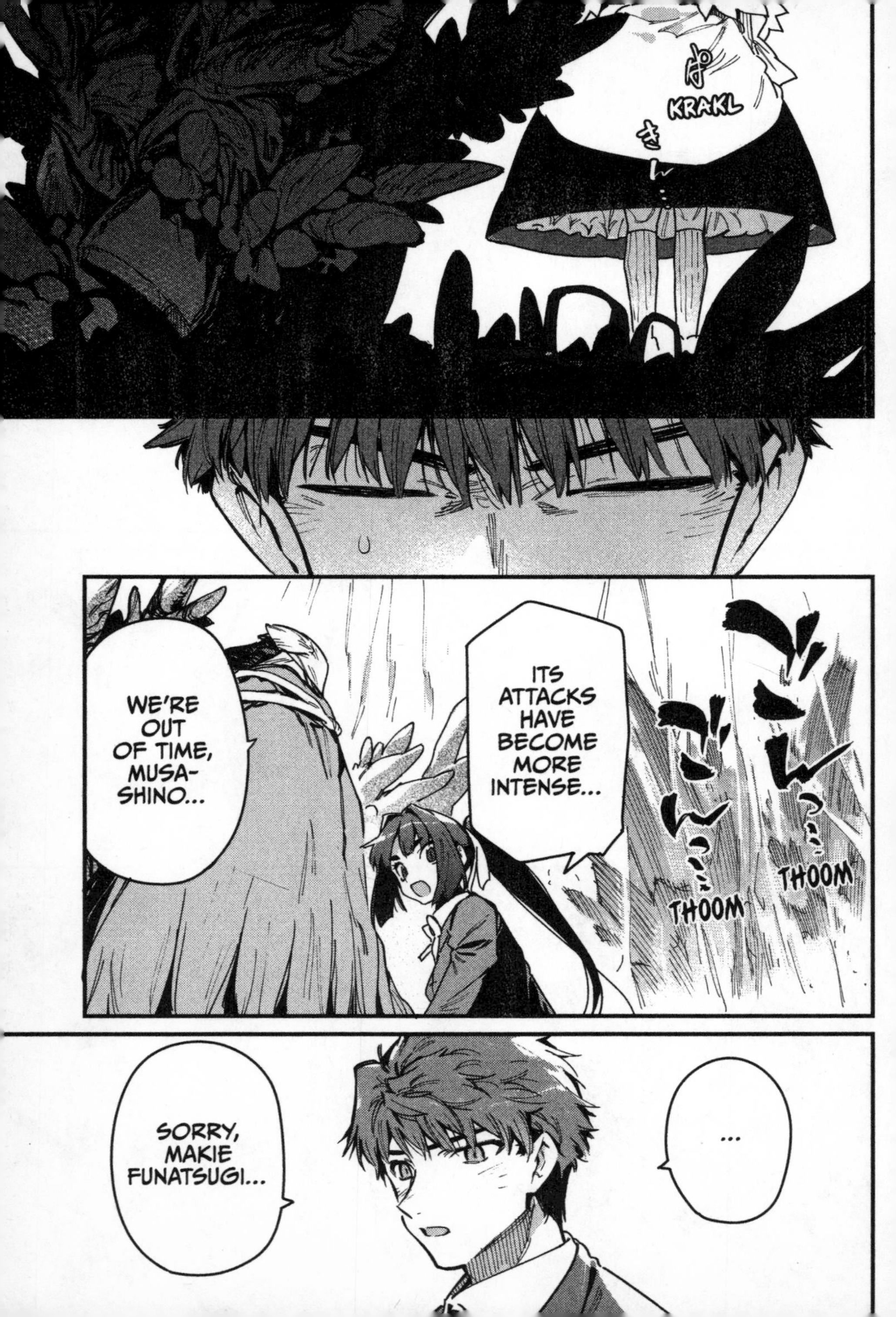
KRAKL
THOOM
THOOM
ITS ATTACKS HAVE BECOME MORE INTENSE...
WE'RE OUT OF TIME, MUSA-SHINO...
...
SORRY, MAKIE FUNATSUGI...

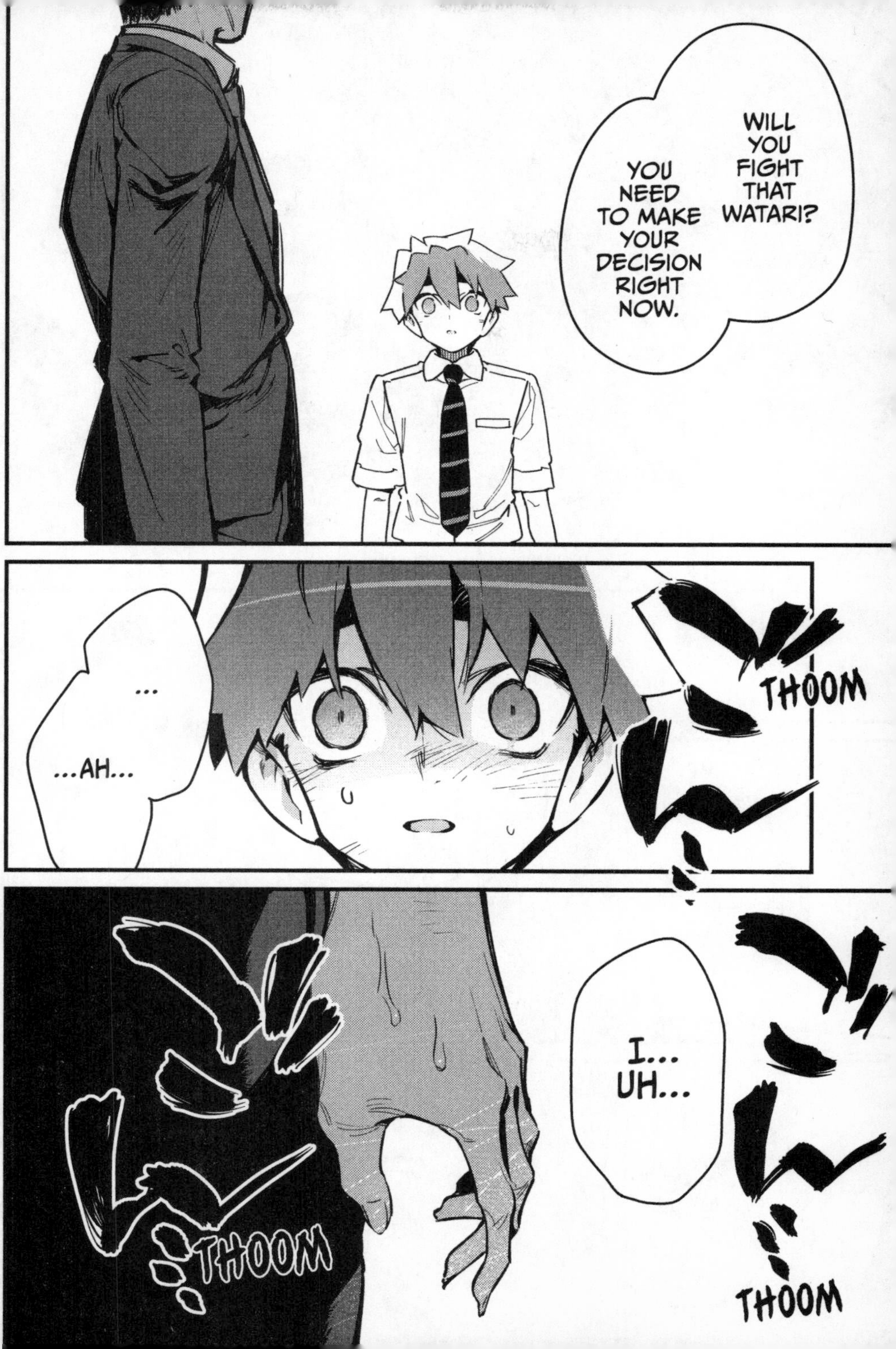
WILL YOU FIGHT THAT WATARI?
YOU NEED TO MAKE YOUR DECISION RIGHT NOW.
THOOM
...
...AH...
THOOM
I... UH...
THOOM

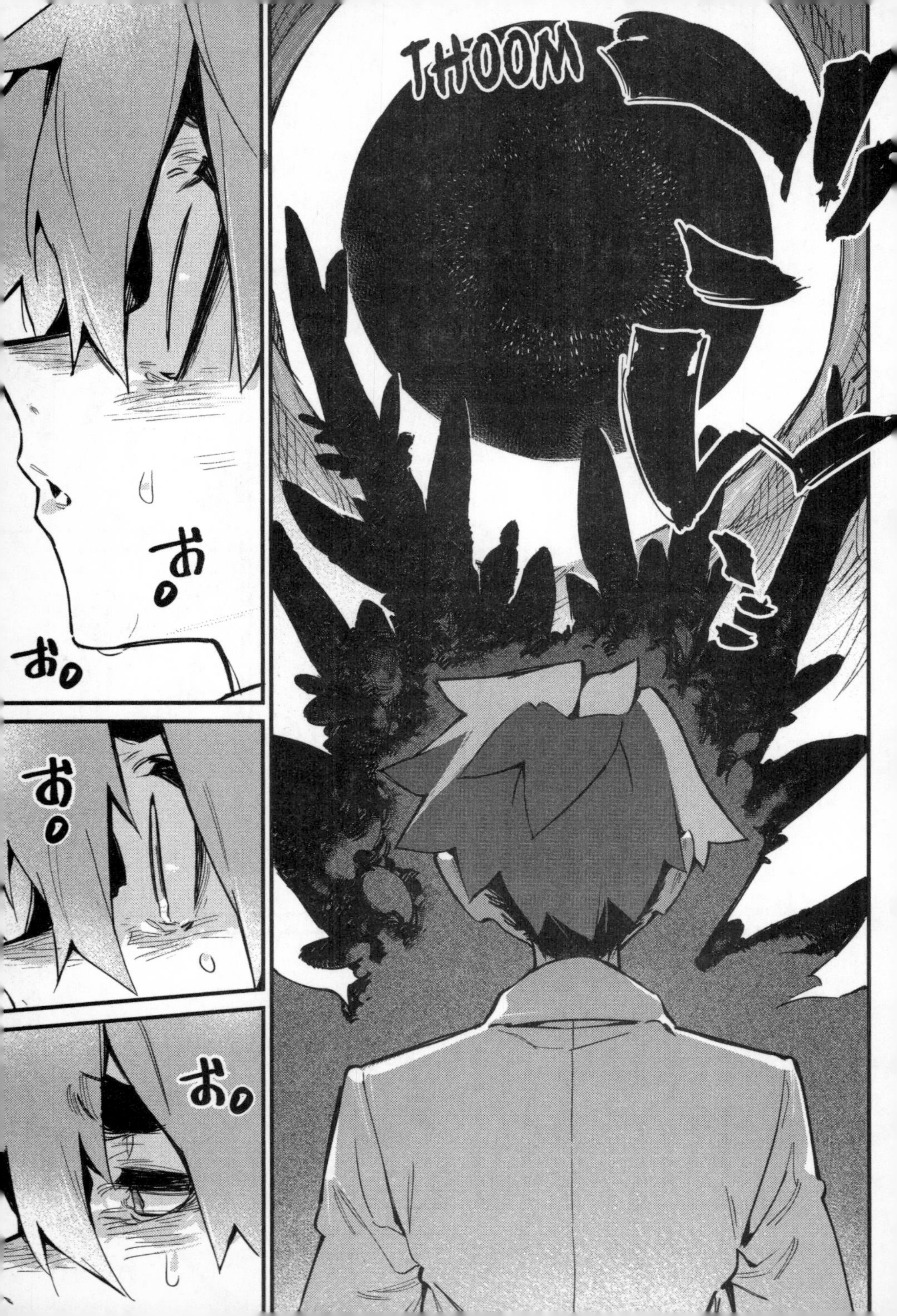
THOOM
お。
お。
お。
お。

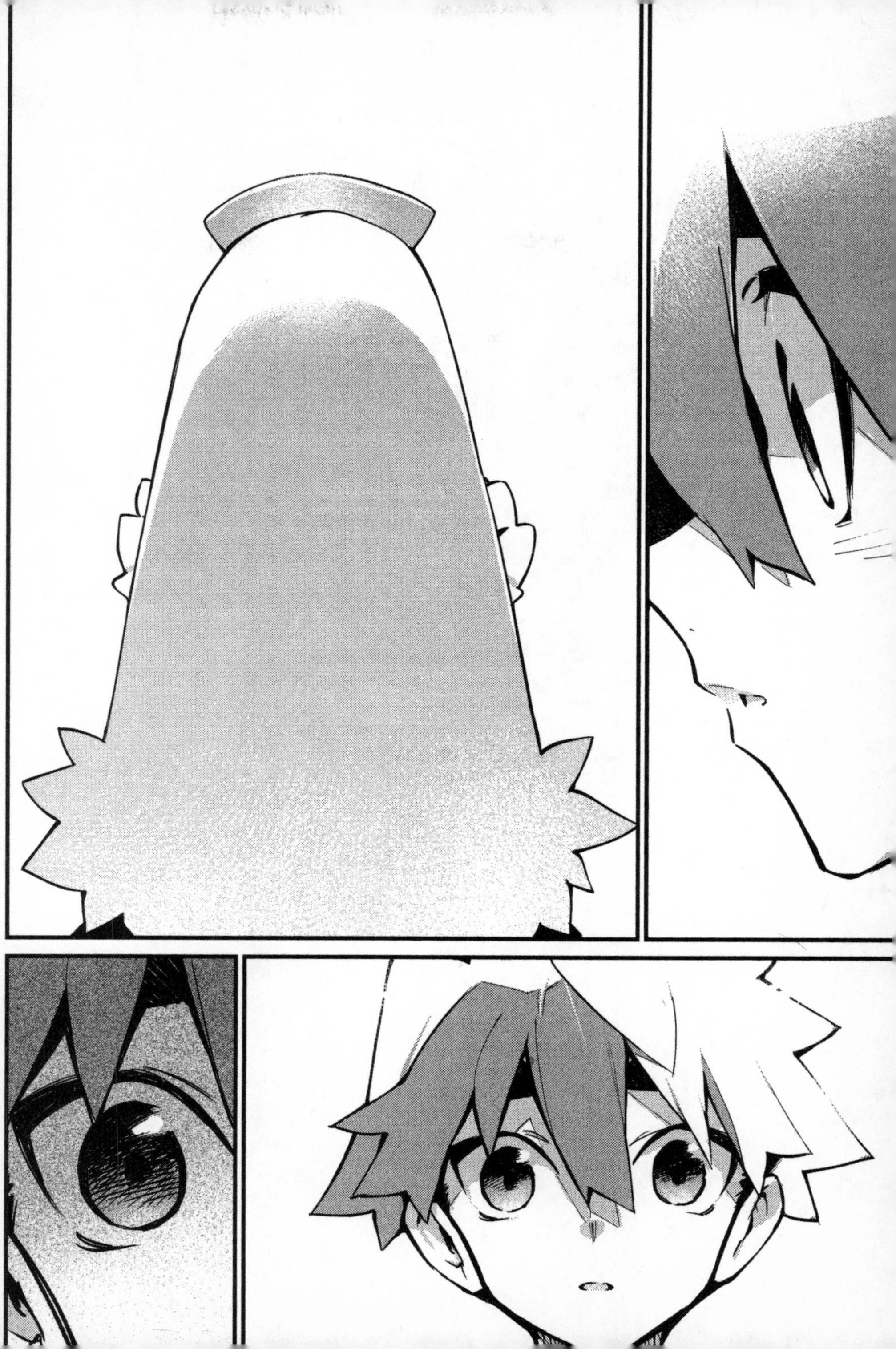

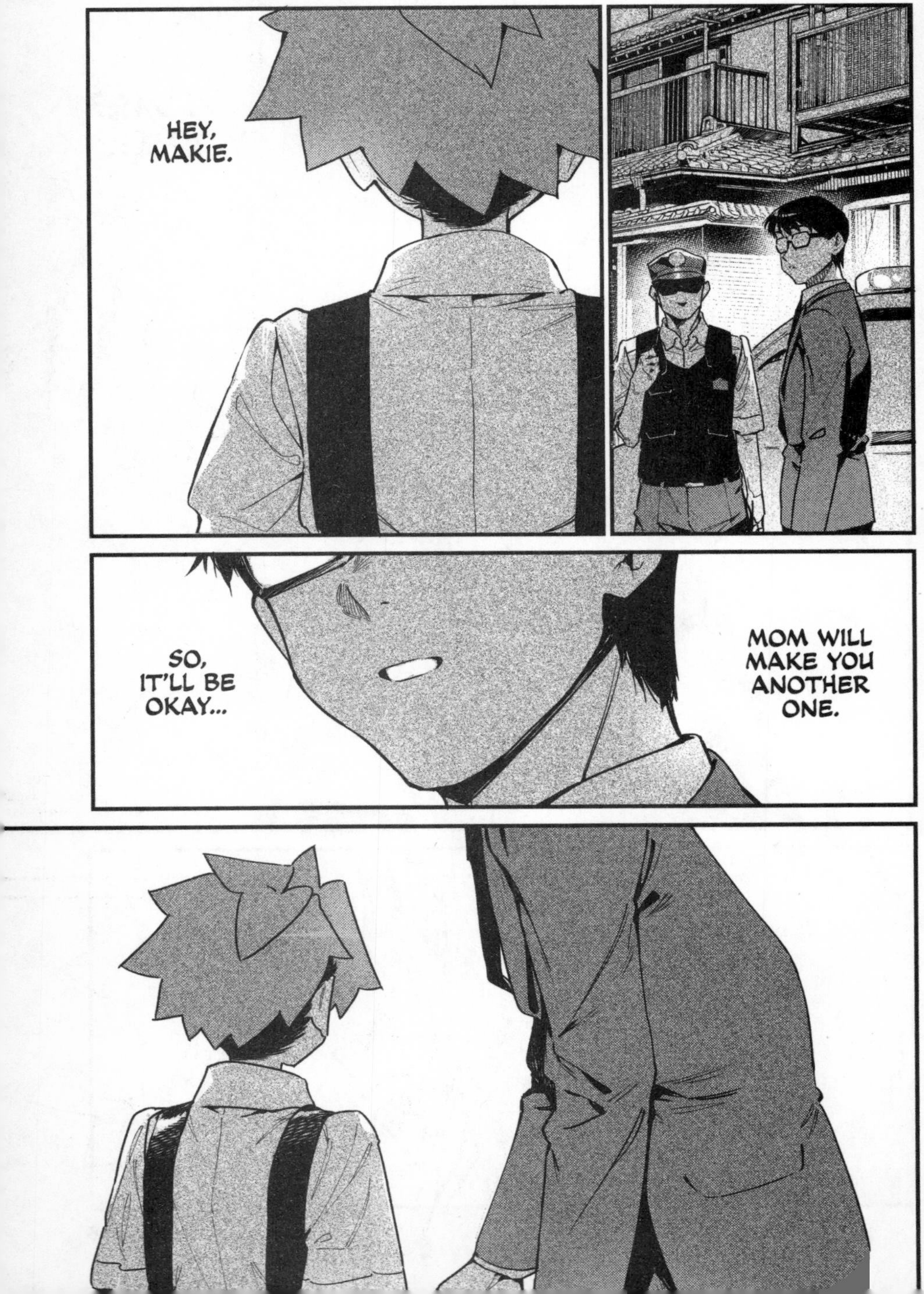
HEY, MAKIE.
MOM WILL MAKE YOU ANOTHER ONE.
SO, IT'LL BE OKAY...

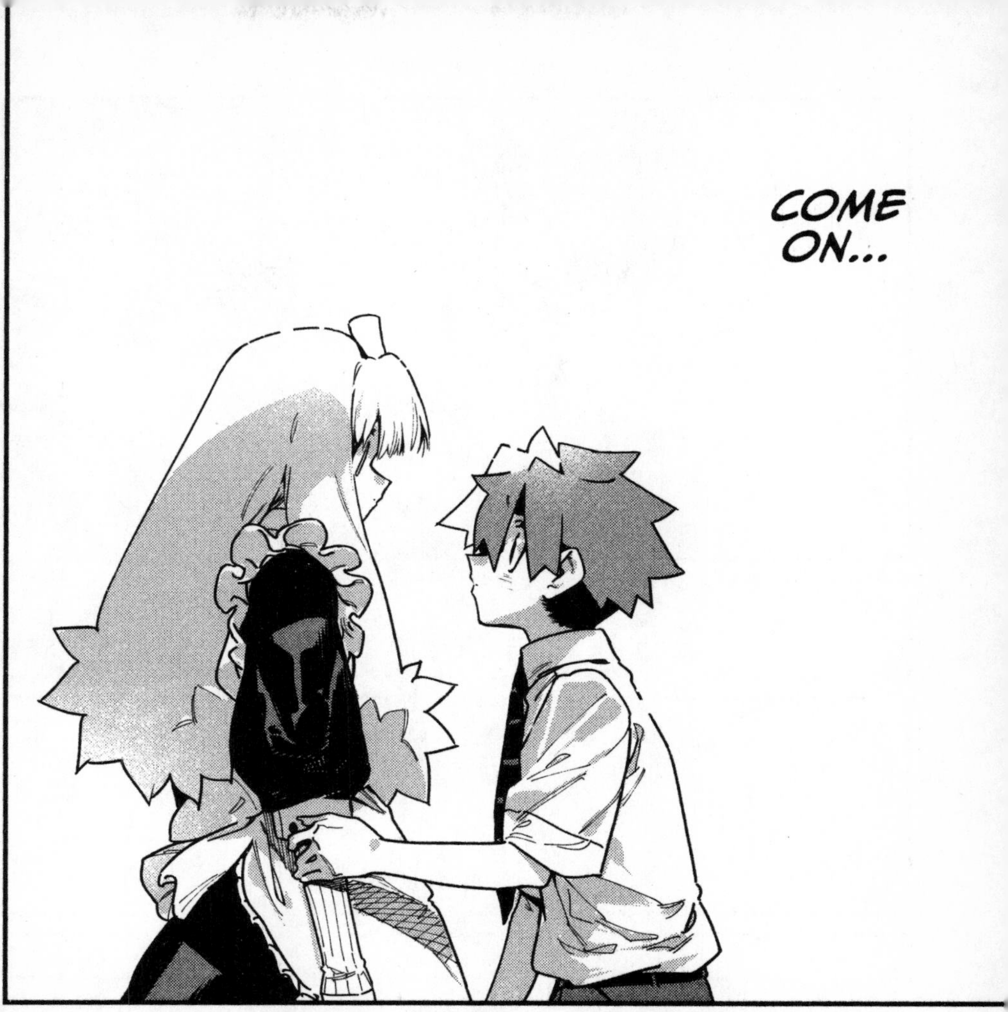
COME ON...
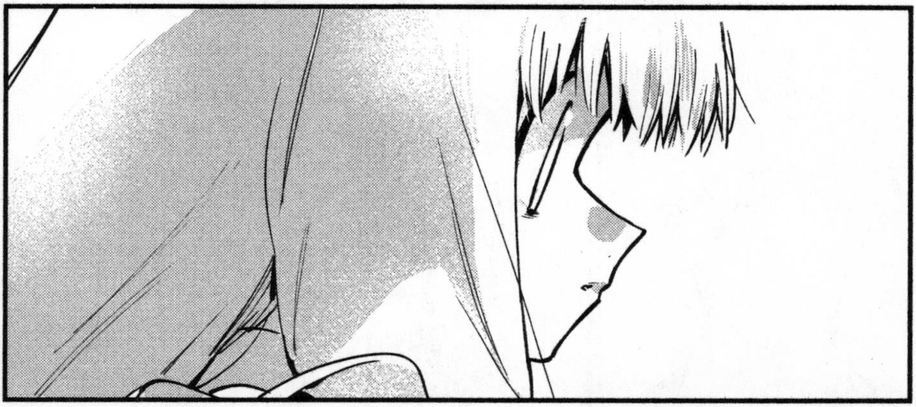

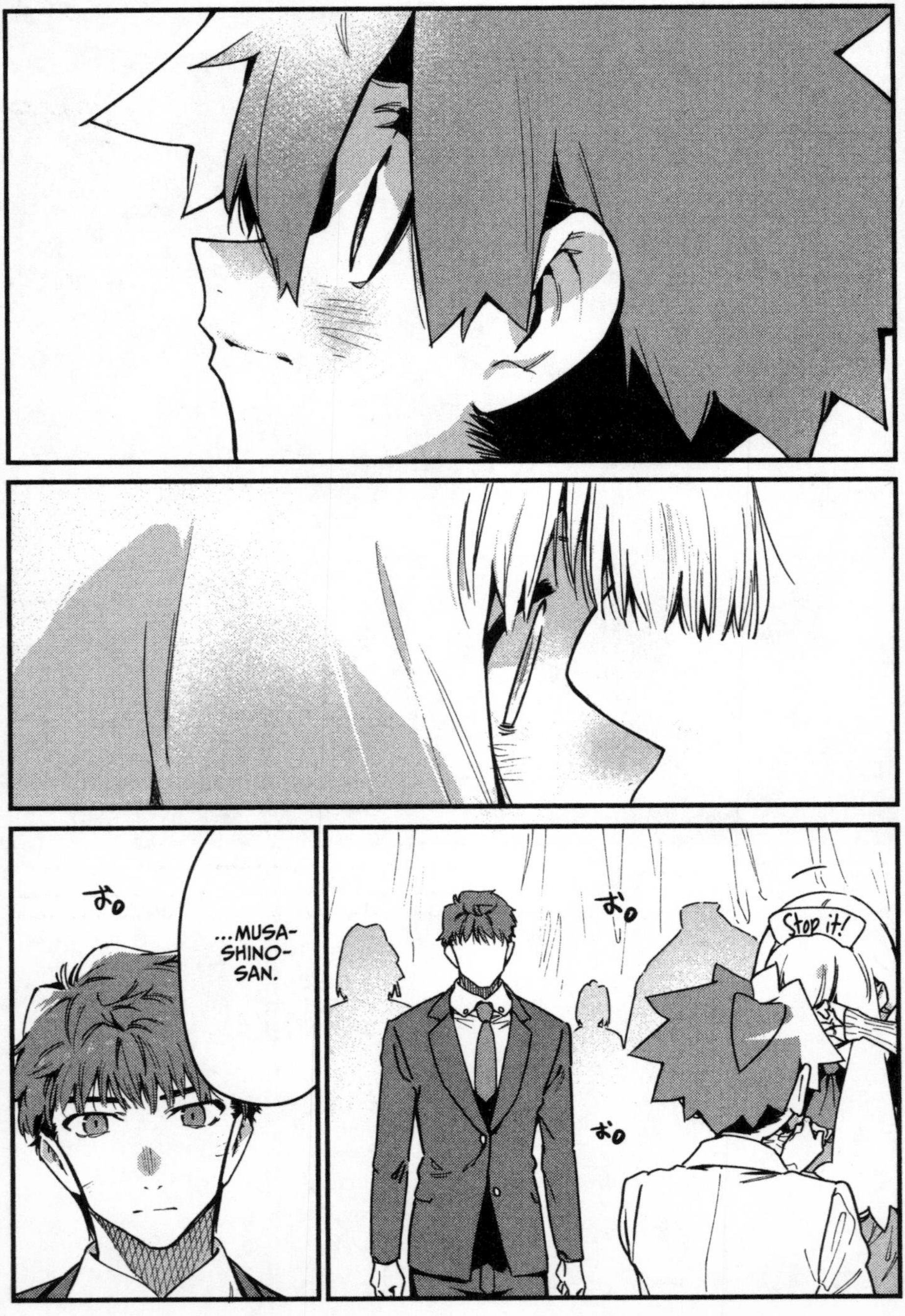
Stop it!
お。
お。
...MUSA-SHINO-SAN.
お。

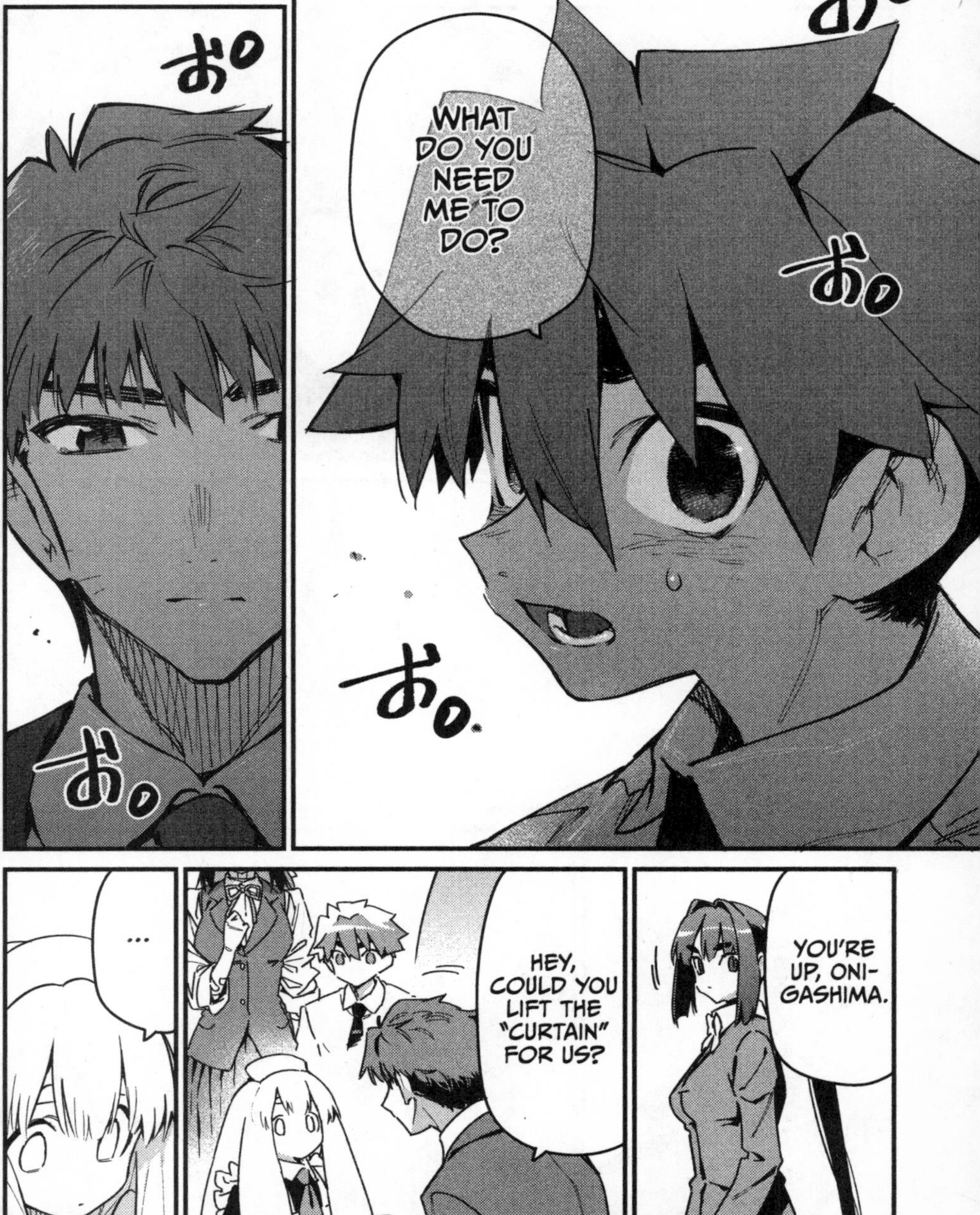
お
WHAT DO YOU NEED ME TO DO?
お
お
お
お
YOU'RE UP, ONI-GASHIMA.
HEY, COULD YOU LIFT THE "CURTAIN" FOR US?
...

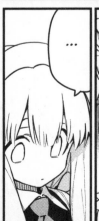

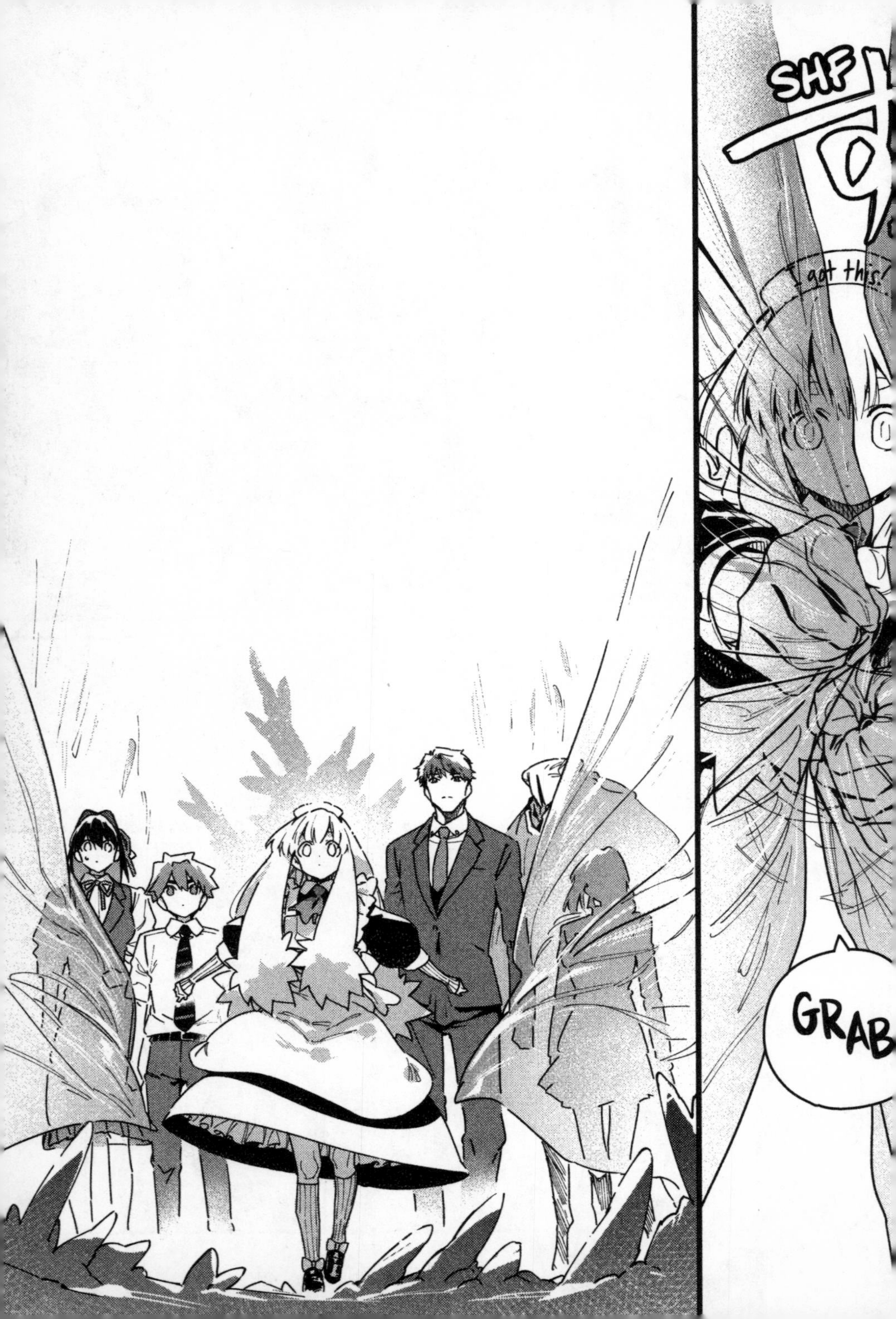
SHF
I got this!
GRAB

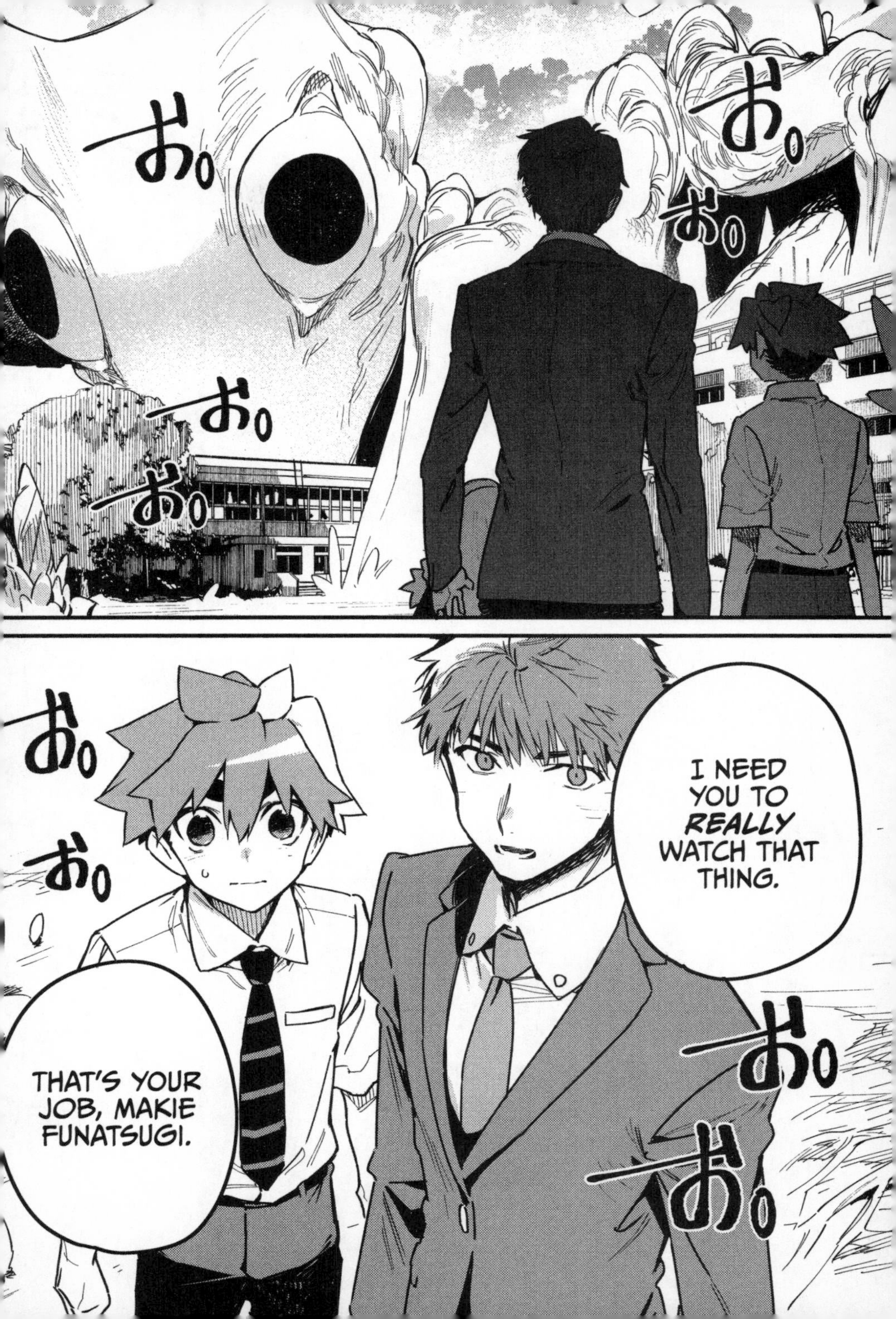
I NEED YOU TO *REALLY* WATCH THAT THING.
THAT'S YOUR JOB, MAKIE FUNATSUGI.

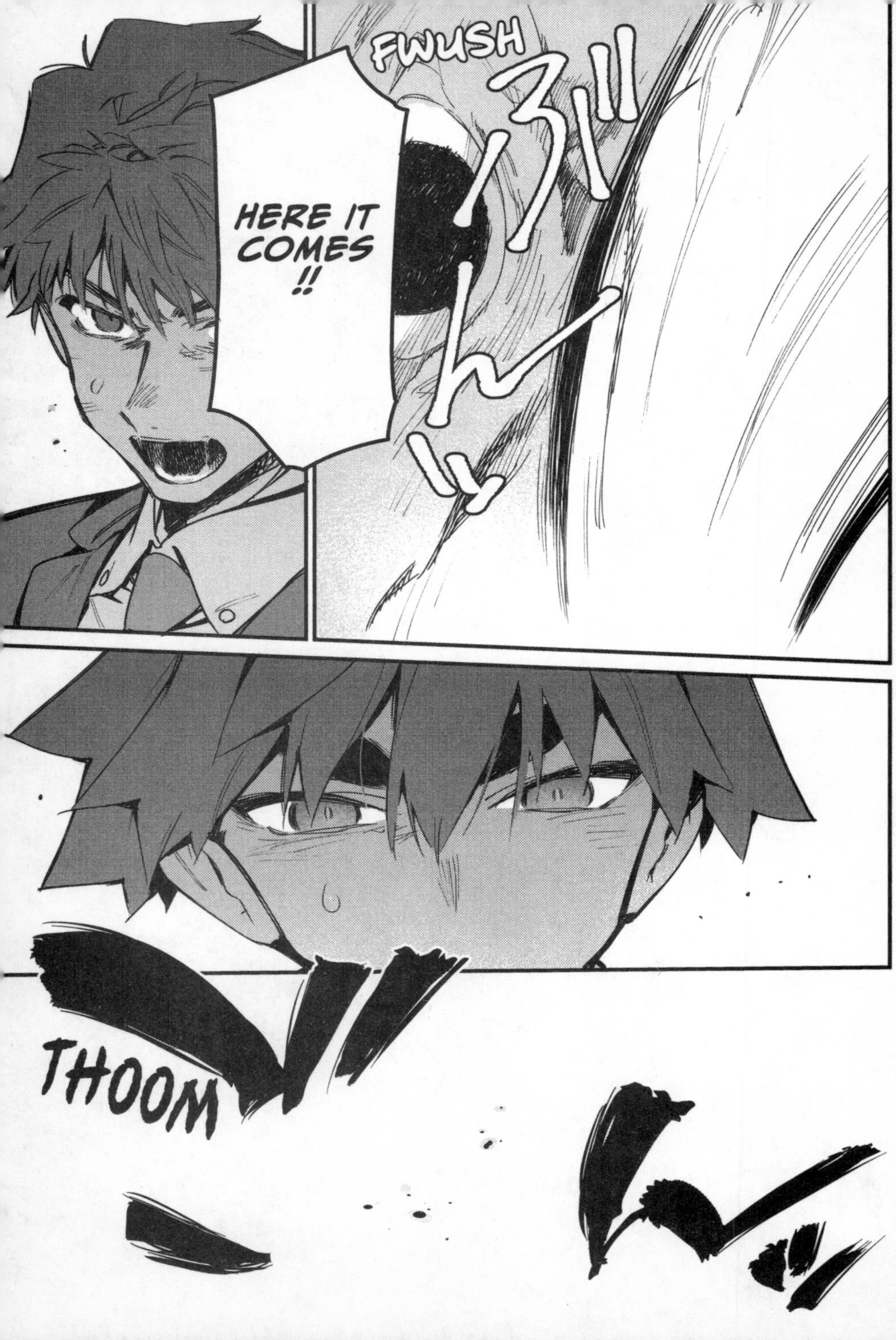
FWUSH
HERE IT COMES !!
THOOM

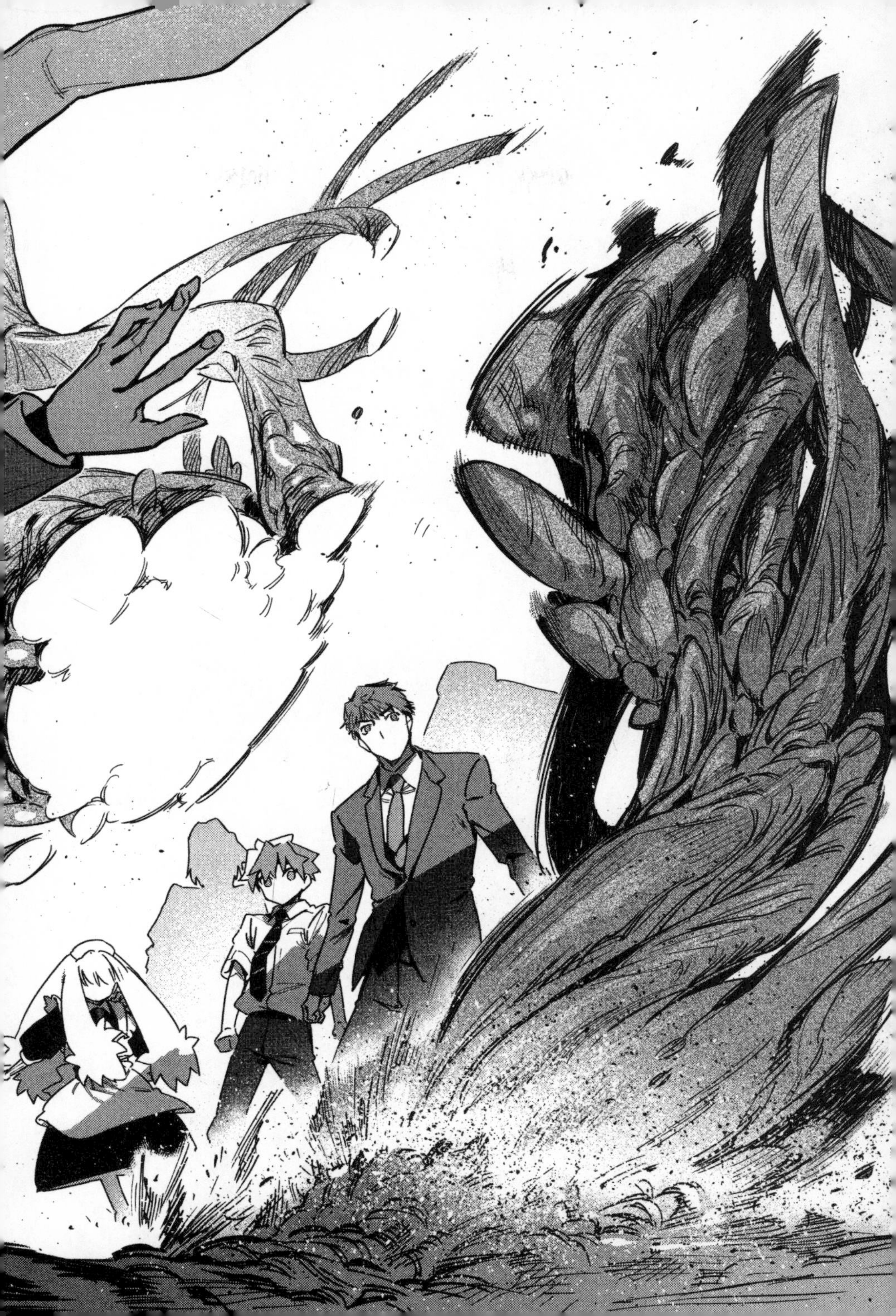

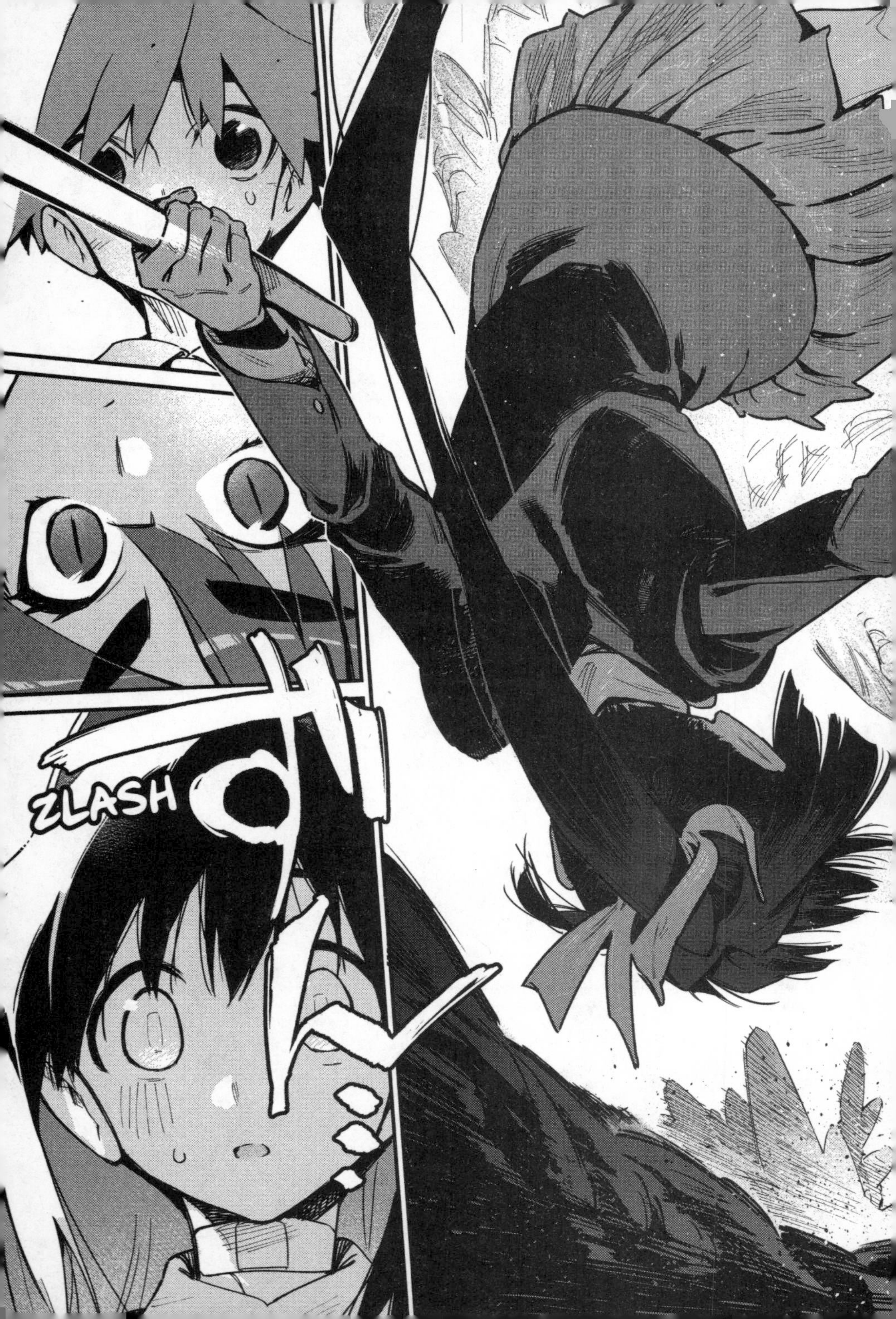
ZLASH

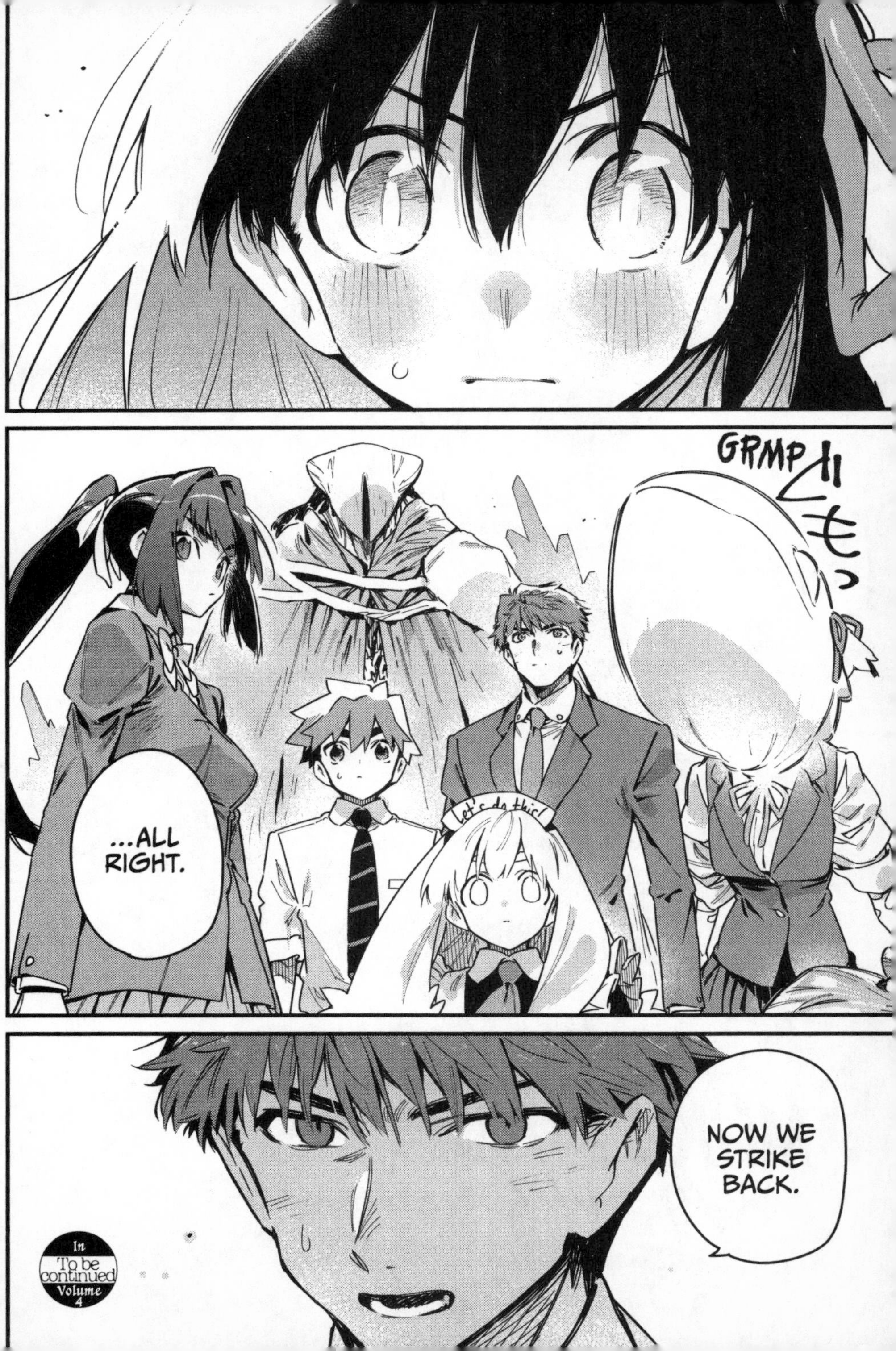
GRMP
ぐもっ
Let's do this!
...ALL RIGHT.
NOW WE STRIKE BACK.
In
To be continued
Volume 4

Sachi's
MONSTROUS
Appetite

Continued in Volume 4

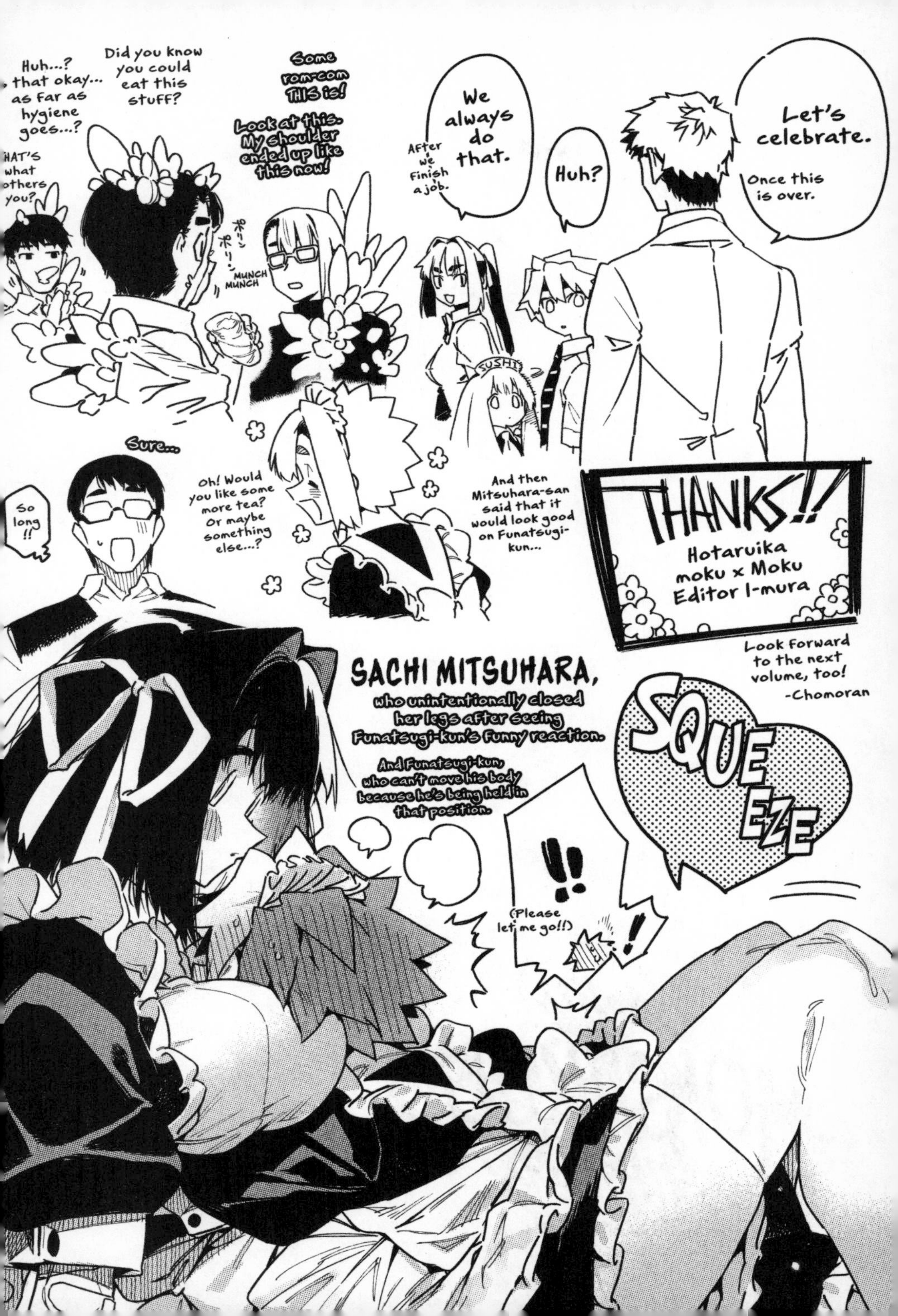

Let's celebrate.
Once this is over.
Huh?
We always do that.
After we finish a job.
Some rom-com THIS is!
Look at this. My shoulder ended up like this now!
ポリ ポリ
MUNCH MUNCH
SUSHI
Did you know you could eat this stuff?
Huh...? that okay... as far as hygiene goes...?
HAT'S what others you?
THANKS!!
Hotaruika
moku x Moku
Editor I-mura
And then Mitsuhara-san said that it would look good on Funatsugi-kun...
Oh! Would you like some more tea? Or maybe something else...?
Sure...
So long!!
Look forward to the next volume, too!
-Chomoran
SQUEEZE
SACHI MITSUHARA,
who unintentionally closed her legs after seeing Funatsugi-kun's funny reaction.
And Funatsugi-kun, who can't move his body because he's being held in that position.
!!
(Please let me go!!)
!

Sachi's
MONSTROUS
Appetite

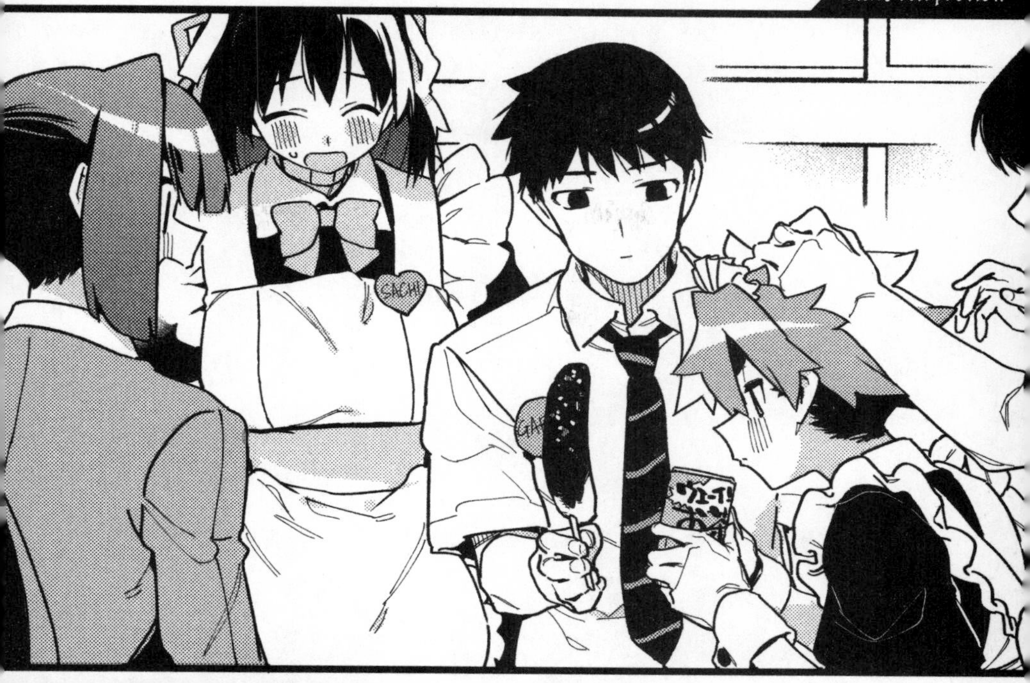
SACHI

Let's take back our Cultural Festival!

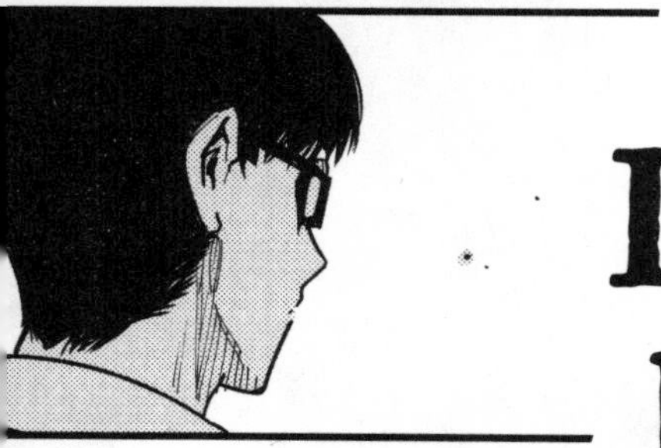

o deal with the colossal *watari*, Iusashino executes an aerial peration. Will Makie be able to ılfill his duties and reunite vith his father?

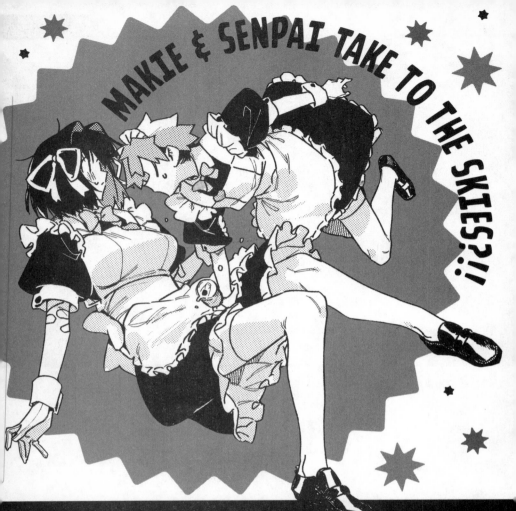

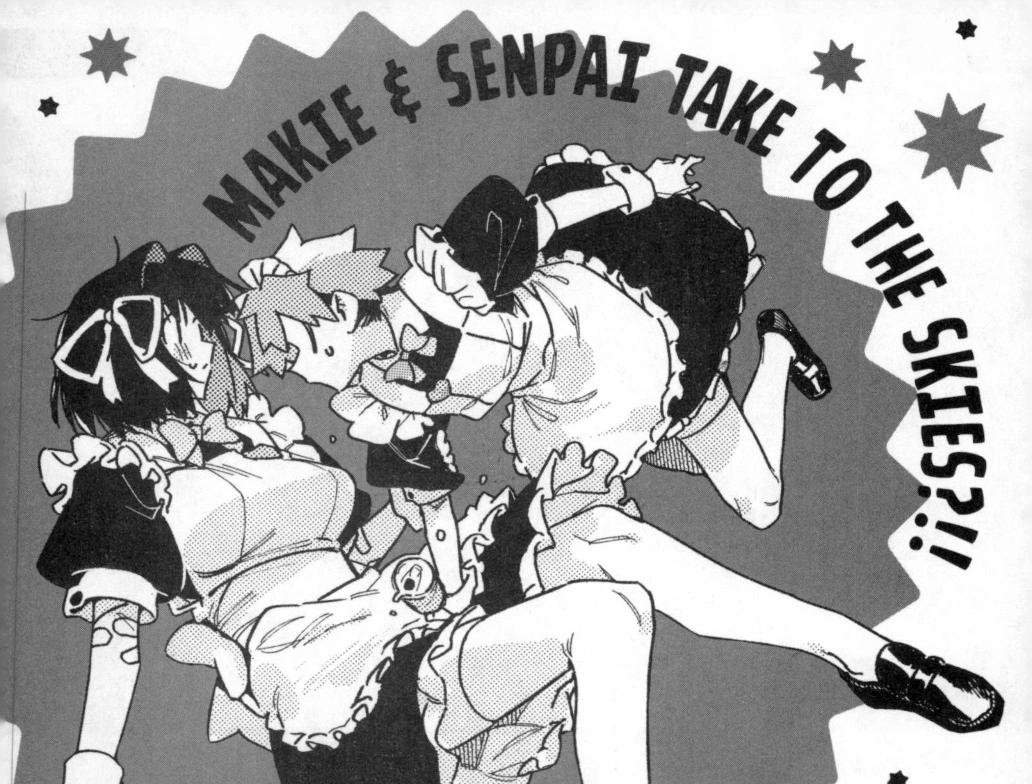
MAKIE & SENPAI TAKE TO THE SKIES?!!

Sachi's MONSTROUS Appetite 4

COMING SOON!

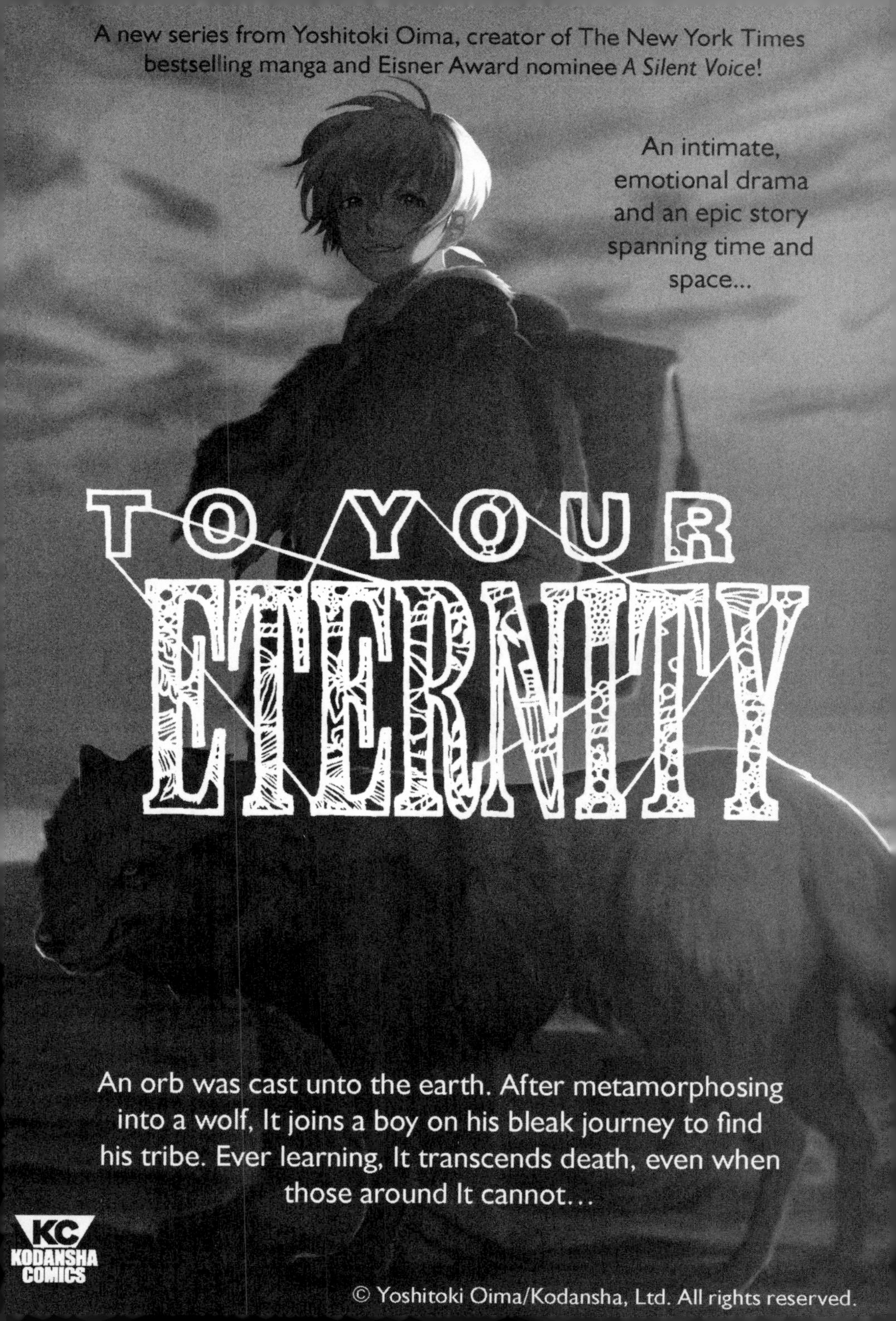
A new series from Yoshitoki Oima, creator of The New York Times bestselling manga and Eisner Award nominee *A Silent Voice*!
An intimate, emotional drama and an epic story spanning time and space...
TO YOUR ETERNITY
An orb was cast unto the earth. After metamorphosing into a wolf, It joins a boy on his bleak journey to find his tribe. Ever learning, It transcends death, even when those around It cannot...
KC KODANSHA COMICS
© Yoshitoki Oima/Kodansha, Ltd. All rights reserved.

KODANSHA COMICS

... most powerful spirit medium delves into the ghost world's greatest mysteries!

Story by Kyo Shirodaira, famed author of mystery fiction and creator of *Spiral*, *Blast of Tempest*, and *The Record of a Fallen Vampire*.

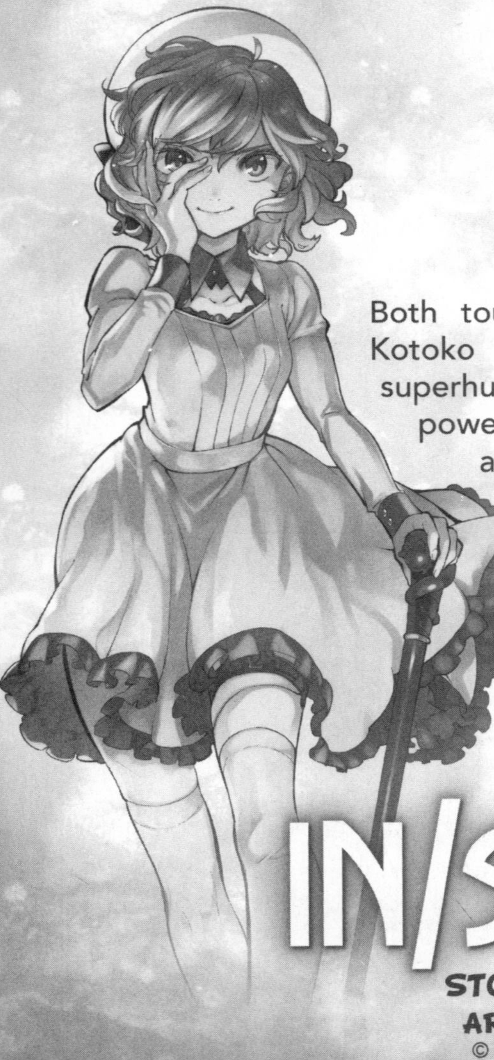

Both touched by spirits called yôkai, Kotoko and Kurô have gained unique superhuman powers. But to gain her powers Kotoko has given up an eye and a leg, and Kurô's personal life is in shambles. So when Kotoko suggests they team up to deal with renegades from the spirit world, Kurô doesn't have many other choices, but Kotoko might just have a few ulterior motives...

IN/SPECTRE

STORY BY KYO SHIRODAIRA
ART BY CHASHIBA KATASE

A Kodansha Comics Trade Paperback Original
Sachi's Monstrous Appetite 3 copyright © 2019 Chomoran
English translation copyright © 2021 Chomoran

Published in the United States by Kodansha Comics, an imprint of
Kodansha USA Publishing, LLC, New York.

Publication rights for this English edition arranged through
Kodansha Ltd., Tokyo.

First published in Japan in 2019 by Kodansha Ltd., Tokyo.

ISBN 978-1-64651-191-4

Original cover design by imagejack danyumi

Printed in the United States of America.

www.kodansha.us

9 8 7 6 5 4 3 2 1
Translation: Ajani Oloye
Lettering: Brandon Bovia
Editing: Haruko Hashimoto
Kodansha Comics edition cover design by Adam Del Re

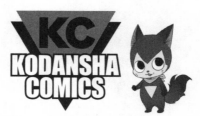

Publisher: Kiichiro Sugawara

Director of publishing services: Ben Applegate
Associate director of operations: Stephen Pakula
Publishing services managing editors:
Alanna Ruse, Madison Salters, Noelle Webster
Assistant production managers: Emi Lotto, Angela Zurlo
Logo and character art ©Kodansha USA Publishing, LLC